Maturing in Hard Times

CANADIAN PUBLIC ADMINISTRATION SERIES

COLLECTION ADMINISTRATION PUBLIQUE CANADIENNE

The Institute of Public Administration of Canada
L'Institut d'administration publique du Canada

This series is sponsored by the Institute of Public Administration of Canada as part of its constitutional commitment to encourage research on contemporary issues in Canadian public administration and public policy, and to foster wider knowledge and understanding amongst practitioners and the concerned citizen. There is no fixed number of volumes planned for the series, but under the supervision of the Research Committee of the Institute, the General Editor, and the Associate Editor, efforts will be made to ensure that significant areas will receive appropriate attention.

L'Institut d'administration publique du Canada commandite cette collection dans le cadre de ses engagements statutaires. Il se doit de promouvoir la recherche sur des problèmes d'actualité portant sur l'administration publique et la détermination des politiques publiques ainsi que d'encourager les praticiens et les citoyens intéressés à les mieux connaître et à les mieux comprendre. Il n'a pas été prévu de nombre de volumes donné pour la collection mais, sous le direction du Comité de recherche de l'Institut, du Directeur général, et du Directeur associé, l'on s'efforce d'accorder l'attention voulue aux questions importantes.

Canada and Immigration:
Public Policy and Public Concern
Freda Hawkins

The Biography of an Institution:
The Civil Service Commission of Canada, 1908-1967
J. E. Hodgetts, William McCloskey, Reginald Whitaker, V. Seymour Wilson

An edition in French has been published under the title *Histoire d'une institution: La Commission de la Fonction publique du Canada, 1908-1967,* by Les Presses de l'Université Laval

Old Age Pensions and Policy-Making in Canada
Kenneth Bryden

Provincial Governments as Employers:
A Survey of Public Personnel Administration in Canada's Provinces
J. E. Hodgetts and O. P. Dwivedi

Transport in Transition:
The Reorganization of the Federal Transport Portfolio
John W. Langford

Initiative and Response:
The Adaptation of Canadian Federalism to Regional Economic Development
Anthony G. S. Careless

Canada's Salesman to the World:
The Department of Trade and Commerce, 1892-1939
O. Mary Hill

Health Insurance and Canadian Public Policy:
The Seven Decisions that Created the Canadian Health Insurance System
Malcolm G. Taylor

Conflict over the Columbia:
The Canadian Background to an Historic Treaty
Neil A. Swainson

L'Economiste et la chose publique
Jean-Luc Migué
(Published by Les Presses de l'Université du Québec)

Federalism, Bureaucracy, and Public Policy:
The Politics of Highway Transport Regulation
Richard J. Schultz

Federal-Provincial Collaboration:
The Canada–New Brunswick General Development Agreement
Donald J. Savoie

Judicial Administration in Canada
Perry S. Millar and Carl Baar

The Language of the Skies:
The Bilingual Air Traffic Control Conflict in Canada
Sandford F. Borins

An edition in French has been published under the title
Le français dans les airs: le conflit du bilinguisme
dans le contrôle de la circulation aérienne au Canada
by Les Editions Chenelière et Stanké

L'Analyse des politiques gouvernementales:
trois monographies
Michel Bellavance, Roland Parenteau et Maurice Patry
(Published by Les Presses de l'Université Laval)

Canadian Social Welfare Policy:
Federal and Provincial Dimensions
Edited by Jacqueline S. Ismael

Maturing in Hard Times:
Canada's Department of Finance through
the Great Depression
Robert B. Bryce

Maturing in Hard Times

Canada's Department of Finance through the Great Depression

ROBERT B. BRYCE

The Institute of Public Administration of Canada
L'Institut d'administration publique du Canada

McGill-Queen's University Press
Kingston and Montreal

ISBN 0-7735-0555-5

Printed on acid-free paper

Legal deposit 2nd quarter 1986
Bibliothèque nationale du Québec

Printed in Canada

Canadian Cataloguing in Publication Data

Bryce, Robert B. (Robert Broughton), 1910-
Maturing in hard times
(Canadian public administration series □ Collection administration publique canadienne, ISSN 0384-854X)
Includes bibliographical references and index.
ISBN 0-7735-0555-5
1. Canada. Dept. of Finance - History.
2. Finance, Public - Canada - History.
3. Canada - Economic policy - To 1930. *
4. Canada - Economic policy - 1930-1939. *
I. Institute of Public Administration of Canada. II. Title. III. Series: Canadian public administration series.
HJ796.B79 1986 354.71062 C86-093632-5

Contents

Tables and Charts

Tables

Charts

Preface

In 1978, after serving the government of Canada for forty years and retiring three times, I decided I would turn to history. I had worried enough about our economic problems during my time with the government. Surely in history, I thought, there was no need to worry—what was done was done. In searching out why it was done, or how, surely it was a matter of finding the evidence, not seeking a solution, or so it seemed to me.

I had no difficulty deciding what I would study and write about. It would be the history of the Department of Finance. I had entered the department in 1938, after some years of study at Cambridge, where I had become a disciple of John Maynard Keynes, and at Harvard, where I had helped to convert others to the use of his system of analysis. I spent much of my working life in the Department of Finance to which I returned as deputy minister in 1963 from the Cabinet Office at the request of the new Liberal government. In 1938 the department was very small and informal, headed by W. C. Clark, who was a brilliant entrepreneur in economic policy when that was very much needed but who had little time or liking for administration. When I retired from the department in 1970, it was large and highly organized but confronted with the new problems of how to deal with persistent inflation to which Keynes's analysis and ideas did not provide many answers.

I wanted to write particularly about the activities of the department during the Great Depression of the 1930s, when it first began to grapple seriously with economic issues, and during World War II, when the department won its spurs under the inspired authority of J. L. Ilsley, one of the finest ministers I have ever known. I had neither the desire to write memoirs nor the diaries or memory to do so. What I have written, with the assistance of my old friend John Garner, has been done the hard way from the files in archives and from publications. In a few places these are supplemented by my memory, and I have so indicated. In some places I have ventured to comment on the wisdom or effectiveness of what was done, with the benefit of hindsight or of my own views at the time. John Garner prepared the chapter on tax collection agreements, a subject on which he had previously worked in the department.

Having written what I had originally intended about the Depression, I then made two substantial additions. One comprises the two chapters on the department's earlier history, which have been researched and written at the suggestion of my friend Ted Hodgetts, the general editor of this series. I enjoyed doing this work, particularly making the acquaintance of men like John Langton, the strong and versatile first deputy minister of finance, and Sir John Rose, the gifted and attractive minister who took over after the brief tenure of Sir Alexander Galt.

The second addition is chapter 3, done at the suggestion of Grant Reuber during his period as deputy minister and also proposed by other readers of my first draft. Surprisingly little seems to be known now about the nature and severity of the Depression; therefore I have tried my hand at a brief account—assisted substantially by the massive tome *Historical Statistics*, edited by M. C. Urquhart and K. A. H. Buckley, and by many who have written about the economic course of the Depression in Canada and elsewhere. The economic situation in 1938 and 1939 resembles in a number of respects the situation in Canada now, when we seem again to be stranded on a frustrating plateau without adequate dynamic forces either in Canada or in the international economy to carry us to a satisfactory level of employment.

The historical project in which John Garner and I have been engaged mostly covers the war period, 1939 to 1945. For those years we have had far more detailed information in the Public Archives, more participants who were still available for information and comment, and, in my own case, many recollections of personal participation and of important personalities. While our research on this period has been largely finished and drafts of potential chapters prepared, we have far more than could be compressed into a second book. To my great regret John Garner was compelled by a serious health condition to cease work entirely on the project in June 1985. We are considering the best way of making this detailed material available to those who would be interested in studying it.

While in writing this book I have had primarily in mind as readers those who work or intend to work in the public services of Canada, it should be of interest to many others concerned with the economic history of Canada in the 1920s and 1930s.

Acknowledgments

I wish to thank the Department of Finance for providing me with access to its papers, and with research and secretarial assistance, and for assigning Mr. John Garner, an experienced officer, to participate as a colleague in both research and writing. In particular I wish to acknowledge my obligation to Mr. Tom Shoyama, deputy minister of finance in 1978, for encouraging me to undertake this project.

I wish also to thank those who have served as my research assistant, first Vera Yuzyk, then David Fransen, and later, in sequence, Mona Hamill, Gisèle Héroux, and now Susan Padmos. All were able to supply an expertise in historical research that I lacked. Especially do I wish to express my appreciation to our secretary Debbie Harrison, who for four years has typed and retyped texts and notes. Alan Donnelly, of the Information Division of the department, has been very helpful at all stages with editorial advice and assistance.

The Public Archives of Canada has been our chief source of information, and I would like to acknowledge particularly the assistance of Mr. Glen Wright, who first taught me how to use it. Much of the published material—even that from the nineteenth century—was available from the Finance library. When it was not, the staff of the library, most notably Roxanne Denault, has secured it for us on loan.

Many old friends have assisted me with recollections of the department and its personalities in the thirties or even earlier. While I probably cannot remember them all, I should mention David Mansur, Ross Tolmie, Harvey Perry, David Sim, the late Gwen Sellar (widow of Watson Sellar), Arthur Annis, George Watts, Elgin Armstrong, Louis Rasminsky, the late Jean Mackintosh (who knew W. C. Clark well), J. R. Beattie, and Jack Pickersgill. O. Mary Hill assisted me not only through her book on the Department of Trade and Commerce but also in conversation. I acknowledge the help of many friends who have read and commented upon early drafts of particular chapters.

I wish to express a special appreciation of the excellent unpublished manuscript by Rod Finlayson, "Life with R. B.: That Man Bennett," in the manuscript collection of the PAC, from which I have quoted. I should note that a few paragraphs and other sentences appearing in chapters 3 and 10 of this book were included in the text of an essay I contributed to *Explorations in Canadian Economic History: Essays in Honour of Irene M. Spry*, edited by Duncan Cameron and published in 1985 by the University of Ottawa Press. That press has kindly given me permission to use these short passages in this book.

I have benefited since the beginning from the advice and encouragement of Professor J. E. Hodgetts. He reviewed in detail the draft manuscript and made many proposals for its improvement. So did Professor William Watson for McGill-Queen's University Press, whose assistance I am glad to acknowledge. The original manuscript had also been reviewed by two anonymous readers. I have taken seriously into account their comments in revising the manuscript. The responsibility for this final text is entirely mine.

It was the suggestion of Professor Hodgetts several years ago that this book appear in the Canadian Public Administration Series of which he is general editor, under the auspices of the Institute of Public Administration of Canada. Maurice Demers, assistant executive director of that institute, has been most helpful in making the arrangements for the publication of the book by McGill-Queen's University Press.

Chapter One

Evolution of the Department to 1920

In July 1867 the Department of Finance of the new Dominion of Canada was formed. Under a provision of the British North America Act, some of the officers and clerks from the former united Province of Canada were transferred to the service of the Dominion. Others remained in the provincial services. The department so formed was made up of two parts, both under the minister of finance. One, directed by the deputy inspector general, had responsibilities for keeping the government's books and for approving and signing cheques, debentures, and currency notes. The other smaller part, the Audit Office, was under the control of the auditor. He reported to the minister of finance through a part-time Board of Audit of which he was chairman and the dominant member. The total number of officers, clerks, and messengers in the department was twenty-eight.[1]

The first minister of finance, Alexander Tilloch Galt, was a strong one. Minister of finance of the Province of Canada from 1858 to 1862 and again from 1864 to 1866, Galt had resigned in 1866 on a question of principle relating to disputes over minority education rights in the Constitution then under discussion. Having been one of the earliest important advocates of Confederation, he had taken a leading role in the conferences on it in Charlottetown and Quebec in 1864 and in London in 1866. He had had extensive business experience in Lower Canada and in the Legislative Assembly in which he represented Sherbrooke.[2] Galt was the obvious choice as finance minister for the new Dominion.

Unfortunately Galt did not remain long as minister. A proud and sensitive man, he felt that his longtime colleagues Sir John A. Macdonald and George-Etienne Cartier displayed a lack of confidence in him in connection with a crisis in the affairs of the Commercial Bank in October 1867. The management of this bank, which was next in size to the Bank of Montreal, had been reckless and incurred heavy losses. Galt had originally turned down a request for government assistance, but when other sources could not be found and there appeared to be a danger of panic if this bank failed, since the Bank of Upper Canada had failed the previous year, Galt decided the government had to act. On October 21 he wired Macdonald for a Cabinet decision that night. Macdonald replied that the information was insufficient to warrant any action. The next morning the bank shut its doors, and a week of panic ensued with runs on other banks. The government then gave an assurance that it and the Bank of Montreal would accept the notes of the other banks at par. This action sufficed to stop the panic. But Galt resigned his portfolio, after staying long enough to see the situation force the government to act. He made a full defence of his position in Parliament on December 12. Galt never took office again, despite requests, but after putting his private affairs in order, he later undertook a number of diplomatic missions.[3]

To succeed Galt, Macdonald was fortunate to find another very able and congenial man, John Rose, member of Parliament for Huntingdon and minister of public works in the Macdonald-Cartier ministry from 1858 until mid-1861.[4] As the *Dictionary of Canadian Biography* states, "Although Rose had been importuned to enter public life since the early 1850s, he had decided not to commence a political career until he had acquired independent means."[5] He was born and educated in Scotland, immigrated with his parents to Canada in 1836, studied law in Montreal, and, to quote from the *Dictionary* again, was "reputed to possess the largest law practice in Montreal by the early 1850s." Rose became minister of finance on November 18, 1867, and was quickly immersed in the business of Parliament, which was then sitting. Within three weeks, on December 7, he introduced the Estimates of expenditures for the nine months ending March 31, 1868, and made a financial statement for that period. The statement dealt not only with expenditure and revenue for the current year, but also with proposals for refinancing the many items of floating debt, an accumulation over many years of amounts owing on various accounts, for example, to the fiscal agents of the provinces. A few days later, on December 12, Rose introduced and secured passage of resolutions to approve new excise duties, to replace all the laws providing for excise duties throughout the Dominion. His colleague, Leonard Tilley, minister of customs, then moved the resolutions respecting the customs tariff, which were more contentious; adoption of a common national tariff would mean increased duties in Nova Scotia because its duties had been lower than those of the Province of Canada.[6] On the other hand, more items would be exempted from the tariff than had been the case previously in Nova Scotia.

Despite his own outstanding ability, Rose could not have prepared a detailed financial statement, the Estimates, and a new set of excise duties, without substantial help from officials. He received it chiefly from the auditor, John Langton, whom he had quoted in the House on the very difficult subject of expenditures. Langton had the reputation of being a most outstanding man, who served not only as the auditor but as the minister's chief adviser. He clearly outclassed William Dickinson, the deputy inspector general, who had equal status in the department. Langton officially became deputy minister of finance and secretary of the Treasury Board as well as auditor general in 1870. This arrangement was at odds with the doctrine of the independence of the auditor general, but it had the great advantage of centralizing influence and administration in the hands of a very capable man, of a quality comparable with that of the best of his successors as deputy minister.[7]

Born in England in 1808, the second son of a prosperous businessman, Langton was educated for some years in Europe and later at Trinity College, Cambridge. He came to Canada in 1833 and settled on a farm near Peterborough; he later owned lumber mills near that town. He took an interest in public affairs and in 1851 was elected to represent Peterborough in the Legislative Assembly. In 1855 he gave up politics to become, at John A. Macdonald's request, the first auditor of the provincial public accounts, under new legislation largely inspired by the reformist zeal of William Lyon Mackenzie, an opposition member and chairman of the Public Accounts Committee. In this new role Langton quickly demonstrated his ability and dedication.[8] After Confederation Langton continued in his auditing role, presiding over the Board of Audit, and reporting to the minister, not to Parliament. His activities and the evolution of this role have been well described by others.

The Department of Finance itself was given its formal status and duties by a statute introduced by Rose in June 1869. The duties were as broad as they could be made: "the supervision, control and direction of all matters relating to the Financial Affairs and Public Accounts, Revenue and Expenditure of the Dominion, which are not, or insofar as they are not, by law or by order of the Governor in Council, assigned to any other Department of the Civil Service, and such other duties as may from time to time be assigned to it by the Governor in Council."[9]

The minister was, as usual, given "the management and direction" of the department, and the auditor general and the deputy inspector general were to be officers of the department. By implication, they were co-equals, each with certain statutory or other specific powers. In the following year, May 1870, the office of Deputy Inspector General was abolished by statute, and the auditor general, as mentioned previously, was also made deputy minister of finance, a bad arrangement in principle but defensible in the circumstances.[10]

The Department of Finance was tied in many ways to another organization given statutory powers in 1869. One of Sir John A. Macdonald's first formal acts as prime minister was to establish by Order-in-Council P.C. 3 of July 2, 1867, "a Board of Treasury with such powers and duties as may from time to time be assigned to it."[11] It consisted of the four ministers with essentially financial duties: the minister of finance, as chairman; the minister of customs; the minister of inland revenue (in those days mainly excise duties); and the receiver general (the formal custodian of funds, whose precise responsibilities were even then somewhat uncertain). To this board the Council (the term then frequently used to refer to the Cabinet) referred a variety of financial and administrative matters for its collective advice and ordered that certain proposals requiring approval by the Governor in Council be sent to Treasury Board for consideration before the Council acted on them. Enough business was done by the Treasury Board in its first year as a committee of Council that Langton was appointed its secretary, with an additional salary of $1,000 a year, commencing January 31, 1868.

The Treasury Board was given statutory constitution and powers in 1869, though not at that time authority to approve matters in place of the Governor in Council. In the passage of this legislation in the House of Commons, there was some criticism of the possible payment of an extra salary to Langton (or anyone else in the service) for his position as secretary to the board, but his outstanding worth was recognized in the debates. The minister of finance is reported as saying, "If there was a man in this Dominion who deserved to be well paid it was Mr. Langton, who was wearing himself out, body and mind, in the public service, working from sunrise till twelve o'clock at night week after week and month after month."[12]

A few months after the statutory establishment of the Treasury Board, Rose secured the approval of the Governor in Council to appoint as chief clerk of the Treasury Board, under Langton, a young Englishman, John Mortimer Courtney, who had been privately educated in England and had had some banking experience in India. Rose had invited this promising young man, another second son, to come to Canada to strengthen the department. In 1878 Courtney succeeded Langton as deputy minister of finance on nomination by Sir Richard Cartwright, the Liberal minister of finance for whom he had worked for about five years and developed both respect and affection.[13]

Accounting Problems in 1867 and 1868

In 1867 the Department of Finance, as distinct from the minister, was almost wholly a bookkeeping, accounting, and auditing organization. The first twenty-two months of its existence, until the Public Accounts for the first fiscal year of the Dominion were submitted to Parliament, put its ability to the test. The financial rearrangements and settlements between the provincial governments and the new Dominion were exceedingly complex and controversial. During the early months, the government at Ottawa, which had most of the experienced and able public servants, collected some revenues and made some expenditures on behalf of provincial governments, as well as on its own account, and also had to work out in detail the new division of responsibilities for expenditures. In addition there were delayed and uncompleted transactions from earlier years. In a letter of December 1867, Langton described some of the difficulties, referring in particular to the division of assets and liabilities between Ontario and Quebec. One problem was the lack of knowledge of the nature and past history of the accounts. As a partial solution, Rose called the two provincial treasurers together and locked them in a room with Langton, who lectured to them for six hours on their assets and liabilities. Langton remarked: "The Treasurer of Quebec who is invalidish [*sic*] was worn out and went away, but he of Ontario stuck it out to the end, and on leaving me said that he had a vague idea that he knew something about it now if he could remember his lesson."[14]

Under Langton's lead, the Department of Finance rose to the occasion. His comprehension and judgment are displayed in two examples: in the preface to the Public Accounts for 1867-68 and in correspondence between the Dominion government and the governments of Ontario and Quebec during 1868 and early 1869, relating to the settlement of accounts.[15]

THE RESIGNATION OF ROSE AND BANKING LEGISLATION

Banking legislation was the most urgent and controversial subject before the first Parliament of Canada. Rose began in 1867 with a modest bill extending the powers of the existing chartered banks to all provinces of Canada. Meanwhile the Senate referred the subject of banking to a select committee, whose report early in 1868 stirred up much controversy, as it included some of the Bank of Montreal's recommendations, which were violently opposed by most of the other banks, as well as by many merchants. Rose proceeded warily; he moved the establishment of what he considered a carefully balanced Select Committee on Banking and Currency. He had prepared in advance for the committee a set of key questions to be put to various knowledgeable and interested people in order to obtain quickly a mass of written and oral evidence. The committee reported in April 1869 with a variety of views, but most were against the policy favoured by the minister and E. H. King, president of the Bank of Montreal. At this time a major conference of representatives of banking and commercial interests from across the Dominion passed resolutions in favour of preserving the existing banking system, which were presented to Rose.[16]

In May 1869 Rose put forward his own proposals in a set of resolutions for consideration and debate in the House. They were much the same in substance as King's proposals eighteen months before, and were necessary, in the minister's view, in order that the currency be placed on a sound and uniform basis. The resolutions were debated for one day only, on June 1. Not only the Opposition but also Ontario members generally and some of the staunchest supporters of the government were hostile to them.[17] On June 15 Rose announced that the government had no desire to force the consideration of these resolutions during the session but would allow time for longer study. Three months later Rose resigned from the Cabinet and gave up his seat in Parliament. Soon after he moved to London where he joined in establishing the private banking firm of Morton, Rose, and Co. For many years he served as the unofficial representative of the government of Canada in England. He prospered in London and was popular.

To succeed his good friend Rose, Prime Minister Macdonald chose a former political antagonist, Sir Francis Hincks, previously a leader of the Reformers (Liberals) of Canada West. Hincks had left Canadian politics when the Liberals had formed a coalition with the Conservatives in 1854. He entered the British colonial service and became governor of Barbados and later of British Guiana, for which he was granted a knighthood, but not an adequate pension. When Hincks was visiting Canada, Macdonald met him and quickly recognized his ability as a potential minister of finance and the political advantage of adding this old Reformer to the government to replace some of the Liberals who had left.[18]

Hincks became minister of finance in October 1869 and immediately began working on the difficult crisis over the banking legislation. In search of an acceptable compromise, he held widespread consultations with bankers, merchants, and others who were interested. The central problem was the note issue, and on this Hincks evolved an ingenious compromise which secured the main objectives of public policy, while leaving the banks with enough powers of issue to meet their interests. The banks were given the authority to issue notes of four dollars or more, while the government would issue Dominion notes for the small denominations of one and two dollars, as well as the very large "legals" used by the banks in settling accounts among themselves.

With the note issue question settled, Hincks introduced and secured approval of his banking legislation in 1870. It involved many changes of detail, but did not alter the basic nature of the Canadian banking system. The following year this new law was consolidated with previous legislation to become the first comprehensive Bank Act, extending the charters of the banks for ten years. Hincks lost his zest for politics, although he continued to perform his duties as minister of finance ably. In February 1873 he resigned from the Cabinet and did not contest a seat in the next election.

SUPERANNUATION—AN EXAMPLE OF GOOD ADVICE DISREGARDED

One serious problem that confronted the government of Canada in its first few years after Confederation was the large number of old civil servants who had been taken over from the provinces. Because of age, many were inefficient, but they were not entitled to a pension or similar benefits on retirement and in most cases had relatively small savings. As a consequence, ministers and the government were reluctant to retire them compulsorily, but tended to keep them on despite their inefficiency, even if that meant hiring others to get the work done. It was decided that some type of superannuation plan should be devised for them.

In 1869 a committee of senior civil servants was appointed, with John Langton as chairman, to examine this widespread and serious problem and propose a solution. Its report of December 4, 1869, surveyed the age distribution of the civil service and compared it with that of the British civil service.[19] Superannuation plans in England and European countries were studied and analysed, with actuarial considerations being taken into account. It then identified and appraised the main problems in setting up a plan in the Canadian public service. On the basis of this sophisticated analysis, Langton and his colleagues proposed a plan for the Canadian service which would meet the problem that was troubling the government, involve fair contributions by civil servants based on actuarial estimates of cost, but would also require appropriations by Parliament (which were necessary because many to be retired in the early years had not contributed in the past).

The government did not accept Langton's well worked-out plan. Instead it brought in a highly simplified scheme to be wholly financed by "abatements" from civil servants' salaries. This rough-and-ready plan led to a series of difficulties and public criticisms that required statutes to change the plan.[20] Finally, in 1898, Prime Minister Laurier, who had criticized the plan for many years, closed it to new entrants and provided for these civil servants only a compulsory retirement savings plan. Only after the war of 1914–18 was a proper new superannuation plan introduced. Meanwhile the government had a difficult time competing with the private sector for able administrators and professionals. This incident gives evidence of Langton's ability but also shows the difficulty of persuading ministers in those early years to undertake complicated long-term proposals that would involve some burden on the Treasury.

The Department in the 1870s

A memorandum by Langton, almost certainly written in November 1873, describes the staff and work of the department at that time. The department had been consolidated under Langton as deputy minister and auditor general but there was an Audit Branch and a Bookkeeping Branch. The total number of staff had grown to thirty-five, including Dickinson, who was doing little, and some who worked only part of the year. The duties were very much as described in 1867. The main increase in workload came from the growth of small, government-operated savings banks, which required detailed auditing. The total of savings deposits, as of June 30 (the end of the fiscal year), rose from $1.7 million in 1868 to $7.2 million in 1874 (including the Post Office Savings Bank at $3.2 million). The only new function that is mentioned is that of a clerk, Mr. Hector, who "has charge of Insurance Companies," probably meaning keeping the reports they submitted. He had worked on this subject for the Province of Ontario but his position there was abolished. Finally Langton's memo states, "Mr. Cross, Junior 2nd class clerk has charge of Bank returns and other statistical matters."[21] Could this have been a beginning of an interest in statistics, if not economics?

Later in the seventies two important changes took place in the functions and organization of the department. In April 1875 two acts relating to insurance were passed in Parliament: one dealt with fire and inland marine insurance and the second with life insurance. Both types of insurance had been developing rapidly in Canada, and the insurance companies had been subject to certain statutory regulation and obligations to file statements of their affairs. The Act respecting Fire and Inland Marine Insurance (chapter 20) consolidated and amended earlier legislation and required detailed statements of each company's affairs to be filed with the minister of finance and with specified courts in each province. What was significantly new in it, however, was the setting up of the position of superintendent of insurance in the Department of Finance "for the efficient administration of the insurance business in the Dominion of Canada and to enforce strictly the provisions of this Act." The superintendent was required to keep records relating to each company licensed to do business in Canada, and also to visit the head offices of each company in Canada each year and examine carefully the statements of condition of the company and report thereon to the minister. If he considered that the assets of the company were insufficient to make it safe for the public to effect insurance with it, he was to notify the minister. If the minister agreed, and also the Governor in Council, an order-in-council could be issued suspending or cancelling the company's licence to operate. A second act (chapter 21) extended similar powers and duties to the superintendent in respect of life insurance. Prior to these acts, the statutes of 1868, amended in 1871, required only the filing of statements and making of deposits by companies licensed to do insurance business. Consequently the department was being given in 1875 an active duty to exercise vigilance and judgment to protect the public against the possible insolvency of insurance companies, many of which had been established in Canada, while others from the United Kingdom and the United States had obtained licences to operate in Canada.

In May 1875 Professor J. B. Cherriman of University College, Toronto, was appointed the first superintendent of insurance at a salary of $4,000 a year, nearly as much as the deputy minister received, including his extra pay as secretary of the Treasury Board. Cherriman's successor, appointed in December 1885, was William Fitzgerald, qualified both as an actuary and as a lawyer; he was paid a reduced salary but was formally recognized as assistant deputy minister and probably was the first with that status.[22] He had two well-qualified actuaries, who assisted him in the work of checking the detailed statements of the life insurance companies, particularly in the difficult task of periodically valuing the policy liabilities of each company.[23]

The second change in the Department of Finance occurred in 1878 and 1879. In April 1878 Parliament passed a new comprehensive Audit Act, patterned on the British Exchequer and Audit Department Act of 1866.[24] The act established the independent office of Auditor General, reporting directly to Parliament, and relieved the Department of Finance of its auditing functions which Langton had exercised. The act provided that the deputy minister of finance should be ex officio secretary of the Treasury Board and should also be deputy of the receiver general. Certain duties and powers of the minister and deputy minister of finance in regard to accounts, debentures, and disbursements were also spelled out in sections of the act.[25]

The new office of Auditor General was filled by John Lorn McDougall when the act came into effect on August 1, 1878. On that day John Langton retired on superannuation at the age of seventy. He was succeeded as deputy minister of finance by J. M. Courtney, whom Langton had trained for the job. Of McDougall and Courtney, Norman Ward has written, "Neither of these gentlemen was less industrious nor less opinionated than Langton, and by the 1890s they were barely on speaking terms."[26]

Just a year later Parliament passed another act abolishing the separate Department of the Receiver General and transferring all its duties and staff to the Department of Finance. The minister of finance was also to be ex officio receiver general, the deputy minister of finance was to be ex officio deputy receiver general, and the separate office of Deputy Receiver General was to be abolished. As a result, the Department of

Finance had incorporated in it the offices of Assistant Receivers General in the provinces and some small country savings banks associated with these offices in Nova Scotia, New Brunswick, and British Columbia. The effect of the Audit Act in 1878 and this one in 1879 was to transfer four persons to the Audit Office from Finance and to bring over, in Ottawa, six from the Receiver General's Department.[27]

THE NATIONAL POLICY OF TARIFF PROTECTION

After the election of September 1878, Sir Leonard Tilley again became minister of finance, as he had been in 1873.[28] This time he was in a government pledged to a National Policy of deliberate protection of Canadian producers by tariffs, if reciprocity of trade could not be achieved with the United States. The National Policy was to a considerable extent the result of a depression in Canada from 1874 to 1878, a time stimulus was clearly needed. The argument was reinforced by the need for greater revenue, as the decline in prices of imports resulted in lower customs receipts under the ad valorem tariffs established by Rose and Hincks. The United States was growing rapidly behind its tariff walls and attracting many Canadians to settle there. Its lower costs of production and falling prices led American businesses to dump many of their goods into the "slaughter market" of Canada, in the phraseology of the day. The two major parties in Canada actively debated the issue. The results of the election in 1878 were an overwhelming victory for the Conservatives, except in Tilley's own province of New Brunswick. But Tilley himself was a protectionist, in agreement with Macdonald. He was elected by the slender majority of nine votes.[29]

It was Tilley, of course, who had to translate the general policy into specific measures. He did this in his lengthy budget of March 14, 1879, after long preparations and ten weeks of discussions with representatives of both protectionism and free trade, as well as drawing upon his own experience as minister of customs.[30] He read out the hundreds of details constituting the new schedules of duties in the tariff. Although there is no need to recount them here, two major points should be noted. First, the new duties included, in many if not most cases, a specific rate of duty per unit of quantity in addition to the ad valorem rate (that is, a percentage of the value of the shipment). This was done to protect the revenue in case prices declined. Second, while the new or increased duties applied to a variety of natural products and commodities as well as manufactured goods, it is notable that they gave substantial protection to the cotton and woollen textile industries and the iron and steel industries.[31]

Did the Department of Finance, apart from the minister, take any part in preparing this very important budget? It does not appear that the personnel of the department included anyone expert in economics generally or the tariff in particular. The new deputy minister was able and motivated enough to have helped Tilley in a general way and probably arranged to have the department try to estimate the effects of the changes in tariffs upon the revenue. In 1879 this endeavour would have been an important and difficult task, with so many and such large changes. One cannot know the normal division of labour then between Finance and the revenue departments in these budget preparations. Tilley made no reference to the department in his speech to the House. Three tariff experts were hired to assist in the budget preparations, telling evidence that the department was unable to cope alone with the preparation of such an important tariff revision and the assessment of its effects. Edward Young, an Americanized Nova Scotian, arrived in Ottawa in late December 1878. He had been chief of the U.S. Bureau of Statistics for eight years and had worked on the American tariff. John Mclean, a longtime journalist, protectionist, and statistical expert, and W.H. Frazer, the secretary of the Ontario Manufacturers' Association, joined Young in January. These three experts helped to draw up the complicated schedules and "obtain all the information possible, both in regard to Tariff legislation in other countries, and to the needs and opinions of men engaged in Industrial and Commercial pursuits."[32]

It is noteworthy that Macdonald had promised the Colonial Office that he would submit these major tariff proposals to London for approval before introducing them. They were sent at the last moment, after Tilley had finished his long work on them. Many higher duties on imports from Britain were included. The reply from the colonial secretary to the governor general was a constitutional precedent: Her Majesty's Government regretted that the effect of the new tariff appeared to be an increase in duties already high, but it deemed the fiscal policy of Canada to be a matter for decision by the Dominion legislature subject to treaty obligations.[33]

Although the Department of Finance may have been involved in the National Policy of tariff protection, it had almost nothing directly to do with the most important and difficult financial legislation and operations of the first half a century of the Dominion: the successful building of the Canadian Pacific Railway (CPR) during the period 1881 to 1885. The railway was Sir John A. Macdonald's own project to knit the country together and open the prairies to settlement. He had lost office in 1873 over scandals during his first try to get it started. When he began negotiations again in 1880, he was careful to consider several possible syndicates to undertake it, but one clearly stood out before all the rest. This group was headed by George Stephen, president of the Bank of Montreal, a resourceful financier who had experience with railroading in the United States. Macdonald negotiated very carefully with this syndicate, first in Ottawa and later in London where he and Sir Charles Tupper, the minister of railways and canals, were able to draw on the expert advice and assistance of Sir John Rose and other friends. In October Tupper and Stephen signed the basic contract, which, of course, would require Parliament's approval and appropriations. Its execution, together with the amendments found necessary as time went on and various crises were surmounted, were to put heavy demands upon the finances of the government.

These great events belong to the history of Canada, not of its Finance Department. Tilley was minister of finance throughout this period, sharing responsibility and having to find the funds for the initial subsidy and later loans. In borrowing some of these funds in London in 1884, he ran into the opposition of organized groups which were against the CPR project. The role of his department, however, was its normal one of assisting in finding the funds, as well as the custodial and accounting operations in connection with the contracts with the railway company.

The Quiet Department, 1879–1906

After its changes in 1878 and 1879 the Department of Finance had a long period of stability under the prudent management of John Mortimer Courtney, who was deputy minister until 1906. Its role was not changed during this time, although the workload and staff of the Insurance Branch grew substantially. Courtney took pride in the ability of the department during the eighties to handle substantial increases in workload without any increases in staff or payroll.[34]

When George Foster became minister of finance at the end of May 1888,[35] Courtney wrote a long memorandum about the Finance Department and described it in some detail.[36] (The auditor general's report as well shows a total of forty-five employees of the department in Ottawa in 1888, plus twenty-nine in the six regional offices of Assistant Receivers General. There were other employees, apparently on a part-time basis, in the many small savings banks.) Courtney praised William Fitzgerald, the superintendent of insurance and assistant deputy minister, and C. W. Treadwell, a lawyer who entered the service as a "shorthand writer" and later took over the secretarial work of the department, where his legal knowledge was used in preparing and examining draft bills, including, in the two preceding years, the proposed changes in tariff legislation. Treadwell also dealt with some of the rapidly growing Treasury Board work, after the resignation of the senior clerk who had done this work before, and he was assisted by Thomas C. Boville, a clerk who had by then acquired a thorough knowledge of it. J. C. Saunders, a junior clerk, also assisted Boville.

In his memorandum Courtney discussed the organization of the department. The Currency Branch, in charge of the note issue, was small in Ottawa, consisting of a chief clerk and two assistants, but it also included the outside offices of Assistant Receivers General in Montreal, Toronto, Halifax, Winnipeg, St. John, Victoria, and Charlottetown. These offices issued and redeemed the currency notes and held specie (gold coin) reserves. A small savings bank was attached to each of these offices, except in Montreal, and it was separate from the more widespread Post Office Savings Banks. Courtney told the minister he was trying to eliminate the savings banks, and had shut some down and transferred the deposits to the Post Office because "my own opinion has always been that the Finance department, like the Treasury in England, should be a Department of Supervision and not be burthened with the details of administration."

Courtney also described the work of the Dominion bookkeeper, M. G. Dickieson, who watched over the expenditures, looked after the revenues, and checked the bank accounts and the debt accounts. Courtney mentioned by name nine "officers" who assisted Dickieson in this work, which also included the preparation of the Public Accounts and the Estimates. Of them Courtney said in his memorandum, "In order to make these men good all round I have from time to time shifted them from one kind of work to another." Later in his memorandum the deputy described vividly his troubles with the government's bank accounts, saying, "Of all the mischievous and wretched systems ever drifted into by a government, the relations of the Treasury with the Banks in Canada are the most wretched." All the banks wanted some share of the government's local bank business.

Courtney went on to write about the work to be done. The first was to settle the Confederation accounts with Ontario and Quebec, which had been outstanding for twenty years. The Public Accounts had to be cleaned up, and obsolete material dropped, if the Public Accounts Committee of the House of Commons could be persuaded. He had suggestions to present to the Treasury Board to streamline the Superannuation Act. Then he wanted to codify all the laws, public and private, relating to the Finance Department. A revision of the Bank Act would have to be introduced before 1891 and he had a brief on the subject ready for the new minister.[37] There was also a lot of "commercial" legislation that had to be considered and revised or initiated, including acts relating to bills of exchange. He hoped the department could help solve the "vexed question" of bankruptcy and insolvency. The acts relating to companies needed revision. Finally he stated that he was putting all these matters on record, as the strain on his health had been very severe.[38]

All in all, this paper suggests that while Courtney was no Langton, he was a worthy successor, an administrator who could keep the department running well and who was providing substantial advice on policy to the minister. In addition he was twice appointed to royal commissions on the civil service. He was an active member of the commission appointed in November 1891, which reported in April the next year, after taking some 643 printed pages of testimony. Upon retiring from the service in 1906, he was made chairman of another royal commission on the civil service in May 1907, which reported in March 1908.[39] On the basis of the comparison he could make with 1892, this second commission reported that the civil service had deteriorated in quality over the fifteen-year period; this was attributed chiefly to the great prosperity in Canada having drawn outstanding men into other vocations, while salaries in the service remained static.

In his memorandum of June 1888 Courtney stated emphatically that for the future the utmost economy must be pursued, not by fits and starts, but by a steady systematic process. He suggested some steps should be taken "either by a Royal Commission or otherwise" to make a thorough examination into all the items included in the Dominion's expenditure. There is no evidence that this advice was taken during the next twelve years.

In a memorandum to his assistant deputy minister on December 14, 1900, Courtney instructed him how to deal with matters that would arise during Courtney's absence overseas, told him to make daily efforts to get in the Estimates from the various departments and to cut down the figures as much as possible, and in particular to approve no new public works. Control over the Estimates was supposed to be a function of the Treasury Board, of which Courtney was secretary, but in fact these decisions were normally taken in the Cabinet. The chief evidence we have of the ineffectiveness of this process during Courtney's period comes from a report the Dominion government received in 1912 from Sir George Murray, a former senior Treasury official in England, who had been commissioned to examine broadly the working of the public service in Canada. In this trenchant report, Sir George summarized the facts he found and his recommendations for change.

Sir George was particularly critical of the Canadian procedures used in preparing and deciding upon the Estimates (which became the appropriations for the next fiscal year). They were prepared in the first instance by each department and its minister, influenced largely by their own interests and pressures from members of Parliament. The Estimates were then examined by the Department of Finance. Owing to pressure of time, this examination was necessarily of a "somewhat cursory character," focusing upon the total of each appropriation to be voted by Parliament rather than important details. Sir George made no reference to the Treasury Board but stated that the final result was arrived at in Council after oral discussion among ministers. He thought this was wasteful of the time of ministers and unlikely to result in effective control, which could only be secured by persistent criticism of details, carried on by correspondence between Finance and the other departments.[40]

Sir George recommended that the Department of Finance should be clearly charged with the responsibility for examining on paper throughout the year the details of what was to go into the Estimates, securing from each department in writing the grounds on which the expenditure was required, and the consequential expenditures in future years if it were approved. The importance of arguments and undertakings being given in writing rather than in conversation was emphasized. He recognized his proposed system would take time, but said nothing about what it would require in the number and quality of the staff in Finance. His report was made in 1912 and seems therefore to confirm that no serious reforms such as Courtney was advocating in 1888 had been made by that time. This is further confirmed by the lack of change in the staff of the department of the kind that would have been needed for a more serious and detailed consideration of expenditure proposals.

COURTNEY'S SUCCESSOR—BOVILLE

In October 1906 Courtney's twenty-eight-year tenure as deputy minister was over. He was succeeded by Thomas C. Boville. At the same time Henry T. Ross, a renowned forty-four-year-old lawyer from Nova Scotia, was appointed assistant deputy minister of finance and legal officer. The superintendent of insurance was thus freed to devote the whole of his time to that office.

Boville was born in Ireland in 1860 where he got his early schooling before the family emigrated to Ottawa. He did well at high school and went on to the University of Toronto on a good scholarship. In the middle of his third year, his father was incapacitated and young Boville had to go to work to support the family. His good academic record had been noted, and in January 1883 Courtney secured the approval of Sir Leonard Tilley to appoint this promising young man to the Department of Finance on the advice of a civil service examiner, as a beginning to building a capable younger staff. Boville became "closely related with the subject of National Budgets," and by 1888 Courtney had him working for the Treasury Board. When Courtney was about to retire, W. S. Fielding, the minister of finance, is said to have looked outside for a new deputy minister with financial experience but could find none at the modest salary of $4,000 a year that was then authorized. Finally with Courtney's support, Fielding asked Boville to take the position. Boville reports he was "dumbfounded and amazed" and asked for time to consult "a number of financial friends" before he accepted the position in November 1906.[41]

Boville took over the department in the middle of the intense prewar boom when imports and Dominion revenues were rising rapidly. Real growth and settlement were taking place year after year, and the prices of exports, imports, and domestic products were also rising. Public expenditures were increasing rapidly, particularly expenditures on western settlements, on railways, and on the public domain. Expenditures on defence were rising too, as a result of tensions in Europe. The public debt of the Dominion was rising but not rapidly, except in 1909 when a short recession caused a drop in government revenue. Large commitments were also being made in guarantees of bonds issued by the expanding Grand Trunk Railway and Canadian Northern Railway systems. The overbuilding of railways (which ultimately led to the Canadian National Railways) seems obvious in retrospect but was part cause and part effect of the booming prosperity of the immediate prewar decade.

Under Boville the Department of Finance grew very little until 1910, apart from the Insurance Branch which was having to expand rapidly to meet an urgent workload, and in accordance with a recommendation of the Royal Commission on Life Insurance. In 1910 the Insurance Branch was separated from Finance and was constituted as the Department of Insurance, with the superintendent being given the status of a deputy head under the minister of finance.[42]

In 1909 Boville brought into the department J. A. Russell, who had had lengthy service with the Customs Department. He was to assist the deputy minister, the assistant deputy minister, and the minister himself in dealing with the tariffs and bounties and trade arrangements with other countries.

THE DEPARTMENT IN 1912

In January 1912 Boville submitted a detailed report on the staff of the department and their duties to the Special Public Service Commission, which was making yet another investigation into the civil service.[43] The total number of staff in the department in Ottawa (the inside service) was ninety-eight, including twenty-one temporary clerks. In the outside service staff numbered forty-three, including six assistant receivers general (in addition to staff at the City and District Savings Bank that served in that capacity in Montreal). Most of the thirty-seven others were clerks helping the six assistant receivers general, including those at the small savings banks associated with their offices. The number of other small savings banks, which Courtney had been trying to reduce, was by 1912 down to thirteen, twelve in Nova Scotia and one in New Brunswick.

In Ottawa there were two main branches of the Finance Department. By far the largest was the Currency Branch with a staff of forty-eight under the comptroller of the currency, J. E. Rourke. Its responsibility was to operate and control the issue and redemption of Dominion notes and silver and bronze coin, which took place through the offices of the Assistant Receivers General. A large central gold reserve was also held in the name of the receiver general against the Dominion notes outstanding.

It is somewhat surprising to find that over half the total number of employees of the department in 1912 were engaged either in Ottawa or in regional centres in what is now generally recognized as a basically central banking function.

The second largest branch of the department was under the charge of the chief Dominion bookkeeper, J. C. Saunders. It had a staff of twenty-eight clerks and a subbranch of which G. W. Hyndman was in charge. The branch had a variety of duties, including the keeping of all the central accounts of the government and the management of the public debt (at that time the debt was held mainly in England and looked after by the Bank of Montreal in London as fiscal agent) and several trust funds. The branch also received from the banks and inspected all the cheques issued by the departments of the government under the authority of letters of credit issued by the Department of Finance, and it adjusted these with the banks' statements.

Besides these main branches there were several small units reporting directly to the deputy minister. One consisted of the senior clerk and junior assistant who helped Boville in serving the Treasury Board. Another, the accountant of contingencies and his two assistants, checked before payment the accounts of the departments for designated types of small expenditures; he also controlled the char service for the cleaning of public buildings in Ottawa. J. A. Russell, the tariff expert, has already been mentioned. Another clerk, R. B. Viets, served Finance Minister Sir Thomas White as private secretary. He had previously served Fielding in the same capacity, despite the fact that they were from different political parties.

From all this staff it would be difficult to identify those who would be giving advice to the minister on general policies, as distinct from individual matters. Deputy Minister Boville and Assistant Deputy Minister Ross must have done so. Documents in the files show Boville's advice to the minister on the terms and time of borrowing, as well as information on, and forecasts of, the government's cash position. Ross was giving legal advice on the interpretation of the law, as well as drafting new bills and regulations. Russell was giving detailed information on the tariff. Saunders and his senior clerks, as well as A. B. Foster, the Treasury Board clerk, and Boville, must have had the duty of assembling and probably of commenting on the Estimates. Against this, we have the clear conclusion of Sir George Murray that their work was largely ineffectual, except insofar as they briefed the minister of finance and his colleagues on the Treasury

Board for the decisive discussions at the Cabinet. On general monetary policy and banking no one on the staff seems to have been trained for advising the minister, but White was qualified in this field by his own experience and had access to many business friends competent to give him advice, though their own interests and business responsibilities must have often influenced their opinions.

Just before World War I, in April 1914, the department acquired a more senior and opinionated tariff expert, R. W. Breadner, who had worked for many years as manager of the Tariff Department of the Canadian Manufacturers' Association. He was to play an important role during and after the war both as an adviser and as an administrator.

The Great War

World War I began for Canada, as it did for Great Britain and the rest of the Empire, at 11 P.M.., Tuesday, August 4, 1914. The minister of finance throughout the war period was Thomas White (Sir Thomas after 1916). Born in 1866, educated in Toronto, he was called to the bar in 1899. Instead of practising law, he entered business and rose to be general manager of the National Trust Company, becoming familiar with the leading financial circles in Canada. In 1911 he was elected to Parliament as a Conservative, opposing the Liberals who were advocating reciprocity in trade with the United States. He was chosen by Sir Robert Borden to be minister of finance on the formation of the Conservative government in 1911. Throughout his period as minister, White looked for advice to the leading bankers in Montreal and Toronto, directly and through the Canadian Bankers' Association.[44]

The war brought about a large increase in the size of the Finance Department. The total personnel of 141 in September 1912 had grown to over 640 by March 1919. In addition large numbers of temporary clerks were employed in Ottawa at the time major loans were being issued.

The largest increase in the department during the war was in what was called the War Finances Branch. This branch carried out the arrangements for printing and distributing and keeping detailed records on the bonds issued in Canada during the war. As well, it was responsible for receiving, redeeming, safeguarding, accounting for, and ultimately destroying the interest coupons on these bonds, and issuing cheques for interest on the registered bonds. This function was new to the department because the issue of Dominion securities before the war had been almost entirely carried out by the government's fiscal agents in London; the department's role had been essentially an accounting and auditing one carried out by the Accounts Branch. As the size of the wartime Canadian bond issues increased, reaching eventually over a million subscriptions in the October

1918 Victory Loan, the scale of these departmental operations grew rapidly, and the necessary senior and junior clerks and accountants had to be trained and carefully supervised. The branch was headed by G. W. Hyndman, who before the war had been a senior clerk under the chief Dominion bookkeeper responsible for the supervision of the Dominion savings banks and the revenue and retirement fund accounts within the department. His managerial and custodial responsibilities in the latter years of the war were very substantial, as the regular staff of the branch had to be assisted at times by experienced clerks from other branches as well as by large numbers of temporary clerks.

Wartime taxation innovations substantially increased the department's work. The business profits tax, introduced in the budget of February 15, 1916, and income tax, introduced in the summer of 1917, were administered as part of the department under the vigorous direction of R. W. Breadner, commissioner of taxation, who had assisted the minister in drafting the legislation.[45] In the spring of 1917 the war situation was grim and after Prime Minister Borden returned from the Imperial War Council in May, the government decided it had to ask Parliament to introduce conscription in order to provide reinforcements. After a divisive and bitter debate in getting this measure approved, Borden and White decided they had to introduce an income tax. The emotions of war, as well as its financial requirements, had overcome both the distaste and the difficulties that had earlier held White back from what is probably the most important financial innovation in the history of the country.

The administration of these new taxes was a major undertaking, in terms of both securing suitably qualified senior staff and decentralizing much of the operation. Offices had to be set up across the country in thirty-five cities and towns, employing approximately two hundred people including temporary clerks. Soon after the end of the war, in March 1919, the number of persons employed in tax administration at headquarters was about one hundred.[46] There was some criticism, at least from Montreal and Vancouver, of the effectiveness of the collection of the business profits tax in 1918, but this is not surprising in view of the novelty and the arbitrary nature of the tax. Breadner seemed able to defend himself against specific examples reported from Montreal.[47]

The work of the Currency Branch of the department increased greatly during the war for two reasons. First, the issue of Dominion notes was expanded in 1914 and later, under the Finance Act and the Dominion Notes Act, 1914, which increased the volume of routine work in issuing and redeeming the notes, both in the offices of Assistant Receivers General in the provinces and in Ottawa. In essence, the Finance Act of 1914 took Canada off the gold standard and established a special wartime currency regime. The banks were authorized to make payment on their own obligations, including deposits, by their own banknotes, rather than in gold or in Dominion notes. In order that the banks have access to enough Dominion notes to meet their needs, the government was authorized to make advances of Dominion notes to them (charging interest) against the pledge of acceptable types of securities as collateral. The obligation of the government to redeem its Dominion notes in gold was suspended.[48] The Finance Act also give rise to a new type of work in the pledging of collateral security for advances and appraising the suitability of the securities offered.

The second and quite unusual task that required a great deal of careful work in this branch was receiving, weighing, safekeeping, and shipping great quantities of gold on behalf of the Bank of England. Early in the war Britain called in balances owing to British banks and other businesses in order to obtain U.S. dollars or gold, which was required to pay for the large British orders for munitions and supplies being placed in the United States. This action led to a large flow of payments to Britain and an increase in the foreign exchange value of the pound sterling. Under ordinary circumstances in those days, such an increase would have been offset by shipping gold, but because of the war risks, it was too hazardous or expensive to ship it to London. Instead the Bank of England requested the Department of Finance, which had large vaults in the East Block and experience in handling gold, to act as its agent in receiving and safeguarding the gold. The department agreed and received huge amounts—$1,200 million worth at the old price of about $20 an ounce—in 1915 and later years from Britain, South Africa, and Russia. Nearly all the gold came in warships, mainly fast cruisers. The gold was to be held until required for transfer to the United States. Three-quarters of it was in the form of bullion rather than coin, which had to be carefully weighed to the nearest one-thousandth part of an ounce. Some of it was "raw" gold not yet refined to the purity required for monetary purposes. A special refinery was built in Ottawa for this purpose before shipment to the United States.

The finance minister was very proud of the way the department handled the task, and he praised it very highly in his book on Canada's war finance. Nearly all of this work, he notes, was done by a few members of the staff of the department, working day and night and weekends.[49] Rourke, the comptroller of the currency in charge of this branch, worked endless hours of overtime on his own tasks and those of others during the war and the years immediately after. His health and nerve failed in doing so, and he committed suicide in December 1921. Sir Thomas White, who had ceased being minister two years before, spoke of Rourke as a casualty of the war.

The Finance Department lost probably its best man in the midst of the war when Assistant Deputy Minister Ross left in March 1917 to become secretary of the Canadian Bankers' Association. As legal adviser and legal draftsman for the department, he had provided advice to the minister and others in the department on the content and application of the law as well. He was also in contact with people outside the government, who were affected by the statutes for which the department was responsible, notably the bankers. Ross explained his advisory role in a letter to the prime minister following his decision to resign.[50] His prospects for succeeding Boville as deputy minister must have been good in 1917, but recent experience probably led him to believe that he could have more influence on policy as well as more pay by being secretary to the association.

Speaking broadly, the war of 1914–18 drew the department into a much wider range of economic and financial operations than it had had before and led its senior officers into a more substantial role as policy advisers to the minister. It was chiefly Breadner and Ross, who had come in as experienced men from outside, who performed this advisory role most fully; many of those who had worked their way up from junior clerks were not fitted for it. R. B. Viets, also trained as a lawyer but employed as private secretary to both Fielding and White, later took over the legal role that Ross had developed. J. C. Saunders succeeded Ross as assistant deputy minister in 1917, but the former Dominion bookkeeper would have been unable to do the legal work. Indeed it would appear that Saunders continued in the role of Dominion bookkeeper, as well as taking on administrative duties generally, for J. G. MacFarlane became head of the Accounts Branch, with the title of assistant Dominion bookkeeper.[51] In retrospect Saunders's advancement proved to be a mistake.

Chapter Two

Performance of the Department in the Twenties

After a sharp inflationary boom in 1919–20, Canada's economy experienced a recession in 1921. Unemployment among trade union members during the spring reached 16 percent, and net domestic income for the year was 24 percent less than that in 1920.[1] Conditions improved in 1922: exports were up, imports were down. Farm prices remained low, but the wheat crop was larger. Construction was increasing.

The year 1922 also saw a new government in power and the return of a very experienced minister of finance. Mackenzie King's first government took office December 29, 1921, and his finance minister was Sir William Fielding, who had been in that office throughout the Laurier regime from 1896 to 1911. Fielding (1848–1929) was born and raised in Halifax and was a journalist for twenty years before entering provincial politics in 1884. He remained minister of finance with King until he retired in 1925 at age seventy-seven.

The Prosperity of the Twenties

The recovery that began in 1922 continued through 1925, with a brief pause in 1924. In May 1923 Fielding reported in his budget: "Suddenly, so suddenly as to leave room for doubt as to a continuance of it, a great revival of business has arisen in the United States. . . . This activity across the border . . . has naturally affected us in Canada. . . . Experience has shown that the United States are usually ahead of us by a few months, perhaps a year, in the change of conditions."[2]

Fielding's doubts were justified; there was a mild and short recession in the United States (and in Europe) in 1924 and a very mild one in Canada. But by 1925 recovery was again under way, led by exports and a mild recovery in business investment. By this time the price of wheat had recovered to satisfactory levels and economic expansion had resumed in the Prairie provinces.[3]

The latter half of the twenties was a period of general expansion and prosperity. Even the Maritime provinces, which had been particularly depressed in the first half of the decade, joined in the expansion, assisted by Dominion tariff and transportation policies, subsidies on coal, and substantial harbour improvements. Ontario and Quebec were developing their own export markets for minerals and pulp and paper, as well as manufacturing for the Canadian market. The development of the automobile and roads for it, extensive production and distribution of electricity, and growing urbanization, all contributed to substantial capital investment, both private and public.

These public investments were in fields of provincial jurisdiction: municipalities and roads, water power, forest and mineral resources, and manufacturing industry in general. The national policies and projects of railway building, western settlement, and the protective tariff, while still proceeding, were less prominent than provincial development and were modified to meet regional interests.[4]

THE GENERAL FISCAL PATTERN

Conscious of the financial burdens of debt and pensions the war had left with them, in addition to the heritage of excessive railroad building, postwar governments in Ottawa were less enterprising and expansive than their prewar predecessors had been. More of the political initiatives were being taken by provincial governments, as reflected in expenditure policies and programs. The only major expenditure program begun in the twenties by the federal government was old age pensions in 1927. Mackenzie King originally undertook this decision in January 1926 as a result of negotiations with Labour and Progressive members of Parliament to gain their support to keep his minority government in office after the disastrous election of October 1925.[5] Even this new program involved very little expenditure in the late 1920s, as the provinces were slow to take up the 50 percent grants available to them if they paid pensions of twenty dollars a month to persons over seventy who could qualify by a means test.

Total Dominion budgetary expenditures were $476 million in 1920-21; they fell to $441 million in 1921-22, and after a decline to $352 million in 1923-24, they gradually rose to $442 in 1929-30. Meanwhile the total current expenditures of the nine provinces more than doubled over this period, from $91 million in 1920-21 to $188 million in 1929-30. The Dominion was able to reduce its net direct debt during the decade from $2,769 million in 1921 to $2,522 million in March 1930, though it increased its indirect debt (mainly guaranteed railway debt) by $706 million. The provinces collectively about doubled their outstanding debt, direct and indirect, from $633 million in 1921 to $1,246 million in 1930. Apart from railway financing, then, it is clear that the fiscal problems of the federal government were not serious during the twenties (after the initial postwar boom and collapse) and it was the provincial governments and their municipalities that were having to finance growth and development.

TAX POLICIES AND TARIFFS

The Dominion government was not inactive in the tax field, however, in part because of the new-found attractions of the sales tax in the first half of the decade, and in part because of the need of Mackenzie King and his ministers of finance to woo the West and farmers in other parts of the country with concessions on the tariff.

In 1922 Fielding increased the sales tax by one-half, as Sir Henry Drayton, the previous minister of finance, had in 1921, making the effective rates 4½ percent on domestic sales and 6 percent on imports, but leaving the cumbersome structure of rates as they had been in 1921. The following year he took note of the many criticisms of the structure of the tax, and he changed the form to a single tax applying on both domestic products and imports, based on the manufacturers' price or its equivalent as determined by administrative rulings. When this new form was adopted, the rate was increased to 6 percent, beginning in January 1924. In his budget a few months later J. A. Robb, acting finance minister, reduced the rate to 5 percent and introduced a number of exemptions as part of Mackenzie King's program to gain the support of the Progressives. King's plan included both expenditure reductions and tax and tariff reductions in 1924, well before the election expected the following year. In the later twenties, successive reductions of 1 percent a year brought the rate of the sales tax down to only 1 percent in May 1930.

Tariff policy also figured prominently in the Liberal program during the twenties, although the overall effects of that policy by the end of the decade did not greatly change the moderately protectionist character of the Canadian tariff as it was after increases imposed during the war for revenue purposes were removed soon after the war. The tariff was reduced during two periods, the first in 1922, 1923, and 1924 when the minority Liberal government was seeking the support of the Progressives. It took the form of material reductions in the duties on farm machinery in 1922 and modest reductions in the high rates on textiles. In 1923 it was reductions in the duty on sugar and minor reductions for equipment used in fishing, mining, and forestry. In 1924 it was farm machinery again, the duties being cut to less than half, and further reductions for the equipment of the other primary industries. These reductions were accompanied by exemption from the sales tax.

Very little change was made in the tariff in 1925, but the finance minister announced the government's intention to appoint an Advisory Board on Tariff and Taxation to inquire into the tariff and other forms of taxation and to advise the minister of finance about these matters. The board was intended to prepare for general or major revisions of the tariff. It was felt to have political advantages if suitable members could be found. As serious difficulties in finding the right men were encountered, the board was appointed only in March and April of the next year, 1926. Indeed Joseph Daoust of Montreal, one of those first appointed, spoke so much in favour of protection in his first interview with the press that he had to be immediately replaced.[6]

The second wave of tariff changes commenced in 1926 when the government had an even smaller minority in Parliament. It began with Robb's prosperity budget of April 15 and consisted of a substantial reduction in the duties on imported automobiles, particularly those selling at retail prices below $1,200.[7] In this same budget, which both reflected and enhanced the new feeling of prosperity in the country, the first major reductions were made in the personal income tax. Personal exemptions were increased by one-half, freeing many people from income tax entirely, and the rates were reduced. Corporate income tax was reduced from 10 to 9 percent.

The next major tariff changes were made in 1928 and were based on a detailed investigation of textile tariffs by the advisory board. Rates were reduced on many cotton and woollen goods and British preferences were widened. In addition rates were reduced on a number of other items, including coal for certain industrial purposes, and a drawback of 50 percent of the duty on seamless iron or steel tubing when used in the transmission of natural gas was initiated—a portent of things to come. Other tariff changes were made during the twenties because of trade agreements, but these were of secondary importance.[8]

The action taken on income tax during the twenties remains to be noted briefly. Despite many complaints about the tax, the rates, as well as personal exemptions, were left unchanged from 1920 until 1926. In 1922 and 1923 the exemption for dependent children was increased from $200 to $300 and then $500. But very few other changes, even of a technical nature, were made during this period, although some had been made in the immediate postwar years.

As already noted, Robb's prosperity budget of 1926 substantially reduced income tax rates and increased exemptions. A number of technical changes were also made, some alleviating the tax, others making it more rigorous. On balance, of course, the whole budget was very popular, as Mackenzie

King had intended it to be, and he claimed credit for it as representing the "fruits of four years of strict economy in management [of the] country's affairs."[9] The increases made earlier in the sales tax, which by that time was yielding much more than the income taxes on persons and corporations together, were not mentioned.

In 1927 income tax was again substantially reduced, the rates being cut by one-tenth, and the sales tax was reduced from 5 to 4 percent. In his budget speech Robb emphasized that the flourishing condition of the Dominion's finances permitted these reductions, while leaving some surplus for the lowering of debt. It was a fitting way for the minister of finance to mark the Diamond Jubilee year of Confederation in a period of solid prosperity.

In the 1928 budget, another reduction of one-tenth was made in the rates of income tax applicable to 1927 incomes (which were payable in 1928). The minister was able to get through the fiscal year, 1928–29, with a surplus and to carry out his declared policy of both tax and debt reduction.

In 1929 there was more of the same. This time the main tax reduction was in the sales tax. Again Robb looked forward to being able to reduce the debt, while holding expenditures in check. When that fiscal year was over, there was a surplus of $45 million of total revenues over all types of expenditures, despite the economic downturn that had occurred during 1929.

It is difficult to determine what role the Finance Department, as distinct from the minister, played in the introduction, amendment, and subsequent reduction of taxes and tariffs from the twenties to the beginning of the Depression in mid-1930. The departmental accountants and the deputy minister were almost certainly involved in estimating and forecasting revenues and expenditures, although forecasts related to economic analysis were generally not given by the ministers in their budgets. The department did not have any economists on its staff and rarely consulted outside economists except on tariff questions. Because of the importance of customs revenues (still much the largest item up to 1929), special attention was paid to trade conditions in budget speeches and no doubt in internal discussions. Some officers of the department, and some from the Customs, also assisted ministers with their knowledge of the complex details of the customs tariff and in the preparation of possible changes in it.

During the postwar period up to 1924, while R. W. Breadner was commissioner of taxation in the Finance Department, with the status and pay of a deputy minister, J. A. Russell continued to carry on his prewar duties of assisting senior officers in the department, and the minister, on matters relating to customs and the tariff. When Mackenzie King became prime minister, and developed a serious personal interest in the tariff, it is likely that he sought information on it directly from Russell and perhaps from Breadner. After the Taxation Division was transferred to the Department of Customs and Excise in 1924, Russell was made commissioner of tariff in the Department of Finance, a position he held until 1930 when he retired. The tariff was so complex, and the interrelation of the rates on various items often so important, that even though the policy involved in it was wholly ministerial, some confidential source of detailed information and analysis was needed.

After the Advisory Board on Tariff and Taxation was established in 1926, it carried on public hearings and made reports recommending new tariff rates. Since Russell's position as the commissioner of tariff was on a confidential basis, he remained separate from the advisory board; however, he assisted it and its consultants from time to time. The board had staff of its own, although this was mainly clerical, as the chairman, W. H. Moore, stated in his report of 1928 to the minister of finance. The board, however, secured technical assistance from civil servants in other departments, and it employed temporarily for special investigations "economists of national reputations," including Professor Gilbert Jackson of Toronto and Professor W. A. Mackintosh of Queen's.[10] Perusal of the board's files and reports indicates its work was of a serious, professional calibre, notwithstanding its partisan origins and associations.

The secretary of the board, Hector McKinnon, appointed in April 1926 by order-in-council on the recommendation of Finance Minister Robb, was a man of ability and good judgment, who had served overseas in the army during the war and at the time of his appointment was the parliamentary correspondent for the *Toronto Globe*. He later succeeded Russell as commissioner of tariff and became one of the outstanding civil servants of Canada. As a correspondent, he had a good practical knowledge of the tariff when he was appointed secretary to the advisory board and must have contributed substantially to the preparation of the constructive, detailed reports of the board.

It should be noted that after the arrival of H. T. Ross in 1906 until 1930, there was always a lawyer in the department but never a trained economist, despite the importance of economic conditions and problems in the department's tasks. Professional economists were relatively rare in Canada in those days and tended to be academic or historical in their interests, though there were such important exceptions as Mackenzie King in the Labour Department and later O. D. Skelton in External Affairs. There were, however, many lawyers in the private sector, even before Confederation, and their varied professional experience often fitted them to become members of Parliament and ministers, and also to be legal advisers and legal draftsmen in departments. Besides Ross, another lawyer in the department was R. B. Viets, who became the departmental solicitor after Ross left, and eventually solicitor to the Treasury. It does not appear, from what one reads in the files, that he was in the same class as an administrator or adviser as Ross was.

Debt Management

Debt was, of course, the main financial legacy of the war, and in the absence of a central bank the burden of managing it fell upon the minister and Department of Finance. The period of the twenties began with fiscal year 1920–21, in which no new direct loans were issued, as a large cash balance was carried over from the proceeds of the 1919 Victory Loan and expenditures had declined by this time to something close to the revenues that could be raised in Drayton's austere budget of 1920. In 1920 there were two issues in New York of guaranteed railway bonds at 7 percent interest, which were sold at a discount. In 1921 there were two more of these guaranteed railroad bond issues, carrying 6½ and 6 percent interest and sold at deep discounts, which the new Liberal minister of finance criticized in his 1922 budget speech.

The first major loan of the decade was issued in New York on May 1, 1922, for $100 million (U.S.). It was a thirty-year bond at 5 percent interest. In December of that year the first tranche of the 1917 Victory Loan matured, and Finance Minister Fielding issued Canadian taxable bonds at 5½ percent to replace it. By late 1923 Fielding and his advisers (who probably included bankers as well as his departmental officials) were prepared to try a large loan in the Canadian market; he sold $200 million of 5 percent taxable five-year and twenty-year bonds to a Canadian syndicate which marketed them to the public. Most of the proceeds were used to meet the $172 million of the maturing tranche of the 1918 tax-free Victory Loan. The following year, 1924, the five-year tranche of the 1919 Victory Loan matured, as well as substantial amounts of British Treasury bills held by the Canadian banks. The minister sold a short-term issue in New York, two short-term issues in Canada, and a $50 million twenty-year refunding loan in Canada to meet these obligations. With these major war loan maturities met, and the budget in surplus, the borrowing operations for the rest of the decade were not notable.

Guaranteed issues were of concern to the minister and department but did not involve the administrative work that the new and refunding direct issues did. Only after the formation of the Canadian National Railways (CNR) in 1923 did guaranteed issues appear regularly, most frequently in New York. On several occasions the CNR issued in New York optional payment bonds, payable either in U.S. or Canadian dollars, and in some cases sterling as well, at the choice of the holder. When the gold standard was the rule, these option provisions seemed to involve little extra risk, but when the value of the U.S. and Canadian dollars diverged, they had special importance.

The servicing and administration of the postwar public debt of $2½ billion, including probably over 2 million bonds, most of them having semi-annual coupons for the payment of interest, involved an enormous amount of routine but careful work. Arrangements had to be made for printing, checking, distributing, transferring, and accounting for the bonds and then for redeeming, checking, auditing, and eventually destroying the interest coupons. Finally there was required the receipt, verification, redemption, accounting, auditing, and eventually destruction of the bonds themselves. An organization chart of the department in 1918 shows about 520 clerks engaged on this work under the charge of G. W. Hyndman.[11] In addition, more temporary clerks were taken on during the months before and after the major bond issues, notably the Victory Loan issues of 1917, 1918, and 1919, and also in the 1920s when the maturing bonds were refunded or paid off. Serious practical difficulties arose in getting competent, trustworthy clerks on short notice. J. C. Saunders described the problem in his evidence to the Special Committee on the Civil Service in 1923.

> During the period of four months from the middle of August to the middle of December the senior officers were obliged to be on duty every night till eleven or twelve o'clock. The junior members of the staff were required to be on duty on alternate nights. . . . The conditions indicated were cheerfully borne by all during the war period but it does not seem reasonable the heads of branches and staff should be compelled by conditions, which ought to be subject to control, to continue under such a strain. The prospect of a yearly recurrence of these conditions prompts an urgent appeal by the Finance Department for a change in the regulations and, if necessary, in the [Civil Service] Act.[12]

The committee recommended what Saunders had requested, but although the law was not changed during that decade, the problem greatly diminished in later years.

Misappropriations of Funds

The strained and overloaded conditions in the War Finances Branch during and after the war probably contributed to two defalcations by officers of the department. The first, during 1916–19, involved the handling of the interest coupons on U.S. dollar bonds issued in New York early in the war. Because of the great workload of the staff administering the bonds, Deputy Minister Boville, arranged that these New York coupons were to be received from the fiscal agent in New York, verified, and held in custody by his own two secretaries, G. J. Artz, an experienced accountant, and Miss G. L. Mainguay. When Saunders succeeded Boville as deputy minister in April 1920, he immediately issued instructions that this irregular practice cease and that the coupons and bonds in the custody of Artz and Mainguay be transferred to the Loans and Interest Branch and be checked and audited in the same way as the coupons and bonds of other issues. An apparent shortage of $53,338.50 in coupons in the account was found. On Saunders's recommendation, the minister brought in an outside firm of chartered accountants to audit this account and all others for loans issued during the war. The audit confirmed the shortage in the New York coupons but no others. After months of investigation by the RCMP, Artz confessed to the theft. Being expert enough to understand the system and its possibilities, and the weakness of double custody with his junior assistant, he would remove some coupons from the packages immediately on receipt and cash them a second time. Because there was always some lag in the cashing of some coupons, he knew that totals did not exceed the number shown as due in the accounts. Artz was arrested, pleaded guilty, and was sentenced to three years in the penitentiary.[13]

The second case of defalcation was more serious and prolonged. In 1922 G. P. Gordon joined the Finance Department as one of a number of experienced and able men whom Fielding brought in shortly after he became minister again at the end of 1921. Gordon's was a political appointment to an unclassified but fairly well paid position. Gordon was a Scot, who earned an M.A. degree from St. Andrews University and won prizes and scholarships there. He taught for a while in Europe and studied business at a commercial college in Britain before immigrating to Canada to work for one and then another coal company in Nova Scotia. He was thirty-five years old when he joined Finance. Although the other men Fielding had brought in left the department after only a short period of service, apparently because of the attitude they encountered there, Gordon was more persistent. He was employed under the comptroller of the currency in inspecting (presumably including auditing) the offices of the Assistant Receivers General for the period 1922 to 1927. Evidence he later gave indicates that he was also doing some auditing and investigating of departmental operations and accounts in Ottawa. During the investigations, Gordon turned up evidence of illegal actions in regard to the misuse and stealing of bonds by G. W. Hyndman when he was comptroller of the currency and later assistant deputy minister.

In 1929 the matter came to a head. Gordon's findings must have convinced Saunders that something very serious had been going on. On July 29 Saunders requested Walter Duncan, a special investigating police officer, to conduct a formal investigation into certain irregularities and defalcations in the department. Duncan proceeded immediately to question under oath many persons in the department, including G. P. Gordon. Within a week he reported to the deputy minister that he had evidence that Hyndman had stolen bonds and obtained a cheque from the department under false pretences. After taking further testimony, and making three interim reports to Saunders, Duncan swore out warrants for Hyndman's arrest and for the search of his dwelling. In Hyndman's house Duncan found an important file and other papers taken from the department. Formal charges were laid against Hyndman and he was found guilty on two of them, was acquitted on one, and pleaded guilty to a fourth. He was convicted and sentenced to seven years in the penitentiary.

Hyndman's behaviour and Duncan's detailed report to the new minister of finance, C. A. Dunning, leave one with an unfavourable impression of the management of the department.[14] The report also cast doubts on the thoroughness of the audits made of the department's accounts by its own officers (other than Gordon) and by outside auditors.[15] At the trial the defence counsel called Gordon W. Scott, chairman of the Board of Audit, in defence of Hyndman, and Scott had to admit there was a discrepancy which his board had assumed was just the result of clerical errors somewhere in the mass of transactions. The losses were small—$10,700—in relation to the many hundreds of millions of dollars passing through the department. Duncan did report that his complete and thorough investigation turned up no evidence of other defalcations.[16] Gordon left the department in August 1930 immediately following the defeat of the Liberals in the election in July that year.

THE FINANCE ACT AND MONETARY POLICY

Another heritage from the war that affected operations of the Finance Department through the twenties was the Finance Act and its implications for monetary and banking policy. It gave the department some of the powers and responsibilities held in more advanced countries by central banks, but without the expert officers and staff, and independence of government, to carry them out.

It may be recalled that the Finance Act of 1914 (and a proclamation made under it on September 5, 1914) suspended the redemption of Dominion notes in gold and, notably, authorized the minister of finance to make advances to the chartered banks of Dominion notes (not backed by gold as under the Dominion Notes Act) on the pledge of securities of such kinds as the Treasury Board determined. The advances were subject to the payment of interest at a rate specified by the board, but it was not to be less than 5 percent.

The effect of the act was the creation of a new, partially managed monetary system, free from the fetters of the gold standard and able to expand money and credit either as a result of inflows of gold or as a result of the "rediscounting" of acceptable assets by the minister of finance. The system was made more expansionary by the decision, taken during the war but continued later, that the rediscount rate on an asset (that is, the rate of interest a bank would have to pay in borrowing from the monetary authorities against that asset as collateral security) would normally be lower than that yielded by the assets or by bank assets in general. This practice was followed by the Federal Reserve banks in the United States, but was contrary to that in London where the bank rate, for rediscounting, would normally be above the money market rates.

During the war, expansion of the system was required, but was held under control by the personal influence of Sir Thomas White, who was knowledgeable in those matters and kept closely in touch with senior bankers. In the dark days of late 1917, however, when British finances were in serious difficulties, White was persuaded to provide by an order under the War Measures Act a special rate of 3½ percent for rediscounting, for the Canadian banks, of British Treasury bill certificates they had bought and held. This special rate encouraged and facilitated more monetary expansion in the remaining year of the war and afterwards. It also set a precedent for bargaining special rates in circumstances that would assist in government financing.

After Sir Henry Drayton took over as minister of finance in August 1919, he was constrained in limiting rediscounting or increasing the discount rate by the continuing need for financing high expenditures during 1919, first by Treasury bills sold to the banks and then by the Victory Loan of December 1919, which required the support of the banks in lending funds to subscribers to enable them to buy the bonds. Afterwards, in 1920, it was the needs of the Market Committee in support of the Victory Loans that inhibited him from increasing the discount rate.[17] By 1921 international deflation was in progress, prices were falling rapidly, and Canada had an adverse balance of payments and a weak exchange rate. Under these circumstances advances under the Finance Act fell rapidly to a low level.

In 1922 and 1923 a new problem arose under the Finance Act. Several banks were in difficulties and needed to obtain Dominion notes to meet their clearing obligations to the Bank of Montreal, which would not accept anything else, except gold. The assets they had available to pledge with the minister of finance for an advance under the Finance Act were of a type that required some knowledge of banking and expert judgment to evaluate. No one in the department had that knowledge. Finance Minister Fielding, unwilling to accept such collateral and make the loans without having it properly appraised, sought to shift responsibility for appraisal to the Canadian Bankers' Association, but it was reluctant to accept the role. He even endeavoured to attract H. T. Ross back to the department from his job as secretary of the association, but with no success.[18] Fielding persisted in efforts to reduce advances to the banks by various means, which added to the difficulties of several of the smaller banks. By one means or another these were saved, until the very different case of the Home Bank came along.

In 1923 an Act to Supplement the Finance Act was passed. A statute such as this was required because the 1919 act (chapter 21), continuing in force the proclamation that was passed under the 1914 act, was to extend only two years after the official termination of the then "present war"; this would be August 31, 1923. The new 1923 act extended indefinitely the power of the minister to make advances to the chartered banks, specified what types of securities could be pledged as collateral for such advances, and removed the lower limit of 5 percent on the interest rate that could be charged on such advances. It permitted the minister to request the advice of the trustees of the Central Gold Reserves, most of whom were bank officials, on the quality of any securities offered in pledge. The act also continued in effect, for three years only, the suspension of the obligation to redeem Dominion notes in gold. This provision meant that unless other legislation was passed, Canada would return to the gold standard in mid-1926. The limitation to three years only was included in the act by R. B. Viets, solicitor of the department.[19] No reference was made to this provision in the House of Commons. Apparently little real consideration was given within the department to its implications.

The 1923 act reflected a lack of understanding of monetary systems and problems by the department and the minister because it provided for a permanent gold standard regime under which the banks could increase their monetary reserves without any additional gold backing. It was passed through all stages in the House of Commons in a debate that occupies only four pages of *Hansard*.[20]

A few weeks after the act was passed, but only by coincidence, the Home Bank failed so seriously that its depositors were about to suffer severe losses. The Home Bank case, the first bank failure since 1914, had an interesting history and important consequences. As far back as 1916 and 1918 Finance Minister White had been warned by some of the directors that the condition of the bank was unsatisfactory. White had made a very discreet inquiry that reassured him and decided not to risk any further action for fear of precipitating a financial crisis that would be harmful in the midst of the war. The situation of the bank gradually grew worse but was not disclosed. The directors did not seek any outside help until the last minute when it was too late. When Fielding became minister, he had been told by Drayton, his predecessor, about the earlier information concerning the Home Bank but he had taken no initiative to deal with the matter. There were confidential files on the subject in the minister's office, of which the deputy minister was unaware.[21]

The report and evidence of a royal commission set up to inquire into the history of the affair were considered by the House of Commons Committee on Banking and Commerce in 1924. The committee concluded that the depositors of the bank had some moral claim for compensation by the government because they had been harmed by White's decision during the war, taken in the public interest. In 1925 Parliament eventually provided some help, though as a gratuity subject to low limits.

A second conclusion of the committee resulted in government inspection of the banks. The Canadian Bankers' Association initially opposed inspection, but when it was clear that something was going to be done, the association prepared draft legislation for consideration by the minister; it undoubtedly influenced the form of inspection. It was an economical arrangement involving an annual inspection of head office accounts by a government inspector general of banks who would have access to all accounts, documents, and securities, the use of the banks' own auditors and their internal reports, and authority to examine bank officers under oath. The legislation was passed in 1924. C. S. Tompkins, former chief inspector of the Royal Bank, was appointed inspector general on November 1, 1924.

Tompkins's association with the department (he reported to the minister) had an important and troublesome effect on Saunders. Prior to that time Saunders readily acknowledged that he knew nothing of economics, as was quite evident in his 1924 testimony to the House of Commons Committee on Banking and Commerce.[22] In Tompkins, however, Saunders felt he had an expert adviser by his side. In fact Tompkins was somewhat limited even in the range of his banking experience. He had little knowledge or understanding of economics in general or of questions concerning monetary systems or policy. Consequently Saunders derived a false assurance from his association with Tompkins, a situation which was dangerous in the years 1926 to 1929.

In 1925 the British returned to the formal gold standard at the old parity of the pound under circumstances that were quite unfavourable. Their action, a matter of controversy for years in which J. M. Keynes was a leading critic, may indeed have been the beginning of Britain's decline as an industrial power. Their action also posed the question of what Canada should do, especially given Viets's three-year clause in the 1923 act that would put Canada back on gold in mid-1926. The prime minister and the minister of finance considered the matter early in 1925, but the leading bankers were opposed to a return to the gold standard at that time and Saunders advised delay. Delayed it was.

The decision had to be faced in 1926. The president of the Bank of

Montreal wrote to Finance Minister Robb that it would be financial suicide to return to the gold standard unless gold reserves were substantially increased. The Royal Bank, however, which was more involved than the others in international banking, favoured an immediate return to gold and circulated a lecture given by its economist, D. M. Marvin, making the case on general economic grounds but including a recommendation that the law should restrict rediscounting under the Finance Act if gold holdings fell below 40 percent of the note issue. The Bankers' Association could give no agreed advice with the Royal opposed to the general view of the other banks. Robb sought other advice, notably from Professor Gilbert Jackson of Toronto. Jackson responded in a long memorandum with three main conclusions: Canada should return to a pre-1914 type of gold standard; there was no serious risk of gold losses; and advances such as those made under the Finance Act should be terminated and used only in an emergency. Saunders studied Jackson's memorandum but was not persuaded that the rediscounting provisions of the Finance Act should be changed. He therefore advised Robb that no further action need be taken and that Canada would automatically go on the gold standard with the expiry of the three-year suspension clause of the 1923 act.[23] Accepting this advice, Robb announced in the House of Commons on May 31 that the government did not intend to introduce new legislation. Canada would therefore be back on the gold standard on July 1.

In the following year, 1927, U.S. interest rates declined as a result of Federal Reserve action designed to ease the pressure on the British pound. The Treasury Board reduced the rediscount rate from 5 to 4 percent on November 1, 1927, allegedly because of the U.S. action.[24] Immediately afterwards, however, on December 1, the rate was again reduced, to 3¾ percent, apparently as part of a deal in which the chartered banks bought $45 million in three-year Dominion notes at 4 percent. This borrowing in Canada at a subsidized rate was done when Robb had already been advised that these funds, required to meet a Canadian dollar maturity, could be obtained in New York, an action which would have been eminently sensible because the Dominion's gold reserves, as the president of the Bank of Montreal had warned in 1926, were really inadequate for Canada to maintain the gold standard, given the nature of its balance of payments and banking system.

These low rediscount rates were most inappropriate for the serious problems looming in 1928 and 1929 as a result of the stock exchange boom on Wall Street. The frenzied buying of stocks on margin gave rise to an intense demand for call loans, at abnormal interest rates, to which the Canadian banks responded, along with many others. The Canadian balance of payments was weakening a little, both on current and capital account, and the exchange market required a significant outflow of monetary gold early in 1928. In response, on June 8, 1928, the Treasury Board increased the rediscount rate on new advances under the Finance Act to 5 percent, with a special provision that banks withdrawing gold in exchange for Dominion notes would have to pay the 5 percent rate on outstanding advances. The banks protested bitterly.[25]

By the autumn of 1928 the exchange situation and rate had eased somewhat. Faced with the need to finance a bumper wheat crop and therefore to obtain increased advances under the Finance Act, the banks asked for and received a reduction from 5 to 4½ percent in the rediscount rate. At the time Robb asked the banks if they would undertake not to demand gold for Dominion notes in order to take advantage of the high interest rates in New York. The president of the Canadian Bankers' Association said that he "did not believe that any of the banks would demand gold under the circumstances."[26]

By the end of 1928 the attraction of New York for funds and therefore for gold was so great that there was a large decline in the gold reserves against Dominion notes in December 1928 and January 1929. As a result, the Finance Department informally embargoed the export of gold by refusing to redeem Dominion notes for that purpose. The Canadian dollar declined in value in New York well beyond the level at which it would pay to sell gold from Canada to get U.S. dollars, indeed to a discount of 1 or 2 percent at times during 1929. Considerable argument ensued over the respective responsibilities of the government and of the banks for maintaining the gold standard and in particular for maintaining the exchange rate by gold sales. Meanwhile the exchange situation was much relieved by the CNR's issue of a guaranteed long-term loan for $60 million in New York in June and another of the same size in October. Then occurred the historic stock market crash of October 1929, which quickly cut down the demand for call loans in New York. By early 1930 the exchange rate on the Canadian dollar was back within the range called for by the gold standard. The large inflow of capital to Canada in 1930 held it there and permitted a modest recovery in the gold reserves.

Events in the monetary and banking field demonstrated the inadequacy of departmental management both in advising the government, such as in the formulation of the 1923 legislation and the decision to return to the gold standard in 1926, and in carrying out operations, such as those relating to rediscount rates and gold movements in 1928 and 1929. The results in the end were not serious at the time—indeed a modest decline in the value of the Canadian dollar in 1929 caused far less economic trouble than a raise in interest rates to compete with the quite abnormal rates in New York would have caused. Even the unsophisticated decision to return to the gold standard in 1926, with inadequate reserves and a lack of effective control over the money supply, seems to have caused no serious harm. What Canada needed most in those years was the ability to borrow in New York when support of its balance of payments was required. Being on the gold standard, if only nominally, probably helped this ability to borrow, even in 1929 when the game was no longer being played according to the rules. It certainly helped in 1930 when the need was greatest and other countries were unable to borrow in New York.

DEPARTMENTAL MANAGEMENT

What this lack of understanding in the monetary field did demonstrate, more than action in other fields, such as setting up the Advisory Board on Tariff and Taxation, was the need to have officials in the Finance Department with an understanding of economics. This was clearly expressed in Parliament in mid-decade by W. C. Good, the member for Brant, who was the president of the Co-operative Union of Canada.[27] On June 11, 1925, speaking on the Estimates for Finance, he said:

> What has impressed me very much since I have been here is the conspicuous difference between the organization in the Department of Finance and the organization in some of the other departments. Take, for instance, the Department of Agriculture, where those in charge of the different branches are specialists in the respective fields. We admit the need of securing the services of experts in these several departments. But in the Department of Finance we have, so far as I can find out no man who has any general knowledge of economics, who has given any special study to the questions that ought to be well known and thoroughly considered in that department. I am sorry to have to make any personal reflections, but the Deputy Minister of Finance, who, I understand, has been acting as secretary of the Treasury board, has been before the Banking and Commerce committee on two or three occasions, and I have also discussed matters with him privately. As I said, I am sorry to make any personal reflections, but I do consider that he is totally unqualified to advise in regard to the many matters which must come before that department, and the minister himself cannot be expected to have gone into a number of these technical matters such as must necessarily be considered by the department. . . . I want earnestly to appeal to the minister to face the situation and apply the same common sense we have applied in our other departments, where we have the good sense to make use of the services of those who have given years of study to their respective specialties.[28]

Good, who had been educated in economics as well as in agriculture, was quite right. In the previous year the minister had defended Saunders as being honest, sincere, loyal to his chief no matter who that chief may be, and a longtime and hardworking member of the service.[29] But the time had come when loyalty, honesty, industry, and seniority were not enough. Perhaps it was this public criticism as well as the internal knowledge of the department that led first the Liberals in 1930, and then Prime Minister Bennett for two years more, to delay in appointing a new deputy minister of finance. The delay was worth it because the department got W. C. Clark in 1932, who was eminently qualified, and in the meantime they had Watson Sellar, a man whose ability to hold the ship on course would soon be tested by the worst economic weather Canada had ever encountered.

Chapter Three

The Economic Course and Impact of the Depression

The problems and performance of the Department of Finance during the 1930s can be understood only with some knowledge of the almost world-wide Depression that developed quickly in 1930 and persisted throughout the decade.

The second half of the 1920s was a period of prosperity and development in most countries, particularly in the United States, Canada, Australia, and Italy.[1] There were notable exceptions, such as Great Britain, whose traditional export industries were growing old and uncompetitive and were handicapped by the re-establishment of the gold standard in 1925 with the pound at its old parity, which was too high. The economy of Germany suffered under the burden of reparations, unemployment, and financial instability, despite the foreign loans it received.

The widespread prosperity of the late 1920s was not accompanied by rising price levels; indeed, on balance, prices were falling gently in the United States and were stable in Canada. Wages were rising slowly. It was only on the stock exchanges, led by New York, that prices were booming in the late 1920s. The stock market boom and the demand for brokers' loans gave rise to increased short-term interest rates in the United States, which drew in short-term capital from overseas, causing financial difficulties for Great Britain, Germany, and other countries. Canada suffered to some degree, but informal restrictions on the export of gold and banking funds kept these outflows from Canada within tolerable bounds.

The price changes of most significance in the latter half of the 1920s were the declines in international commodity prices—food and raw materials—in non-European countries. This downward trend in prices was clearly visible in the case of wheat, a commodity of overwhelming importance in international trade. The high wheat prices that emerged immediately after the war stimulated production in the United States, Canada, Australia, and Argentina, which became the great exporters, aided by the mechanization of large-scale wheat farming. During the 1920s production expanded in Europe as well, behind high tariffs and other more direct forms of protection for the peasant farmers. This increased worldwide production exceeded prewar levels. Prices fell until 1923, when crops were small, and then declined steadily after 1925. The 1928 crop was large in both importing and exporting countries, especially Canada and Argentina, and the world wheat prices declined substantially as stocks increased. The decline led to widespread government action to protect the farmers in importing countries and to some holding back of supplies in exporting countries in efforts to avoid further price declines.

Such declines in prices and increases in stocks applied to sugar, coffee and tea, and other foodstuffs. Many raw materials were similarly affected, notably cotton, wool, silk, rubber, and tin. The declining prices and inadequate markets led to lower incomes for producers and to serious problems in the balance of payments for some of the overseas countries heavily dependent on exports of these products. In a number of countries, notably Argentina, the situation led to depreciation of their currencies.

In the United States, the downturn in industrial production began in mid-1929. Construction was at high levels from 1923 to 1929. Residential construction, however, reached its peak in 1925, declined slowly to 1928 and sharply in 1929. Automobile production and sales, largely financed by instalment credit, were very substantial in the late 1920s (by the standard of those days), reaching their peak in March 1929. Indeed, the high and sustained levels of construction and production in the United States in the 1920s were largely based directly and indirectly upon the effects of the mass purchase of automobiles, which influenced the growth of cities and suburbs as well as many supporting industries. But despite the prosperity, serious weaknesses in the American economy made it vulnerable.[2] The stock market crash of October 1929 in which share prices fell by 30 percent over a few months was such a spectacular and shocking setback to the public faith in continuing prosperity, and in the ability, and credibility, of business and businessmen, that it must have had serious effects on the willingness of businesses to make long-term investments in plants and equipment, and of consumers to spend on durable goods like cars.

The downturn in industrial production, in wholesale prices generally, and in international trade took place in most countries in Europe and North America at various dates in 1929. Indeed, the nearly simultaneous downturn was a part of the problem, since there were few large prosperous economies to help cushion the shock. Germany was the first major country to get noticeably worse; it had had many economic troubles and much unemployment before 1929. France, on the other hand, was doing well, largely because of its undervalued currency; industrial production there did not decline until 1931. Britain's economy had been less prosperous in the late 1920s; it turned down in 1929 but declined less rapidly after mid-1931 and had levelled off by 1932.

After a short pause early in 1930, world industrial production fell rapidly throughout that year and the next and reached very low levels in 1932. By then the United States had declined furthest (apart from Germany), to 53.8 percent of 1929 levels, according to the annual indexes published by the League of Nations,[3] but Canada was close behind at 58.1 percent, along with Poland, Italy, and a number of the smaller European countries.

World production of agricultural products did not decline in the 1930-33 downswing, except for crop yields in particular areas, but their prices declined drastically. The wholesale prices of farm products in the United States, based on the 1929 average as 100, fell to 97.1 by the end of that year, to 71.7 in December 1930, to 53.1 in December 1931, and to 42.0 in December 1932.[4] An index of world agricultural prices, based on 1923-25 as 100, declined to a level of about 70 in the third quarter of 1929; the pace then increased and the decline during 1930, 1931, and 1932 was 40, 28, and 12 percent, respectively, bringing prices to 24.4 percent of that base period by December 1932.[5]

World production of raw materials, other than farm products, fell rapidly in 1930, 1931, and 1932 to a level of 63 percent of that of 1929.[6] This decline was greater in North America than elsewhere. Although the prices of particular commodities varied widely, their decline was substantial but less than the decline in prices of foodstuffs.

Between 1929 and 1932 manufacturing production in Europe fell to 78 percent of the 1939 level, which was significantly less than in North America where it dropped to 58 percent of the 1929 level.[7] In the United States the wholesale prices of finished goods declined substantially less than those of raw materials and semi-finished goods.[8] The same was true of other countries. Internationally this difference in the rate of decline of prices was visible in the comparison of export and import prices of the overseas agricultural and raw material producing countries, including Canada.[9]

Another general feature of the Depression was that production of investment goods for producers declined much more than production of current consumer goods. While this situation was most marked in North America, where the decline occurred even more severely in construction, it was also evident in the major European countries, but in their case building activity was better maintained than the production of business investment goods.

Perhaps the most important feature in the whole process was the very great decline in world trade. In part this decline was the result of decreased production and demand in importing countries. But a large part of the reduction was caused by increased tariffs and other barriers imposed after the downturn had begun. The most serious of these new barriers was the Hawley-Smoot tariff, a radical increase enacted by the U.S. Congress during late 1929 and the first half of 1930. This legislation increased tariffs on both agricultural and manufactured products to the highest levels in history. The greatest market in the world was being fenced in without any concern for the well-being of the other nations which would certainly be affected by this action. Inevitably it led to widespread retaliation and imitation by other countries. Canada, one of the countries most affected, responded with widespread, severe, and arbitrary protectionist measures within three months.

As a result of the depression in incomes, aggravated by these severe restraints imposed by many countries, the value of world trade, expressed in U.S. dollars, fell by more than 60 percent from 1929 to 1932. These figures include the effects of the fall in prices; estimates made by the League of Nations of the volume of world trade, valued at constant prices, show a decline of 25 percent from 1929 to 1932.[10]

The decline in production and trade naturally led to unemployment on a massive scale. Unfortunately data on unemployment at that time were quite inadequate except in a few countries. In the mid-1930s the International Labour Office estimated that for the Western world as a whole unemployment in 1932 was about three times what it had been in 1929.[11] In the United States it was seven times greater; in Britain, about two; in Germany, about three; in Canada, about four; in Australia, about two and one-half times greater. These figures do not include the huge numbers of underemployed farmers and their families, particularly those of western Canada and the United States, many of whom were just as destitute as the unemployed.

The International Monetary Crisis

The international monetary crises of 1931 in Europe ultimately led to the end of the gold standard.[12] Germany had been burdened with reparations, occupation, hyper-inflation, serious unemployment, and subsequently deflation. It had been getting along with the help of large amounts of short-term borrowing and was very vulnerable if those loans were not renewed. Its neighbour, Austria, had mismanaged its finances for years, and its weak economy was dependent on trade with Germany and short-term banking credits from the major countries. In May 1931 the largest bank in Austria, the Credit-Anstalt, found itself unable to carry on without substantial help from outside. A run on the bank developed while efforts were being made through the Bank for International Settlements to line up credits from major central banks. Too little was obtained too late.

The run on the Austrian banks spread to others in central Europe, including Germany. By June the German banks were in serious trouble. President Hoover managed to arrange a moratorium for twelve months on intergovernmental debts and reparations but this action was not enough to stop the rot. After other efforts, Germany introduced exchange controls which made it possible to block foreign credits. Neither the British nor the Americans were then willing to provide further loans to Germany or to guarantee private loans.

The pressure shifted to Britain, which was heavily indebted in sterling to external creditors, including central banks. It had large claims on Germany that were frozen. Two official reports gave some support to concern about Britain's financial strength—the Macmillan Commission report on monetary and international exchange matters and the report of the May Committee on the state of the British budget and measures to improve it. The need for some foreign loans to support sterling was evident but getting them raised serious questions of policy. The Labour government broke up over these issues of budget and exchange policy on August 24, 1931, and a National (coalition) government was formed with Ramsay MacDonald continuing as prime minister. Early in September a new balanced budget increased taxes and reduced expenditures. But there were also new bankruptcies in Germany which made the European markets nervous and they withdrew funds from London. Dangerous rumours were circulating about trouble in the Royal Navy as a result of pay cuts. The withdrawals accelerated. But the bank rate was not increased beyond that of 4½ percent established on August 30. On September 21 the British government decided to abandon the gold standard and let sterling decline in the market, an action widely regarded as a national disgrace and calamity. But it permitted Britain within a year to have a new, sensible, easy money policy and to convert its massive internal war loan from 5 to 3½ percent. By 1934 Britain's industrial production was above the admittedly unsatisfactory 1929 level. Building activity and automobile sales were well above their 1929 levels.

This experience in 1931 illustrated vividly that Britain could no longer lead and stabilize the world economy as it had before 1914. It still possessed the necessary institutions and the skills, but it lacked international financial strength and reserves. That role would have to be assumed by the United States and eventually was, in 1947. But in the 1930s the United States was neither ready nor willing to lead and stabilize the international economy.

Indeed, the United States was itself a source of instability for four reasons: the vicious barriers of the Hawley-Smoot tariff of 1930; the massive decline in private domestic investment from $16.2 billion in 1929 to $1.0 billion in 1932;[13] the precipitous fall in the index of wholesale prices from 95.3 in 1929 to 73.0 in 1931 and 64.8 in 1932, with farm prices falling much more;[14] and the banking failures and crises of 1931, 1932, and 1933, which reduced the volume of money and credit, culminating in a complete closure of all of the banks by Roosevelt immediately after his inauguration on March 4, 1933, to permit remedial action to be taken to safeguard them. American exports fell until 1932, thereby reducing American incomes and employment. Imports to the United States also fell rapidly until 1933, reducing incomes and employment in other countries. Net farm income in the United States fell from $6.1 billion in 1929 to $2.0 billion in 1932, despite the priority given to agriculture in the trade and support policies of the Hoover administration. Unemployment in the worst years, 1932 and 1933, has been estimated at 24 and 25 percent of the civilian labour force, from which it slowly came down to 14 percent in 1937 and only returned to pre-Depression levels in 1942 when the United States was at war.[15]

THE DOWNTURN IN CANADA

While 1929 stands out as the year of highest prosperity, production, and incomes in Canada before the Depression—but just barely better than 1928 when farm income was much higher—it is clear in looking at the figures that the Canadian economy in general turned down in about May of that year. By late autumn the decline became evident in employment and in production and exports. Yet apart from the stock market crash which occurred in Canada as well as in New York, there was little to indicate that more than a modest recession might be ahead.

As in the United States, however, there were good reasons for concern about the state of the Canadian economy in 1929. Both its largest manufacturing industry, pulp and paper, notably newsprint, and its great agricultural staple, wheat, were experiencing serious marketing problems. Moreover the Hawley-Smoot tariff was in the making.[16]

The production of newsprint in Canada had tripled during the 1920s, based on the huge growing market in the United States and advantages in supply arising from cheap wood, cheap water power, and proximity to main markets. The industry had been very profitable in the mid-1920s, even though the price of newsprint was declining, because costs were also declining. As time went on, however, the building of additional plants led to excess capacity and low operating ratios of 80 percent or less in the late 1920s. A number of mergers took place and much of the growth in capacity had been financed by bonds and debentures. Canadian exporters were confronted by large American newspaper companies and chains who could play one supplier off against others. In such a situation excess capacity was bound to lead to instability of prices and unsatisfactory operating results.

The trouble was not long in coming. Production of newsprint reached its peak in 1929, but at prices only about 86 percent of what they had been in 1926. In 1930 production declined by about 8 percent, but prices were held close to 1929 levels by a cartel which pooled contracts and divided production according to capacities. The cartel did not last beyond that year. Prices and production both fell in 1931 and much more in 1932. Major companies went into receivership.[17]

Difficulties were also encountered with wheat exports. In 1929, on the eve of the Depression, the Canadian wheat situation was unusual because of the size and quality of the two preceding crops at a time of overproduction in the world and growing protection in many European importing countries. In the 1927–28 crop year, world crops had been good, world year-end stocks had risen to relatively high levels, and world prices had declined significantly. Then came the bumper crops of 1928. Canada harvested a huge crop, but one of poor quality, with relatively little of the hard wheat on which the good reputation of Canadian wheat rested. As this fact became recognized in the autumn of 1928, coupled with relatively poor prospects for the 1929 crop, Canadian opinion began to expect a shortage of higher grade wheat and its price in Canada rose relative to general wheat prices in Liverpool and other overseas markets. This excess premium discouraged purchases overseas and resulted in a decline in Canadian exports early in 1929. The decline continued during the 1929–30 crop year, and the price fell steadily from the sharp peak of $1.60 a bushel in July 1929 to 95 cents in July 1930. (No. 1 Northern at Ft. William). When that crop year was over in mid-1930, exports of wheat (and flour) amounted to only 186 million bushels compared with 333 and 408 million bushels in the two preceding crop years. The carry-over stock on hand was 111 million bushels compared with 104 million the previous year.[18]

THE DRASTIC DECLINE TO 1933

In Canada the economic decline that began in May 1929 continued until April 1933—four years later—although for most of the world outside the United States the bottom was reached in 1932. Canadian affairs were so much affected by those in the United States, both directly and psychologically, that the final months of the U.S. banking crises and uncertainty during the transition from Hoover to Roosevelt delayed the end of Canada's decline and the beginning of recovery until after Roosevelt's inauguration on March 4, 1933.

It is convenient to describe the decline in terms of components of the gross national product (GNP) and gross national expenditure (GNE), even though these measures were not normally used in those years. At the time the main developments were recorded in trade and balance of payments figures (measures which were well developed), and in various measures or indexes of production and prices, farm income, and construction and capital expenditures. These statistics are given in tables 1-5.[19]

The scale and rapidity of the decline show up in the annual figures for the main aggregates and selected components of national income and expenditure in table 1. The value of the gross national product declined by about 43 percent between 1929 and 1933, much of the reduction owing to the fall in prices. In terms of "constant dollars" the decline in gross national expenditure (which by definition is equal to the GNP) in 1933 was 30 percent of that of 1929, and the implicit GNE deflator—the most comprehensive measure of prices—fell about 13 percent over these four years. The fall in many important prices, however, was much more severe. The cost of living index declined by about 22 percent, the wholesale prices of farm products by 51 percent, and the index of export prices generally by 38 percent. Most damaging was the fall in the average farm price per bushel of wheat. For the crop of 1929 the average was $1.05; for the crop of 1932 it was 35 cents—one-third as much.

Among the key components of gross national expenditure, the most important, in terms of its widespread effects on incomes and employment, was the fall in the receipts from exports of goods and services. They fell from $1,632 million in 1929 to $804 million in 1932—just less than half. The rapid decline in the basic support of what was essentially an export-oriented economy, with one-third of its labour force engaged in farming, was devastating.

The second main component in the decline of gross national expenditure was that of business capital expenditures on fixed assets: construction, machinery and equipment. This item declined by 20 percent between 1929 and 1930 but was offset to some extent by an increase that year in government expenditures on construction largely on projects already started. Business investment declined by a further 33 percent from 1930 to 1931 but public sector investment expenditures fell by only 21 percent. By 1933, however, business fixed capital investment had fallen to 20 percent of its 1929 level and public sector investment to 32 percent of that level.

Expenditures on consumption declined relatively less than the other major items of gross national expenditure. Allowing for the fall in prices, the level of consumption in constant dollars declined by 1933 to 81 percent of the 1929 level. This level was made possible only by negative personal savings, that is, in aggregate, consumers were drawing upon previous savings or going into debt. (It is worth noting that the decline in purchases of automobiles was very severe, falling by three-quarters from the prosperity levels of the late 1920s to the bottom of the Depression.)

The relatively modest decline in total real consumption when agricultural incomes were so low, and so many were unemployed, means that many

TABLE 1

SELECTED COMPONENTS OF GROSS NATIONAL PRODUCT AND GROSS NATIONAL EXPENDITURE (AT MARKET PRICES), 1929–1939
(MILLIONS $)

Calendar Year	Wages, Salaries and Other Labour Income	Corporate Profits	Accrued Net Farm Income	Gross National Product and Expenditure	Consumer Expenditure	Government Expenditure on Goods and Services	Business Gross Fixed Capital Formation: New Residential Construction	Business Gross Fixed Capital Formation: Other New Construction	Business Gross Fixed Capital Formation: New Machinery and Equipment	Business Gross Fixed Capital Formation: Total	Exports of Goods and Services	Imports of Goods and Services
1929	2,948	396	392	6,134	4,621	640	230	490	441	1,161	1,632	-1,945
1930	2,794	144	343	5,728	4,367	721	191	384	351	926	1,286	-1,645
1931	2,416	13	94	4,699	3,773	688	158	265	199	622	967	-1,142
1932	1,983	-98	104	3,827	3,194	584	90	121	108	319	804	-901
1933	1,796	73	66	3,510	2,984	462	72	78	84	234	826	-828
1934	1,947	191	167	3,984	3,182	503	92	91	115	292	1,018	-948
1935	2,088	237	218	4,315	3,338	542	107	116	146	369	1,143	-1,017
1936	2,250	314	199	4,653	3,549	544	131	148	179	458	1,428	-1,183
1937	2,547	432	280	5,257	3,884	619	164	188	281	633	1,591	-1,409
1938	2,524	334	353	5,278	3,897	666	148	170	274	592	1,356	-1,257
1939	2,633	521	362	5,636	3,984	683	174	164	254	592	1,451	-1,328

SOURCE: M. C. Urquhart and K. A. H. Buckley, *Historical Statistics of Canada*, series E1-12, "National income and gross national product, by components, 1926–60," and series E13-27, "Gross national expenditure, by components, 1926–60," pp. 130–31.

TABLE 2

PRICES AND PRICE INDEXES, 1929–1939

Calendar Year	Cost of Living Index, 1935–39 = 100 (1)	Wholesale Price Indexes, 1935–39 = 100: General (2)	Farm Products (3)	Wood, Wood Products, Paper (4)	Nonferrous Metals and Their Products (ex. gold) (5)	Gross National Expenditure Deflator, 1949 = 100 (6)	Export Price Index, 1948 = 100 (7)	Import Price Index, 1948 = 100 (8)	Terms of Trade (9)	U.S. Dollar in Canadian Funds (average, in Canadian cents) (10)	Sterling in Canadian Funds (average, in Canadian cents) (11)
1929	121.6	124.6	140.8	130.3	134.9	67.7	64.4	61.9	104.0	100.76	489.38
1930	120.8	112.9	119.5	123.1	109.7	66.0	54.0	54.0	100.0	100.16	486.98
1931	109.0	94.0	78.9	109.7	87.9	62.1	44.8	45.4	98.7	103.81	470.78
1932	98.9	86.9	65.5	95.9	80.2	56.3	40.3	44.4	90.8	113.52	398.01
1933	94.3	87.4	69.3	87.2	87.5	55.2	39.9	42.5	93.9	108.74	460.73
1934	95.6	93.4	83.5	90.7	87.5	55.9	42.6	45.3	94.0	99.00	498.91
1935	96.2	94.1	89.2	89.9	92.5	56.2	43.4	45.5	95.4	100.51	492.68
1936	98.1	96.7	97.9	93.6	96.3	58.0	45.8	46.4	98.7	100.06	497.45
1937	101.2	108.4	117.4	102.5	114.6	59.6	53.4	50.9	104.9	99.99	494.32
1938	102.2	101.9	102.9	106.9	98.3	59.5	47.1	47.3	99.6	100.56	491.62
1939	101.5	99.0	92.6	107.5	98.1	59.1	45.1	47.3	95.4	103.70	461.05

SOURCE: Column 1, M. C. Urquhart and K. A. H. Buckley, *Historical Statistics of Canada*, series J139-146, "Cost of living index, 1913–52," p. 304; columns 2, 4, and 5, ibid., series J34-44, "Wholesale price indexes, chief component material classification, 1867–1960," p. 293; column 3, ibid., series J75-83, "Wholesale price indexes of Canadian farm products, 1890–1960," p. 298; column 6, ibid., series J153-164, "Implicit price indexes of gross national expenditure, 1926–60," p. 305; column 7, ibid., series J108, "Export price indexes, 1913–60," p. 301; column 8, ibid., series J118, "Import price indexes, 1913–60," p. 302; columns 10 and 11, ibid., series 619–630, "Foreign exchange rates, 1910–60," p. 276.

NOTE: The figures in column 9 are those in column 7 divided by those in column 8.

TABLE 3
INTERNATIONAL TRADE AND PAYMENTS, 1929–1939
(MILLIONS $)

Calendar Year	Exports to U.K.	Exports to U.S.	Total Exports (Merchandise)	Exports of Non-monetary Gold	Tourist and Travel Receipts	All Current Receipts	Merchandise Imports	Interest and Dividend Payments	All Current Account Payments	Net Current Account Balance	New Issues of Canadian Securities	Retirement of Canadian Securities	Net Capital Movement
1929	224	519	1,178	37	198	1,646	1,272	322	1,957	-311	297	-150	311
1930	174	397	880	39	180	1,297	973	348	1,634	-337	400	-110	337
1931	139	254	601	57	153	972	580	330	1,146	-174	200	-202	174
1932	149	169	495	70	114	808	398	302	904	-96	104	-105	96
1933	188	177	532	82	89	829	368	264	831	-2	134	-166	-11
1934	234	226	648	114	106	1,020	484	268	952	68	111	-169	-114
1935	258	285	732	119	117	1,145	526	270	1,020	125	117	-256	-152
1936	342	369	954	132	142	1,430	612	311	1,186	244	106	-270	-241
1937	385	391	1,041	145	166	1,593	776	302	1,413	180	90	-170	-172
1938	337	268	844	161	149	1,361	649	307	1,261	100	89	-151	-106
1939	332	344	906	184	149	1,457	713	306	1,331	126	155	-251	-136

SOURCE: M. C. Urquhart and K. A. H. Buckley, *Historical Statistics of Canada*, series F57-71, "Canadian balance of international payments, all countries and by major areas, current account, 1936–45," pp. 160–61; last two columns from ibid., series F91-103, "Canadian balance of payments, all countries and by major areas, capital account, 1927–37," p. 164

TABLE 4
WHEAT PRODUCTION, ALL CANADA, CROP YEARS 1928-29 to 1939-40

Crop Year Beginning August 1	Wheat Production (millions of bushels)	Average Yield/ Seeded Acre (bushels)	Average Farm Price/Bushel ($)	Exports of Wheat and Flour (millions of bushels)	Cash Income from Wheat Production (millions $)
1928-29	567	23.5	.80	408	451
1929-30	302	12.0	1.05	186	334
1930-31	421	16.9	.49	259	165
1931-32	321	12.2	.38	207	95
1932-33	443	16.3	.35	264	120
1933-34	282	10.8	.49	195	118
1934-35	276	11.5	.61	166	142
1935-36	282	11.7	.61	254	146
1936-37	219	8.6	.94	210	146
1937-38	180	7.0	1.02	96	139
1938-39	360	13.9	.59	160	179
1939-40	521	19.4	.54	193	217

SOURCE: Dominion Bureau of Statistics, *Handbook of Agricultural Statistics*, parts 1 and 2.

TABLE 5
INCOME FROM ALL AGRICULTURAL PRODUCTION, 1928-1939
(MILLIONS $)

Calendar Year	Cash Income	Income in Kind	Realized Net Income	Realized Net Income from All Farm Production by Regions				
				Maritimes	Quebec	Ontario	Prairies	British Columbia
1928	1,064	241	666	35	88	160	363	21
1929	932	246	545	32	85	155	250	22
1930	642	226	277	30	69	115	45	18
1931	472	182	155	19	51	85	-11	11
1932	409	149	110	14	37	53	-3	9
1933	420	154	142	19	38	62	13	11
1934	503	161	210	21	46	72	58	13
1935	533	166	234	25	50	80	66	14
1936	587	175	288	28	59	93	92	15
1937	638	177	318	29	60	104	107	18
1938	650	174	329	27	66	107	111	18
1939	712	177	377	25	74	111	149	18

SOURCE: M. C. Urquhart and K. A. H. Buckley, *Historical Statistics of Canada*, series L67-72, "General statistics, income from farming operations, Canada, 1926-60," p. 356, and series L83-87, "General statistics, realized net income of farm operations, by region, 1926-60," p. 357.

of those who were steadily employed were able to keep up their standard of living despite the Depression. For example, Dominion civil servants, even with a reduction in their salaries and higher income tax and other taxes, were probably not forced to curtail their living standards. Few people in the Prairie provinces, however, would have been able to maintain their living standards, whatever their occupations.

Despite austerity at all levels, government expenditures on goods and services in 1930 and 1931 remained above the levels of 1929—partly because of the need to finish many capital projects and partly because a large amount of relief for the unemployed in 1931 was in the form of work projects that were included in this component. The projects were cut back in 1932 and 1933 because of their cost, and, instead, money was spent on direct relief. Besides the expenditures on goods and services, there were large government expenditures on transfers (including interest on debt). These amounted to $236 million in 1929, and they increased steadily to $355 million in 1933, owing to direct relief payments and the growth of interest on the public debt in Ottawa and in the provinces and municipalities.

The most striking item of the gross national product in table 1 is the decline in net farm income from $392 million in 1929 (in the three previous years this item was $600 million or higher) to $104 million in 1932, and to a catastrophic $66 million in 1933 when ruinous drought coincided with depressed prices in the Prairie provinces. Table 5 sets forth farm income in cash and in kind, with regional figures for realized net farm income. The basic problem was the disastrous fall in farm prices, which resulted from restricted export markets and from the reduced buying power of unemployed and underemployed Canadian consumers.

Table 1 also indicates that corporation profits before tax in 1930 fell to less than half their 1929 level and by 1932 there was, in aggregate, a substantial net loss for corporations, after taking into account depreciation on capital used as well as other costs. This decline naturally inhibited an upturn in business capital expenditures, both because of its direct effects on the financial situation of the businesses and because of its implications for possible investment projects.

The largest element in gross national income, the component wages, salaries, and other labour income, was $2,948 million in 1929. It fell relatively slowly in 1930 but by 1933 was down to about 60 percent of its 1929 level. This decline was due mainly to the fall in the number of persons with jobs paying wages or salaries. Figures published in the *Canada Year Book* of 1939 show a decline in the number of wage earners employed from 2,444,000 in 1929 to 1,788,000 in 1933—about 27 percent. The number employed in 1933 was about 74 percent of the total number of wage earners in the gainfully occupied population that year, implying that 26 percent of these wage earners were unemployed.

The definition of "wage earner" excludes employers, persons working on their own account (including farmers), and persons who have never worked for money even though they may be employable and seeking work (for example, young people and wives).

Using modern concepts of the labour force and the unemployed seeking work, the Bureau of Statistics worked out and published retrospective statistics in 1957. These have been extended back to the 1931 census, which showed a total labour force of 4,151,000 persons, of whom 1,216,000 were working in agriculture and 2,454,000 in other occupations, as either employees, employers, or self-employed. Another 481,000, estimated as persons without jobs but seeking work, that is, "unemployed" by our current definition, amounted to 11.6 percent of the total labour force of that day. About 30 percent of that labour force, however, was more or less permanently engaged in farming, poor though that was at the time, and not seeking, or, indeed, in most cases unable to seek, other work. It would be more appropriate to compare the number of unemployed with the number of the labour force outside agriculture, which gives a percentage of unemployed for that census year of about 16 percent. For 1932 and 1933 these labour force estimates show figures of unemployment amounting to 25 and 27 percent of the labour force excluding farmers.[20]

Canada's balance of international payments was not a source of any serious trouble during the downswing of the Depression, despite the drastic falls in the value of exports of grain and other products. Between 1929 and 1930 exports fell sharply, but so did imports, and the large deficit in Canada's current account of receipts and payments was more than adequately covered by an inflow of capital, including the proceeds of a record-breaking volume of Canadian security issues in New York. In 1931 and 1932 the decline of exports was more than matched by the decline in imports, and inflows of capital in those years reduced to relatively small figures the deficit that had to be met by monetary gold and the external assets of the banking system. By 1933 the current account was almost in balance, and a small net outflow of capital was readily met from bank and gold reserves.[21]

The most noteworthy monetary development during this period was the partial depreciation of the Canadian dollar in terms of the U.S. dollar (and gold) after the pound sterling was devalued in September 1931. The only action taken by the government was to formalize the informal control and restriction on exports of gold. It did not establish a positive exchange rate policy. The market simply carried the exchange rate of the Canadian dollar in New York about halfway as far down as sterling had fallen. This intermediate position seemed to be an acceptable compromise between the interests of the many Canadian public and private debtors with U.S.

dollar obligations and the interests of Canadian exporters who were suffering so much from low prices in markets outside Canada.

Sustaining Employment and Income

From 1930 to 1932 efforts were made by the Canadian government to sustain employment and earnings. These measures took the form of what had previously been the chief instrument of economic policy, the customs tariff. Immediately after he took office in August 1930, Prime Minister R. B. Bennett called a special session of Parliament to enact emergency relief measures and widespread increases in the customs tariff, as well as to give much broader powers to the minister of national revenue for setting arbitrary values on imports and levying special dumping duties. These powers were quickly used to protect the Canadian manufacturing industry. A further long list of tariff increases was introduced in the budget of June 1931. New trade agreements were negotiated with Great Britain and other parts of the Empire at the Imperial Economic Conference in Ottawa in July and August 1932. These agreements secured at minimal cost increased access to British and other "Empire" markets for Canadian products, including farm products, providing in exchange improved access for British manufactured goods into the Canadian market.

Little of a financial nature, apart from tariffs, was done by the government in trying to slow the decline of incomes, prices, and employment in the years 1930–32. Fortunately the Canadian commercial banking system was strong enough to withstand the strains of the declines in prices and incomes and in the ability to pay off its various debtors. The banks' business and private loans outstanding in Canada, including call loans and current loans other than to governments and municipalities, declined from $1,665 million in 1929 to $1,004 million in 1933, an overall reduction of 40 percent, slightly less than the 43 percent reduction in gross national product.[22] This decline of $661 million was offset by an increase of $413 million in securities, most of which were Dominion or provincial government securities. The supply of money in Canada, currency plus bank deposits, was $2,331 million in 1929. It fell to $2,025 million in 1933, a decline of only 13.2 percent. The cash reserve ratio of the banks in 1929 was 8.3 percent, decreased to 8.2 and 8.1 percent in the next two years, and rose to 8.8 and 9.8 percent in 1932 and 1933.[23]

In November 1932 bank reserves were increased by a concerted borrowing by the banks of Dominion notes under the Finance Act, with an understanding that these advances would remain outstanding. This action, however, had only a small monetary effect. Early in 1933 the government tried to persuade the chartered banks to reduce their interest rates on savings deposits (on which matters the banks operated in concert exempt from the combines law). The government saw it as a necessary step towards reducing the interest rates on bank loans, mortgages, and bonds in order to stimulate business. That year savings account rates were reduced ½ percent and certain lending rates were correspondingly reduced. It was one of the first small monetary steps in promoting economic recovery.

In 1929 the yield on long-term bonds had been around 5 percent and the average interest rate on mortgages, about 7 percent. Before Britain's departure from the gold standard in 1931, the yield on government bonds, long- and short-term, had drifted down, while the yield on corporate bonds had gradually edged up. The British crisis led to a sharp decline in prices and increases in yields of Canadian bonds. Corporate bond yields exceeded 7 percent for a short time in mid-1932 and again early in 1933. Long-term government of Canada bond yields reached a peak of 5.47 percent early in 1932 and then declined slowly in that year and 1933. The decline became more rapid early in 1934, breaking through the 4 percent level by mid-year and finally touching 3 percent in 1936. Short-term government bond yields fell very rapidly during 1934, touching 2 percent in 1935 and falling well below that figure during 1936. Corporate bond yields moved down gradually and irregularly during 1933 and then steadily down until they reached 4 percent at the end of 1936. Mortgage rates varied among the provinces and according to the quality of the security, but the average renewal rates remained close to 7 percent during the first three years of the Depression, declined a little in 1933 and 1934, and fell substantially in 1935.[24]

WHEAT AND DROUGHT: A SPECIAL CASE

The decline in the market for Canadian wheat of the 1929 crop and its abnormal price caused the holding back of stocks for which the western wheat pools had paid an initial price of $1 a bushel to their farmer members.[25] The international price fell almost continually through 1930 and confronted the Canadian producers and their three western pools with a very uncertain and gloomy outlook. The 1930 crop was of normal yield and acreage, but the average farm price was only 49 cents a bushel—less than half the $1.05 realized the year before.[26] In the United States, the Federal Farm Board also accumulated stocks of wheat that year.

In 1930, both before and after the election of early August, methods of marketing Canadian wheat were debated at length. The new prime minister had a close knowledge of the grain trade and quickly became convinced of the need to centralize the marketing of the wheat held and received by the large pools. After many discussions, Bennett agreed with the heads of the western pools on November 26, 1930, to appoint John

I. McFarland, his close friend and former business associate, to manage the marketing of the pools' wheat through the Canadian Cooperative Wheat Producers Limited. Although this was not a government appointment, it was very important, and McFarland, who was experienced in the grain trade, worked closely with the prime minister, who took direct responsibility for formulating government policy on the sale of wheat. Bennett conducted several discussions on wheat in England and France when he went overseas to attend the Imperial Conference in the fall of 1930. At the end of the year he reported to the Canadian public as encouragingly as he could, stating that the Dominion government would provide financial guarantees required to forestall enforced selling of the pools' unsold wheat. He and McFarland managed as best as possible to see that Canadian wheat was sold for as good a price as could be negotiated under the circumstances.

The selling agency was retained until 1935 in order to dispose of the unsold carry-over of the 1930 pool deliveries and to be the channel for the government's market support operations managed by McFarland. The three provincial pools operated separately as before and their farmer members were to be free to sell to them at market prices or for thirty-five cents a bushel plus participation in profits. Most farmers sold for cash.[27] McFarland's operations were given legal authority and financial resources by an order-in-council under the 1931 Unemployment and Farm Relief Act.

McFarland's operations in holding the unsold 1930 wheat and supporting the market with purchases of wheat (largely in the form of futures, thereby replacing the normal role of the speculative purchasers, who were understandably cautious in those years) were continued until the Canadian Wheat Board was set up. That board was established by legislation passed in mid-1935 immediately before Parliament prorogued for the election. Bennett had proposed a board that would be the exclusive marketing agency for both wheat and coarse grains and would end the main role of the Winnipeg Grain Exchange. After much consultation with western interests and lengthy interparty bargaining, Bennett agreed that initially at least the board would deal only in wheat and would not have a monopoly in the purchase of it from producers. The Grain Exchange would continue to operate. The remaining 205 million bushels of McFarland's wheat in store and futures contracts were turned over to the Wheat Board, which managed to liquidate the stocks over the next two years at a net profit of about $9 million.

The dramatic decline in wheat prices prompted many of the countries seriously affected to seek an international solution to their problem. During the first half of 1933 officials of the main exporting countries discussed the possibility of arranging an international agreement which would regulate production, exports, and surpluses at least among the four principal exporters, Canada, Argentina, Australia, and the United States, and perhaps also among some lesser exporters and some major importing nations. An agreement was finally reached which included undertakings by the governments of the four main exporters to limit their exports in the 1933–34 and 1934–35 crop years according to certain formulas and understandings.

The agreement, however, never really brought about any significant restraint on exports and production. Drought and market forces severely reduced Canadian production and exports. In the United States the acreage reduction plan under the Agricultural Adjustment Act reduced production so much that exports were below those agreed for 1933–34, and that country became a net importer for the 1934–35 crop year. By late 1934 the acreage restriction in the United States and the droughts and rust in Canada in 1933 and 1934 had removed the burdensome carry-overs of wheat.

In these circumstances wheat prices strengthened. The market price rose to eighty cents a bushel and the average farm price for the 1934 crop was sixty-one cents, as it was for the 1935 crop. The trouble now was more fundamental than prices; it was the low yield per acre resulting from drought, rust, grasshoppers and other insects, and disease. Occasional drought, such as one in 1929, had to be expected in much of the relatively arid south prairie lands. A worse drought in Saskatchewan in 1931, combined with the ruinous farm price of thirty-eight cents a bushel, caused widespread hardship and put many thousands of farmers on relief. Nature relented in 1932 and the average yield in the Prairie provinces was nearly up to the average of the 1920s but in that year the farm prices of wheat reached their lowest levels. In 1933 a five-year period of serious drought began. The worst came in 1937 when in Saskatchewan the average yield per seeded acre was only 2.6 bushels compared with 16.6 on average from 1920 to 1929.[28] The Royal Commission on Dominion-Provincial Relations vividly described the relief problem in Saskatchewan.

> The area affected by successive crop failures was about equal to one-quarter of the total improved farm acreage of Canada. It contained nearly one-half the rural inhabitants of Saskatchewan. In 1931, one-half; in 1933–4–6, one-third; and in 1937, two-thirds of the total farm population of the Province was destitute. Not only was this large section of the population dependent for livelihood upon public charity, but the operating expenses of from one-third to two-thirds of Canada's largest export industry had to be met by the Government. It was the latter which chiefly distinguished Saskatchewan's problem from that in the other provinces. In the other provinces it was mainly a matter of providing food, fuel, clothing and shelter for unemployed wage-earners. In the case of the Saskatchewan wheat farmer the failure of a crop involved not merely the loss of the means of livelihood but also the working capital invested in that crop. This working capital had to be made available before there was another chance of the farmer becoming self-support-

ing. The provision year after year of seed, feed, fodder and supplies to tens of thousands of large-scale farmers entailed a huge financial burden not encountered in the relief of industrial unemployment.[29]

While Saskatchewan was by far the worst hit of all the provinces, the disastrous effect of ruinous wheat prices and droughts were shared by Manitoba and Alberta. In 1930 Saskatchewan had a wheat acreage of 14.3 million, Alberta of 7.2 million, and Manitoba of 2.5 million.[30] But Manitoba suffered more than Alberta mainly because of the effects of the general situation upon Winnipeg, the centre through which the wheat sales and merchandise purchases of the Prairies were funnelled and where the unemployed and dispossessed congregated. So heavy was the impact of the Depression on the finances of the Prairie provinces (and British Columbia) that they were unable to borrow on their own credit and the Dominion had to finance their borrowing requirements from 1932 until early 1936. The provinces in turn had to help their municipalities with loans and special grants for relief and other purposes.

In retrospect it is surprising that the Prairie provinces were able to keep up their revenues and expenditures and the provision of education and other public services through these years of great adversity. Historically, most other areas of the world that experienced droughts similar to those in Saskatchewan and parts of Alberta in the 1930s suffered famines. Yet Saskatchewan survived; those educated there in these lean years have provided Canada with many leaders and the province itself has gone on to take a lead in social programs, efficient government, and now a strong diversified economy, still based to a very large extent on producing wheat efficiently for export.

Relief Measures for the Unemployed and Others

While the need for relief in the drought areas of the Prairies was the most extreme, the needs of the unemployed and their dependants were the most general and became the major financial problem for municipalities, provincial governments, and the Dominion.[31] The constitutional responsibilities for social assistance are described in chapter 10 of this study. The municipalities were held responsible for providing aid to those in need, including the unemployed, and the provinces were responsible for seeing that they did so and, if necessary, for assisting them financially. The Dominion government was quickly drawn in to sharing the costs with the provinces. In 1930 the aid for the unemployed was in the form of municipal work relief projects to which the provincial and Dominion governments contributed. The projects continued into 1931, but by this stage it was necessary to supplement such works by direct relief, both urban and rural, on a substantial scale. In the fiscal year 1931–32 total expenditure in this area was $95 million of which the Dominion contributed just over half.

By 1932 the number of unemployed had reached over half a million, and the outlook was for more. The Department of Labour began keeping track of the number on relief, which it analysed in yearly reports. The estimated number of persons without jobs and seeking work peaked at about 828,000 in 1933, and the estimated number of employable persons on unemployment relief also peaked that year at about 321,000. Including dependants and those on drought area relief, the total number of persons receiving direct relief that year was about 1,228,000—about 1 in every 8.7 persons in the population.[32]

In all provinces except Saskatchewan, where a special commission was established, relief for the needy, excluding transients and other minor categories, was administered by municipalities, which were required to contribute a share of the outlay as well as administration costs. There was a great variety of standards in the scale of assistance provided and in the quality of its administration, both of which were inadequate in very many municipalities. More is said in chapter 10 about the Dominion-provincial agreements for financing relief and the disputes over them.

The Beginning of Recovery, 1933–1935

Recovery of the Canadian economy began in April 1933 after Roosevelt's actions to deal with the banking crises in the United States and to initiate various monetary, agricultural, and industrial reform measures. In Canada some improvement had taken place in certain industries during 1932, notably mining. Construction activity, however, fell rapidly in the second and fourth quarters of 1932, as well as during the first half of 1933.

The first influence on Canada of the U.S. actions in March and April 1933 was on expectations and confidence. Canadian stock exchange prices rose in April, May, June, and July. More tangible was the increase in mining production that went on through the year and in manufacturing production during the second and third quarters, although the latter fell back a little in the autumn, as it did in the United States. Construction, however, really hit bottom in 1933. Investment in new physical assets, construction, and machinery and equipment reached its lowest level that year. New business investment in fixed assets was less than half the depreciation allowances on past investment, which meant that Canada was running down its capital. Inventories were still being reduced. Personal savings were negative, but consumer expenditures were still declining; many consumers, too, were living on their capital. Net income from farm production was at its lowest level of the Depression, although wholesale prices of farm products rose strongly during the middle of the year, probably a reflection of the new farm programs being introduced in the United States. General wholesale prices were rising as was the index of total industrial production. Total incomes and the balance of payments were supported by increasing exports, particularly to Great Britain and other Commonwealth countries, but also in some small measure to the United States. It was, all in all, a very bad year, but by its end the tide had turned.

In 1934 and 1935 there was more general expansion, based mainly on exports, particularly those to Great Britain which by 1935 were at levels above those of 1929, despite the lower wheat prices. The tariff preferences negotiated at the Imperial Economic Conference in Ottawa in 1932 were bearing fruit, assisted by the expansion in the British economy made possible by going off the gold standard. Exports of automobiles to the other dominions were increasing rapidly. Exports to the United States were also rising, in spite of the barriers to that trade; the tourist business was increasing, and gold mining was booming spurred on by the greatly increased price of gold in United States. But the general recovery was slow and employment was lagging; about 20 percent of wage earners were unemployed and over 10 percent of the population was on relief. While exports to the United States were far below what they had been in the 1920s, a new reciprocal trade agreement with that country had been signed by Mackenzie King at the end of 1935.

The main drag on the economy was the low level of new investment by business and governments in durable assets: construction, machinery and equipment. The total volume of such investment in 1935 was only 39 percent of what it had been in 1929, even when the fall in prices is eliminated. By far the largest part of the decline was in business investment, mainly in manufacturing industries, utilities, electric power companies, and railways. The level of current demands on these industries was well below their capacity, and there were few incentives for new investment, even when interest rates had fallen and credit was available.[33] Domestic demands could be expanded only by more autonomous investment, that is, in new industries or innovations, or else by further increases in exports. Consequently expansion of trade was vital.

The Dominion and provincial governments were hard pressed to find enough revenue or sources of credit to meet their essential regular expenditures, as well as those for relief. In addition the Dominion government was burdened by the need to finance the very large deficit of the Canadian National Railways, which in 1935 was about half of the Dominion expenditures on relief. In July 1934 Bennett had initiated a special program of public works to provide jobs and accelerate the recovery of the economy, which was to be financed in a somewhat unorthodox manner by a final expansion in the Dominion note issue before the Bank of Canada commenced operations. But the expenditure on such works was limited to $40 million and was mostly made during 1935, adding only perhaps about one-tenth to the total expenditures on new construction that year.

The Slow and Incomplete Recovery, 1936–1939

In the election of October 14, 1935, Bennett was overwhelmingly defeated, despite his change of strategy in January of that year. He had introduced a new program of economic and social reforms, most of which intruded into provincial jurisdiction. Mackenzie King became prime minister again on October 23, and included in his Cabinet numerous strong ministers who were to become well known during the next twenty-two years of Liberal government.[34] But the economic situation and outlook in late 1935 were enough to daunt any government. The potentially strong Cabinet was handicapped at the beginning by a very conservative economic and financial policy in which King, influenced by his comfortable economic experience in the prosperous 1920s, devoutly believed. He selected Charles A. Dunning, another believer strong enough to carry out a program of financial restraint, to be minister of finance. Both King and Dunning favoured lower tariffs obtained by trade negotiations as the chief instrument of recovery.

In his budget of May 1936 (so different from his complacent optimism expressed in his budget of May 1930), Dunning had to begin with these serious qualifications: "The most welcome feature in the fiscal year which has just closed has been what it indicates of a movement toward recovery. I do not wish to exaggerate the extent of that recovery, for to those who are charged with the responsibilities of government in these hard times the distance yet to go and the problems still to be solved are the features of our economic record which are most impressive—and at the same time most distressing."[35]

In the previous year the government's deficit had been $160 million. Dunning announced a new policy of making "an immediate approach to a balanced budget," which would "show that complete equilibrium can be reached within a reasonable time," a policy which he identified as "a doctrine of deflation."[36] To this end he imposed new restrictions on expenditures and increased the rates of both income and sales tax. This mistimed austerity had been conceived a few months after the appearance of John Maynard Keynes's *General Theory of Employment, Interest and Money*, a work that provided the intellectual foundation for a framework of analysis which would show that such a doctrine of deflation and the measures giving it effect were quite wrong in the circumstances of 1936.

Notwithstanding Dunning's budget, 1936 was a year of modest recovery—the gross national product in real terms increased by about 4½ percent, despite the worst wheat crop since 1919, caused by a disastrous drought. The stimulus to recovery came from increased exports to the United Kingdom and the United States and increased income from gold mining and the tourist trade. The surplus in the current account of the balance of payments was nearly a quarter of a billion dollars—the highest for any year during the 1930s. But it was used mostly to repay debts to the United States and Great Britain, while new capital investment in Canadian business remained far below the levels of the prosperous years. Total expenditure by all levels of government on goods and services, as well as transfers, such as relief, remained close to the 1935 levels.

Recovery in 1937 was better but unstable. Real gross national product increased by about 10 percent again despite the almost complete failure of the western wheat crop because of drought. Exports also rose, mainly owing to large increases in the price of many items. Gold production and tourist receipts from nonresidents climbed up. But in that year imports increased more than exports, and the current international account surplus declined. Price rises were fairly general but moderate, except at the wholesale level where prices, particularly on raw materials and farm products, increased sharply under the influence of international markets. Wheat prices rose rapidly through 1937 as world stocks declined. Business investment in new construction, machinery, and equipment grew by a substantial 38 percent between 1936 and 1937, but about a quarter of this rise was due to cost increases in materials, imported equipment, and even wages.

At this point it is worth noting the main sources of expansion between the depths of 1933 and the high-water mark of 1937. Gross national product as a whole increased by about half, or $1,750 million, of which roughly one-sixth was due to the rise in prices. About $765 million of this amount came from an increase of exports of goods and services, a vivid illustration of Canada's dependence on trade. About $300 million was in response to the rise in business investment in construction and equipment. About $160 million was from larger expenditures by government on goods and services. These were the relatively stimulating expenditures. Consumers, having received higher incomes, increased their expenditures on goods and services by $900 million. These four sources of increased demand amounted to $2,125 million. Deducting from this total the $580 million increase in imported goods and services—for to this extent increased demands were met from outside Canada—leaves a net increase of expenditure on Canadian goods and services of about $1,545 million.[37] These figures indicate that recovery was largely due to export demands rather than to increases in business capital investment or in government expenditures on goods and services.

It has been estimated that in June 1937 about 2,776,000 persons had jobs in nonagricultural occupations, an increase of about 27 percent over 1933. But there was still a very large number, 411,000, of persons without jobs and seeking work, which is how unemployment is now defined statistically. This number amounted to 9 percent of the total labour force including farmers, or 12.9 percent of the labour force excluding farmers. Thus, in 1937, the year of the highest level of employment (outside agriculture) during the late 1930s, Canada was clearly far from "full employment." Subsequent wartime experience corroborated this fact. In 1941, when Canada was still far from fully mobilized for war, 270,000 more people were employed in nonagricultural industries than in 1937, and 290,000 more in the armed services.

The year 1937 marked the culmination of the recovery from 1933 and was followed by a plateau of two years at approximately the same levels of employment and production in aggregate terms. These annual aggregates, or averages, however, mask an important short business cycle which reached its peak in July 1937 and its trough around October 1938. In Canada this short cycle affected mainly the manufacturing sector, particularly the manufacture of durable products (such as automobiles and steel) and the trade and transportation industries that served this sector.

The Canadian business cycle of 1936–38 was very largely a reflection of a more serious one that occurred in the United States at almost the same time. Some differences, however, did exist. In the United States the peak was reached two months earlier in 1937, and the trough about four months earlier in 1938; the decline was considerably greater (about 33 percent in manufacturing compared with about 24 percent in Canada) and the fall in gross national product and expenditure between 1937 and 1938 was significant (about 7 percent) but negligible in Canada. Also, in Canada net income from farming in 1937 was substantially less than in 1938 because of drought, while in the United States both farm and industrial incomes reached a peak in 1937.

The Canadian recession of 1937–38 was longer and milder than that of the United States not because of any particular policy action (for that came too late), but because the recovery in 1937 was restrained by the seriously low agricultural incomes in the Prairies and because exports to the United Kingdom and other overseas countries held up better in 1938 than exports to the United States had.[38] In addition, gold production was substantially higher in 1938. Most importantly, Canadian gross business investment did not fall nearly as much in proportion from 1937 to 1938 as did that in the United States. Two major Canadian industries suffered a serious decline in volume of production in 1938. One was the newsprint industry. Buyers of newsprint built up their inventories in 1937, believing the price would rise substantially in 1938. There was such an increase but the price of 1938 was only 70 percent of the average price of 1926–29, when most of the mills were being built and the debts incurred. In that important industry no large additions to capacity were made after 1930 until the postwar boom in the 1940s. In the other case, the automobile industry, domestic purchases of both passenger cars and trucks, after a peak in 1937, declined in both 1938 and 1939. Total registration of passenger cars in use continued to increase substantially, but production fell from 133,000 in 1937 to 90,000 in 1939.[39]

Relief Reconsidered

In the 1935 election campaign King did not try to match Bennett's "New Deal" promise of an unemployment insurance program. He preached financial restraint, and as well was no doubt conscious of the limits of Dominion jurisdiction in a program such as Bennett's unless the provinces agreed to a constitutional amendment. But King was aware of the inadequacies of the existing relief system, despite his reluctance to increase Dominion expenditures. His selection of Norman Rogers, a young, ambitious, and energetic professor of political science from Queen's University, as his minister of labour was evidence of his seriousness in approaching the relief system.

Rogers quickly set about making some reforms, beginning with the most criticized of all federal relief programs, the relief camps organized and run by the Department of National Defence. He managed to find alternative arrangements within six months. Because of the extreme drought, special assistance also had to be given to the Prairie provinces in 1936 and 1937. Apart from these two changes, Rogers carried on with the programs initiated under Bennett's government.

The most important action that Rogers took in his first six months was to win the provincial governments' support for establishing the National Employment Commission, which was given a broad mandate to carry out a national registration and classification of all relief recipients, to establish standards and regulations which the provinces should meet to qualify for federal assistance, to supervise the distribution of that assistance, and to plan and coordinate a consistent program of public works and employment projects. The duties and powers of the commission were established by the National Employment Commission Act approved in April 1936.[40] More is said about this commission in chapters 6 and 10.

The Wheat Situation, 1938–1939

A substantial change in the world wheat situation in 1938 led to revisions in policy and practice in Canada. Early that year it looked as if the world crop would be large and surplus stocks would reappear, especially in the United States. Prices began to fall in the spring and then plunged from well above $1.20 to just above 86 cents a bushel by summer.[41] With the October futures (the market's appraisal of what the new crop could sell for) at about 77 cents a bushel and falling, the government had to reconsider its wheat marketing policy in late July.

At a series of Cabinet meetings and with the approval of Dunning, who was ill, it was decided that the Wheat Board would initially pay 80 cents a bushel. The payment would mean a large loss for the board, one which in the end the government would have to assume. The result of this action was that western farmers sold all of their available crop to the board. To make clear its intention to sell wheat at competitive prices, the government announced that all wheat would be sold on the world's markets as fast as it was received, a radical departure from the withholding policy of 1930. But despite the government's intent, the board had to accept deliveries of more wheat than it could sell in that crop year. On July 31, 1939, the end of the crop year, the Wheat Board held 86 million bushels of wheat in stock, about 30 percent of the amount it had purchased. This carry-over was not fully sold until May 1940, and, as a result, its sale overlapped with that of the much larger 1939 crop in the restricted wartime markets.

In 1939 new legislation on the Wheat Board provided for an initial payment of 70 cents a bushel on a limit of 4,000 bushels from any one producer. The setting of this lower initial payment was accompanied by the passage of the Prairie Farm Assistance Act, which set up an elaborate type of compulsory crop insurance for western wheat producers. It provided for payments based on a farmer's acreage, but at a rate determined by the average yields per acre in the township. This plan was to come into effect during an emergency year (that is, when the price of wheat was less than 80 cents a bushel) or a crop failure year (that is, when the average yield was 5 bushels an acre or less in a defined number of townships in the province). Assistance would thus be provided in a fairer way than increasing the price or paying a bonus on sales, as had been done in 1931.[42]

The Final Failure to Recover

Despite the mildness of the decline in Canada between 1937 and 1938 and some improvement in 1939, particularly in agriculture, Canada did not achieve a satisfactory level of employment, production, and incomes before World War II began. Even the war, though it began in September, did not have much effect upon the economy by the end of 1939 (except the decision to depreciate the exchange rate by 10 percent). Gross national product and expenditure for 1939 were about 8 percent below the pre-Depression levels mainly because in 1939 prices were lower.[43] Figures for 1939, adjusted to 1929 prices, were much lower for business investment in new construction (including housing) and machinery and equipment—barely 54 percent of 1929 or two-thirds of the average level during the 1926–29 period. It was this low level of business capital investment at the end of a decade of depression, and in spite of a recovery of corporate profits back to or above pre-Depression levels, which was most serious.

In 1939 the labour force is estimated to have grown by 123,000 persons over that of 1937; 40,000 of these found jobs in agriculture, which was a little less depressed than it was in 1937.[44] But 35,000 fewer are estimated to have had jobs in nonagricultural industries, and the remaining 118,000 are believed to have been added to the number of those without jobs and seeking work. A total of 529,000 were unemployed and seeking work, or 11.4 percent of the total labour force (including the 30 percent of the labour force still in agriculture). The labour force was growing at a rate of about 1.4 percent a year, just slightly less than the growth rate of the population over fourteen years of age. Few among the major industries had increased their employment over that of 1929. The manufacturing sector as a whole showed employment at 1 percent less than in 1929.[45] The railroads, which had overexpanded in the 1920s (like automobiles and newsprint), recovered very little from the drastic decline to 1933. Only the metal mining sector was booming at the end of the decade, employing twice as many persons as at the beginning, but its 46,000 employees in 1939 were too few to offset substantially the lack of vigorous recovery elsewhere, particularly in the construction sector (where unfortunately good employment figures are lacking).[46]

The economic situation that emerged in Canada in 1938 and continued until the outbreak of war was reasonably stable, although of course it was a time of acute international tension and turmoil. This was a period of underemployment equilibrium, such as Keynes had argued was possible and even likely in his book *The General Theory of Employment, Interest and Money*. By 1938 the relevance of Keynes's analysis to the current situation had been explicitly recognized by President Roosevelt in the United States and more quietly by the National Employment Commission and the Cabinet in Canada.[47] But recognition was not enough. What were the causes of the lack of recovery?

Few efforts have been made to analyse the reasons for the failure of recovery in the Canadian economy after 1937, perhaps because the adverse effects of the 1937 crop failure and the subsequent collapse in international wheat prices were so obvious, and perhaps because the serious conditions of provincial and municipal finances and the Royal Commission on Dominion-Provincial Relations deflected attention. Only A. E. Safarian has analysed the subject at length in his book *The Canadian Economy in the Great Depression*, first published in 1959. In his concluding chapter he notes that most of the analyses of the Depression of the 1930s in Canada have placed primary emphasis on external factors. But he locates the key problem of incomplete recovery in the late 1930s as lying in the area of domestic investment—principally business investment in nonresidential construction, machinery and equipment, and, to a lesser degree, housing.

In analysing the persistently low level of such investment, Safarian makes a useful distinction between "induced" investment, which is made in order to meet an increase in market demand for the goods or services the investment will produce, and "autonomous" investment, which is usually related to innovations in products, marketing, resources, or technology. Insofar as induced investment was concerned, recovery in the demand for

Canadian exports, or for consumption goods in the domestic market, did not proceed far enough in general to eliminate the excess capacity that existed in many industries, notably, automobile production, newsprint, electric power, and railways. As long as excess capacity existed in a wide range of industries, recovery in investment would be depressed. Safarian set forth a host of external and domestic conditions that would cause businesses to be cautious in these circumstances. Most of the autonomous investment, Safarian states, was made in the 1920s—the first and indirect effects of the mass production of automobiles, the electrification of North America based both on hydro and on thermal power, the development of cheap newsprint in Canada for export, and the opening up of major mining areas. Because these major innovations were fully exploited during the late 1920s, there was little left to be done in the 1930s, except in mining. Moreover, there were no major new innovations to give rise to such autonomous investment in the 1930s. He concluded, "The crucial point is that autonomous investment did not play a significant role in any part of the upswing."[48]

Safarian's conclusions are correct, although he does not give enough emphasis to the effects on Canada, both in exports and in psychology, of the sharp recession suffered in the United States from 1937 to 1938. Moreover, it would seem appropriate to attribute more economic importance to the cautious fiscal policy followed by the Dominion government in 1937-39.

One surprising feature of the situation in 1938-39 was that the Canadian economy was so little affected by preparations for the impending war in Europe. It is true that Canada's own defence expenditures doubled from 1936-37 to 1938-39, but even in the latter years they were only about $34 million, too small to have much economic effect. Nor was there any serious effort made to build up a war industry,[49] although the British government placed a few relatively small contracts for weapons and munitions. Only in the fledgling aircraft industry did the defence program have any significant industrial effect and even there it was not important economically. The main economic effect of European preparations for war was to increase the demand for Canadian exports of nickel, aluminum, copper, and lead,[50] although even the greater demand did not lead to much prewar capital expenditures on expanding capacity to produce these metals.[51]

Thus, Canada entered the war with a great reserve of untrained manpower and surplus general industrial capacity, a large excess of wheat (which ultimately was needed), and many smaller export trades and industries vulnerable to the effects of the war upon their markets. Beyond the war lay a long period of expansion, diversification, and prosperity such as Canada had never known—but who could possibly have foreseen it in 1939?

Chapter Four

Bennett and the Department's Interregnum

At the beginning of 1930 the Department of Finance was in disarray. C. A. Dunning had just been appointed minister, following the death of Robb in November 1929. Deputy Minister Saunders was ill and entered hospital in January; three months later he died. Assistant Deputy Minister Hyndman was in the process of being convicted of stealing bonds and money from the department. For the next two and a half years the department was without a deputy minister and was run, nominally, by a five-man committee during the crucial period of having to cope with the impact of the Depression and adapt to the major policy shifts of the incoming Bennett government. The man Dunning chose to be in charge of the department and whom he appointed in February 1930 as assistant deputy minister was Watson Sellar, who had been private secretary to Robb since 1924.[1] Fortunately Sellar was a man of ability and good judgment, who had learned much about the department from the vantage point of the minister's office.

On tariff matters, which were very important at the time, Dunning was assisted by Hector McKinnon, who in March 1930 became commissioner of tariff after J. A. Russell retired. As stated previously, the minister also received considerable advice and assistance on tariff matters from the Advisory Board on Tariff and Taxation, of which W. H. Moore, a former Liberal MP, was chairman, and McKinnon was secretary. The advisory board had just completed a comprehensive report proposing a revision of the lengthy and detailed iron and steel schedules in the tariff. Despite the help of Sellar and the others, Dunning nevertheless remarked in a letter to a friend that his situation was "exceedingly difficult."[2] King, too, acknowledged privately that Dunning had his work cut out for him.

DUNNING'S BUDGET OF MAY 1930

The Liberal party's conservative approach to Canada's economic problems influenced the Dunning budget of May 1930. Although there is little in the departmental files about its preparation, the diary of Prime Minister Mackenzie King gives a colourful account of his involvement and that of Dunning in this politically important budget.[3] That changes in the tariff would dominate the budget had become evident very early. On January 16, 1930, King had Dunning and a political friend to dinner, and the prime minister spoke to Dunning of "free breakfast table—no duties on tea, etc."[4] On January 20 King wrote in his diary, "It begins to look as tho we had better wait till after Easter to bring in our budget and then deal sharply with U.S. as well as increase Br. preference." (It was at this time that the Hawley-Smoot tariff bill was before the U.S. Senate.)

By February King had decided for a variety of reasons that he should call an election as soon as possible.[5] On February 11 he told Dunning "to get a real budget in readiness," by which he apparently meant one that would help in the election. Two weeks later, after work had proceeded on tariff matters, King recorded in his diary that he had Dunning and Billy Moore to dinner and discussed the "Tariff Board" and the budget.[6] On March 12 the Liberal caucus discussed tariffs, and King noted: "I spoke at some length endeavouring to conciliate and pacify and explain and believe I succeeded in bringing about a certain amount of harmony. I have saved, too, I think an unsettling effect re changes in tariffs on motors, etc. I tried to point out how impossible in a country like Canada it is for all to see and think alike."

By March 22 the Liberal Cabinet was fully occupied with the detailed work of the budget. King wrote: "Went to the East Block [where the Cabinet Room was] at 11 and spent till about 2 in Council. Time taken up discussing budget proposals. . . . I favour a little retaliation on fruits and vegetables if U.S. puts up tariff on our agricultural products." These discussions were continued on March 29. Summarizing the progress made, King noted in his diary:

> Have had a long day in the Cabinet today. From 11 to one, and again from 2:45 to 6:45, most of the time was spent listening to Dunning going over changes in Tariff schedules on Iron and Steel and products into which they enter. It is a revision of the tariff schedules as worked out by the Tariff Board. Increasing British Preference wherever possible, without raising duties vs. the U.S. in a few cases raising duties vs. the U.S. but in some few cases lowering and abolishing them (in latter re hospital supplies). It is a far reaching revision, really wipes out large slices of protection. It will be a real bombshell into the Tory camp. They will certainly try to keep us here as long as they can and we will almost certainly be obliged to dissolve and go to the country on the budget.

On April 5 King wrote of yet another long Cabinet meeting at which the ministers reviewed the details of the tariff proposals. They were nearly unanimous in increasing duties on vegetables to protect against U.S. dumping. They also intended to increase the British preference on nearly everything on which tariffs on American goods were increased. King observed, "We were practically unanimous for 'countervailing' duties against US." Tariff changes were discussed again at Cabinet meetings on April 9 and 10. It is remarkable how much time and effort were devoted to the details of the tariff. However, the tariff had been at the heart of Canadian politics and the Liberals were determined to created a politically appealing budget.

King made an important, indeed surprising, entry in his diary for April 10.

> I sent tonight a message to Ramsay MacDonald, Snowdon and Thomas [the British prime minister, chancellor of the Exchequer, and Dominions secretary, respectively] not to prejudice Canadian wheat and flour in Br. market by requiring percentage of British content. I gave them our Budget plans in outline, told them with a word from the Chancellor that he was keeping Canada in mind, I wd. assure him a budget here that would be rec'd with enthusiasm in Grt. Br. It is taking a risk to send this message in code, a mighty big risk—but it would be fatal to our success if the Br. budget hits Canada in any particular just at this time.

King reiterated the essentials of the message orally to the British high commissioner and, enjoining the utmost "secrecy," asked him to cable London.[7]

Dunning was unquestionably under considerable pressure during the preparation of the budget. In mid-April King noted that Dunning expressed fear that the Tories would not let the budget through without strong opposition and that an election was inevitable. King thought that Dunning was apprehensive about losing his Regina seat. Privately the prime minister wrote in his diary that even if Dunning and the Liberals lost the election, he would find the minister a seat in the House. Dunning continued to worry. At a Cabinet meeting on April 25, King noted that Dunning "almost broke down" as a result of attacks on him by the protectionist element in the Cabinet. Remarking on the minister's behaviour, the prime minister wrote that Dunning was inclined to be censorious and querulous, thereby bringing these attacks upon himself.

Aside from the extensive changes in the tariff, the principal measure in the budget was the reduction of the sales tax from 2 to 1 percent. This was bound to be popular and required little technical or policy assistance. It would cost the Treasury some $22 million, but fortunately the accounts of the fiscal year just ended showed a surplus of revenues over all expenditures of more than double this amount.[8]

There was no reduction in income tax rates—they had already been substantially reduced in 1926, 1927, and 1928—but four popular measures by way of exemptions and deductions were introduced. Cooperatives were exempted from income tax, as they had requested, after prior attempts by the income tax authorities to tax certain types of cooperatives and their transactions. Exemptions for dependants were extended beyond children to dependent parents, grandparents, brothers, sisters, and certain other relatives. Government or other "like" annuities were wholly exempted from income tax to the extent of $5,000, which looks in retrospect to be a large exemption, relative to income levels in 1930. Finally, it was proposed that donations to any church, school, university, or hospital be deductible from income up to 10 percent of the net income of the taxpayer. Besides these measures, several amendments were made to the corporate income tax to block loopholes which permitted evasion of the tax. On these income tax changes, the finance minister probably looked for advice and assistance to the senior officials of the Income Tax Division of the National Revenue Department, notably the commissioner, Chester Walters, and the chief legal counsel, C. Fraser Elliott. Viets, the solicitor in the Department of Finance, may have acted as a conduit for information in income tax matters but he did not possess the expertise required to provide much assistance himself.[9] No doubt Dunning, who clearly trusted Sellar, sought his opinion on taxes and other subjects.

Normally the Department of Finance was expected to forecast revenue and expenditures in the new fiscal year for which the minister was budgeting. Although forecasts might have been done for the fiscal year 1930–31, Dunning did not include any in his budget. For this he would be roundly condemned by the leader of the Opposition, but under the economic and political circumstances it was probably felt it would not be prudent to hazard such forecasts.

Dunning revealed the full contents of his budget to the Cabinet on April 30, and the next day he presented it to the House of Commons. King felt his judgment was vindicated by the reception it received from the Liberal members: "There was tremendous applause on our side. The effect of the budget was electrical in a moment it became clear our men were delighted. . . . The cheering in the lobbies after was very great. Dunning was put on a table and asked if they were now ready to fight and all said they were."[10] With sublime overconfidence, the prime minister wrote: "This budget will be far reaching in its consequences. It will, I believe, win us the election. It is now apparent the party will welcome a fight forthwith. All opposition to an immediate appeal to the people has vanished. Our forces are as one."[11]

In the House, almost all the discussion of the budget and the tax resolutions and bills focused on the tariff measures. During the debate on the tariff details, with the House sitting in committee, Dunning was visibly assisted in explaining them by McKinnon, who sat at a small table on the floor of the House in front of Dunning's desk, as was the custom. In the relatively brief discussions on the income tax measures, Dunning was finally persuaded by Bennett to widen the purposes for which donations would be deductible, which the minister decided they could do by stating simply that the donation could be "to any charitable organization," a phrase which had been adequately defined by English legal usage. It is tempting to speculate that if proper departmental research had been done, this solution could and should have been reached in time to include it in the budget.

THE NEW CONSERVATIVE GOVERNMENT

The skill of King in tariff making and the other attractions of the budget were not enough to overcome the unpopularity of a government when the times were tough. In the election of July 28, 1930, the Liberal government was defeated and the Conservatives won 137 of the 245 seats. Bennett formed his government on August 7 and occupied the portfolio of Finance as well as External Affairs. He had promised many things during the election campaign, including quick action to deal with unemployment. As he had pledged, the new prime minister called a special short session of Parliament for September 8 so that urgent business could be done before he sailed to attend the Imperial Conference in London at the end of the month.

Even before the House met, Bennett took action that affected the work of the Department of Finance. An order-in-council abolished the Advisory Board on Tariff and Taxation, which had been established by a Liberal government. Bennett regarded it as a very Liberal body, to such an extent that he suspected the motives and objectivity of McKinnon, its secretary. McKinnon was allowed to retain his position as commissioner of tariff in the department. But for advice on tariff and customs matters, Bennett turned to R. W. Breadner, then commissioner of customs in the Department of National Revenue, who shared many of the protectionist views that Bennett held, who had worked for the Canadian Manufacturers' Association from 1908 to 1912, and who was still highly regarded by industrialists. Bennett asked McKinnon to work under Breadner's direction and McKinnon agreed, although his status must have been humiliating. McKinnon gradually won the respect of the prime minister by his knowledge of the tariff and related matters and by his objectivity and dedication.[12]

The first urgent business Bennett brought before the special September session was a bill to deal with the problem of unemployment. Its main section provided that a sum not exceeding $20 million be appropriated and paid out of the consolidated revenue fund of Canada for such purposes as were approved by the Governor in Council for the relief of unemployment. This was a blank cheque, but justified by the circumstances. The debate in the House indicated the government intended that the money would be used mainly for relief work projects to be carried out by either the provinces, the municipalities, or the departments of the Dominion government. Provisions also allowed it to be used to reimburse provinces and municipalities for a share of other expenses incurred in providing work or direct relief for the unemployed, including destitute farmers. An equal sharing of expenses by the provinces and municipalities was contemplated. Although they were held to be primarily responsible, the scale of the problem was then making it a matter of national concern. Expenditures made under this relief act were eventually to amount to about $18 million. But despite the urgent need for action, only a quarter of this amount was actually disbursed by the end of March 1931. The balance was paid out later on commitments made by that date.

It seems unlikely that the Department of Finance was significantly involved in the preparation or administration of this legislation. It was to be administered by the Department of Labour, and in its early preparation Bennett had taken advantage of the Employment Service Council of Canada, which had been organized in 1920 as an expert advisory body but had gradually become inactive. He had had a meeting of this council called in order to consult the provincial, trade union, and business representatives on it about the scale of unemployment and to secure their recommendations on what should be done.

The special session also passed several technical amendments to strengthen the anti-dumping clauses of the Customs Act. Some of the provisions gave the minister of national revenue arbitrary powers to determine the value for duty of imported goods, especially those imports believed to prejudicially or injuriously affect the interests of Canadian producers or manufacturers. If the value for duty exceeded the price at which goods were invoiced, a dumping duty was to be levied equal to the difference (up to a specified amount), in addition to the regular duty. The dumping duty was aimed primarily at imports from the United States. These arbitrary powers were later modified by trade agreements with that country.

A third statute of September 1930 amended the customs tariff itself. Bennett had come into office pledged to use the protective tariff vigorously as the principal weapon to fight depression. He argued that, given the high level of unemployment, only goods that could not be produced in

Canada should be imported, insofar as was reasonably possible. Revision of the tariff, he stated, should exclude goods that Canadians could make if protected from competition.[13]

The tariff bill changes were confined largely to the general and intermediate tariff rates, applying to goods from the United States and countries outside the Empire. Bennett stated that it "deals only with such items in the tariff as it is believed will ensure additional employment to a large number of men and women in Canada."[14] He spoke of an increase of 25,000 in employment. Although he planned a general revision of the tariff at Parliament's next session, this preliminary bill increased the rates substantially on well over a hundred tariff items.[15] Bennett's later tariff measures and negotiations are described in chapter 5.

More Effective Control of Expenditures

Bennett introduced two other major changes while he was minister of finance. These he was able to accomplish because he was also prime minister and in undisputed command of the government. In making these changes he relied substantially upon the advice and assistance of the senior officers of the Department of Finance.

First, he reorganized the accounting and cheque disbursing process throughout all government departments. Immediately after taking office, he had turned his mind to the control and reduction of the ordinary expenditures of the government, with a view to both limiting the deficit that would arise from the decline in revenues and diverting funds to emergency requirements like unemployment relief. When he sought figures on the expenditures of the departments so far during the fiscal year and on contractual commitments they had entered into, he found the Department of Finance was unable to give him up-to-date figures on either. The reason was the nature of the arrangements for the accounting and control of expenditures under the various appropriation "votes" granted by Parliament. These arrangements had remained virtually unchanged for over a half century, having been reformed in 1878 to conform to the British practice. Each department, excepting the revenue departments, was from time to time given a letter of credit by Finance authorizing it to draw cheques up to a specified limit on one of the government's accounts. Such cheques, after being honoured by the requisite bank, were delivered to the Department of Finance, where they were inspected and checked each month against the departmental vouchers and the bank statement. Finance then reimbursed the bank for the verified or adjusted total. The Department of Finance thus did not know the expenditures made under various appropriations until it received the vouchers from the departments and cleared the cheques from the bank. Nor was it informed and apparently did not normally ask what contractual commitments for future expenditures departments had made under their appropriations. Indeed the departments were not required to keep proper accounts of such commitments, though some naturally did so for their own information and management. Several of the officers of Finance had been conscious of these shortcomings and had considered possible changes but no reforms had occurred.[16]

Alarmed at this lack of knowledge and control, Bennett instructed the senior officers of the Finance Department to devise modifications that would each morning provide it with a report on the commitments and disbursements made by all departments the previous day. This instruction was addressed to the Executive Committee of the Finance Department of which Watson Sellar, as assistant deputy minister, was chairman. The Executive Committee included four other members. The most senior was B. G. McIntyre, comptroller general, whose duty it seems to have been to assist Sellar in coordinating and overseeing the work of the main branches of the department. The next was Bennett Roberts, who in his early days had been private secretary to Finance Minister Fielding, then was secretary of the department, and after March 1931 the comptroller of government guarantees. Sellar, McIntyre, and Roberts were able men who were eventually to reach most senior positions. The other two members were W. C. Ronson and R. B. Viets. Ronson was director of Estimates, the chief officer engaged full time on Treasury Board work, and was later to become assistant deputy minister in that role; Viets was the solicitor of the Treasury and as such was the department's legal officer.[17] This committee in effect ran the department under Sellar's leadership until a new deputy minister was appointed in November 1932.

The Executive Committee reached agreement fairly quickly on a plan to meet the objectives Bennett had set and submitted a report to the prime minister on December 15, 1930. It found that the existing accounting system afforded an acceptable degree of protection of public funds against defalcations and that the accounts were adequate for informing Parliament and the public about expenditures and revenues through the auditor general's report, the Public Accounts, and departmental publications.[18] The accounts, however, were not adequate to safeguard against expenditures exceeding the amounts authorized by Parliament, as they did not furnish information on expenditures and commitments early enough to permit corrective action. Indeed, the chief weakness of the system was that it did not "provide the Administration with adequate and timely information throughout the fiscal year."[19]

The committee suggested these weaknesses could be remedied without new legislation, by action under existing law relating to the transfer of duties,[20] and without adding many persons to the civil service. Control of the accounting and disbursing officers and clerks in the departments could be transferred from their departments to the minister of finance, while each continued to carry on the same duties in the same location and at the same salary. These officers would make no attempt to influence the nature of the expenditures but would see to it that the charges to any vote in the appropriations conformed with the intention of Parliament and that the total expenditures and commitments did not exceed the amount appropriated by Parliament. In the Department of Finance, control ledgers would be set up in which the up-to-date totals of the expenditures and commitments in all appropriations would be brought to account for the daily information of the minister and the government. Operation of the plan would require appointing a senior officer of the Department of Finance, with possibly one or two assistants, to supervise the accountants serving in the various departments.

The Executive Committee believed that its proposals, were they given the backing of the government, would accomplish the prime minister's objectives on expenditure control. But it warned the prime minister that its proposals might evoke strong opposition from administrative officers throughout the public service.

The prime minister, apparently influenced by Harold Daly, a Conservative informal adviser, thought this relatively simple solution did not go far enough and that there should be a greater legislative centralization of the accounting, pre-audit, and cheque-issuing functions with statutory powers and responsibilities. Bennett determined to bring this about by sweeping amendments to the Consolidated Revenue and Audit Act of 1878. A powerful position of comptroller of the Treasury would be established under the minister of finance, and the comptroller would be in charge of a large staff of Treasury officers and clerks posted in all departments. For the most part these posts would be filled by those who had previously carried out the accounting and clerical duties in the departments concerned.

Bennett directed Sellar to have such new legislation prepared by the Departments of Finance and Justice and circulated to the heads of all departments.[21] After a few changes, it was introduced in the House of Commons on June 19, 1931. Apparently a great deal of opposition within the government administration arose, and Sellar is quoted as saying, "If we had had to depend on another minister as minister of finance, we would never have gotten it."[22] Moreover, it seems clear that the prime minister had discussed his proposals with Mackenzie King in advance and received some assurance of support.[23] Further, King quickly supported the bill on second reading and thereby blocked potential Liberal opposition to it.

The bill was passed at the 1931 session and came into effect April 1, 1932. Having been appointed comptroller of the Treasury two months before that, Watson Sellar quickly secured authority and made arrangements to transfer about one thousand persons from various departments to his staff.

While technically the comptroller was an officer of the Department of Finance and reported to the minister of finance and Treasury Board, in fact he and his very considerable organization, which grew to include many thousands of employees by the end of World War II, were never regarded as part of the Finance Department under the control of the deputy minister. The comptroller had many statutory duties and powers, and was from time to time given others by the Treasury Board. The history of this office has already been written in a lengthy, detailed study by Roderick D. MacLean and will not be included here.[24]

Since Watson Sellar continued to act in the place of a deputy minister of finance and as chairman of the Executive Committee until a new deputy minister was appointed, his name and activities will continue to come up in this narrative. B. G McIntyre became the chief assistant to Sellar as the comptroller of the Treasury and in 1940 succeeded to the office when Sellar became auditor general.

Strengthening the Treasury Board

The second major change Bennett introduced while he was minister was the invigoration of the Treasury Board. When John A. Macdonald set up the board as a committee of ministers in 1867 and made Langton its secretary, it appears he intended that it would be a strong committee of the Cabinet. But during its first fifty years, it dealt mainly with the form and nature of accounts, the transactions criticized by the auditor general, and the details of personnel administration.[25] It had a small staff under the direction of its secretary. It does not appear to have dealt substantially with the Estimates during this period. The board began taking an interest in the Estimates only after 1908 when the establishment of an independent Civil Service Commission relieved the board of a good deal of the detailed personnel work.[26] In his report on the public service of Canada in 1912, Sir George Murray recommended that the Treasury Board be abolished and its work be taken over by the Finance Department and its minister. In 1919 the Senate Committee on the Machinery of Government paid little attention to the Treasury Board, although it did recommend major changes in the Cabinet, including the establishment of a Cabinet secretariat.[27]

During the 1920s the Treasury Board continued to deal with a variety of subjects, apparently at a leisurely pace.[28] These included personnel matters that fell outside the Civil Service Act of 1918, superannuation questions, remissions of custom duties, taxes, and penalties, special authority for certain insurance company transactions, as well as the few potentially important monetary decisions relating to advances to banks under the Finance Act. Sir George Murray undoubtedly was right; most of this work could have been done by officials and individual ministers, but the few efforts to introduce the reforms he had proposed came to nought because of the war. It was not until the late 1920s that the Treasury Board became an active agency within the executive of the government. And, according to W. C. Ronson, it was not until the beginning of the Depression in 1930 that the board became actively engaged in policy.[29]

But despite its indifferent record, Bennett saw the Treasury Board as the machinery by which he could exercise strict controls over expenditures. A former civil servant who worked with him at that time stated: "Bennett . . . rode the economy horse hard and ordered the secretary of the Treasury Board to cut all expenditures. Bennett took a personal hand in this as Minister of Finance and he conscientiously attended all Board meetings. There were so many influences to increase both expenditures and the size of the civil service that the Board had to act as a counter influence and it started issuing letters of refusal as well as Treasury Board minutes as authorities."[30]

This new economy drive was reflected in the Main Estimates for 1931-32, the first prepared by the Bennett government. They showed decreases in nearly every department and a decrease of $37 million out of a total of $241 million of controllable items to be voted by Parliament (that is, excluding statutory items such as interest on the public debt and subsidies to the provinces). This reduction must have taken a serious effort. But special expenditures on relief and other urgent items to deal with the Depression and its effects ultimately caused a small increase in total expenditures compared with those in the previous fiscal year, and left a budget deficit of about $114 million. In addition there was the need to finance, by loans, the Canadian National Railways which in 1931 had a deficit of $62 million and as well required another $34 million for capital expenditures on projects then under way.

Bennett introduced more severe economies in 1932. The Speech from the Throne opening Parliament on February 5 was low key but ominous; it forewarned the House of Bennett's intention to enforce "a policy of rigid economy."[31] Four days later the prime minister dropped his "block-buster." After referring to the fall in revenues and the success of the government in spending less than the amount appropriated by Parliament for the year nearly finished, he stated that his government had decided that to achieve the degree of economy desired, it would request Parliament to pass a statute reducing by 10 percent the salaries of public servants and the indemnities of members of the Senate and House of Commons. He asserted that this action was essential to enable the country to have a balanced budget, which was necessary in the interests of the people. It is important to note his reason:

> First and foremost we must maintain the national credit, because this new, young country can only go forward into the future if it has credit in the money markets of the world. There is but one money market of the world that is left, practically, and that market is indeed conscious of the high regard we have for our credit obligations, for we have met every contractual obligation of the provinces, the dominion and the municipalities in the money market of New York in the terms of our contract, and that we will continue to do.[32]

It should be remembered that he was speaking in February 1932, after Britain had left the gold standard and restricted access to her capital market and before the United States had had its banking and monetary crisis of March 1933 and cancelled the gold clause in all contracts under U.S. jurisdiction.

The reduction in salaries and indemnities of which Bennett gave notice on February 8 was carried out by the Salaries Deduction Act, introduced by resolution on February 26 and given Royal Assent on May 26. The plan had been worked out in the Department of Finance, which had started on it before October 1931.[33] Bennett introduced the resolution himself, as Edgar N. Rhodes, the recently appointed minister of finance, was ill. During the debate Bennett reported that there had been an average reduction of 14.4 percent in the cost of living since 1926, and "so far as wages and salaries generally are concerned, the statisticians report that the average reduction throughout the country is approximately ten per cent or perhaps a little more."[34] These declines in living costs and private sector salaries implied that the arbitrary deduction of 10 percent was equitable in the circumstances. It should be noted that for employees receiving less than $100 a month the government assumed the cost of the 5 percent employee contribution to the Superannuation Fund, thereby making the net deduction for this lowest paid group only 5 percent. The Labour members of Parliament opposed the bill as did many, but not all, of the civil service organizations. King, the astute leader of the Opposition, said his party could accept the principle of the bill but opposed some features of it. The Liberals voted against the resolution.

The Treasury Board had been busy cutting expenditures in many forms, and in his budget of April 6, 1932, Finance Minister Rhodes was able to say that the reductions in appropriations recommended to the House of Commons for the 1932–33 fiscal year marked a "considerable contribution" towards achieving a balanced budget. He stated that it was his government's intention to reduce controllable expenditures for the year by $35,800,000, about 20 percent.[35] There is no doubt that these economies were more severe than any others instituted before, and in retrospect they look very unwise.

To achieve economies in expenditures, the Treasury Board also introduced staff control regulations in June 1932.[36] This order-in-council abolished all permanent positions then vacant and restricted promotions severely; it set up procedures to reduce the number of temporary employees and to restrict the appointment of new or additional staff, and generally assigned to the Treasury Board responsibility and authority to ensure that these directives were enforced.[37] It was a blunt policy of economy by attrition. As Hodgetts and colleagues remarked in their history of the Civil Service Commission, "In retrospect, this Order in Council represented a most decisive break with the 1918 [Civil Service] Act. Clearly the CSC's responsibility for personnel management was being radically reduced."[38] The Treasury Board was not staffed to take over the detailed task of personnel management from the commission. Its methods were rough and ready. They were later described by Ronson to the Royal Commission on Administrative Classifications in the Public Service: "The whole idea was to obtain economies wherever possible . . . by austere methods; but that is the only way you can get them in the Civil Service."[39]

Bennett's budget of June 1931 and Rhodes's of April 1932 will be discussed, along with subsequent budgets, in chapter 6.

THE IMPERIAL ECONOMIC CONFERENCE OF 1932

Economic issues and in particular the subject of inter-Empire trade dominated the agenda for the Imperial Conference held in London from October 1, 1930, until November 14. King had looked forward to attending but, of course, Bennett went in his stead.[40] In his opening speech, Bennett endeavoured to get the 1930 conference to approve in principle a system of imperial tariff preferences. What preferences he offered the British in the Canadian market were in substance not very appealing to them and were contrary to the free trade policies of the Labour government. The only point of agreement was the decision to hold an economic conference in Ottawa in 1931.[41] In June 1931, however, the conference was postponed until 1932 because Australia could not send a delegation until then, though it probably also suited Bennett to postpone it in the hope of getting a more sympathetic government in Britain.[42]

As host government (this was the first time Britain was not host), Canada was responsible for proposing the agenda for the July 1932 conference and consulting with the other governments about it. Bennett was very slow in doing so; it was only on May 24 that he telegraphed his proposed agenda to the British and the other dominion governments. He wanted to discuss trade, of course, but also currency arrangements and policies. The agenda came as no surprise to the British, as the House of Commons in Ottawa, with the government's support, had approved on February 25 a resolution saying that the Canadian representatives should initiate and support measures for the stabilization of the currencies of all British countries.[43] This action reflected in part a concern over the low price of silver by H. H. Stevens, minister of trade and commerce, who represented British Columbia, the leading silver-mining province. To cover the subject in his proposed agenda, Bennett suggested a very broad item entitled "Monetary and Financial Questions."[44] The British were reluctant to discuss their policies on sterling with India and the dominions in the sterling area, and sought a narrower subject, which Bennett rejected. He succeeded in getting their acceptance of this item: "Consideration of existing inter-relationships of the various currencies and monetary standards of the Empire, and of the desirability and feasibility of taking steps to restore and stabilize the general price level and to stabilize exchange."[45]

While these preliminary discussions about monetary issues, as well as about trade questions, were taking place, a large interdepartmental committee, of which O. D. Skelton was chairman, was preparing in Ottawa for the Canadian participation in the conference. It was already evident that Canadian ministers were going to need to be briefed on monetary questions and there was really no one in the public service competent to do so. Skelton, presumably with Bennett's approval, approached W. C. Clark, his former student and longtime friend, to prepare a group of briefing papers. Clark took on the assignment and produced what he referred to as a "bulky volume."[46] Included was a very good paper on the possibilities and problems of the remonetization of silver, which was clearly intended to deal carefully and as constructively as possible with the views of Stevens. No doubt Bennett and Skelton saw Stevens's position as an important part of the problem of the Canadian delegation in any discussion of the monetary subjects on the agenda. In addition, Clark submitted voluminous background papers on the international gold standard, the sterling exchange standard, the objectives of monetary policy, and monetary reconstruction, which included a discussion of Canada's special interests and problems.[47] Clark was appointed special economic adviser to the Canadian delegation and financial adviser to Watson Sellar, senior representative of the Department of Finance.

One committee set up by the conference dealt with monetary and financial questions. It included mainly finance ministers, with Bennett representing Canada. He had arranged that Stevens should be chairman of the committee, because Stevens was highly interested in the general level of prices as well as in silver.[48] The committee heard lengthy statements from the main representatives, including Bennett (who spoke largely on the iniquity of current world price levels and their effects on debtor countries like Canada); they emphasized long-term objectives rather than immediate measures. The committee was brought down to earth when it learned from the British chancellor of the Exchequer, Neville Chamberlain, that the United Kingdom had "no intention of returning to the gold standard unless we can be thoroughly assured that a remedy has been found for the maladjustments which led to the breakdown of that standard last year."[49] On the possibility of stabilizing exchange rates within the Empire, he said the U.K. representatives would be glad to discuss any proposals that might be put forward but warned that world conditions were singularly unfavourable to stability. Meanwhile, he recommended "easy money" domestic policies and the reduction of interest rates, including the issuing of "conversion" loans to refinance callable outstanding debt.

The conference eventually accepted and endorsed the British view, but went on to recognize the ultimate aim as the restoration of a satisfactory international monetary standard. This matter was to be discussed the following year at an international conference then being organized by the League of Nations. Agreement on such a standard, and operating system, was not to be achieved until a dozen years later at Bretton Woods. It was adopted as a postwar measure at a time the U.S. dollar was the one pre-eminently strong currency.

THE APPOINTMENT OF W. C. CLARK

Clark's work at the conference, as well as his briefing papers, must have impressed Bennett. Years after, officials who had been there recalled that Bennett had been particularly impressed by the tactful but effective way in which Clark had dealt with the silver issue. About two months after the conference, Bennett asked Clark to accept appointment to the vacant position of deputy minister of finance. Since the academic year had just begun and Clark was a key member of the faculty, the offer led to some problems at Queen's. Recognizing the importance of Bennett's proposal and no doubt prodded by Skelton, the university, however, made arrangements which permitted Clerk to take up his duties in the department on November 4, 1932.

Clark was qualified by education, experience, and character for the job. Born in Glengarry County, Ontario, in 1889, he grew up on a farm near Martintown and entered Queen's at the age of sixteen. He started to study mining engineering, but within a few weeks he shifted to the more intellectual fields of the honours arts courses in Latin and French, earning an M.A. by securing first class in both courses. His great potential was recognized and he was encouraged to complete in the next two years the honours courses in English, history, and finally political and economic science. He was much influenced and stimulated by O. D. Skelton, the brilliant young professor of political and economic science, who was the under secretary of state for external affairs in Ottawa from 1925 to 1941. After three years of postgraduate work in economics at Harvard, where he was a favourite of the renowned Professor Frank Taussig and won senior fellowships, Clark returned to Queen's in 1915 to join Skelton in teaching applied economics, including international trade and banking. In 1923 he left Queen's to become one of the earliest business economists in the United States, as an officer of S. W. Straus and Co., which specialized in financing urban development. The firm shared the disasters of the collapse of the U.S. boom at the end of the 1920s, and Clark was left with his health impaired. He returned in 1931 to teach again at Queen's.[50] At this time he was substantially in debt because the value of the house he had bought near New York before the crash fell quickly to far less than what he had borrowed to pay for it.

By 1932 Clark had a wide knowledge of and interest in economic and financial affairs. He had joined in discussion and writing about international monetary affairs and as far back as 1920 had been interested in the establishment of a central bank in Canada.[51] At Harvard he had chosen to write a doctoral thesis on the Canadian grain grade but never found time to complete it.[52] A hard worker, who read voluminously, Clark relaxed principally by talking at length to a variety of people who had occasion to visit him. He originated ideas and would argue both for and against them until he made up his mind, and then he would defend his conclusions tenaciously. He did not mind being in a minority of one, and was often right. Throughout his career he saw problems that needed to be solved and was ingenious in devising solutions to them. At home he had a most understanding and helpful wife and two sons and two daughters.

It is said on good authority that Clark agreed to become deputy minister of finance only when he had found out that the prime minister was prepared to accept in principle the establishment of a central bank for Canada and the introduction of unemployment insurance.[53] Bennett did establish the central bank, and he did try to introduce unemployment insurance, only to have his legislation nullified by the courts.

Clark was fortunate to have entered the Finance Department under an able and congenial minister, who had been largely overshadowed by Bennett during the events of 1932. Rhodes had already had a long and distinguished political career before he became minister of finance in February 1932. Born in Nova Scotia in 1877, educated at Acadia and Dalhousie universities, and called to the bar in 1902, he joined the Conservative party and was elected to Parliament in 1908. He was elected Speaker in 1917 and in 1918, and sworn in as a member of the Privy Council in 1921. In the election of 1921, his constituency of Cumberland went to the Liberals. In 1925, following the provincial election, Rhodes became premier of Nova Scotia, a position he held until 1930, when at Bennett's request he accepted the portfolio of Fisheries in the new Conservative Cabinet. Rhodes was well suited to his new role. As R. K. Finlayson, the prime minister's private secretary, has written in his unpublished biography of Bennett:

> Rhodes was one of the best Speakers ever to occupy that post in the House of Commons and later as a Minister of the Crown, no one knew procedure better than he and no one else could, with such ease, trip up the usually competent parliamentarian, W. L. Mackenzie King. A man of more than ordinary capacity, he had an uncanny sense of where the line should be drawn between a Minister and his advisers. In Rhodes' view, the function of a Minister was to make decisions and accept before the public the responsibility for doing so while that of his advisers was to bring him assembled facts and ideas upon which he could form a judgment. He conducted his work with a leisurely self-confidence that led some of his colleagues, including Bennett, to believe he was indolent. Rhodes, as federal Minister of Finance beginning in 1932, earned the respect of the business community, as well as such a representative and cosmopolitan group as the Canadian Legion. He enjoyed the confidence of members of the different parties and of all people who came in contact with him. He had often been mentioned as the possible successor to R. B. Bennett, but before 1935 his health had failed.[54]

With Clark's appointment, the interregnum in the department was over. During that time the government had made two decisions which enlarged the department. After consultation with the British government, it was decided that operations of the Ottawa Mint, built in 1905–7 as a branch of the Royal Mint of Great Britain, should be transferred to Canada and become a branch of the Department of Finance. An act of Parliament established the Royal Canadian Mint, effective December 1, 1931.[55] The staff, including the master of the Mint, J. H. Campbell, were transferred from the British to the Canadian civil service.

The second addition was made in October 1932. In response to widespread criticism led by the Canadian Bar Association, Parliament that year reviewed the Bankruptcy Act. A special select committee heard evidence on the matter and made a unanimous report, approving with amendments a bill that had been introduced by the minister of justice. The unsupervised working of the act had led to numerous abuses and high costs, which reduced unreasonably the amount of bankrupt estates available for creditors or for the bankrupt person or firm. It was therefore proposed that a superintendent of bankruptcy (who eventually had a staff of about ten persons to assist him) scrutinize the administration of bankrupt estates by their trustees. Since the government felt that the central problems were those of financial administration rather than of law, it was decided that the superintendent should be part of the Department of Finance, not Justice.

Organization in November 1932

When Clark arrived in November 1932, he was given an organization chart (chart 1) showing the main elements of the Finance Department, their chief officers, and the number of persons in each. It gives a total of 494 staff members, including the Mint but excluding the comptroller of the Treasury and his offices. Three-quarters of the total worked in three routine operating units: the Loans and Interest Branch with 172; the Currency Branch with 133, which included 66 in the offices of the Assistant Receivers General in each province; and the Mint with 83.[56] There was no assistant deputy minister at this time; the heads of all the units reported directly to the new deputy minister. It was not until April 1935 that Clark had Bennett Roberts appointed assistant deputy minister.[57] Clark was not greatly interested in organization and management, and it is possible that he relied on Roberts informally to assist him in managing the department during 1933 and 1934 when he was very busy on conferences, policy, and legislation. Nearly the whole of the department in those years was engaged in what were essentially operating functions or in accounting, which did not give rise to policy problems. The officers in those branches were not of much help in dealing with the policy problems with which Clark himself was most concerned, apart from W. E. Hunter in connection with financing relief expenditures and Roberts in the financial relations with the Canadian National Railways. Ronson at the Treasury Board dealt directly with the board and the minister, following general policies already laid down. An analysis of the conflict between Clark's lack of interest in administration and his entrepreneurial zeal for devising new policies is included in the reflections in chapter 13.

CHART 1

DEPARTMENT OF FINANCE, NOVEMBER 2, 1932

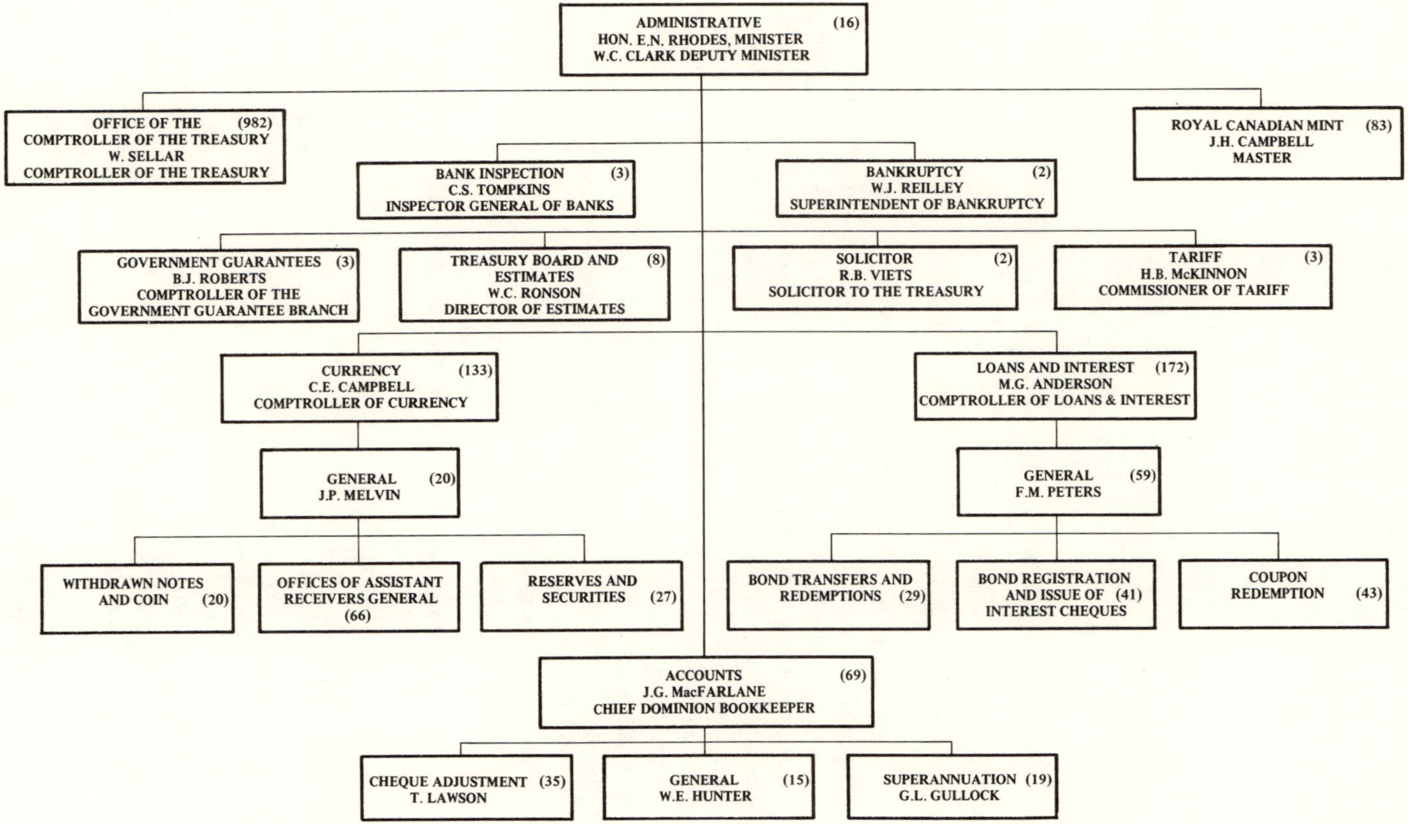

Copied from chart found in PAC, RG55, vol. 643, file 3-9.
Number of staff, November 2, 1932: general 411; Comptroller of the Treasury 982; Royal Canadian Mint 83; total 1,476.

Chapter Five

Tariff Policies and Negotiations

Canada entered the 1930s without tariff agreements with either the United Kingdom or the United States, its two main trading partners. Most Canadians still regarded the country as part of the British Empire, and Britain, its keystone, predominantly still followed a free trade policy initiated almost a century earlier. Towards Britain Canada had voluntarily extended a system of tariff preferences, which applied also to the other dominions, India, and the colonies, but were modified in some cases by bilateral agreements. With the United States, reciprocity in the trade of natural products had once existed, but had been jettisoned in the 1860s by the United States. It might have been revived on a wider scale had not the election of 1911 overturned the Laurier government which had negotiated a new reciprocity agreement. There had been no agreement since. Indeed, in the first half of 1930 the U.S. Congress was putting the finishing touches on the wildly protectionist Hawley-Smoot tariff. Canada had bilateral trade agreements with a score of European countries and one with Australia, which was to be revised. These agreements, however, did not largely influence or constrain Canada's general tariff policy in 1930, as the Liberals and then the Conservatives reacted to the rapid decline in employment and trade and the threat of the new U.S. tariff.

Dunning's budget of May 1930 had been the first reaction, and a very carefully calculated one, which strengthened the discriminatory rather than the protectionist features of the tariff through stronger British preferences, introduced the principle of measured retaliation against the United States by countervailing duties, and modernized the whole iron and steel sector without much net overall addition to the weight of the tariff. Bennett's September tariff measures were rough and ready. Fashioned for him by the Canadian Manufacturers' Association and R. W. Breadner to deal with the unemployment and farming crises, they provided widespread protection against imports from the United States and other non-Empire countries of anything they believed could be made in Canada.

By the time he introduced his budget on June 1, 1931, Bennett had had more time for preparation, but he faced a more desperate unemployment situation and the need for more revenue. He did not have his complete revision of the tariff ready, but he did have another large instalment of the same sort of widespread protection that he had introduced in September 1930. The automobile industry was one of his principal targets. He introduced a high rate of duty, 40 percent, on "luxury cars" imported from the United States.[1] The most important measure imposed severe restrictions on drawbacks, that is, refunds of duties, allowed to manufacturers importing parts to be incorporated in cars made in Canada. Thus more protection was afforded to a wide range of the Canadian parts manufacturing industry, including the makers of tires. Used cars, which were flooding into Canada as the Depression deepened in the United States, were prohibited entry, a provision that remains to this day. Many other commonly used items were subject to increased duties, such as coal from the United States. Leather goods too were subject to higher rates even under British preference rates. Magazines and periodicals were subject to duty by the pound, with the Governor in Council being able to exempt what he saw fit. Even tea, which of course could never be produced in Canada even under Bennett, was made subject to duty under the British preference rates—clearly a revenue measure, as apparently was the case for a number of other items. Increased revenue from imports was mainly to come from a special excise tax of 1 percent on all imports, whether subject to duty or on the free list.

The tariff measures in this budget brought the tariff to the highest level in Canada's history. Bennett seems to have had some qualms about this himself, for, in concluding his tariff proposals, he said: "It is an unfortunate thing perhaps, but it is true that all the countries of the world are now protected countries, and Canadian products may find access to their markets only by paying very high tolls. Can this country afford to be an unprotected country against the competition of the protected countries of the world? We have answered that question in the way I have indicated and by that answer we stand or fall."[2] Can we infer from this statement that Bennett, who was already planning the Imperial Economic Conference of 1932, had in mind bargaining away some of these very high duties in order to get better access for Canadian goods in other markets in the future? Probably not at that time—even higher rates against U.S. exports, which would be used as a means of increasing the British preference, were still to come. But over a long period of years, these atrociously high tariffs of 1931 were in fact bargained down in return for reductions in the equally atrocious Hawley-Smoot and other high rates in the United States and elsewhere.

APPROACHING THE 1932 CONFERENCE

After the 1931 budget, the Canadian government did not change its tariff laws again before the 1932 conference. It did, however, increase the special excise tax on all imports from 1 to 3 percent as a revenue measure in Rhodes's budget of April 6, 1932. After much hard bargaining, it also revised its trade agreement with Australia in June 1931. In the new agreement Canada gained a number of relatively minor reductions in the rates on manufactured products and, more importantly, increased preferences on lumber and canned salmon; Australia gained concessions from Canada in the duties on meat and poultry and the promise of new preferences on rice and peanuts. During times that Australia could meet all of Canada's requirements for rice and peanuts, new duties would be applied to these products from other sources.

In January 1932 Canada made its first trade agreement with New Zealand. Before that time, New Zealand had been given the rates provided for Australia, which included imports of butter into Canada at the low duty rate of one cent a pound. This arrangement was terminated when so much butter poured into Canada in early 1930 that controversy arose. Under the trade agreement of 1932, butter was subject to a rate of five cents a pound, a safe rate in those days but lower than the British preference rate of eight cents. New Zealand granted Canada its British preferential rates on all but six items, which restored the situation that had prevailed before 1930 without an agreement. Stevens, the minister of trade and commerce, had a major role in working out these two agreements and appears to have relied upon H. B. McKinnon of Finance, as well as his own officials, in doing so. In November 1932 he stated in a letter to Sir George Perley, minister without portfolio: "Mr. McKinnon is one of the very few men in the Government Service who are qualified to deal with tariff matters in the preparation of trade agreements."[3]

Bennett was not yet making adequate use of McKinnon's qualities, however. He looked first to Breadner, the old die-hard protectionist, for advice, as he had in raising the tariffs in 1930 and 1931. But he went much further in this wrong direction by seeking information and advice directly from the Canadian Manufacturers' Association (CMA) on the very important and difficult question of the concessions to be offered or made to Britain for the bilateral agreement which was to be the centrepiece of the 1932 conference.[4] Bennett began meeting with the CMA in December 1931 and continued meeting and corresponding with members of the association right up to the eve of the conference in July, though by this time he was exasperated and disillusioned with their dilatory and obstructionist tactics.[5]

The British government as well had a hard time making up its mind on trade policy both for the 1932 conference and generally. A coalition government had been formed in late August 1931 to save the pound. Though it failed in that task, it was reorganized and re-elected in October. All the while, confusing debates went on within as well as among the three main parties over free trade versus protection. Prime Minister Ramsay MacDonald was by then regarded as a renegade from the Labour party. Stanley Baldwin led the Conservative majority, and Neville Chamberlain, another Conservative, became the chancellor of the Exchequer and emerged as the most powerful minister. Walter Runciman, a strong National Liberal, served on the Board of Trade as a counterweight to Chamberlain, who apparently had inherited his penchant for protectionism.

In February 1932 Chamberlain consulted Bennett by telephone on Britain's general plan. Bennett suggested to him that the United Kingdom impose a general nonpreferential tariff, but one that would not be applicable on goods from the dominions until after the Ottawa conference. Chamberlain accepted the suggestion and sold it to most of his colleagues. The basic plan of a general revenue tariff to remedy the imbalance of trade had already been more or less accepted on Runciman's initiative in December 1931. Combining these two ideas, the British government placed before its Parliament a bill that became the Import Duties Act, which imposed a general duty of 10 percent on imports not already dutiable (as a few manufactured goods had been for many years, including some from Canada,) but deferred until November 15 its application to imports from the dominions. The bill provided free entry for a few important items, notably, copper, wheat, and meat, a provision which was to be the subject of special discussions at Ottawa. Agricultural protectionism was developing at this time in Britain, and the government there was not ready early in 1932 to decide on food import policies. On its industrial exports, however, the British government, with its expert advisers and industrial contacts, was quickly able to formulate the concessions it would seek from each dominion. It sent out a list of them to the governments with which it would be negotiating and repeatedly sought discussions of these before the conference. It did not succeed in getting any formal replies from Canada, although the British high commissioner generally discussed the matter with the Canadian Cabinet soon after the list was delivered in February.[6]

Early in 1932 the Canadian government established a Cabinet committee to consider policies for the conference and help draw up the agenda.[7] As mentioned previously, the main work of organization and preparation was assigned to an interdepartmental committee, based mainly on the Departments of External Affairs, Trade and Commerce, Finance, and National Revenue, their first major collaborative effort. But this committee was not intended to produce a tariff policy in advance of the conference.

There was a subcommittee on tariff preparations chaired by the redoubtable Breadner, but since he had been sick and McKinnon was vice chairman, the subcommittee did not function as intended.[8] R. K. Finlayson, the prime minister's private secretary, and William Herridge, the Canadian minister to Washington, as well as Breadner, were advising Bennett on the preparations for the negotiations with the British, while Dana Wilgress of Trade and Commerce, Norman Robertson of External Affairs, and McKinnon of Finance, as well as Breadner, were preparing Minister of Trade and Commerce Stevens for discussions with the other countries.[9]

Bennett did not decide on the main requests he wanted to make of the British until the last moment. It was not until July 11, two days before the British delegation sailed to Canada, that he cabled a list of Canada's demands to London. They were put only in general terms—something on wheat, flour, meat, cattle and dairy products, tobacco, fruit, vegetables, timber, pulp, and base metals. These demands were probably not unexpected by the British experts, but the generality of the requests gave them little to work on during the voyage.

Trade Negotiations at the 1932 Conference

Bennett had said to those accompanying him to the 1930 Imperial Conference that he felt the British Empire had reached a critical point in its history. Its political continuation would depend on whether its statesmen could work out some plan of tariff preferences among the countries of the Empire so that each could enjoy, as much as possible, a market for its products.[10] This seems to have been his broad purpose in proposing the Ottawa conference of 1932.

When the time came, the objective was complicated by the compelling economic circumstances and political problems of the principal participants. Bennett himself combined this imperial objective with the desire to give up as little as possible of the protection he had created for the Canadian manufacturing industries in exchange for as much preference as possible in the British market for Canada's exports of farm products, lumber, metals, and fish, nearly all of which had lost important markets in the United States. To accomplish this, he intended to increase Canadian tariffs on imports from the United States and other foreign countries whose exports competed with those coming to Canada from the United Kingdom. His intentions were opposed by the British ministers who wanted lower Canadian tariffs on their manufactured goods with the least cost to Britain in providing preferred access for Canadian food and raw materials, and with a minimum of new tariffs or restraints on imports from other countries in the British and other Empire markets. Australia, the other major participant, also wanted preferred access to the British market, especially for its meat, which had to compete with that from Argentina. It, too, had a highly protected domestic manufacturing sector to which it wished to allow the British only very limited access.

The conference was a very large international gathering and involved the most complex trade negotiations that had ever taken place. Moreover, preparations had been inadequate, except perhaps on the part of the Australians. Too much had been left to be negotiated in the month allowed for the conference itself. The British arrived with strength in numbers and experience, but with some important policies unsettled. Their seven ministers included most of those in the Cabinet who were involved with trade policy and they had been granted full powers to act. They represented a national coalition government, and included Conservative, former Labour, and former Liberal ministers. They were supported by a large number of officials and advisers and accompanied by representatives of all the important British interests likely to be affected. The Australian delegation of seven was led by Prime Minister Stanley Bruce, who could be just as tough as Bennett, with whom he in fact conspired against the British at times during the conference. He could risk a failure of the conference, while both Bennett and the leading British ministers really could not because they had staked too much of their prestige on its success. New Zealand was represented by its prime minister, South Africa by its minister of finance. The others present included the Irish Free State, India, Southern Rhodesia, and Newfoundland.

The Canadian delegation was huge—thirteen ministers, sixty-four departmental advisers (three from Finance), and seven special advisers. Of course the rest of the Cabinet was nearby as were many representatives of special interest groups. The press was also there in profusion, although the press arrangements, as in many later Commonwealth conferences, were unsatisfactory. The agreed official policy was to say very little, but the British had brought along the able and attractive son of the prime minister, Malcolm MacDonald, MP, parliamentary under secretary in the Dominions Office, who briefed the British press very skilfully each night. Meanwhile, at Kingsmere, a short drive away in the Gatineau hills, Mackenzie King was happy to be available to chat with his many acquaintances among the delegates and thus keep track of what was happening and float what rumours he wished.

The conference opened on July 21, elected Bennett as its chairman, and adopted his agenda as modified in advance consultations. It heard brief opening statements from the leaders of each delegation, who, though dealing in generalities, revealed real conflicts of interests. Five main committees were set up for discussion of broad issues, including the promotion of trade within the Empire, customs administration, methods of economic cooperation, monetary and financial questions, and commercial relations with foreign countries. The discussions were later to lead to conference resolutions of good intent but with no binding power.

The real work was the negotiation of bilateral trade agreements, particularly those between the United Kingdom and Canada and between the United Kingdom and Australia. Agreements between the United Kingdom and the other dominions and India would not present serious difficulties so long as these two were settled. The United Kingdom extended its preferences to all the dominions, India, and the colonies, but the other countries had to negotiate their own preferences with one another. These negotiations were also carried out during the conference. The agreement between Canada and South Africa involved some serious difficulties and was settled only on the final day. Canada made a similar agreement with Southern Rhodesia, and a simple exchange of British preference rates was undertaken with the Irish Free State.

It was the negotiations for the agreement between Canada and the United Kingdom that caused the most difficulties and nearly resulted in breakdown. Bennett proclaimed imperial sentiments and principles but was neither a skilful diplomat nor a tactful chairman. The British press mercilessly criticized him to the point that Malcolm MacDonald felt he had to apologize and state that he had not inspired the unfavourable statements. Chamberlain recorded in his diary that Bennett "has strained our patience to the limit."[11]

Bennett, with all his bullying, was not the only one to blame. Despite Australia's preparatory conversations, Bruce was very aggressive in demanding preferences in the British market on meat and nearly broke off negotiations to get them. The British ministers, as previously stated, had come to the conference without having reached agreement among themselves on food and agricultural policies and contributed to the delays, crises, and allegations of bad faith, as they struggled to formulate their own position on the more controversial matters.

On the substance of the Anglo-Canadian negotiation, the British sought two main concessions from Canada. First was tariff concessions of the normal varieties: reduction in protective rates or increased preferential margins. The British ministers found Bennett persistently unwilling to be specific on this matter, despite the proposal in his opening speech "that the United Kingdom have free entry into Canada for her products which will not injuriously affect Canadian enterprise."[12] Similar differences were encountered between Britain and Australia. It appeared that the United Kingdom would not succeed in getting enough additional employment in manufacturing to justify the preferences already provided in the Import Duties Act, much less the further concessions being sought by the dominions. Casting about for some way out, Chamberlain was attracted to the idea that a formula or principle might be put into the agreements that would lead to further gradual reductions. This led the British to propose a second major concession which they called "domestic competition," derived at least in part from the Indian protective tariffs. Canada (and Australia) would be asked to submit their tariffs, specifically the British preferential rate, to an impartial Tariff Board to determine the rate of duty on British manufactured goods that would be necessary to offset the lower costs of production in industrial Britain in comparison with costs in Canada.[13] The British also proposed that Canada include in its trade agreement a clause stating that once this rate was determined, Canada would not impose any higher protective tariffs on British goods. The British ministers told Bennett that his public statements had really implied the acceptance of this principle. Although Bennett agreed that the principle could be put into the agreement, he objected for some time to the inclusion of the right of British firms to appear before the Tariff Board and the obligation of the Canadian government to accept the findings of the board. After some days, on August 10, Bennett acceded and articles 10 to 15 of the agreement were drafted.

On the immediate changes in tariff rates, progress was much slower and more erratic.[14] Here Bennett was subject to the influence of Breadner as his chief official adviser, the right wing of his Cabinet led by C. H. Cahan of Montreal and E. B. Ryckman of industrial Ontario, and the numerous industrial lobbyists from the CMA and elsewhere. The proposals he was grudgingly putting before the British were being rejected as much too little, indeed derisory, in terms of the additional employment they would provide in the United Kingdom.[15]

Bennett became convinced, apparently some time in the second week of August, that he would have to make substantially more concessions and turned to the experienced and objective Hector McKinnon for advice. He had McKinnon take along the list of concessions Bennett was then prepared to make for discussions with Sir Horace Wilson, the principal industrial adviser to the British government. As expected, Wilson rejected the proposal. Bennett then requested McKinnon, with Dana Wilgress from Trade and Commerce and Norman Robertson from External Affairs, to draw up a list they thought the British would accept. H. H. Stevens later stated that he had worked with these three to devise the compromise. The revised proposal was at first rejected in part by the Canadian Cabinet, but the British delegation would not accept the changes and Bennett yielded. Just when agreement seemed in sight, Bennett changed one important item at the request of a major steel manufacturer and this piece of impetuousness momentarily fouled the entire deal. The prime minister soon withdrew it to enable agreement to be achieved on the last day.[16] The British got a better market in Canada for their iron and steel products, textiles, chemicals and drugs, glass, and other manufactured products. To be precise: "In 132 cases duties on British goods were reduced, and in 83 cases increased margins of preference were secured by raising foreign tariff rates. In 79 cases goods from the United Kingdom were placed upon the free list [apparently included in the 132 above]."[17]

In return, Canada asked for concessions or more assured markets for wheat and flour, bacon, cattle, timber, pulp, base metals, cheese, apples, and a variety of lesser exports. Bennett pressed hard for some kind of effective restraints on Russia, which was dumping lumber (and wheat) on the British market—a serious situation, as the Russians were in dire need of foreign exchange and had to sell at distress prices goods they really needed at home. After much hard bargaining, complicated by some ideological arguments, Canada and Britain consented to prevent sales "through state action on the part of any foreign country" at prices that would frustrate the preferences provided in the agreement.[18] This required the British to terminate their existing trade agreement with Russia and negotiate a new one.

Canada got most of what it was seeking in preferred access to the British market. New preferences on wheat, butter, cheese, apples, and some other food items were granted. The preferences created by duties on foreign wheat, copper, zinc, or lead could, however, be removed if Empire suppliers were unable or unwilling to offer their exports for sale in the United Kingdom at prices not exceeding world prices or in quantities sufficient to meet U.K. needs. Such was the case with copper because of an effective cartel.

On the most controversial category of all, preferences for Empire meats in the British market, it was Australia and New Zealand that were bargaining hard and agreement was reached only in the last few hours of negotiations, when the British agreed to impose quotas on foreign lamb, mutton, and beef. Canada got a duty-free quota on bacon without much trouble.

The agreements of the United Kingdom with Australia and New Zealand were signed just before midnight on Friday, August 19, and the one with Canada shortly after. The plenary closing session of the conference took place the next morning.

THE TARIFF BOARD

After the major effort of 1932, tariff changes in the budget of 1933 and 1934 were relatively minor, both in number and in significance. Many simply clarified the wording of items. Most of the others were reductions, especially in the British preferential rates, though some items in the general and intermediate tariff were reduced as well. What few increases were made were usually explained as recommendations of the Tariff Board, which had been organized in 1933 in accordance with the Tariff Board Act passed in 1931.

The board had begun work on its reports in mid-1933 in response to requests from the minister of finance, as the law required. Most arose out of demands by the United Kingdom for review of particular items or groups of items, but later they came on the initiative of the minister, no doubt arising in part from requests from Canadian industry or as a result of preliminary study by Canadian officials. The board was required to hold inquiries in public. Another function of the board was quasi-judicial: to hear appeals from rulings of the Department of National Revenue on customs and excise decisions, such as those relating to value for duty on the rate of duty applicable. It had a small but competent staff of economists of whom Phyllis Turner was the most senior.[19] Hector McKinnon acted as secretary of the board during its early years, as well as being commissioner of tariff in the Finance Department.

Finance Minister Rhodes tabled the first group of reports by the Tariff Board when he delivered his budget of 1934. Thereafter he and Dunning normally tabled reports at subsequent budgets, usually implementing the board's recommendations.

A Trade Convention with France

A trade treaty with France, which had been in effect from 1923, was abrogated late in 1931 after fruitless efforts to revise it. This action had to be taken to clear the way for the major negotiations of the Empire trade agreements in 1932. Once these were enacted, preparations began, under direction of the prime minister, for a new trade convention with France. Much of this work was done by Wilgress in the evenings during November 1932.[20] Bennett asked C.H. Cahan, the bilingual secretary of state, to take up the proposals with the French when he was in Europe for a League of Nations Assembly, but he ran into unexpected difficulties. Negotiations were adjourned to Ottawa early in 1933 where agreement was reached in May. Each side obtained improved access to markets of the other for a wide range of products. Canada could not, however, provide concessions on French wines because South Africa refused to accept a reduction in its preference for wines in Canada. In compensation Canada lost its preferred rate in France for wheat. As these and other aspects of the 1933 agreement were unsatisfactory, Bennett himself negotiated a supplementary agreement when he was in France in 1934. More progress was possible because South Africa had withdrawn its earlier objection.

The First Agreement with the United States

Even while preparing for the Ottawa conference of 1932, Bennett was beginning to think about an approach to the U.S. government on trade matters. His private secretary, R. K. Finlayson, reported that Bennett asked trade officials to prepare "material" to be submitted as a trade proposal to the United States, probably as a result of suggestions by W. D. Herridge, the Canadian minister to Washington.[21] There is some indication that Herridge talked to Raymond Moley, Roosevelt's chief adviser, either before the U.S. election of 1932 or shortly after. Bennett met officially with Roosevelt in April 1933. The press communique of that meeting stated, among other matters, that they had "agreed to begin a search for means to increase the exchange of commodities between our two countries, and thereby promote not only economic betterment on the North American continent but also the general improvement of world conditions."[22] The following February, in 1934, Bennett reported in Parliament that "in the nine months which have elapsed since that statement was made, informal conversations with Washington have been continued."[23] Nothing could be done, however, until June when Congress passed the Reciprocal Trade Agreement Act, giving the president authority to negotiate agreements.

The first definite move came in November 1934. On instruction of the Canadian government, Hume Wrong of the legation drafted a long, formal note and Herridge submitted it to Cordell Hull, the secretary of state of the United States. It concluded with a five-point outline "as a suitable basis for negotiation of a trade agreement."[24] One point was "the mutual concession of tariff treatment as favourable as that accorded to any other foreign country; this means that Canada would extend to the United States its intermediate Tariff."[25] This was a key point, as the U.S. law required the "most-favoured nation" treatment in agreements and Canada was seeking to have the British preferences excepted from that clause. The intermediate tariff was the lowest one, apart from the British preference rates.

The United States officials were somewhat embarrassed by this early Canadian initiative, as they were not ready for the important points it raised. Hull accepted the proposal on December 27, but added to the points for negotiation "value for duty practices," which was a serious problem for the United States because of Bennett's protectionist customs laws.[26] The Americans, however, dragged their feet on the matter and negotiations did not officially commence until August 1935, after Congress had adjourned. Following this meeting, at which the United States had given its views, Bennett sent a telegram to Wrong in Washington, expressing concern at the omission of any probable improvement in the access to the United States for a number of important Canadian products including codfish and cattle. By the time of the second meeting of officials, the Canadian election had been called, and it was decided to suspend negotiations.

When King was overwhelmingly returned to office in the election on

October 14, 1935, he was committed by his campaign promises to conclude an agreement with the United States before the end of the year. Immediately after taking office, he informed the U.S. minister in Ottawa that he wished negotiations to resume at once. They did, "in great haste," as Wilgress, one of the negotiators, later described it.[27] King himself visited Washington two weeks after taking office and met with Hull and Roosevelt to expedite the agreement. O. D. Skelton stayed on to help finish the deal. The agreement was signed by King on a second visit a week after his meeting with Roosevelt. The speed was possible largely because of the form of the deal, at least on Canada's part. It consisted mainly in the granting of the intermediate tariff schedule instead of the general one, and, as Wilgress remarked, it did not need to be sweetened by many specified reductions.[28] Canada did not get all it wanted from the United States, especially on products from the Maritimes. However, it accomplished two important and related objectives: it put Canada firmly on a most-favoured-nation basis with the United States and it obtained U.S. acceptance of the British preferences as a recognized exception to the most-favoured-nation clause. In addition King himself felt that he had established a close and warm relationship with Roosevelt, which would help in many other matters.

Neither Dunning nor Clark appear to have had anything important to do with this trade treaty, but McKinnon was a key member of the three-man negotiating team in Washington, along with Robertson and Wilgress. McKinnon and Robertson have not written publicly about these matters, but much of what is known about the negotiations and their effects has come from Wilgress. McKinnon also had a hand in settling the rather bitter dispute with Australia over the effects of the Canada-U.S. agreement on its preferences in Canada and its exports.[29]

TARIFF ACTION IN 1935 AND 1936

Quite apart from the agreement with United States, both Rhodes's last budget in March 1935 and Dunning's in May 1936 contained a number of changes in the tariffs, mainly reductions. Rhodes reduced further some of the British preference rates, putting twenty items on the free list. A dozen reductions affected all three schedules of rates, the intermediate and general tariffs and the British preference. Only four items were subject to increases, a result of Tariff Board findings. It was a careful pre-election budget, made after Bennett, who was by then on good terms with the British, asked if they had any changes to propose.[30]

In 1936 Dunning, as might be expected, put a more Liberal stamp on his tariff policy. He described his proposals as both extensive and important, even though they immediately followed the Canada-U.S. agreement. A number of the more important changes were based on Tariff Board recommendations on motor vehicles, cotton products, gasoline, and artificial silk. The board had also made an interim report on furniture, recommending no change at that time. Serious disputes in the Cabinet resulted, as W. D. Euler, the protectionist minister of trade and commerce, pressed strongly for increased protection but did not succeed.[31] The intent of several complicated and conditional tariff items on automobiles was to maintain the industry in Canada and encourage a high degree of "Canadian content" in the completed vehicle in order to improve the auto parts industry. The consumer, the driver of the car, was helped by a reduction in the duty on gasoline from two and a half to one cent a gallon. Most of the other reductions were in the British preference rates and reflected the Liberal policy of "giving" these concessions rather than bargaining with them. Dunning made clear the British were expected to take the gift into account. A popular item in the budget was the exemption from duty three times a year of $100 worth of personal purchases by tourists, which had been included in the agreement with the United States but would now be generally applied. One of the most politically interesting changes was the reduction in duties on farm implements, which had been decided by Cabinet at the last moment. The duty, negotiated with the United States some months before at 12½ percent, was reduced in the budget to 7½ percent, in part at least because the reduction made in the U.S. trade agreement had led not to a lower but to somewhat higher prices in Canada.[32]

In 1936 major negotiations were held with the United Kingdom. Dunning himself was the leader of the delegation, and the concessions to be given by Canada were the central feature of the agreement, along with reductions in the number of fixed margins of preferences on both sides in order to permit each to negotiate related agreements with the United States later. The structure of the Canadian tariff would be much affected, and not only McKinnon but Hugh Scully, the commissioner of customs, Robertson, and Wilgress went to London a month ahead of Dunning to begin the renegotiation of the Canada-U.K. 1932 agreement. It is said that Robertson, in particular, "felt very deeply about the bad way we treated the British in '32 and he wanted to make it good without it appearing to be a one-sided deal."[33] Dunning, who seems to have gone along with this attitude, reported to King at the end of July that there was not likely to be serious difficulty over the British requests. The main problem turned out to be the British treatment of Canadian farm products, as Britain moved towards protection of its domestic agriculture, using quotas and restriction to accomplish this goal. The principal products involved were beef and cattle, eggs, poultry, cheese, butter, and other milk products. As a result, the final negotiations were protracted over details, and the agreement was not signed until February 23, 1937, just in time to be tabled with and explained in the budget of February 25.[34] No less than thirteen columns of *Hansard* dealt with Dunning's speech to the House on the agreement and its relation to Canadian-British trade—testimony to its importance in the economic recovery taking place in Canada and the complexity of the tariff and other trade arrangements.

One administrative matter relating to these negotiations illustrates the austere economy in staff in those days. In a cable from London in late July 1936, Dunning reported that the consolidation of the details that had been agreed upon into a draft tariff schedule would require a fortnight's work for McKinnon, Scully, and Robertson—three of the most able and senior trade officials of the government were engaged in this tedious labour, apparently without assistance.

Canada-U.S.-U.K. Triangular Negotiations

Once the revised Anglo-Canadian agreement had been approved, attention both in London and in Ottawa turned to Washington. From Ottawa, Skelton in February 1937 sent an excellent dispatch about the new British agreement to Sir Herbert Marler, Canadian minister in Washington. It had been the result, Skelton noted, of a successful effort to bring the forty-year-old policy of imperial preferences into line with the international commercial policies which the U.S. and Canadian governments were promoting. He said, "I need not emphasize the vital importance to Canada of confirming, for a further period of years, the assurance of unrestricted free entry into the United Kingdom market, which perhaps more than any other single factor has been responsible for Canadian economic recovery, the maintenance of this country's stable exchanges and its solvent financial position."[35] The United States would also benefit by this agreement, Skelton added, since it would increase the purchasing power of its best customer. Canada had managed to keep open a door in danger of closing, that of farm products to the United Kingdom. The intention of the dispatch was, of course, to explain the U.K.-Canada agreement to the United States and to indicate that it would make Canada freer to negotiate a more wide-ranging agreement with the United States, subject to the effective limits of the law defining what the United States could concede in trade agreements.

By mid-1937 British officials were in Washington for preliminary talks about a possible U.K.-U.S. trade agreement that would require Canada and the other dominions to give up some of their preferences in the U.K. market. When he heard of this requirement, King made clear to the British that Canada would have to be consulted and compensated. The British then proposed that Canada should enter into concurrent direct negotiations with the United States. Washington invited Canadian officials to discussions at which Robertson, McKinnon, and Wilgress laid the basis for the tripartite negotiations of 1938.

Wilgress has described these 1938 negotiations in his memoirs.

> We travelled to that city in March for a very different kind of negotiation from that of three years previously in Washington. It was much more thorough and more leisurely. . . . The British used to meet the Americans in the morning and our turn came in the afternoon. When the preferences exchanged between the United Kingdom and Canada were under discussions we held tripartite meetings. . . . [At these] the British were surprised at the friendly feelings that had developed between ourselves and the Americans, not experienced in the more formal meetings between themselves and the Americans.[36]

He has also recounted how Canadian ministers were kept informed, even under some handicap because of illness. McKinnon had first reported progress to Dunning in Atlantic City, where the minister was recuperating from a heart attack he had suffered during the budget debate. Wilgress continued:

> In September, 1938, the three of us went to Ottawa to report to the government. Mr. King was laid up at the time but we saw him at Laurier House and outlined the situation to him. Then we met with the whole cabinet, presided over by T. A. Crerar, who was Acting Prime Minister. We met morning and afternoon for four days in the Langevin Block, where Crerar had his office. For a day and a half I outlined the concessions we expected to obtain, then for the next two and a half days McKinnon discussed what we proposed to give to the United States in return. Instructions were agreed upon in relation to points deliberately left open.[37]

One departmental detail is of interest in connection with these negotiations. In mid-1936, W. J. Callaghan and Arthur Annis had been appointed to McKinnon's staff as "tariff investigators." In 1938 McKinnon had Annis go to Washington to assist the negotiators, not attending the meetings but working in the hotel supplying needed information and, as Annis said, "keeping the score."[38] In postwar multilateral trade negotiations, this kind of staff assistance was to become the general practice both for Finance and for Trade and Commerce. Other departments were also to have representatives on hand.

In 1963 Wilgress wrote that in the 1938 negotiations the first use was made of the bargaining power created by the high duties Bennett imposed in the early 1930s.[39] There were to be several more rounds in which they would serve the same purpose. Wilgress also recalled that the bound margins of preference were a serious problem for both Canada and the United Kingdom, especially those bound in agreements with other Commonwealth countries. Canada gave up the preferred rate of duty on wheat in the United Kingdom; it was really ineffective, since Canada had so much for export that competitive prices had to be determined in other markets where there was no preference. The most difficult item turned out to be lumber, which the United States wanted to export to Britain on better terms and which Canada wanted to sell to the United States. Eventually a complicated and ingenious solution was worked out. Both the Canada-U.S. and the U.K.-U.S. agreements were concluded rapidly after the mid-term congressional elections were held early in November.

As part of the negotiations, Canada agreed to give up, on imports from the United States, the 3 percent excise tax imposed early in the 1930s on all imports (the tax had been removed from imports entering under the British preferential tariff in 1934 and 1935). In 1939 this action was extended to all imports entering Canada at duties less than the general tariff rates. Because of the revenue aspects, Clark was involved in this part of the negotiations and it was implemented in the budget of April 25, 1939. The agreement as a whole had been approved by Parliament a few weeks earlier, after an extensive debate, but most of it, the tariff rates, had come into effect on January 1 by order-in-council. This was Canada's last major trade agreement before the outbreak of World War II.

Wilgress later commented on its significance: "The successful outcome of the triangular negotiations of 1938 served to stabilize trade relations with the two chief outlets of Canadian products. A goal had been achieved towards which Canadians had been striving ever since the days of Canada's immaturity as a nation. In reaching this goal Canada had won the respect and high regard of her trading partners. The basis was laid for that partnership which would take the lead towards the promotion of world trade through multilateralism."[40]

By the end of the 1930s, tariffs had become less controversial and more a matter of skilled international negotiation than partisan doctrine. In his 1938 budget speech, Dunning recognized that Canada should not reduce tariff rates on a unilateral basis when the reduction could be used to bargain down obstacles to Canadian exports. This approach reached such a point that on one occasion McKinnon expressed serious concern to the minister of finance because the Cabinet had decided, without consulting officials, to put into effect an old campaign pledge to reduce substantially the tariff on farm implements—an action which McKinnon felt could have been used to very good effect in tariff bargaining.[41] Tariffs also became less controversial because of the role of the Tariff Board. As an expert, quasi-judicial body which conducted impartial studies of tariff questions, with public hearings and published reports, the board helped to defuse the potential controversy and to open up the policy-making process in what had been a very political and sensitive field.[42]

In the Department of Finance the use of civil service staff experts in tariffs and trade grew substantially during this decade. During the war this expertise was supplemented by the wide knowledge and wisdom of W. A. Mackintosh, as well as by the specialized knowledge of the grain trade which Mitchell Sharp contributed. However, the main increase in the numbers of persons in the department working on international trade problems, which then involved quotas and nontariff barriers, took place after the war, when John Deutsch was in charge of trade policy matters.

During the war, much thought was given to long-term trade policy and its relation to the international monetary regime and international lending. Canada was to play an abnormally important role in developing these ideas because so many of the major countries were shattered by the war. Robertson was to turn from trade negotiations to more general foreign policy and diplomacy. Wilgress, too, became a senior diplomat and government executive. McKinnon left the Department of Finance to become chairman of the Tariff Board in 1940. From that vantage point he participated in many of the postwar discussions which carried forward the kind of policies these three men had applied to their negotiations in Washington and London from 1935 to 1939.

Chapter Six

Budgets, Taxes, and Fiscal Policy

The budget has traditionally been the annual highlight of the work of the minister of finance and his department. Although the archives relating to the budgets of the 1930s are scant, an account of the activities of the Finance Department can be reconstructed from the budget speeches and debates, the legislation enacted, and the knowledge and comments of the few surviving officials of the department. One official has said that Bennett in fact gave orders that the papers used in the preparation of the budgets should be destroyed after the debates and legislative actions were finished.[1] This may have been the case, although a few papers have survived. Others recall that the main advice and information, apart from revenue estimates and draft legislation, were usually given to the minister and deputy minister orally, either in group discussions, which often included senior officials from the Department of National Revenue, or in individual interviews.

This chapter is addressed primarily to readers interested in the main events and policies, rather than details and figures.[2] For convenience of reference and to spare the text, the main figures relating to each budget, both in forecasts of revenue, expenditures, and deficits and in the actual outcome as shown by the accounts, are set forth in table 6. This summary table facilitates comparison of one year with another and brings out the effects of the sharp economic decline and the slow and incomplete recovery.

The budget of May 1930 has already been described in chapter 4 at rather more length than most of the others will be chiefly because, as a result of his participation in creating it, Mackenzie King meticulously recorded the lengthy process in his diary. Only in tariff policy did this budget reflect the reaction of the Liberal government to the changing economic situation. The tax reductions Dunning introduced were essentially a continuation of the policies followed in the late 1920s and reflected the anticipation of an early election. In retrospect, they were more suited to the economic situation as seen in terms of modern Keynesian analysis than were the tax measures in the budgets that followed, including Dunning's of 1936 and 1937, but this seems to have been more accidental than deliberate. The minister said next to nothing about economic affairs in his relatively cheerful budget speech.

BENNETT'S BUDGET, 1931

Bennett, as minister of finance, introduced his one and only budget on June 1, 1931. In a long, detailed speech, he said nothing about the general policy on expenditures, but announced three increases: a raise in the Dominion share of old age pensions from 50 to 75 percent for one year only; higher rates of subventions for the freight rates on coal, as had been promised during the election campaign; and payment of a subsidy of five cents a bushel on that year's wheat crop.

Taking Dunning and previous Liberal finance ministers to task, deservedly, for not forecasting revenues and expenditures, he made his own for 1931-32 (see table 6), including $78 million he hoped to raise by increasing taxes. He left out any realistic expenditure forecast for unemployment and farm relief, however, for which he soon after introduced legislation which amounted to a complete blank cheque. In the tax field his main action was to increase the sales tax from 1 to 4 percent (where it had been in 1927). A new 1 percent special excise tax was applied to all imports, and the income tax rate on corporations was raised from 8 to 10 percent.

Bennett also put forward, rather hastily as it turned out, several new income tax proposals. One was a 2 percent withholding tax on interest and dividends payable to nonresidents of Canada; he said that all other countries of which he was aware had such a tax and that those who pay such a tax to Canada, at least those in Britain, France, and United States, could take credit for it against their own country's tax. On July 16, however, Bennett withdrew this resolution, along with the others. Explaining his action in the House of Commons, the prime minister admitted, "Repercussions of the present conditions in Canada began to be realized fully after the middle of June and it is the most inopportune time in the world to present such a resolution in view of these repercussions in Europe, as may be found from a perusal of the Times and continental papers of repute in Paris and elsewhere."[3]

The other resolutions withdrawn were to amend and consolidate the Income War Tax Act—the name still applied to the income tax law—which included an increase in personal exemptions and a wholly revised rate schedule, as well as several more technical changes. In his budget speech Bennett stated, "Mr. Walters was asked to prepare with the aid of his officials what he conceived to be a proper tax rate for this country, having regard to known conditions. He has done so, and the government proposes to adopt his recommendations."[4] Chester Walters, the commissioner of income tax, was under the minister of national revenue, not finance, indicating that the Finance Department was unable to do this work for its own minister.[5]

The effects of the changes on individuals at various income levels were not illustrated in the speech and perhaps had not been clear even to the minister himself. During the budget debate, it became evident that not only was the maximum rate reduced from 40 to 25 percent but a new substantial exemption was provided for dividends. It was also shown that while the tax was removed from, or reduced for, those with the lowest incomes, and increased for those with annual incomes above $8,000 up to $137,000, it would be reduced for anyone with an income of $140,000 or more, of whom there were reported to be sixty-nine in the fiscal year 1930–31. Consequently, the budget was open to criticism on grounds of equity, since the poor and those of middle incomes would shoulder the great burden of tax increases, coming from the higher sales tax, customs duties (for example, on coal), and the general excise tax on all imports. This distribution hardly accorded with the stern quotation from the *Chronicles of the Pilgrim Fathers* calling for the equitable sharing of burdens, with which the prime minister concluded his budget speech.

Bennett was known to be a wealthy, perhaps even a very wealthy, man, and there had been a few personal attacks made, arguing that he was proposing to "relieve himself and his wealthy friends of 25% of their income tax."[6] Bennett referred to these comments in the House on July 16 when he asked leave to withdraw his resolution on changes in the personal income tax. He defended his own position eloquently and received much support against any imputation of personal motives. Some members, however, thought if he believed the proposals were right, he should proceed with them. After relatively little debate, however, his request for leave to withdraw was carried without division. As he pointed out, an early budget in 1932 could bring in revised proposals to apply in 1932–33, based on the incomes of 1931, as was customary in those days.

Bennett did not talk explicitly about what today would be regarded as fiscal policy. He implied that the budget should be balanced which, he later explained, was necessary to preserve Canada's credit in the New York capital market.[7] In a period of great depression, however, departures from customary methods of taxation should be as few as possible to dislocate business as little as possible. Taxes, he claimed, should be as light as the situation permitted. He then added, "One of the paradoxes of a situation such as the present one is that when money is required most, the people are least capable of paying it in the form of taxation."[8] The orthodox faith in the need to balance the budget was just beginning to seem irrational. It was, in fact, unattainable. When the year was over, there was a deficit of $114 million—about one-quarter of total expenditures, even without taking into account the CNR deficit. Meanwhile the higher taxes, especially on the poor, were helping to deepen the Depression.

RHODES'S 1932 BUDGET

In his budget speech on April 6, 1932, Finance Minister Rhodes began by recounting a number of the serious international financial crises and troubles of 1931.[9] He took not unjustified pride in the way Canada had managed to meet all its external debt and interest obligations, in part by the use of gold purchased from mines and the reserves and in part by borrowing in New York. The Dominion government had advanced funds to the four western provinces to meet their maturities in New York, as they were unable to borrow for the purpose. Formal licensing of gold exports from Canada was introduced some weeks after sterling was forced off gold, and the Canadian dollar fell to a substantial discount in terms of the U.S. dollar, while remaining at a premium in terms of sterling. Canada's internal financial markets had remained in good order, thanks to the strength of the banking system and the general stability of financial institutions. Two major Dominion bond issues had been successfully sold: a very large conversion issue in May 1931 and the National Service Loan of November. Consequently the government had ended that year of financial crises with quite substantial cash balances, which would be needed in 1932-33 when the deficit and other cash requirements became very large.

In budgeting for the new year, 1932-33, Rhodes felt "the absolute necessity of placing our financial house in order" and the need to "preserve our national credit in the eyes of an observant financial world."[10] However inappropriate as fiscal policy for the worst year of the Depression, this course was understandable after the crises of the previous year. All Rhodes aimed for was enough revenue to meet "the usual current expenditures of government." Although severe reductions had been made to hold expenditures to a total of $370 million,[11] the minister of finance found it necessary to propose tax increases.

In regard to the personal income tax, Rhodes's proposal ran no risk of incurring the criticism levelled at Bennett's. He retained the previous rate schedule but removed the 20 percent reduction on the schedule rates that had been in effect since 1928, added a surtax of 5 percent of the tax on net incomes over $5,000, and reduced the personal exemptions by one-fifth. The top rates on the very rich were thereby increased from 40 to 52.5 percent, in addition to the income taxes the provinces and some municipalities levied. This time the minister did include a table showing the effects of the proposed tax at various income levels compared with those of the current tax.

With the desperate need to maintain revenue as incomes, expenditure, and trade declined, the minister proposed a further increase in the sales tax from 4 to 6 percent, with the deletion of some foods from the exempt list. The special excise tax on all imports was increased from 1 to 3 percent. Other special excise taxes were raised and applied to new items. The corporation income tax was raised again from 10 to 11 percent. Despite all these austerities and taxes, when this dreadful fiscal year was over, Dominion revenues had reached their lowest level of the decade, the accounts showing a record overall deficit of some $221 million (including the writing off of loans made to the CNR in 1931 to finance its deficit that year; see table 6).

The finance minister reported, in his 1933 budget, that during 1932-33 "the dominion has been able to arrange for the orderly financing of all requirements during the year, including provisions for maturing securities and the financing of the Canadian National Railways."[12] External borrowings were for meeting maturities only. The government's cash balances in Canada were drawn down by more than $50 million. By these means it financed the worst fiscal year of the Depression. The policies and measures were orthodox in the extreme, tempered by the realization that a fully balanced budget, after financing relief needs and the appalling railway deficit, was simply out of the question. The bankers still played a major role in advice and in lending but were soon to be made subject to the expert leadership of the Bank of Canada and the tough bargaining ability of W. C. Clark, who had become deputy minister in November 1932. Meanwhile financial events and measures in the United States, including Roosevelt's New Deal, were to make expansionary economic policies in Canada appear to American and British financial markets as no more dangerous than those at home.

RHODES'S 1933 AND 1934 BUDGETS

What can be seen of Clark's hand in the next budget, that of March 21, 1933, the first in which he participated? Not a great deal, even to those who knew him well, apart from some improvement in the style of the speech and the review of economic conditions. In regard to expenditure policy for 1933, an unsigned memorandum in the Finance Department, probably from W. C. Ronson, set forth possible further economies of a drastic and arbitrary nature, beyond those which Rhodes had been able to work out with other ministers. Rhodes felt that more cutbacks should be made, but Clark urged that more time should be taken to work out the additional economies. This situation was reflected in the budget, in which it was stated that expenditures as shown in the Estimates for 1933-34 would be reduced by some $14 million, about 10 percent of the controllable expenditures. Although Ronson reported to Rhodes in June 1933 that these further reductions were "at a standstill,"[13] it would

TABLE 6

BUDGETS: FORECASTS AND OUTCOMES, 1929–30 TO 1939–40

(MILLIONS $)

	1929–30 Robb Mar. 1, 29	1930–31 Dunning May 1, 30	1931–32 Bennett June 1, 31	1932–33 Rhodes Apr. 6, 32	1933–34 Rhodes Mar. 21, 33	1934–35 Rhodes Apr. 18, 34	1935–36 Rhodes Mar. 22, 35	1936–37 Dunning May 1, 36	1937–38 Dunning Feb. 25, 37	1938–39 Dunning June 16, 38	1939–40 Dunning Apr. 25, 39
Budget Forecasts											
Revenue before tax changes	–	–	325	319	287	–	–	388	485	–	–
Effects of tax changes	-25	-22[2]	78	55	70	–	12	29	nil	–	–
Total revenue forecasts	450	–	403	374	357	360	392	417	485	502	490
Expenditure:											
Ordinary	–	–	392	370	355	351	371	–	–	–	–
Relief	–	–	13	–	35	–	–	–	–	–	–
Railway deficit (–)	–	–	–	–	-48	–	–	–	–	–	–
Total expenditure	–	–	430	–	[438]	–	–	517	520	525	550[10]
Expected deficit (–) or surplus	60[1]	–	-27	–	-[81]	–	–	-100	-35	-23	over -60[11]
Actual Results (Accounts)											
Revenues:											
Customs duties	180	131	104	70	66	77	74	84	93	79	104
Income tax	69	71	61	62	62	67	83	102	120	142	134
Sales tax	45	21	41	57	61	72	78	113	138	122	141
Total taxes	379	296	275	254	272	304	317	387	449	436	468
Total revenues	446	356	334	311	324	362	373	454	517	502	562

Expenditure:											
Ordinary	358	390	373	350	347	360	373	387	415	413	398
Capital	23	28	17	9	6	7	7	4	4	5	7
Relief	–	4	38	37	36	61[5]	80[6]	78	69	47	62
Railway deficit (–)	7	7	7	62	59	48	47	43	42	54	40
Other noteworthy items	–	–	11[3]	68[4]	–	–	23[7]	18[8]	–	25[9]	27[12]
Total expenditure	398	440	448	532	458	478	533	532	535	553	681[13]
Budget deficit (–) or surplus	48	-84	-114	-221	-134	-116	-160	-78	-18	-51	-119
Loans to provinces in need	–	–	23	16	13	23	42	15	16	15	13

SOURCES: For forecasts, refer to budget statements. For actual results, see tables of accounts in the second succeeding budget.
NOTE: Figures enclosed in square brackets are inferred.
[1]Robb stated, "The revenues will meet all expenditure obligations and also provide for the redemption of the loan maturing in August next."
[2]Cost of reducing the sales tax from 2 to 1 percent.
[3]Bonus payment on wheat of 1931 crop.
[4]Loans of 1931–32 transferred to inactive, including $41 million CNR deficit ($41 million + $62 million = $103 million up to 1932–33). The $7 million in preceding years was the deficit on the eastern lines operated for government account.
[5]Includes $9 million for special public works.
[6]Includes $30 million for special public works.
[7]Wheat payments for earlier crops.
[8]Dominion contribution to debt adjustment in drought area relief.
[9]Reserve for loss on 1938 wheat marketing guarantees.
[10]To this figure should be added $29 million of capitalized defence expenditures which were not in fact capitalized.
[11]See note 10 and include some probable loss on wheat marketing guarantees as well.
[12]Reserve for losses on wheat marketing guarantees.
[13]Includes $118 million for war expenditures.

appear from the figures in the budget speech of the following year that ordinary expenditures had been held within the limit proposed, despite some unforeseen requirements, and that the deficit on ordinary account arose from a shortfall in revenues below expected levels. Of course, a large overall deficit was anticipated because of special expenditures for relief for the unemployed and farmers and the CNR deficit, items not included in "ordinary" expenditures. In fact, the overall deficit, and the consequent increase in net debt for 1933–34, amounted to $134 million.[14]

Tax policy in the 1933 budget was broadly more of the same, but not too much. The basic sales tax was not increased, but the exemptions from it were narrowed and some items were shifted from the half rate list to the full rate. The income tax on corporations was raised again, to 12.5 percent from 11. The basic exemptions for the personal tax were reduced, and the schedule of rates were increased moderately. A withholding tax of 5 percent on all dividends and on interest payable in Canadian dollars, paid to nonresidents by Canadian debtors (other than the government of Canada), was introduced. A similar tax at 12½ percent on royalties paid to nonresidents was also imposed. It would seem that Clark must have persuaded the prime minister and Rhodes that the time was now more propitious for such withholding taxes than it had been in 1931 (despite the financial crisis in the United States) and that most nonresident shareholders and creditors could offset this tax against their domestic income taxes. A more unusual withholding tax of 5 percent was also imposed on interest and dividends payable and paid to Canadian residents in a currency that was at a premium in terms of the Canadian dollar. It may have been implemented partly because of the widespread existence of optional payment bonds in Canada, payable in two or three currencies at the holder's choice. When the gold standard ruled, these option provisions were mainly a convenience, but they became especially valuable when the Canadian dollar depreciated.

Various special excise taxes were introduced, including one on malt for brewing and, in particular, a tax of two cents a pound on all refined sugar. Great controversy and trouble arose over the tax on sugar, as it apparently could not be applied in practice to the sugar content of imports such as candy and confectionery. Indeed, the situation became so difficult that the minister of finance some months later wrote to the prime minister, protesting that the Customs Department was refusing to collect the tax on the sugar content of imports as the law required.[15]

By April 1934, the time of Rhodes's next budget, things were at last looking up, but conditions were still very bad. Employment had increased substantially and so had the depressed commodity prices, especially farm prices. But unemployment was still very high, and the total number on relief in March was over 1.5 million (including dependants), about 14 percent of the population. Foreign trade was beginning to improve, but the volume of exports and imports remained very much below pre-Depression levels. Current international payments were about in balance. The U.S. dollar had been devalued and the Canadian dollar was close to parity with it and near the old relationship with sterling. Noting these facts in his budget, the minister of finance was able to claim some progress in doing something about the Depression. In particular, interest rates were being nudged down and the investment market was strong, permitting the conversion of high interest bearing debt to issues at lower rates. Moreover, a new public works program was being undertaken, to be financed, as it later developed, by an expansion in the note issue.

In these circumstances, the minister foresaw the probability of an improved budget position without new tax measures and with some reduction in special expenditures for relief and railway deficits. While his expectation about relief proved to be wrong, the budget position improved without any major tax changes or new austerities in expenditures.

The only contentious tax change was one intended to replace the revenue lost in cutting in half the troublesome tax on sugar. It imposed a levy of 10 percent on newly produced gold. The price of gold had risen from twenty to thirty-five dollars an ounce as a result of the devaluation of the U.S. dollar, creating large windfall profits for what had already been a prosperous industry. An unsigned memorandum sent to the minister from the department, almost certainly with Clark's approval, suggested these profits could legitimately be taxed. As considerable resistance arose from the gold mining industry, supported by the minister of mines of Ontario (then a Conservative), some modifications were made to lighten its impact. The tax lasted only a year, but it was replaced in 1935 with a "compensating" reduction in the generous depletion allowances that had been previously allowed to both precious metal mining companies and their shareholders.

The preparation of the 1934 budget was assisted by the appointment of Kenneth Eaton in January 1934 as a specialist in the field of tax policy.[16] Clark assigned him the task of preparing papers for use by the minister and others involved in discussion of the budget, including an annotated list of proposals submitted from businesses and others for tax changes. His presence, ability, and role soon came to be well known, and many businessmen would bring their problems and proposals to him. He was able to comprehend these quickly and anticipate questions that Clark and the ministers would raise. In addition he established close contacts with senior officers of the Department of National Revenue with whom he could discuss problems they had encountered in the law as well as proposals being made to the minister. In these ways Eaton relieved the burden on Clark in a field with which he was not very familiar and provided the foundation on which an expert tax staff would later be built.

RHODES'S 1935 BUDGET

The budget of March 22, 1935, Rhodes's last, was introduced after Bennett had announced his "New Deal" measures, which were virtually unopposed by the Liberals in the expectation that they would be thrown out by the courts. It was a pre-election budget but had few of the characteristics of one. The minister took note of the continued recovery in production, trade, and employment (but not prices), and admitted that "conditions in agriculture still leave much to be desired."[17] The total number on relief (including dependants) was about 1,230,000 in February.

Rhodes emphasized the progress in domestic financial markets, which was considerable, and the decline in interest rates (even before the policies of the Bank of Canada, which had just commenced business earlier in the month, could have effect). He reviewed, probably for use in the election, the progress in trade and trade agreements and in financial legislation, including the important Farmers' Creditors Arrangement Act. He was able to claim for 1934-35 "the first surplus on ordinary account since 1929-30,"[18] but had to report an overall deficit (and increase in net debt) of $118 million, again owing almost entirely to relief expenditures and the deficit of the CNR, which had improved only slightly over the preceding year. For the year ahead he was able to see some continued increase in revenues at current tax rates but had to take into account increased expenditures, some a result of the partial restoration of salaries, which had been reduced in 1932, others a result of new provincial grants and programs, while the relentless load of relief and the railways still had to be faced. Consequently, and despite the impending election, he felt it necessary to resume the increasing of taxes, which had been suspended in 1934.

The main tax increase was a cumbersome surtax on "investment income," which did not apply to any income less than $5,000 a year but to all income, whatever its source, in excess of $14,000—only between these limits was it properly a tax on investment income. The corporation income tax was moved up yet another notch, to 13.5 percent from 12.5. A new tax on gifts was introduced supposedly to reinforce the income tax, and the provincial inheritance taxes, by discouraging gifts within family groups. The rates were so low as to cast doubt on its effectiveness for the purpose stated, but this point was not raised in Parliament. No significant change was made in the sales tax, but the special excise tax on imports was abolished on goods entering under the British preferential tariff. One notable reduction was made: the excise duties on liquor were lowered from seven dollars a gallon to bring them in line with U.S. rates and to secure increased revenues by diverting into legal channels purchases being made illegally. In this way the Canadian consumer was to benefit from the practised art of bootlegging developed during Prohibition in the United States.

Why did Rhodes increase personal income taxes in the clumsy way he did, and bring in an ineffectual gift tax, to gain only a small increase in revenue, much of which was lost by removing the remaining 1½ percent excise tax on imports from Empire sources? It is tempting to speculate that these changes, coming immediately after the Bennett "New Deal" and before the election, were intended to be seen as "reform" measures to tax the well-to-do more heavily and lighten the load on the poor, rather than serve any fiscal or economic purposes.

THE RETURN OF THE LIBERALS

When the Liberal party returned to power after the election of October 14, 1935, Dunning again became minister of finance, though the prime minister himself took a considerable interest in financial policy, particularly in relation to the provinces, during the first eight months after the election.

In his budget speech on May 1, 1936, Dunning announced that it was "the declared purpose of the government to end in the shortest practicable time the era of recurring deficits."[19] This statement embodied the orthodoxy of King and the finance minister, subject to that prudent word "practicable." Explaining this position, Dunning said that such a policy would "contribute more effectively to the solution of the problems of unemployment and depression than any other single thing that governments can do."[20] Here was the orthodox faith forthrightly expressed just a few weeks after the publication of J. M. Keynes's *The General Theory of Employment, Interest and Money*, which was to replace this orthodoxy within a few years. Moreover, this attitude was taken when the credit of the Dominion stood high both at home and in the New York market.

To cope with the immediate budget prospects and show some progress in reducing the deficit, Dunning relied primarily upon increases in the general sales tax from 6 to 8 percent and in the corporation income tax from 13.5 to 15 percent—the last increase in both before the war. What Dunning said about expenditure policy was general and procedural. His forecast of 1936–37 expenditures was slightly lower than the outcome for 1935–36, but comparison is complicated by several factors, particularly some controversial transactions relating to wheat marketing, as well as by some of the kind of bookkeeping actions that are tempting when governments change. Eventually, it turned out that although total expenditures in the two years were almost exactly equal (about $532 million), the deficit in 1936–37 was only about half that of 1935–36, partly because of the tax increases, but mainly because of the increase in national income, as Dunning explained the next year.

The principal economic measure in the budget was the introduction of a "temporary" exemption from corporation income tax for new mines in their first three years of production. This measure, probably designed by Eaton of Finance, was apparently a concession to T. A. Crerar, who had been brought back by King to be minister of mines and resources in 1935.[21] It was passed by the House of Commons with no real discussion of its substance or merits. Along with allowances for depletion, it was very popular with the mining industry for many years afterwards.[22]

DUNNING'S 1937 BUDGET

Dunning's 1937 budget, on February 25, was one of the main events of an abnormally short session of Parliament, but it occasioned far less controversy than did the really rather modest increase in the Defence Estimates from approximately $19 million in 1936–37 to approximately $34 million for 1937–38. Expressing grave concern over the startling increase in expenditure on arms when so little was to be spent on social security, the Co-operative Commonwealth Federation (CCF) moved an amendment on this subject. A long debate ensued and the amendment was defeated 17 to 191.[23] The controversy having been anticipated by the government, a "hard" debate had taken place in Cabinet during December 1936 in which Dunning's financial objections to this increase were defeated,[24] although the Chiefs of Staff got little more than half of what they had proposed.[25] This debate had been only part of a long series of Cabinet discussions of the Estimates for the 1937–38 fiscal year, in which King and Dunning strove to hold the line on expenditures, while many ministers were showing growing dissatisfaction with the continuing policy of fiscal austerity as the economy and the revenues based on it were expanding.

Little of this struggle over expenditures showed up in the budget speech. The record for the fiscal year nearly completed showed that after a proper adjustment for the write-off of certain earlier advances to farmers in the drought areas of Saskatchewan and Manitoba (as part of a cooperative program by various creditors to cancel what were clearly unjust and uncollectable debts), aggregate expenditures in 1936–37 had actually declined from those of the previous Conservative year. The overall deficit had come well within Dunning's target of "less than $100 million," mainly because revenues had increased by a good deal more than had been forecast. In looking forward to the new fiscal year, Dunning spoke of the "consistent pressure which is being exerted to effect economies and hold down expenditures."[26] Optimistic about the trends in economic activity, however, he announced that the government would recommend to Parliament the ending of the 5 percent deduction from salaries, effective for the new fiscal year. (When the Bennett government in April 1935 had cut the original 10 percent deduction in half, there had not been much increase in the cost of living or wage rates.)

Dunning forecast an overall deficit of about $35 million for the new fiscal year and proposed no tax increases to reduce this small amount. He thought economic recovery would make it possible to wipe it out altogether the following year, "the goal which we must steadily keep in sight."[27]

CHANGE IN FISCAL POLICY, 1938

The year 1938 was one of crisis in fiscal policy, although little of this is evident in the rather lacklustre budget Dunning brought down belatedly on June 16. As in 1937, troubles began at the turn of the year in determining expenditures. Defence expenditures were not a major problem, despite the increasingly obvious approach of war, because it was possible to hold down the Defence Estimates by sustained pressure in Cabinet on a relatively weak minister of national defence. In November 1937 the prime minister had warned his colleagues in Cabinet that he wanted to keep expenditures down so that the 1938 budget could be balanced and tax reductions brought in before the election expected in 1939.[28] This view was reiterated in a strong, confidential letter to all ministers on January 12, 1938, in which the political motive for economies in expenditures was bolstered by an appeal for restraint on expenditures, based on the danger of a temporary recession—a danger that proved exaggerated, but a policy that was mistaken in any case. Most ministers replied in a polite, perfunctory way, but several mentioned possible difficulties. Only Crerar objected to the policy itself and urged positive expenditure policies to increase the national income, notably by programs that would promote mining development and the tourist trade. His letters of January 19 and 27 were probably drafted by Charles Camsell, the highly respected deputy minister of mines and resources.

A special committee of Cabinet, instructed to reduce the proposed Estimates, gave Dunning some support in this effort. The results came back to Cabinet late in January when even more was whittled away by King and Dunning before they were settled and tabled on February 3. In May the battle would resume with greater intensity over the Supplementary Estimates.

As deputy minister, Clark had urged Dunning to take a strong position in holding the line on expenditures for 1938–39. On January 4, 1938, he sent the minister a memorandum entitled "Estimates and Budgetary Policy for 1938–39" and included a forecast of revenues for the current fiscal year compared with revenues of the preceding year.[29] Because of the economic downturn in Canada (and particularly in the United States) late in 1937, he feared a decline of revenue of 4 percent, despite some increase in income tax payments, which in those days were based on the income of the preceding year. There were the strongest possible reasons, he said, for insisting on a balanced budget that year, after a series of eight successive deficits aggregating about $900 million. There would be grave disappointment if there was not a balance, which would have an important retarding effect on the economy and on the cost of financing. He went on to say that "even if we do not aim so high," the reductions which should be made in the Estimates as submitted were very substantial, and certainly the minister should contemplate $500 million as the absolute maximum of expenditures.[30] While Dunning needed no urging by Clark to take this attitude, and King, too, had his own reasons for wanting a severe restriction on expenditures, this memorandum is evidence of the continued strict orthodoxy of Clark's views at a time when a faltering and incomplete recovery really required a more constructive policy of the sort advocated by Crerar and later by others. Incidentally, Clark increased his revenue forecasts substantially by the time he worked on the budget in June, and he wrote a reasonably optimistic account of the economic outlook at that time.

Recommendations on general expenditure policy in the final report of the National Employment Commission, issued in April 1938, contributed to a prolonged debate in Cabinet over the Supplementary Estimates.[31] W. A. Mackintosh, a leading member of the commission, had been reading Keynes's *General Theory*, which had appeared about the time of the commission's appointment, and, as he later reflected, "In reporting on the role of public expenditures in contributing to the stability of the economy, the Commission . . . was evidently strongly influenced by Keynes' *General Theory* as well as by discussions in the United States."[32] As a result, the commission included in section 2 of its report a relatively modern Keynesian but nondoctrinaire analysis of the impact of the Depression on Canada and a consideration of broad policies to induce recovery, paying careful attention (as Mackintosh always did) to the particular structural and trade problems of the Canadian economy. Later in its report, the commission discussed public expenditure policy in general and said that "there is sound economic ground for urging a policy under which public expenditures might be expanded and contracted to off-set fluctuations in private expenditures, but any such policy must be subject to the most careful management and good judgment lest it create more problems that it solves."[33] After cautionary observations about the timing and nature of expenditure programs,[34] it recommended a program of development and conservation works for certain specified purposes to expedite recovery from the Depression. It is clear that the commission expected that such a program might involve budget deficits. It emphasized, however, the need to hold public expenditures in check and reduce debt during periods of prosperity so that spending could safely be increased during a depression.

This recommendation of the commission appealed very much to Norman Rogers, the minister of labour, and to a number of other ministers who felt that the state of the economy and of public opinion made some such positive action highly desirable, even though it might lead to another or larger budget deficit in the 1938–39 fiscal year. Dunning, who remained committed to the policy which King had stated in January, was resolutely opposed to such a program. It is not evident whether the Department of Finance was continuing to advise Dunning to take this strong position.[35] It is likely that W. C. Ronson and his staff felt it their duty to support and assist the minister in pruning the Supplementary Estimates, but it would be surprising if Clark did not share some of the views expressed by Mackintosh, with whom he was very close, and by Crerar. Knowing the minister's strong views, however, Clark may have felt constrained to say little.

The debate in Cabinet over the Supplementary Estimates stretched from April 1 to May 20, the morning of the day they were tabled, at which time the prime minister had achieved sufficient compromises and consensus to close off the discussion. King had begun on March 30 by urging Rogers to work out a long-range program for promoting and developing the tourist trade and carrying out reforestation as Canada's method of dealing with unemployment (which, King added, the commission had been appointed in large part to do). The prime minister assured Rogers that he would back him in Council towards this end.[36] As soon as the Cabinet began to discuss the plans for the "Supps," however, a strong line of cleavage developed between the minister of finance and the others. King records that he personally was strongly in sympathy with Dunning, but "other members of the Cabinet were all for more in the way of expenditures, to save a situation of which they have grown very fearful."[37] It should be recalled that the economic effects of the western drought of 1937 and the recession in the United States were showing up in the early months of 1938, particularly in construction, which declined by some 25 percent from the level reached in early 1937.

Early in April the prime minister appointed a committee of five, excluding Dunning, to review what the government had done since 1935 in the nature of a national development program and to recommend what should be done. The information was to be used in preparing the Supplementary Estimates over the next six weeks. A month later, King talked to Dunning about the move to increase expenditures considerably for relief purposes (which may have included the development program). He said he would "stand with Dunning in trying to reach the point where we can reduce taxation."[38] On May 5, however, the ministers had what King described as a very trying day in Cabinet over Supplementary Estimates, with Rogers showing a good deal of impatience at any suggestion of seeking to have the budget even approximately balanced or at anything that would reduce the program he and the committee had in mind. King thought that Dunning might resign if he were forced beyond a deficit of $30 million. King also noted that the deceptive part of the business was that the "Supps" in themselves really contained all the items that should be included, apart from an additional $25 million program the committee had in mind. Tired from the day's exertions, King reflected, "Nothing wearies me like contentions in the Cabinet."[39]

The next day the debate in Cabinet continued, but King observed, "The discussion, save at the close, was not quite so tense as yesterday. . . . Some progress has been made in getting each side to come a little nearer to the center."[40] Talks resumed on May 9, 10, and 12, and a little progress was made in segregating the special conservation and development program from the construction of "endless unnecessary public buildings in small communities" and other routine items.[41]

On May 16 the Cabinet returned to the Supplementary Estimates and the situation again became very tense. Dunning said he had been prepared to accept a certain size of deficit and had been generous in accepting it, but he would go no further. He offered to leave the room if his colleagues felt he was an embarrassment, but he thought it wrong to imitate Roosevelt, who had just approved a large public expenditure program. King told him to stay. Rogers then intimated he would have to consider his position in the government if his stand was not upheld. But King saw no necessity for that sort of position; the Cabinet had a common purpose and could work towards it. He talked about the possibility of a dissolution "if I found we were going to have cleavage in the Cabinet which would result in divisions in the Party that would affect its future."[42] He was not going to remain head of a government unable to hold itself together.

After these threats and counterthreats, the Cabinet resumed efforts at compromise, and Crerar, Rogers, C. D. Howe, and J. G. Gardiner all made concessions under King's pressure. Dunning, too, accepted in the end rather more than he had intended. Reflecting on this resolution of differences, King wrote, "I think we have a well balanced program and one which will be well accepted by our Party in the House and by the country, though it means following the example of priming the pump to a greater extent than one would like."[43] Fiscal policy had changed, but how great a change it was is hard to say. Dunning was never a strong force in the Cabinet again, and he collapsed with a heart attack during the debate on his budget some weeks later. Afterwards he was ill from time to time until he finally resigned the following year. His budget in April 1939, however, certainly suggests that his views also had changed by that time.

The 1938 budget—delayed until mid-June in the vain hope of having some announcements on tariff changes that were under negotiation with the United States—contained no hint of the lengthy internal struggles over the Supplementary Estimates and fiscal policy generally. Dunning reported that the recession had interrupted recovery in the United States and to a lesser extent in Britain; Canadian business, however, had begun to recover again in February and was showing up well compared with that of the two major countries to which Canada exported. The dreadful drought in the West in 1937 and its many effects were noted as was the decline in construction during early 1938. Construction, particularly housing, was singled out as the first priority in recovery policy.

Some important technical changes were proposed in the income tax, but no changes were made in rates. Lump sum contributions by employers to pension funds to cover past services of employees were to be deductible over a period. Dividends from foreign subsidiaries of Canadian corporations were to be exempt from Canadian tax under specified circumstances, but, on the other hand, Canadian taxpayers were to be prevented from evading taxes by artificially locating income outside Canada. The gift tax was amended by a generous and unusual deduction related to after-tax income, and the rates were raised well above the low ones imposed by Rhodes in 1935.[44] All these measures suggest that the Finance Department was becoming more sophisticated in tax policy.

The only important economic measure in the budget was intended to stimulate construction. All major products used in the building of houses (including, for example, lumber used for all purposes) were exempted from the sales tax. Whether this timely and popular measure was worked out by the Department of Finance is not clear. Probably the department did not initiate it. Only three days before the budget speech the prime minister had urged Dunning to reduce the sales tax generally from 8 to 6 percent. The next day Dunning suggested the tax on building materials be cut in half, but a day later he told King he had decided he might as well take the tax off these goods altogether. King recorded, "I told him I thought that was, in every way an admirable stroke; It will help to offset any talk of tariff changes, and . . . help so to encourage construction."[45]

The budget was discussed by Cabinet only a few hours before it was delivered. J. L. Ilsley opposed the sales tax exemption, but it went through without King having to intervene.[46] In the budget, Dunning forecast an overall deficit of "approximately $23 million."[47] King wrote in his diary that he thought Dunning would end up the year with a surplus, but he was wrong.[48] In April 1939 Dunning reported a deficit of $31 million for 1938-39 and to that he felt he had to add "an arbitrary figure of $25 million" as a reserve against possible wheat marketing losses on the 1938 crop.[49]

The First "Keynesian" Budget

The budget of April 25, 1939, reflected the turn that had occurred in fiscal policy the previous year. By then Dunning was ready to accept the need for deficit spending to promote recovery from depression. In the House he argued the case carefully but forcefully in a speech that indicated the evolution in departmental views as well as his own thinking:

> We are, of course, well aware of the arguments for pump priming in times of depression, and we have had to increase government expenditures substantially as a partial offset to the gap in private investment. But we have never believed that public spending could be a substitute for private enterprise. We have realized that public spending could only be a relief and not a cure, unless one is prepared to take the whole of business into government hands. . . . Under our present system government expenditures are likely to leave the situation no better, and perhaps worse, when they are withdrawn. If they are carried too far they are likely to undermine confidence in the country's financial position and thereby to retard employment in private industry to an extent much greater than the new employment which they create. Nevertheless, a government cannot stand idly by and allow the ravages of depression to take their toll because of the too slow revival of private investment. In these days, if the people as a whole, and business in particular, will not spend, government must. It is not a matter of choice but of sheer social necessity. The alternative is a greater burden of relief and greater dangers from deflationary forces. . . . When private investment expands, not only will we find our need for government expenditures less, but also our revenue receipts will be so much increased that debts can be reduced and taxes lowered.[50]

Elsewhere in the speech Dunning emphasized this vital role of private capital expenditures and the need to increase them, both by private initiative and by public policy. He reviewed the positive contribution of monetary policy in recent years and of the special measures to stimulate house building and renovation, under the Home Improvement Plan (of guaranteed loans), the long-term low rate mortgages provided under the National Housing Act, and the exemption of building materials from the sales tax. He urged private business to invest more at that time and argued that the state of the Canadian economy quite justified it, despite the sluggish state of world trade and the looming threat of war.

The measures he introduced in the budget were in accord with these views. The only outright tax reduction was the formal removal of the 3 percent excise tax on imports, which had been pledged in the U.S. agreement in 1938 and which Parliament had already approved in principle. Dunning defended the existing level of taxation as not onerous. He proposed the extension of the three-year income tax exemption for new metalliferous mines to sustain that booming industry. He also proposed, as a broad incentive to business capital expenditure, a tax credit of 10 percent of the amount of such expenditure incurred during the next twelve months, to be credited against taxes over the next three years in which the firm had a taxable income. This credit was the forerunner of many types of "expansionary" tax measures introduced in many countries in the decades since World War II. It had been devised in the department, endorsed by Clark, and accepted by Dunning and subsequently by Parliament.

This budget anticipated a deficit of more than twice that foreseen in the budget of 1938, which had occasioned such a struggle, but it worried Dunning much less. He made a much more reasoned defence of the long-term need for achieving a balance, but explained, in terms of both defence needs and fiscal policy, why a deficit was necessary at the time. Even so, the forecast for defence expenditure had been artificially reduced by having about $30 million of those expenditures "capitalized" with a special sinking fund.[51] The results of the April budget were never apparent because of the war expenditures undertaken after the war began and the war tax measures of the September budget.

Tabled with the 1939 budget were the usual several reports from the Tariff Board. The finance minister paid eloquent tribute to George Sedgewick, chairman of the board since its formation, who had just died. Nearly a year later, Hector McKinnon replaced Sedgewick, an appointment that led eventually to changes in the handling of tariff matters within the Department of Finance but that retained for the government the advice and negotiating skill of one of its quietest yet most valuable public servants.

This budget inaugurated the custom of tabling a separate White Paper, which contained a detailed review of revenues and expenditures in the fiscal year just closing, with tables of comparisons, and a review of economic and financial conditions in Canada. The minister explained that this practice, which had been borrowed from the United Kingdom and Australia,[52] would make it possible to shorten the budget speech by eliminating much tedious detail. The modest growth in the staff of the Finance Department made possible the preparation of a comprehensive review of this kind, along with the budget speech itself.

It should be noted that this was the first budget on which the author worked after joining the Finance Department early in October 1938. The department was so small that, despite my junior status, I participated in the discussions of the budget measures, drafted several portions of the speech, and did most of the work on the economic portion of the White Paper—but all under the critical eye of Clark. My arrival as a committed disciple of Keynes, just after the crisis over fiscal policy in 1938, was a coincidence, not a consequence of the debate. Clark never told me the story of the 1938 disputes in Cabinet. By 1939 Clark was quite prepared to listen to Keynesian arguments, indeed he asked for them. He remained, however, very careful in their application to the Canadian economy because it was such an open one and its financial community did not yet understand the essence of Keynes's analysis.

Chapter Seven

Monetary Measures and the Bank of Canada

It was in the monetary field that the activities of the Department of Finance and its ministers showed the greatest change from the 1920s to the 1930s. Indeed the change began immediately, despite the illness and death of the deputy minister early in 1930 and the absence of the former assistant deputy minister. Dunning, it will be recalled, had placed Watson Sellar in charge of the department. Sellar was no monetary expert but neither had been Saunders, deputy minister during the 1920s. Moreover, Sellar had a more realistic knowledge of the limitations of C. S. Tompkins, the inspector general of banks.[1] Sellar had a clear head, common sense, and political judgment; he had watched closely from the sidelines the monetary manoeuvres of Saunders and Tompkins with Robb during the late 1920s, especially in 1929, and he had little fear of the bankers.[2]

The remarkable improvement in the Canadian balance of payments made it possible to conduct monetary policy along more orthodox lines in 1930 than in 1928 and 1929. The improvement in international payments was all on the capital account; on current account there was a deficit of $267 million, the biggest of the Depression years. But the U.S. capital market was particularly receptive to Canadian issues in 1930, and relatively few Canadian obligations matured that year. Moreover, Canadians exported much less capital in the purchase of securities outside the country. As a result the favourable balance on capital account was $316 million, yielding an overall surplus of $49 million, much of which resulted in a return flow to Canada of monetary gold that had gone to the United States in 1929.[3] By the end of the year the chartered banks were able to reduce their advances under the Finance Act, while restoring their cash reserves to 1928 and 1929 levels.[4] The banks' total Canadian deposits at the end of 1930 were only 6.6 percent below those at the beginning of 1929. Their current loans in Canada increased during 1929 and until September 1930 but then declined gently and steadily, while holdings of Dominion and provincial securities increased.

Early in 1930 the president of the Canadian Bankers' Association, following discussions among the banks in 1929, wrote to the minister of finance, urging an increase in the gold reserves against Dominion notes.[5] More specifically he suggested that full gold "cover" should be provided for the $16 million of notes issued in 1915 against securities of railway companies that had since disappeared into the CNR and also for the $10 million issue in 1915 not "covered" by any asset. In addition, he proposed that the $20 million increase made in 1914 in the basic fiduciary issue with only 25 percent gold cover should be subject to full gold coverage. Altogether the increase in the required gold reserves would amount to $41 million. Nothing was said about the need for gold reserves against the notes advanced to the banks under the Finance Act; indeed, one can infer that the banks wanted the fuller gold reserves against the basic issue of notes to minimize the likelihood of requiring limits on gold reserves against these Finance Act issues, even though they were the feature in the Canadian system most contrary to the traditional gold standard. That standard related the internal supply of money to the stock of gold held by the monetary system and thereby related changes in the supply to inflows or outflows of gold. The Finance Act permitted increases in the internal supply of money to be made without any increase in the gold reserves, indeed even if the reserves were at a dangerously low level, as they were in 1929.

In a long memorandum to Dunning, Sellar related these proposals to the arbitrary nature of the statutory gold reserve ratios. Experience had shown, he said, that the serious problems really arose from the use of the Finance Act and that more severe statutory restrictions on the reserves held against the basic note issue would tie down gold and prevent its use for supporting the exchange market. He urged that there be no legislation such as that proposed. Rather, the gold reserves should be built up gradually by purchasing gold produced in Canada and, meanwhile, the practices regarding advances under the Finance Act should be reviewed.[6]

Apparently accepting Sellar's advice, Dunning informed the banks that their proposals would not be pursued. Moreover, in April 1930, when the annual limits for advances to the individual banks under the Finance Act were normally set, the Treasury Board reduced the figures below levels of the previous year. When Sellar so informed the Bankers' Association, the bankers became alarmed and sent the secretary of the association to plead their case for no reduction. He not only gave the reasons the banks felt more might be needed in those difficult times, but stated that in future the banks' power of drawing advances would be "exercised lawfully and for legitimate purposes. Banks can be trusted not to abuse power if privilege [is] granted."[7]

By this time Sellar, with the help of the balance of payments, had made his point. Larger lines of credit were authorized in June (but below those in 1929). In fact they were not needed or used on a large scale. Meanwhile the gold reserves continued to increase as a result of the department's purchase of gold from Canadian mines as well as from the reversed flow of gold from the United States to Canada.

CANADA AND THE GOLD STANDARD

On September 15, 1930, Watson Sellar prepared a memorandum on the gold position for the newly elected government of Bennett. He described the difficult situation in 1929, when the gold reserves against Dominion notes had fallen to about $61 million. To prevent jeopardy to the gold reserves, the Finance Department had refused to redeem Dominion notes, secured by the banks in large supplies under the Finance Act, to provide gold destined for the New York market. He stated that "conditions are now adjusted":[8] the gold reserves had risen to $88 million and were over 60 percent of the note issue. Canadian-produced gold should still be acquired, he suggested, and the banks could now be allowed to redeem Dominion notes for gold for such purposes as they desired. Apparently, Bennett so informed the banks because the first large-scale redemptions of Dominion notes since the 1928–29 crises took place a few weeks later.[9]

During 1931 the balance of payments situation weakened substantially. Exports and imports both fell sharply, but on balance the deficit on the current international account was only $125 million. The capital account, however, was much weaker. Maturities of external debt more than doubled from 1930 and new issues were little more than half the record amount made in that year. Because the small net capital inflow was not enough to meet the current deficit, it was necessary to sell nearly $47 million in monetary gold and run down somewhat the net bank asset position outside Canada in order to settle the accounts. The cash reserves of the banks in Canada fell back from the high level at the end of 1930, and after mid-year the banks were again drawing advances of Dominion notes under the Finance Act to bolster their reserves.

Even early in 1931 the Dominion government's revenues were declining, despite the increases in custom tariff rates, and its expenditures were rising, despite efforts to economize. Faced with this worsening financial situation, the prime minister mentioned at a meeting with bankers in April a possible small increase in the Dominion note issue subject only to a 25 percent gold reserve. The bankers reacted quickly against any such solution to the government's problem. In May Sellar prepared a lengthy memorandum for the prime minister, urging caution regarding anything that would be construed as inflationary, such as increasing the amount of the "uncovered" issue of Dominion notes or tying up gold that might be needed for supporting the exchange rate.[10] He suggested developing a Treasury bill market in which the banks could invest surplus funds instead of putting them into Dominion notes. He also suggested that the government should institute a more scientific approach to managing operations under the Finance Act, in particular one that could keep discount rates under the act more in line with those in the United States. Although Bennett did not proceed with any action on Dominion notes, he began the issue of Treasury bills in 1932 and implemented a new and ingenious application of the Finance Act, which will be discussed later.

The forced departure of the British pound sterling from gold on September 21, 1931, after all the frantic efforts of the British authorities to avoid it, came as a shock to the Canadian government as it did to others around the world. The crisis caught the government in Ottawa without a policy and without economists in its public service qualified to advise on one in the radically new situation created by a floating pound sterling, with two dozen other currencies following in its wake.[11] The problem of policy was far beyond what Sellar could be expected to solve.

Bennett's immediate reaction was to state that Canada would maintain the gold standard. He did not elaborate, and it seems likely that he did not really understand what was meant by maintaining the gold standard. The Canadian dollar had opened that day, September 21, in the New York market at a discount of 3 percent, which fell to 6¼ percent. The following day, after Bennett's statement, it declined to a discount of 11 percent, being quoted at 89 cents (U.S.)—only moderately above the relative price of sterling in New York. By the end of the week, however, sterling had declined to $3.50 (U.S.) in New York—72 percent of its par value—while the Canadian dollar was back up to 91 percent of par in a foreign exchange market described as "completely demoralized."[12] On October 3 the International News Service asked Bennett to clarify the situation of the Canadian dollar and the government's intentions. His reply was interesting if not precise: "Canada has not altered the position taken when the announcement [was] made that England had departed from the gold standard, nor do we contemplate so doing. We have appealed, and not in vain, to Canadians to conserve our gold supply to meet whatever strain may be placed upon our resources by reason of our foreign commitments, which are payable in gold and will be honoured accordingly."[13] Bennett implied, but did not confirm, that Canadians were being persuaded not to cash Dominion notes for gold.

In a memo prepared about this time, Sellar said that although Canada was technically on the gold standard, it was an academic question. Legally gold could be had for Dominion notes and exported, he wrote, but patriotic appeals by the government and the banks were being brought to bear on Canadians not to exercise this right.[14] In fact, however, Bennett's files contain long lists of those who were refused the redemption of notes in gold by the assistant receivers general. The obligations to pay gold to Canadians were not being met in order to be able to meet the more important obligations to pay gold to foreign creditors in future. It was a realistic policy, but it was not the gold standard. Within a few more days, the Department of Justice drafted an order-in-council, under the broad authority of the relief act of 1931, prohibiting the export of gold without a licence from the Department of Finance. The order was approved by the Governor in Council on October 19; Canada was then officially off the gold standard. Canadians were being refused redemption of Dominion notes in gold; it was made clear that if they got gold, they would not be allowed to export it nor would those to whom they might sell it. (It is probable that smuggling of gold into the United States would eventually have taken place on a large scale had Dominion notes in fact been redeemed in large amounts.) Gold produced in Canadian mines was bought by the government at the New York value, after some short delay.

In modern terminology the Canadian dollar was "floating" in the market without intervention by the Canadian government or any other agency. This did not mean, however, that Bennett was not offered advice on what the government should do about its currency. The first expert proposal came from S. R. Noble, assistant general manager of the Royal Bank of Canada, who was very experienced in foreign currency and exchange problems.[15] The Royal was the most modern and sophisticated of the chartered banks at that time. In a letter to Bennett on September 26, Noble stated, "My experience convinces me not only of the seriousness of the present situation but also of the possibility of turning it greatly to our advantage."[16] In his enclosed "Notes on the Present Financial Situation," he argued that it would take a very large reserve of gold to restore to par the Canadian dollar, which was then selling below ninety cents (U.S.). He considered it was much more desirable to let the Canadian dollar fall further, until the premium on the U.S. dollar was 25 percent, before attempting to stabilize it. He went into the arguments for and against further depreciation and came out clearly in favour of it. He recognized, but played down the importance of, the increase in costs to Canadian debtors with U.S. dollar or gold obligations, believing that these would be more than offset by the favourable effects of the higher prices obtainable on Canadian exports and the higher domestic price levels. Depreciation would also impair Canadian credit in New York to some degree, but relatively few maturities had to be refinanced in the near future and the harm done to future borrowing would not be great. Noble did not go into the processes necessary to bring about or manage this depreciation.

Bennett sent these notes to Sellar and, apparently, to O. D. Skelton (whom Noble had given as a reference) for comment. Sellar's statements show that he hardly recognized that the Canadian dollar was already "off gold" because nothing had been done officially to establish this status. He felt Noble exaggerated the benefits of depreciation, although he himself did not display much knowledge of the subject. Eventually there would have to be an international solution, he thought, and Canada might want a central bank that could be a member of the Bank for International Settlements.[17]

An unsigned memorandum that appears to be from Skelton (it is clearly not from the Finance Department) recognized the facts more clearly and indeed questioned perceptively the whole future of the gold standard after Britain's action. Although the author also felt that Noble had exaggerated the advantages of depreciation, noting possible American countermeasures, he was sympathetic to the economic case Noble had made. He warned of the dangers, however, particularly the difficulties of controlling the level of the Canadian dollar in the market once the government began intervening. Since Canada's organization for managing the gold standard had proven wholly inadequate, he doubted that it could manage the value of its currency in the exchange market. The Canadian government had little alternative but to admit that the dollar was off gold and would be for some time. He advised that the value of the dollar should be allowed to fluctuate as the market dictated until conditions improved, at which time the government could borrow enough foreign exchange to stabilize the rate.[18]

Neither memorandum encouraged Bennett to take Noble's advice. It would have required a brave man to do so in the circumstances. After the British crisis, Bennett had explored the possibility of borrowing in New York, but a sensible report from the Bank of Montreal had warned against it.[19] He also had some rather amateurish inquiries made about obtaining an exchange stabilization loan from the Federal Reserve authorities in the United States, only to learn that loans were made solely to other central banks. Rather impetuously, he decided to discuss with some of the Canadian bankers the desirability of setting up a central bank to have access to such assistance; he received, of course, no encouragement.

Soon after the British crisis, Bennett had sought the advice of Professor T. E. Gregory of the London School of Economics, an expert on the gold standard. Gregory's memorandum is dated October 10, 1931; it is not clear when it reached Bennett.[20] He realistically stated that Canada was off the gold standard and to get back on at the previous par value would cost a lot of gold, with no assurance of permanence. A return to par that proved only temporary would be worse than not going back at all. Although gold exports could be checked by administrative devices, it would be difficult to evade legal obligations and there would be danger of discrimination. Legal control over exports would be better, he suggested, and could be implemented quickly. Legal restriction on conversion of notes might be better for some purposes (for example, to counter smuggling.) Gregory advised that gold reserves should be centralized in the Department of Finance and that the laws on the required gold reserve against Dominion notes might be changed. As long as Canada remained off the gold standard, he stated, the gold should be used for meeting obligations payable in gold or for managing the exchange rate to prevent abrupt changes.

EXCHANGE RATE DEVELOPMENTS

If, as Gregory expected, Canada was not to return to the gold standard in the near future, it would be necessary to decide whether to stabilize the premium on U.S. dollars, which was about 10 percent, or to allow it to rise still further before stabilizing. On the whole Gregory thought that some increase would have favourable effects, if it did not destroy confidence or add appreciably to the difficulties of financing in the New York market. In view of the general nervousness in all countries, Gregory believed that it might be unsafe to allow the premium to rise much, if any, above 20 percent (surprising advice from an Englishman, since the pound had depreciated more than that). Finally, he proposed that if Canada wished to borrow in New York, a loan council should regulate all its borrowing in New York and carry out all negotiations for loans. All in all, Gregory's advice, apart from this last impractical point, was not all that different from Noble's.

Despite the similarities in their recommendations, Bennett did not act on the advice of Gregory or Noble. Having been ill, he went overseas to recover. The Canadian dollar in New York was left to float and reached its low point in December 1931 when the premium on U.S. dollars averaged 21 percent. On December 22 J. A. McLeod, president of the Canadian Bankers' Association, issued a statement that discussions between the association and the prime minister had resulted in the conclusion that "immediate steps should be taken through the banks, brokers, trust companies and investment houses, to control in so far as they might be able, the purchase abroad of securities by residents of Canada."[21] By January 17, 1932, McLeod was able to say that the "control" had had "a remedial effect" and the restrictions on the sale of foreign exchange by the banks would be relaxed.[22] The premium on U.S. funds declined during the first quarter of 1932, and throughout the rest of the year the Canadian dollar floated roughly midway between sterling and the U.S. dollar, which was still on gold.

Canada's financial standing at that time does not appear to have been impaired by the performance of its currency. A memorandum dated March 15, 1932, from Sellar to Rhodes, stated that Kuhn, Loeb, and Co. in New York had offered its services to negotiate a long-term loan with some French interests. Sellar had replied that it was nice to know that Canadian credit was so highly regarded, but at the moment there was no need to borrow. Sellar also reported that a representative of the Chase Company was in Ottawa, hoping to discuss the refunding of the $40 million Treasury notes which would mature in New York on December 1 and that he intended to put him off by saying that money was getting cheaper and the minister was tied up on parliamentary business.[23]

An important suggestion on exchange rate policy was put before Bennett in mid-April 1932 by C. S. Tompkins, the inspector general of banks. He gave the prime minister a memorandum prepared by G. F. Towers, assistant to the general manager of the Royal Bank, for Sir Josiah Stamp, a British financier then in New York.[24] Towers noted the decline in the Canadian dollar to just under 80 cents (U.S.) in late 1931 and its recovery since that time to 90½ cents. Left to itself, Towers said, the Canadian dollar would probably return to par, as in 1920–21. However, the business situation in the United States was extremely serious; low price levels had so reduced the value of real assets that they could not support the liabilities of the banks, with the result that there would be continued banking pressure towards liquidation and deflation. The rise in the value of the Canadian dollar, Towers explained, was dragging the Canadian business situation in the same direction. Consequently, Canada should either manage its own currency or "join" sterling.

Towers suggested that because Canada had little experience in managing its own currency, a lack of confidence and a fear of further inflationary action might result. On the other hand, joining the sterling bloc would be regarded as an acceptable, clearly defined goal, since confidence was again reposed in the pound. The depreciation of the Canadian dollar by 22 percent in terms of gold, equal to that of sterling at the time, was justified by the decline that had taken place in Canadian prices. Here he went into some detail. He thought the difficulties for governments from the effects of such depreciation on foreign debts could easily be exaggerated. Unless Canada acted, 1932 would be a much worse year than 1931, as Canadian prices followed U.S. prices down. Consequently, Towers recommended linking the Canadian dollar to the pound and relying on British skill in managing the exchange position of the pound. To get on the sterling basis, Towers continued, the Dominion government would simply buy and accumulate pounds sterling through the Canadian banks and hold it until the exchange rate got up close to par with the pound, at which time there could be an announcement of the intention and the authorization of an additional issue of Dominion notes to be held against deposits of sterling in the Bank of England. If at some point the Canadian dollar weakened against sterling, the sterling holdings could be used to buy Canadian dollars in the market, which could in turn be used to reduce the issue of Dominion notes made to acquire the sterling.

This carefully conceived proposal of Towers did not persuade Bennett any more than Noble's and Gregory's had. The debtor mentality—the concern to protect the country's credit rating—was so widespread in Canada that it reached right up through the Finance Department to the prime minister. Bennett and Rhodes did not wish to take action that would increase the premium on the U.S. dollar and gold in which many of the debts of Canadian governments and businesses were expressed. Bennett told Tompkins he was not convinced that the benefits of the higher prices would outweigh the losses sustained in buying exchange to service foreign-held debts, private, public, and corporate. No one seems to have been asked to calculate the effects in quantitative terms—and in those days the information to do so may not have been available.

It should be added that around this time W. C. Clark prepared a short memorandum for Bennett and the others, entitled "A Suggestion as to Canada's Immediate Problem." He argued that Canada should maintain monetary autonomy for the time being, refusing to enter into any hard-and-fast relationship either with sterling or with the American dollar. Formal arrangements to join the sterling area would be undesirable because British policy on sterling exchange "has not been formulated with sufficient clearness and courage" to provide assurance that it would bring about cessation of price declines, then some "reflation" of prices, and, thereafter, stability.[25] The first step, he thought, should be the improvement of the means of exchange rate and credit control, so that Canada, acting alone or in cooperation with others, could halt the downward course of prices and encourage an upward trend. The only structural change Clark recommended was an amendment to the Dominion Notes Act making it possible to use balances of sterling or U.S. dollars as partial "cover" for Dominion notes. Possibly, however, he suggested, it might be prudent to make a unilateral, temporary tie-up with sterling from which Canada could withdraw at short notice. Thus, at this early stage in his connection with the Finance Department, Clark's advice on exchange policy resembled that of Towers, although he was more careful to avoid commitments to stay with sterling. But he, too, failed to persuade Bennett and Rhodes to intervene in the exchange market or even to change the legislation to make that possible.

Monetary Expansion, 1932

During 1932 Bennett, Rhodes, and Sellar arranged for the first of two domestic monetary expansion measures, which made ingenious use of the Finance Act. Until that time, individual banks had taken the initiative in securing advances under the act, although the interest rate to be charged on the advances against particular issues of securities had on several occasions been settled by discussion between the banks collectively and the finance minister or department. Usually the bank repaid the advances as soon as it had sufficient reserves in Canada to do without the Dominion notes obtained. Consequently, the Finance Act, although often leading to monetary expansion when that suited the banks, was not an instrument the government could readily use when it thought monetary expansion was desirable.

In 1932 Bennett decided the act should be used for this purpose. Just when he did so is not at all clear. George Watts, an officer of the Bank of Canada, who enjoyed Towers's confidence, recalls Towers saying that it was he who had made this suggestion to Bennett in 1932.[26] Such a suggestion would have been consistent with his general attitude shown in his April memorandum. It would also explain the silence of M. W. Wilson, general manager of the Royal Bank, at a meeting of the bankers with Rhodes on September 27, 1932, when representatives of the Bank of Montreal, the Banque Canadienne Nationale and some others argued that they had sufficient reserves and would not need to borrow under the Finance Act. It would also be consistent with a memorandum by Sellar written May 30 on the financing schedule for the year in which, speaking of a new issue of securities to refund the 5½ percent renewal loan maturing November 1, he said: "As to the $34,000,000 maturing on November 1st in Canada, and the $9,000,000 of Manitoba Northern Notes, my present view is that we should force the banks to take this and, if they want to, have them discount it under the Finance Act. In other words, inflate our currency."[27]

The Manitoba Northern Note to which Sellar referred was held by the Royal Bank and had been guaranteed by the Canadian National Railways. In mid-1932 consultations had to be held with the Royal Bank over the settlement of this old, short-term loan, which in fact was paid off by the CNR, on instructions from the government, in two instalments in June and August. Once this was done, only the $34 million maturity of the 1922 loan had to be refinanced on November 1. In the end it was refinanced from a long-term issue on October 15. Meanwhile agreement was reached with the banks on the sale of two-year 4 percent Treasury notes at par and on an interest rate of 3 percent on advances made to them under the Finance Act against the security of these notes (the general rate on advances had been 4½ percent since 1928, but with certain exceptions relating to the securities pledged as collateral). The terms for what was essentially a borrowing operation, with a special rate of discounting under the Finance Act, were approved by Order-in-Council P.C. 2407 of October 28, 1932.

In addition, apparently there was an oral agreement, more or less forced on most of the banks by "moral suasion" of the prime minister,[28] that the banks would draw advances of Dominion notes up to the full amount of the two-year notes they had purchased and that they would not repay such advances until those notes matured. This meant that at least $35 million would be outstanding as part of the reserves of the banking system for this period. No formal announcement of this arrangement seems to have been made, but it leaked out quickly to the press. As a result it was reported that the government had resorted to an inflationary means of financing, a statement apt to be misunderstood and exaggerated. It was just at this point that Clark arrived as the new deputy minister. He drafted a statement for Bennett (at this time no longer the minister of finance) to make in Parliament on November 8, which explained and justified this expansion in bank reserves and compared it with central bank operations and policy in Great Britain and the United States. He noted that it was the only way open to the government to bring about an increase in bank reserves, which he termed a monetary measure to encourage recovery.[29]

The initial reaction to this unusual measure was a small decline for a few months in the Canadian bond market and an 8 percent decline in the foreign exchange value of the Canadian dollar, which in itself was beneficial. Finding their reserves thus increased, the banks paid off their other advances under the Finance Act, which had been low on average in September and October 1932. The November 1 operation kept the total of bank cash during 1933 and 1934 at a level substantially above the low ones of 1931 and 1932, despite the serious banking situation in the United States. While it improved the reserve position of the banks and thereby relieved any need to liquidate loans and, indeed, permitted some increase in their investments, it did not increase the general level of Canadian deposits, which was to come only after the secondary expansionary measure in 1934.

In 1933 declines in interest rates began. They showed up in short-term government bonds in the second quarter and in long-term bonds in the third quarter.[30] More important, however, were the reductions on May 1, 1933, in the rates of interest on savings deposits from 3 to 2½ percent paid by the chartered banks, the Post Office Savings Bank, and other savings banks.[31] It seems clear that the government nudged the banks into this action, not to improve their earnings, but to enable them to reduce correspondingly the interest charged on loans to "public bodies and to agricultural borrowers."[32]

WORLD MONETARY AND ECONOMIC CONFERENCE

In 1933 attention centred on the prospects and preparations for the broad World Monetary and Economic Conference to be held in London in June and July under the auspices of the League of Nations. Much was hoped for from this conference. It was to deal with the major subjects of international finance and trade, which were in a state of chaos in early 1933. Elaborate international preparations were made, including a detailed annotated agenda prepared by a panel of experts. The agenda itself took in monetary and credit policy, prices, the resumption of capital movements, restrictions on trade, tariff and treaty policies, and the organization of production and trade. Led by France, the gold bloc countries in Europe were urging early restoration of the gold standard before they would dismantle their many trade and payments restrictions; the British were not prepared to go back to gold until they could be assured that the conditions that had forced them off that standard were corrected. The great uncertainty was the policy of the new Roosevelt administration in the United States, which had taken office only in March of that year, at which time the U.S. banking system was in a state of collapse and its economy in the deepest trough of depression.

Canadian preparations for the conference were brief and informal by comparison with those made for the Ottawa conference in 1932 partly because the elaborate background papers of 1932 were still useful, needing only to be supplemented by more recent information. In addition many documents were prepared by the League of Nations itself, some from the expert economic branch of the staff, which included Louis Rasminsky, a Canadian who later became the third governor of the Bank of Canada.

During April and May there were many discussions and messages between the major European countries, Britain, France, Germany, and Italy, and the United States. The U.S. president invited Ramsay MacDonald, who was to be chairman, and Edouard Herriot, a former premier of France who was to head the French delegation, to discuss the business of the conference with him. While they were at sea en route to Washington, Roosevelt stopped issuing gold export licences, effectively taking the United States off the gold standard. This action, of course, complicated and frustrated the planning for the conference as well as the working out of interim monetary arrangements. Indeed, the confusion over currency and related financial policies arising from the actions and statements of Roosevelt and his many conflicting advisers made effective negotiations nearly impossible both before and during the conference.[33]

In late April 1933, when the confusion was at its height, Roosevelt invited Bennett to discuss some of these monetary and other economic matters. For this purpose, and as background for the conference, Clark prepared for the prime minister an eighteen-page memorandum, "Monetary Problems." He covered particularly the conditions precedent to the ultimate restoration of the international gold standard, possible measures to raise the world level of prices, the British program, the U.S. program (on which Clark was inevitably out of date), and suggestions on Canada's attitude to the issues in these fields. How much Bennett used these notes when he met with Roosevelt on April 29 is not clear. Their joint statement to the press touched lightly on the need to increase the general level of prices and to restore as soon as practicable an international monetary standard. They said they had also examined "proposals for the more effective employment of silver" and "agreed to begin a search for means to increase the exchange of commodities between their two countries."[34]

The prime minister took with him to the London conference a relatively small but strong delegation including Finance Minister Rhodes; Howard Ferguson, the Canadian high commissioner in London; Clark of Finance; Wilgress of Trade and Commerce; and Robertson and Lt. Col. Georges Vanier of External Affairs. The Canadians played an active but not prominent part in the Monetary and Financial Commission and its two subcommissions, and in the Economic Commission and its three subcommissions dealing with commercial policy, commodity problems and arrangements, and other measures affecting trade. The conference as a whole, however, was abortive, frustrated mainly by the unreadiness of the Roosevelt administration to deal with these very important issues so early in its term of office and at a time of such difficulty at home.

Two subsidiary results of the conference were of some importance to Canada. An agreement was reached on silver, the low price of which was causing problems to countries producing it and those holding it as monetary reserves. Subcommission 2 of the Monetary and Financial Commission approved unanimously a resolution that stated in part: "That an agreement be sought between the chief silver producing countries and those countries which are the largest holders or users of silver with a view to mitigating fluctuations in the price of silver; and that the other nations not party to this agreement should refrain from measures which could appreciably affect the silver market."[35] Pursuant to this resolution and detailed negotiations in which Clark participated for Canada, an agreement to purchase silver was entered into among the governments of Australia, Canada, the United States, Mexico, and Peru, as producers, while China, India, and Spain, as large holders of silver, agreed to limit its sale during a five-year period. The agreement was subsequently ratified and entered into force. In Canada the price of silver increased as did the volume of production. The silver that Canada agreed to buy was acquired and held by the Bank of Canada as part of its reserves after it was established.

Canada also joined a Declaration on Financial and Monetary Policy made by the delegations of the British Commonwealth following the end of the conference. The declaration acknowledged the beneficial effects of the actions taken and conclusions reached at the Ottawa conference in 1932 and the continuing validity of the conclusions about financial policy. It was reaffirmed that the ultimate aim of monetary policy should be the restoration of a satisfactory international gold standard and that the problem with which the world was faced was to reconcile the stability of exchange rates with a reasonable measure of stability, not merely in the price level of a particular country, but of world prices. The delegations recognized that such stability would depend on international cooperation, but in the meantime, it was important to achieve stability in exchange rates within the Empire in the interests of trade. They declared, finally, that in working for the economic recovery of the countries of the Commonwealth, it was especially important to reduce the rate of interest on long-term loans. This declaration, despite its vague generalities, was helpful to Canadian ministers because of the distinguished endorsement it gave to policies the government would subsequently adopt which would be controversial in conservative financial circles at home.

CREATION OF THE BANK OF CANADA

As announced in the budget of March 21, 1933, the government had decided to set up a royal commission to study the organization and workings of the entire Canadian banking and monetary system and to consider whether a central bank should be established. During the spring and early summer, the prime minister and the minister of finance, in consultation with Clark, gave extended consideration to possible members for the Royal Commission on Banking and Currency, as it was correctly foreseen that there would be controversy and a division in Canadian opinion. They thought it necessary to have a distinguished impartial chairman from outside Canada with a broad knowledge of financial institutions, and another member with expert knowledge of central banking, as well as some Canadian financiers and at least one person with a debtor's view of financial institutions as members. Numerous names were considered,[36] and it is interesting to note that at an early stage Clark suggested an American expert. While at the conference in London, Bennett approached Lord Macmillan, the distinguished British jurist, who had been chairman of the recent major British inquiry, the Commission on Finance and Industry. Macmillan agreed to serve as chairman and suggested as a second member Sir Charles Addis, who had had both commercial and central banking experience.

Having secured Macmillan by June 30, Bennett then endeavoured to complete the appointments as soon as possible by cables from London. He had previously obtained the agreement to serve of Sir Thomas White, the respected wartime minister of finance and, later, banker. Beaudry Leman, a leading French-Canadian banker, was reluctant but finally agreed to become a member. After some persuasion and hesitation, the Honourable J.E. Brownlee, then premier of Alberta, joined the commission, representing western Canadian views on these controversial subjects. The commission was finally appointed by an order-in-council of July 31, 1933, with broad terms of reference, but it was clearly intended to focus on "the advisability of establishing in Canada a Central Banking Institution."[37]

Macmillan acted promptly. He arrived in Canada on August 4 and the commission first met on August 8. B.J. Roberts of the Department of Finance was appointed secretary, with A.F.W. Plumptre, a young but talented economist from the University of Toronto, as assistant secretary. Macmillan had brought along John Fisher from the Bank of England as his personal assistant. Later, Raymond Kershaw, who was an expert on Commonwealth central banks, came over and in fact supplied much expertise needed by the commission. He drafted key sections of the report and its detailed appendix of suggestions on the constitution of a central bank for Canada. Hearings commenced August 8 and were completed by September 11. The report, with dissents by White and Leman and a memorandum by Brownlee, was in the hands of the government by September 28. The job had been done with admirable dispatch and constituted a breathtakingly close decision. But Bennett and Clark got what they wanted.

Clark had appeared formally on the second day of the public hearings of the commission. He filed with it memoranda on facts and figures concerning the Canadian legislation on banking and currency and gave oral testimony on the workings of the Finance Act, the Dominion Notes Act, and other related matters, but he did not express an opinion on the desirability of setting up a central bank. Later that day, however, he testified at a "private" sitting, along with a number of senior bankers. In this confidential setting, Clark elaborated on his earlier testimony and gave his views in answer to questions from the commissioners. In this testimony, he stated quite clearly that he personally would favour some institution to perform the central banking functions that Macmillan had described. In response to a question on whether as administrator of the department he would welcome it "for your assistance," Clark responded "very much so. I think it is becoming a real and embarrassing burden upon a political department to operate the Finance Act."[38] While the evidence, seen from half a century later, does not make clear just why a "political" department would find it so embarrassing, there seems no doubt that Clark had the departmental performance of the 1920s in mind, as well as the very constructive role that he felt an independent central bank could play. He emphasized the need for cooperation from the commercial banks and the importance of the senior personnel of the central institution, particularly the initial personnel, in giving it the prestige that would be essential to perform its function.

Within about a week of publication of the commission's report, the prime minster, in a national radio broadcast (which he paid for out of his own, very ample pocket because his use of the national network had been criticized) announced the intention of the government to proceed, at the next session of Parliament, with the establishment of a central bank.[39]

The legislation to establish the Bank of Canada was prepared very largely by Clark and drafted in its legal form by Fred Varcoe of the Department of Justice. To a large extent, Clark followed the details recommended by the royal commission and summarized in the appendix of the report, but there were many additional details to be decided and a few departures from what the commission suggested. The bank was to be owned by shareholders, who were to be Canadian individuals or companies, and no one (except the minister of finance) could own more than 50 of the 100,000 shares. The shareholders were to elect seven directors from "diversified occupations" who were themselves shareholders and who, together with the governor and deputy governor, would compose the Board of Directors.[40] The initial governor and deputy governor were to be appointed by the Governor in Council for a term not exceeding seven years, and subsequent appointments were to be made by the directors with the approval of the Governor in Council.

The legislation provided in detail for the organization of the bank, its management and direction (including an Executive Committee of the board), its powers (including the issue of currency notes), and certain duties (notably to be the fiscal agent of the government in paying the interest and principal of the public debt of Canada). These latter provisions implied taking over immediately from the Department of Finance the work of its Currency Branch, and, as soon as practicable, that of the Loans and Interest Branch, two of the main routine and troublesome operations of the department. Detailed provisions dealt with the issue and redemption of notes and with reserves of gold, silver, and foreign exchange to be held against the notes and deposit liabilities. A substantial provision required that each chartered bank hold a reserve of not less than 5 percent of its Canadian deposit liabilities in the form of notes of, and a deposit with, the Bank of Canada. The chartered banks also had to transfer all the gold they owned and held in Canada to the Bank of Canada when it began business.

The forty-three sections of the act, which incorporated numerous amendments made by Parliament, many suggested by the Opposition, did not contain any directives on how the bank was to use its powers in the conduct of monetary policy, or any explicit provisions on the relationship between the policy and operations of the bank and the policies of the government of the day. It would, of course, have been difficult to give specific statutory directions and would have been contrary to the traditions of central banking. Clark persuaded the prime minister to include in the bill an artfully worded preamble, incorporating some but not all of the tasks which the royal commission had described as falling to the lot of a central bank.[41] Clark's now well-known preamble was approved by the government and Parliament and became, in effect, a set of nonmandatory objectives for the bank:

> Whereas it is desirable to establish a central bank in Canada to regulate credit and currency in the best interests of the economic life of the nation, to control and protect the external value of the national monetary unit and to mitigate by its influence fluctuations in the general level of production, trade, prices and employment, so far as may be possible within the scope of monetary action, and generally to promote the economic and financial welfare of the Dominion: Therefore, His Majesty, by and with the advice and consent of the Senate and House of Commons of Canada, enacts as follows: . . .[42]

The Bank of Canada Bill provoked much active debate in Parliament. The Opposition supported the principle of creating a central bank; indeed, in the Throne Speech debate at the beginning of the 1934 session, Mackenzie King emphasized at length that he had advocated the establishment of a central bank in September 1932 and had argued extensively for it in Parliament in February 1933. The Liberal leader decided to press for a government-owned and -controlled central bank,[43] and the debate centred on that issue, including the importance of the government's appointing at least most of the directors. While King ultimately got his way when he became prime minister again, and was probably right in principle, the emphasis given this issue looks excessive. In fact, the governor and the deputy governor and their staff have nearly always determined monetary policy, with a varying degree of influence by the other members of the Executive Committee, depending on the personalities involved. Parliament amended the original bill to provide that the deputy minister of finance should be a nonvoting member of the board and Executive Committee; the lack of a vote mattered little (even as a put-down) as long as he had a voice and enjoyed the confidence of the governor, as Clark most certainly did.

The only public part that Clark played in the parliamentary consideration of the bill was to defend, in the Committee on Banking and Commerce, the proposal that the gold transferred from the chartered banks to the Bank of Canada should be at the formal value determined in the Currency Act rather than at the much higher external market value at the time. The brief of the banks had argued that since all of their gold was essentially held as a reserve against external liabilities and foreign exchange transactions, they should be paid the going international market price. Clark presented a long, masterly memorandum, rebutting the banks' points one by one and presenting positive arguments, in terms of Canadian law and recent practices in regard to gold (both in Canada and in other countries), showing why the proposed legislation on this issue was justified.[44] He easily carried the day in defence of the legislation he had drafted.

THE ISSUE OF RESPONSIBILITY

Clark was less successful in advising Bennett on another major issue. Because of the controversial decision that the bank was to be privately owned, and the directors elected by the shareholders, the question of the authority of the government over monetary policy quickly arose. The issue was first raised by a western CCF member; if the central bank adopted a policy contrary to that of the government of the day, whose authority would prevail? Using a legal argument, Rhodes replied that unquestionably it would be that of the governor and directors of the bank. When he was then challenged about responsible government, Rhodes replied that the authority of Parliament is always supreme, that it was delegating the power to the bank, but that if an abuse should arise, Parliament could always correct it. Much later, during the committee stage of debate on the bill, Mackenzie King brought up the issue again in the broader context of a problem arising from "a conflict between financial [meaning monetary] and fiscal policies": "If a government . . . has placed certain policies before the people and the people have endorsed those policies, returning the party to power in order to enforce them, it seems to me that no institution should be created by the state which could interfere with the will of the people as thus expressed . . . in Parliament."[45]

Bennett seemed to see that such a situation could arise and undertook to consider the matter before the next day's sitting. He consulted Clark and received a memorandum which very much played down the possibilities of conflicting policies, relating the issue to questions on trade and the "currency unit."[46] In light of this advice and his own reflections, Bennett stated first that "the national policy is the policy of the government of the day and a central bank serves the government, that is, the policy which it enunciates."[47] The context indicates that he was referring to the external value of the currency. When he turned to monetary and fiscal policy, he sidetracked the issue by denying that private bankers would be in control and said that "for the first time in the history of Canada we are setting up an organization in which the control of the government over credit is real." He saw no possibility of the central bank operating "to the detriment of any policy, fiscal or otherwise, which the government of the day might have."[48] These answers did not resolve the issue which Mackenzie King had raised.

In 1936 the Liberal government had Parliament amend the act to give the government control of the board of the bank by having majority ownership of the shares and appointing directors with a majority of the votes on the board. Naturally, the question of government control of policies of the bank arose, but the control was increased only by the greater government powers of appointment of voting directors. If the bank as reconstituted was not responsive in major matters of economic policy to the will of the then existing Parliament, Finance Minister Dunning said he would expect the government to bring forward amendments to the law to carry out its wishes. In 1938 Dunning rather reluctantly introduced further amendments to the act making the bank wholly owned by the government and providing that all the eleven directors would henceforth be appointed by the government for terms of three years. Again Dunning stated that the broad policy of the bank had to be in harmony with the desires of a majority of Parliament; if not, the government could propose to Parliament and carry through such changes in the legislation as the majority considered desirable. Thus, the amendments and the debates on them did not provide or assert that the government had itself any legal control over the policy of the bank. The implication was that Parliament had given the bank full authority and responsibility for monetary policy, and the government did not need to accept responsibility for it, except insofar as it was prepared to have Parliament change the law.

The bank did not agree. The deputy governor, J. A. C. Osborne, publicly raised the issue in 1938: "No respectable central bank would accept from its government a policy with which it differed fundamentally."[49] Dunning was able to put this remark aside by saying that any man who was asked by the government to do something which in his opinion was fundamentally wrong ought to get out of the public service rather than do it.[50] The governor, Graham Towers, made a more clear and careful statement on the matter in March 1938.

> It becomes apparent, also, that the matter is of such great national importance that it cannot be dealt with by a number of unco-ordinated agencies. Some one body must be assigned the duty of exercising control, and have no other interests which would clash with its responsibility for the regulation of currency and credit. This is the reason why there are central banks in operation in most countries. Instead of hav-

ing central bank functions performed by a department of government, the governments have preferred to intrust these functions to specialized institutions. The laws under which they operate vary. But the banks all have one thing in common: their monetary policy must conform to the policy of their respective governments. No other conception of the situation is possible in this day and age, nor would any other state of affairs be desirable in view of the vital effect which monetary policy can have on the affairs of a country.

Strangely enough, the supreme control of government in matters of monetary policy does not lessen by one iota the responsibility of central bank executives and directors. If things go wrong, in a monetary sense, while they are in charge of the affairs of a central bank, they are in no position to pass the responsibility on to the government. For it must be assumed that the policies which have been followed are in substance policies which they endorsed and recommended. If they did not agree, they should have said so. And in those circumstances they would, no doubt, have been replaced by others who did not share their objections.[51]

Towers implied that the government of the day could, if it wished, determine monetary policy, if necessary by using what he later called "various ways and means by which directors and management can be got rid of," and therefore he felt ministers of finance should be prepared to accept responsibility for supporting monetary policy.[52] During the 1940s and 1950s, however, there was a tendency for ministers to deny that they had any statutory power over the bank's policies and actions and to use that as a reason not to accept responsibility for defending them. Finance Minister Ilsley did so, first in a quick answer to a question, though he was persuaded to recant in an important statement on June 13, 1941.[53] After Towers retired and James Coyne became governor in December 1954, Finance Ministers Walter Harris and later Donald Fleming were less prepared to accept responsibility. The serious crisis that developed over Coyne's actions and statements, and the efforts of the Diefenbaker government to get rid of him in 1961, showed that Towers's rather subtle interpretation of the relations between a government and the bank could not always be relied upon. Therefore when Louis Rasminsky became governor in August 1961 after Coyne's resignation, he put forward a proposal, the substance of which was incorporated in the Bank of Canada Act in 1967. Provisions of that legislation required consultations between the governor and the minister of finance and stated that "the Minister may, after consultation with the Governor and with the approval of the Governor in Council, give to the Governor a written directive concerning monetary policy, in specific terms and applicable for a specified period."[54]

Rasminsky had said in his original proposal: "If this policy . . . was one which the Governor felt he could not in good conscience carry out, his duty would be to resign and to make way for someone who took a different view."[55]

This legal provision and the stated position of Rasminsky are satisfactory means of defining the subtle relationship that exists and should exist between a parliamentary government and the central bank. It puts the governor and deputy governor, if they are men of stature, as they should be, in a stronger position than deputy ministers usually believe they have, probably stronger than that of most Cabinet ministers. However, it places responsibility squarely on the government either to accept and defend the policy of the bank or to find another governor who will accept the government's policy and carry it out and who will be powerful enough to command public confidence. The real strength of the position of the bank derives not from the law but from its reputation in the capital and exchange markets in which it operates and with the informed public at home and abroad.

THE BANK BECOMES ORGANIZED

The Bank of Canada Bill received Royal Assent July 3, 1934. The decennial revision of the Bank Act, which had been postponed a year, also took place that summer. It took into account the Bank of Canada Act and some consequential changes, for example, the gradual phasing out of the banks' right to issue notes. A ceiling of 7 percent on interest rates on loans was retained after some consideration by the government of the mixed views of the members of the Macmillan Commission. In the Finance Department the work on the Bank Act in those days, as now, was done mainly by the inspector general of banks. While he was an independent officer with statutory duties and powers, one may assume that the new deputy minister also took some informed interest in the preparation of the bill.

Two other statutes following from the Bank of Canada Act are worth noting. The Dominion Notes Act had to be repealed effective on the date the Bank of Canada started business, which turned out to be March 11, 1935. Included in the bill to repeal the act were two provisions to be effective in the transitional period. One authorized the purchase and holding of silver pursuant to the agreement made the previous year in London and included such silver as "an additional security" for the redemption of Dominion notes.[56] This silver was sold to the Bank of Canada when it commenced business. The second provision was more important: it increased from $50 million to $120 million the amount of Dominion notes that might be issued with only 25 percent gold cover, in addition to those with full gold cover and those under the Finance Act. This permitted an increase of $52.9 million in the amount of notes that might be issued, which was said to be required for "a strictly limited interim elasticity" in the note issue pending the commencement of Bank of Canada operations.[57]

The Finance Act was also being repealed effective the same date, which would require the repayment by the banks of the advances outstanding under it; in the meantime, Bennett stated, the banks might feel some hesitancy in using the Finance Act. To reassure the House, and the financial markets, that this currency expansion was not a radical inflationary step, Bennett referred at length to a resolution passed at the World Monetary and Economic Conference the previous year which held that 25 percent gold cover should be sufficient for a central bank's legal reserve ratio in future. He pointed out that the Canadian coverage was then 40.6 percent and the requirement for the Bank of Canada was to be 25 percent.

Bennett had a good use for most of the new money permitted by this expansion of the note issue. He linked it to a program of public works amounting to about $40 million to be undertaken "throughout the Dominion from the Atlantic to the Pacific."[58] In the circumstances of 1934 this program was eminently sensible and its unusual financing apparently gave rise to no apprehension in the monetary centres of the world. The Canadian dollar was selling in the exchange market at a modest premium over the U.S. dollar, which had been gradually depreciated during 1933 and formally devalued on January 31, 1934.

With the legislation passed, the most important and urgent need was to appoint a governor for the bank. The nationality of the governor had been a matter of debate in the House of Commons, with a broad demand that he should be Canadian, although Bennett had originally believed that no Canadian was qualified by experience for the post. In fact there was one: Graham Towers was selected and appointed by early September. Apparently no other person was seriously considered. It is said that Clark proposed Towers to the prime minister.[59] Towers was an obvious candidate. He was assistant to the general manager of the Royal Bank of Canada and about to be promoted to assistant general manager. Educated as an economist, he had had banking experience in both Canada and abroad. He was thirty-seven years of age. His appointment was widely supported in Canada and also quietly approved in the Bank of England itself.[60] It had been recognized in Parliament that if the first governor was a Canadian, the deputy should probably be an experienced central banker. J. A. C. Osborne, on loan from the Bank of England, was appointed to that post late in 1934 for a term of up to five years.

With these appointments made, the role of Clark and the Department of Finance in the organization of the bank became more routine. The

Currency Branch was transferred to the bank early in 1935 as was the Public Debt Division in 1938, which reduced the size of the department quite materially during the 1935-39 period. Clark served actively on the Executive Committee of the bank as well as on the board, and was frequently in contact with Towers, Osborne, and Donald Gordon, the secretary, about the policies of the bank as well as those of the government. Clark was not afraid to speak his mind and to advocate policies. He probably had some measure of influence on monetary policy, but there is no way to tell how much he really swayed Towers, who was just as intelligent and strong a character.

Clark was frequently involved with other officers of the bank, notably Kenneth A. Henderson, the securities adviser. Within the department, Clark relied upon the assistance of George Lowe, a senior clerk. Lowe later became Clark's administrative assistant, dealing with the issue and servicing of securities.[61]

Throughout his term as deputy minister, Clark continued to keep largely to himself the contacts of the department with the senior officers of the bank on monetary questions. However, other officers in the department were able to benefit from reading, on a carefully controlled basis, some of the memoranda that Clark received from Towers and others at the bank on general economic and monetary conditions, as well as on particular matters. Usually they were unsigned and frequently undated, but officials in the Finance Department quickly learned to recognize their source, not only because of the content and context, but also because they were typed on higher quality typewriters than the government used in those austere times.

Chapter Eight

Expanding Traditional Activities

Although borrowing and debt management had always been the responsibility of the Finance Department, before 1914 the government's fiscal agents in London had carried out nearly all of these duties. The Post Office and other savings banks, described in chapter 1, had handled most of the rest. These activities increased greatly in importance during the war of 1914–18 when Sir Thomas White was finance minister.[1] It was at that time, with the sale of large public war loans and victory loans, that the bond market in Canada was really established. During the 1920s both the total debt and the funded debt outstanding declined,[2] and debt management primarily involved refunding. During the 1930s, a time that international capital markets were very disturbed and restricted, however, there was a continuous need to borrow to meet chronic deficits (including those of the CNR) and to refund a large volume of maturing war loans.

On March 31, 1930, the total funded debt of the government of Canada was $2,227 million of which $1,804 million was in Canadian dollars, $257 million (equivalent) in sterling, and $166 million in U.S. dollars.[3] Nine years later the total had risen to $3,316 million, including a small rise in the sterling portion to $336 million and a large rise in the U.S. dollar portion to $469 million. The government-guaranteed railway debt in the hands of the public also increased from $806 million in 1930 to $1,055 million on March 31, 1939. Of the direct debt outstanding in 1930 some $826 million was tax free, having been issued during World War I when the income tax was thought to be a temporary wartime measure. All this debt was retired before 1939 and no new tax-free securities were issued.

A troublesome feature of the Canadian bonded debt in 1930 was that a large amount of it was payable in U.S. dollars or sterling: "Over one-half of the total debt of all Canadian governments and over four-fifths of the bonded debt of Canadian corporations were either solely or optionally payable in a foreign currency [though a large portion of these optionally payable securities were held in Canada]. Because of their payment features these obligations constitute a huge mass of international securities which readily flow back and forth across the boundaries, according to financial conditions in Canada, New York and London."[4] The existence of this large amount of external debt was, as noted earlier, an important influence on both monetary and fiscal policy during the 1930s because it necessitated conducting affairs in a manner that would maintain Canada's ability to borrow for refunding in New York and, to a much lesser extent, in London.

Another potentially troublesome feature of the outstanding debt at the beginning of the 1930s was that much of it—both domestic and U.S. dollar debt—was payable in gold coin, an inheritance from the gold standard days. Debtors with bonds payable in the United States in gold were relieved of this obligation (when that became important because the United States left the gold standard) by a joint resolution of the U.S. Congress approved June 5, 1933.[5] As far as the bonds payable in Canada were concerned, the tight restraint on the export of gold and the inability to sell it in Canada for its export value inhibited the holders of these securities from asking for payment in gold.

This indirect inhibition worked until 1937 when a legal decision by the House of Lords in London held that an obligation to pay gold implied an obligation to pay money equivalent to the value of the gold. For Canada the significance of this decision was that the Judicial Committee of the Privy Council, in dealing with appeals from the Supreme Court of Canada, would likely follow it and thus in due course it would become the applicable law in Canada. The provincial governments were seriously concerned about the effects of this change on their obligations under outstanding bonds. As a result, Parliament passed the Gold Clauses Act in 1937 which provided that obligations governed by the law of Canada and payable in gold or in an amount of money measured thereby could be discharged by payment of the nominal amount of the debt in legal tender of the country in whose money the obligation was to be paid. To overcome legal difficulties arising from decisions of the Judicial Committee of the Privy Council, this act was repealed and replaced by a more complex one in 1939.[6]

Borrowing in the Early 1930s

In the early 1930s, before Clark's arrival in the Finance Department, borrowing in Canada took the form either of negotiated sales of short-term notes to the banks or of large public issues of bonds, sold with the aid of a management committee representing banks and investment houses, usually with the president of the Bank of Montreal, then still the largest bank, as chairman. The most notable was the large conversion loan of May 1931 when some $639 million of long-term bonds maturing in 1931, 1932, 1933, and 1934 were successfully converted at par into 4½ percent bonds maturing twenty-five years later than the original bonds (but callable after fifteen years).

A large public issue to raise cash in Canada was sold in November 1931. This National Service Loan was oversubscribed and raised $221 million, even though the banks withdrew their subscriptions when the government decided that it was in the national interest to give preference to small investors.[7] The second such public issue was made on October 15, 1932. It was for $80 million, with a 4 percent coupon. Some sales resistance was mentioned for a twenty-year tranche offered at 93.45 percent, but the loan was all sold. It was just at this time, November 1932, that the special and controversial issue of $35 million of two-year 4 percent notes were sold to the banks on the understanding that they would be discounted under the Finance Act.

Borrowing U.S. dollars was important in 1930–31 when Canada's gold reserves were low. In October 1930 the government was able to sell a large issue of $100 million thirty-year U.S. dollar bonds in New York through a banking syndicate at a time very few foreign loans were being sold there. These bonds were the last to be issued by Canada that were payable in gold coin. (This part of the obligation was abrogated two and a half years later by the congressional resolution mentioned earlier.) The CNR was able to sell a $50 million guaranteed issue the following year in New York when international markets were in the crisis leading to the British devaluation. The government arranged a short-term loan of $60 million in New York in October 1932 for refunding purposes.

BORROWING IN CLARK'S PERIOD, 1932 TO 1935

From November 1932 until March 1935, Clark was effectively in charge of debt management. Within the Finance Department he had the assistance of M. G. Anderson, the comptroller of loans and interest, and his branch, which kept the registers of the loans and handled the details of issuing and servicing the debt. In addition, he had the advice of the able comptroller of the Government Guarantees Branch.

Clark started cautiously in May, July, and August 1933 with negotiated sales of two issues of Treasury bills to the banks in Canada and one in New York for refunding. In March 1934 Clark introduced the sale of three-month Treasury bills in Canada by auction. These sales were continued later in 1934 and became a regular practice.

There were two sales of "registered stock" in London during this period: one for £15 million in August 1933 and another for £10 million in May 1934. The first was negotiated personally in London by Clark after the unsuccessful World Monetary and Economic Conference in July. He had the assistance of the Bank of Montreal's London branch, which was the government's fiscal agent there, and dealt with Lord Glendyne of Messrs. Nevisson and Co. Business was conducted smoothly and quickly. The loan was "sold" in sixty seconds, the press reported the next day, and was oversubscribed by three times. Clark later spoke of the informality and friendliness of the London process compared with the elaborate complexities and formalities of borrowing in New York. He never said much about the terms of the London transaction, but a file in the Public Archives of Canada reveals his concern, after the issue had been sold, that it was too successful—that he had sold it at too low a price.[8] In writing to Pope, the manager of the Bank of Montreal in London, on August 11, he said "a premium of 2⁵⁄₁₆ yesterday gives one pause."[9] Later, on September 1, he wrote that he expected criticism of the price and had dictated a memo (not to be found) of six points to answer it.[10]

From 1932 to 1935 two large public bond issues were sold in Canada. The first, dated October 15, 1933, was issued without the use of a management committee representing bankers and security dealers, after a good deal of study of this matter by Clark himself.[11] The issue was for $225 million, offered in three tranches: two, six, and twelve years. Nearly all the new issue was used to refund or retire the Victory Loan maturing November 1 and to pay off Treasury bills sold to the banks earlier that year, with only $15 million being left for current purposes. The second large issue, the refunding loan of October 15, 1934, was offered primarily to refund the 5½ percent Victory Loan maturing November 1 of that year. It was sold in four tranches, with lower coupons and yields than those of the 1933 issue. It was notable for the publicity given to it; indeed, subscribing to it was considered a public duty, at least according to the many leading businessmen who spoke in support of the loan on the new facilities of the Canadian Radio Broadcasting Commission. Perhaps as a result, the issue was oversubscribed, but only the stipulated total of $225 million was accepted, which was enough to convert or pay off all of the Victory Loan, as well as the six-month Treasury bills maturing November 30, and to leave about $16 million to meet current expenses.

In 1933 the government felt it necessary to guarantee $60 million in loans from the chartered banks to the Canadian Pacific Railway to enable it to meet capital costs and indebtedness in Canada and the United States, at a time the company could not issue securities in the normal way.[12]

THE BANK OF CANADA'S ROLE IN BORROWING

From March 1935 until the outbreak of World War II, borrowing was a joint responsibility of the Department of Finance and the Bank of Canada, under the overall responsibility of the finance minister, and of the government, from whom authority for the size and terms of loans had to be obtained by orders-in-council. Many bonds and very many more Treasury bills were issued during this period.[13]

The Bank of Canada served as the fiscal agent of the government, advising it on the marketing of its issues. The department continued until March 1938 to maintain the registers of the new loans and process subscriptions and payment of interest and principal, but the bank took over the marketing functions. Kenneth Henderson, a partner in a securities firm in Montreal, was appointed securities adviser at the Bank of Canada and appears to have had the full confidence of Towers. It was Henderson who usually discussed borrowing needs with Clark and suggested the timing, form, and pricing of issues, usually after consultation with Towers.[14] One important function of the department in regard to borrowing was (and still is) the forecasting of cash receipts and disbursements of the government in order to estimate the amounts of borrowing required to maintain its bank balances at adequate levels.

During this period, there were normally two public issues of bonds a year in Canada, even though budget deficits were declining, compared with one a year in the earlier 1930s. The issues were for lesser amounts and almost always included two or three tranches. Interest rates had already declined before the start of this period, and the cost to the government on the twenty-year tranche of the first issue, which was dated June 1, 1935, was only 3.10 percent. The yield on subsequent long-term issues in Canada varied between 3.07 and 3.35 percent. There were no special management committees or publicity arrangements to help sell issues until the war.

One notable feature was the fairly regular use of the New York market to issue long-term public loans. Between 1935 and 1939, four issues were made: $76 million U.S. in August 1935, $48 million in January 1936, $85 million in January 1937, and $40 million in November 1938. Canada's current account in international payments was in modest surplus at this time, but there were large maturities of Canadian securities in the United States, including direct and guaranteed bonds of the Dominion. All four issues were essentially refunding loans. They required registration under the U.S. Securities Act, which was a complicated, tedious process involving many lawyers and the painstaking assembly of the required detailed information on Canada and the government's financial position. The loans were underwritten by numerous U.S. investment houses and managed by Morgan Stanley and Co. in 1937 and 1938. The London market, too, was used to sell a long-term issue in January 1938 to pay off outstanding sterling stock maturing July 1.

One issue during this period was an innovation which was never repeated and which in retrospect probably caused more trouble than it was worth.

In a lengthy memorandum to Towers in August 1936, Henderson proposed an issue of perpetual bonds by the government, as well as a policy statement holding out the expectation of the setting up of a general sinking fund to provide for the gradual amortization of the public debt. His suggestion was based on British practice and inspired by the view that interest rates had declined to levels that justified issuing the longest possible maturities. Towers approved the proposal and sent it to Clark, who showed interest in it. The question arose whether a perpetual issue was legal under the applicable Dominion statutes. The deputy minister of justice finally decided it would be legal provided that it was callable after some date, at the government's option. Clark recommended the issue to Dunning, and a perpetual loan at 3 percent was approved in the amount of $55 million, which sold well at a price to yield 3.11 percent to the holder. Moreover, Henderson had proposed and it was agreed that bonds of $100 denominations be included in the offer so that it would appeal to small buyers.[15]

Thirty years later, in 1966, the bonds became callable. Because current long-term interest rates, influenced by inflationary tendencies, were then about 5¾ percent, the perpetuals were selling at prices far below par. The government had no incentive to call them. Thousands of holders of these bonds knew little about securities markets and could not understand why they would never get their money back, but only interest at a low rate and in money that was steadily shrinking in real value. Many holders had expected the bonds to be called when they became callable and resented being told that it was better from the government's point of view just to leave them outstanding. Other more sophisticated holders had bought the bonds at a large discount in the hope that the government eventually would be persuaded to call them. In March 1973 the government decided to call these bonds, though only in 1996. Thus holders of them were put into a position similar to that of holders of other long-dated bonds, yielding a similar rate of return over an equal period.

The Bank of Canada, on behalf of the government and to serve its own open market operations, continued throughout the later 1930s to develop the market for Treasury bills. Regular fortnightly auctions were started in 1937, and by March 31, 1939, there were six issues of three-month bills outstanding, all sold at yields of less than 0.7 percent.

The success of the borrowing policies and operations carried out during the 1930s was a credit to the Finance Department and its ministers and to the Bank of Canada when it came into operation. Moreover, these operations eliminated the inequitable and expensive tax-exempt bonds, and reduced greatly the amount of the hazardous optional currency bonds. In 1939 a statute ended the antiquated and potentially dangerous gold clause obligations. In his last budget in April 1939, Dunning was able to report: "Although our dominion funded debt has increased substantially since 1930, the annual interest burden of that debt, allowing for elimination of tax-free securities, is lower than in any year since the war. So the increase in dominion debt has not required any increase in taxes to carry it. Economic conditions have made the increased debt well-nigh inevitable, but a careful regard for our credit and the improvement of our financial machinery have enabled us to meet this economic necessity without increasing the burden of our debt."[16]

FINANCING THE CNR

The issue to the public of guaranteed securities had been a major means of financing the Canadian National Railways (and indirectly its nearly one hundred subsidiary or component companies) during the 1920s. There were also a few guaranteed issues for other purposes.[17] The minister and Department of Finance participated in the authorization of and accounting for such securities and the preparation and passage of frequent acts of Parliament approving the CNR issues. At the peak of this activity in the 1929 session of Parliament, thirty acts had related to the CNR, mainly approving construction or acquisition of lines, as well as usually authorizing the issue and guarantee of securities. It is no wonder that in April 1931 one of the senior officers of the Finance Department, B. J. Roberts, was appointed comptroller of government guarantees.

Throughout the thirties as well, financing the CNR was a major problem for the minister of finance, beginning with the completion of the very large 1929 construction program. Thereafter large annual deficits had to be financed and relatively modest amounts of maturing issues held by the public had to be refunded, including those of its predecessor companies, the Canadian Northern and the Grand Trunk, which had been absorbed in the CNR. The scale of the problem and its possible reduction led Bennett to appoint a Royal Commission on Railways and Transportation in Canada, with Mr. Justice Lyman Duff as chairman, in November 1931. Its report of September 1932 criticized the past extravagance of the CNR and urged that the management of the company be emancipated from political interference and community pressures.[18] For this purpose it recommended that the direction and control of the company and all its subsidiaries should be vested in a group of three trustees in place of the previous board of directors. Among other measures it also recommended that operating deficits should not be met by loans but that Parliament should vote appropriations each year to cover them. These proposals were implemented by legislation in May 1933.

When the government changed in 1935, C. D. Howe became minister of railways and, in 1936, minister of the new Department of Transport. One of his first undertakings was a second reorganization of the CNR, reversing that of 1933. The role of a board of directors was restored and the board, with a full-time chairman, was placed in the control of the railway, but a president responsible to the board for operations was appointed as well. He also nominated better directors than those in the past. In the next year, 1937, Howe and his Department of Transport, as well as the CNR itself, after extensive consultation with the minister and Department of Finance, put forward a bill that ultimately became the Canadian National Railways Capital Revision Act, 1937. The essence of this proposal had been suggested by others in earlier years but it required Howe to grasp the nettle. The purpose of this act was to remove from the books of the CNR many debts owed to the government of Canada, which the government had earlier regarded as unlikely ever to be paid and had transferred from the category of "active" to "nonactive" assets in its balance sheet. (The "active" assets were those deducted from the gross debt of the government in determining its "net debt," and amounts disbursed in acquiring active assets each year were not included in determining the budget deficit or surplus.) Included in the obligations to be wiped off the company's books were some loans for capital purposes later judged to be worthless, all loans made to meet operating deficits, and all interest that had accrued on loans from the government that had been unpaid. In eliminating the outstanding, inactive debt, the government's equity in the company as its proprietor was increased. In addition the government transferred to the CNR various railway lines and assets it had acquired or constructed in the past, including, for example, the Intercolonial Railway, which it had not treated as active assets.

The result of these very complicated transactions was to remove the misleading and exaggerated view which Howe believed foreign financial analysts perceived in the overall debt position of the government. Previously the net debt of the government had been increased by writing down the value of loans to the railways, while at the same time the very large nominal debts of the government-owned railway to the government itself were still conspicuous in the CNR reports.[19]

This complex bill was referred to the House of Commons Standing Committee on Railways and Shipping, which heard testimony from many experts before approving it. W. C. Clark testified for Finance, mainly to explain the effects of the measure upon the government's own accounts. "What is being done here," he said, "is essentially, in large part, to consider the Dominion government as owner . . . of the Canadian National Railways and the advances that have been made in the past to that railway for capital purposes . . . will be equity of the owner in the property."[20]

The Capital Revision Act of 1937 did not affect the need of the CNR to borrow funds, which it continued to do with the support of government guarantees. Before the act was passed, the Department of Finance and the Bank of Canada had studied in 1936 the relative cost of borrowing in the Canadian market by the issue of government-guaranteed CNR bonds versus direct government of Canada bonds, the proceeds of which the government would lend to the CNR. The detailed studies made by the bank led it and Clark to believe that a direct government bond could be sold at a better price. Clark recommended a direct issue, both to reduce the cost and to increase the government's control over CNR capital expenditures. Dunning and the Cabinet, however, decided on a guaranteed CNR issue, perhaps because they wanted the CNR to appear as less of a drain on the government.[21] In the following prewar years substantial loans required by the CNR were usually obtained by the issue of guaranteed bonds made through the Bank of Canada as fiscal agent, as were the direct bonds of the Dominion itself, or through agents in New York; small amounts required were temporarily advanced by the government.

THE STRENGTHENED TREASURY BOARD

The Treasury Board did not become a strong arm of the government until 1930 when Bennett, then minister of finance as well as prime minister, became its chairman. As leader of the newly elected Conservative government, he concluded that decisive action was needed in restraining and reducing expenditures to limit the deficits caused by the Depression and thus maintain Canada's credit in external financial markets. As described in chapter 4, he used the Treasury Board and its small secretariat as his instrument in achieving major economies in the Estimates for 1931-32 and by the Salaries Deduction Act. When Rhodes took over as minister of finance and chairman of the Treasury Board in February 1932, he received Bennett's support in continuing to develop at the board special economy measures to meet the situation. In particular he brought in the staff control regulations, also described in chapter 4.

During these first two years of the Bennett regime, first Bennett and then Rhodes worked directly with W. C. Ronson, who, though he carried the formal title of director of Estimates, was de facto secretary of the Treasury Board. Watson Sellar may have been used as intermediary on some matters. Ronson had both the information and attitude his political masters required. He had a vast knowledge of the public service and public expenditures, based on many years' experience dealing with the details at the Treasury Board. He was industrious, intelligent, conscientious, and decisive and believed it was essential in his job to be "rough and ready," which he was. Though this annoyed and frustrated the departments seeking approval of proposals from the board, Ronson felt it was unnecessary for him, as secretary speaking for a board of ministers, to give reasons for its decisions, and consequently did not do so. His approach to his own organization was in keeping with the board's policy of austerity; to be beyond criticism from elsewhere in the public service, he kept the secretariat small and positions within it classified at a low level.[22] Despite this domestic frugality, the members of his staff were contented and loyal to him. He took a personal interest in them and his pride in his work was infectious.

When Clark arrived at the Finance Department late in 1932, he became ex officio the secretary of the Treasury Board. He rarely attended the meetings of the board, however, nor did he usually see the papers going before the board, other than the proposals for Estimates and a few other papers of special significance. He did intervene occasionally to give the minister of finance advice on matters coming before the board, especially on Estimates and on broad policy relating to the public service, but not on details of public service administration or other administrative work.[23] In fact there is little evidence that Clark took any active part in supervising Ronson in carrying out his duties at the board, including advising the ministers, which was mainly done orally. There were good reasons for this. First, it was quite apparent that both Bennett and Rhodes (and later Dunning) had given Ronson direct instructions to enforce economy in public expenditures, both in revising Estimates and in approving administrative details. Second, the matters coming before the board, especially those concerning the public service and administrative practices, required a detailed knowledge of the workings of the service, which could be obtained only by long experience, which Ronson had, or by demanding, full-time study (which I had to undertake when I succeeded Ronson in 1947). Clark initially knew nothing about the working of the service and had no time to spare for detailed study of it. He had much more important matters to handle, and in any event realized he could not intervene effectively in detailed administrative policies.

Ronson had had a close relationship with Watson Sellar when Sellar was assistant deputy minister, and their relations continued to be close when Sellar became comptroller of the Treasury. The same was true of Ronson's relations with B. G. McIntyre, who became Sellar's second-in-command and, later, his successor as comptroller. In general the officers of the comptroller of the Treasury served as a source of intelligence for Ronson, and as a source of suggestions and advice, in addition to being the enforcement arm of the board in a number of administrative matters.

On the other hand, Ronson's relations with the Civil Service Commission and its staff were much less harmonious. Friction was almost inevitable once the Treasury Board became active and severe in its role as the committee of Cabinet dealing with personnel matters. In the easy days of the 1920s, the Civil Service Commission had had the personnel field largely to itself, but during the austerity after 1930 problems in this area arose for many years between the commission and the board. The detailed work on the organization, classification, and pay of the positions in the civil service was handled by the large Organization Branch of the Civil Service Commission, although not to the satisfaction of the departments or of Ronson and the Treasury Board. The logic of Ronson's general views in the 1930s should have led to the transfer of this work and staff to the board, but he did not want either, feeling that his main concern was the Estimates and that his staff should remain small.[24]

Ronson gave an informative, although hardly balanced, account of the work of the Treasury Board in his testimony before the Royal Commission on Administrative Classifications in the Public Service in 1946.[25] He noted that it was necessary to have substitute members to get at least a quorum of three for its weekly meetings. In the 1930s Finance Minister Rhodes and then Dunning (until his illness in 1938 and 1939) attended fairly regularly, but after the war ministers from other departments frequently presided.[26] There were, Ronson said in 1946, an average of four hundred recommendations, most of them routine, before each meeting. During the 1930s the figure would have been much less.[27]

Staff of the Board and Its Work

In the mid-1930s the Treasury Board had only a very small staff to deal with the substantial number of cases coming before it. Ronson's chief assistant was W. Smellie, who became the clerk of Estimates in 1936. He was a careful man, who had had many years of experience as an accounting clerk. There were as well two other senior clerks and three or four stenographers. As the workload expanded in 1937 and 1938, and perhaps with some prodding from Clark, Ronson hired three outstanding young university graduates, E. B. Armstrong, C. J. Mackenzie, and G. V. Loughead, as clerks grade 4. In later years they had successful careers with the board and rose to senior positions in other departments.

The assembly, scrutiny, and reduction of the Main Estimates and the several sets of Supplementary Estimates were the largest and most important functions of the Treasury Board. It was, of course, highly seasonal work on an annual cycle. During their terms as minister of finance, Bennett, Rhodes, and Dunning all took part in the scrutiny of the Estimates and in securing the agreement of their Cabinet colleagues to reductions in those they had proposed. During the 1930s, particularly in 1937 and 1938, important discussions and decisions on them took place in Council. Ministers and their officials appeared before the Treasury Board to explain and defend their proposed Estimates, even when the decisions were made by the Council as a whole.[28] It is impossible to judge how successful the Treasury Board itself was in reducing the Estimates, since the records do not give the reductions made by the board as distinct from those made by the Council.

In 1938 Dunning succeeded in rationalizing somewhat the form of the Estimates. Until that time items for which a particular minister was responsible appeared under a number of general headings, such as "Civil Government," "Miscellaneous," "Aviation" (which included the Air Force as well as civil government air operations, though not all civil aviation items). Sometimes parts of the costs of the same unit of a department were included under different headings. Experienced clerks in the departments as well as the Treasury Board staff could assemble the figures on specific services or for which a particular minister was responsible, but it was not easy for members of Parliament or even the Cabinet to get a clear picture of the expenditures budgeted for the various operations of governments. Dunning, probably urged by Clark, had the Estimates rearranged to show all the amounts to be voted on separately by Parliament (and also those already authorized by statute) for each department or unit, such as the Civil Service Commission. This arrangement facilitated the understanding of the expenditure budget and identified the minister and senior officials responsible for its elements. The new format also provided, under "Details of Services," considerably more information about expenditures other than the salaries of permanent employees, which had always been included. These details were given for each vote under various "objects of expenditures" headings, which later were standardized and extended, and are still to be found in the Estimates. Thus began a more efficient form of expenditure accounts, which has since been developed much further.

Much of the routine business of the Treasury Board was in the field of personnel administration. Some matters were trivial in the extreme, such as the authorization of retirement benefits according to the detailed formulas in the statutes or the extension of service of those who had reached retirement age. Some were more substantial but still minor, such as the salaries to be paid to the staffs of ministers,[29] while others involved major decisions, such as the approval of the detailed organization of the new combined Department of Mines and Resources on November 30, 1936. Just what input the small staff of the board could make to such a large reorganization is not clear, though they usually did try to satisfy themselves and the members of the board that the organization conformed with the general directions on austerity in personnel. In the later years of the 1930s, as rigid staff control measures were relaxed, more discretionary changes in organization and salaries were permitted, and more staff members were needed for the board to scrutinize the requests submitted by the departments and the Civil Service Commission.

Under various Dominion statutes, the Treasury Board was given certain powers and responsibilities relating to insurance, trust, and loan companies. These statutes concerned mainly the permissible types of assets such companies could acquire or hold and the assets that foreign companies had to deposit to safeguard their Canadian policyholders or creditors. The board was given power to make temporary exceptions for specified reasons. During the early years of the Depression, serious problems arose about how these assets were to be valued, particularly in the case of the Sun Life Assurance Company, which had acquired large amounts of U.S. corporate equities for which the market value had declined precipitously. It was also necessary to judge whether the amount of certain types of assets could be above the stipulated limits, especially real estate obtained by foreclosure of mortgages. On these matters the board was advised by the superintendent of insurance, G. D. Finlayson, who ran the industry with an iron hand. It is not clear why the statutes required the approval of the Treasury Board rather than that of the minister of finance, but this was no more open to question than many of the statutory requirements for the Governor in Council to authorize transactions and rules that individual ministers might well have treated more seriously were one alone responsible.

Until 1934 the Treasury Board also had responsibility under the Finance Act for approving the lines of credit of the chartered banks and the terms of advances made to them—a responsibility of some potential importance to policy, which was largely neglected. It also had some routine responsibilities under the Bank Act.

In its search for economies, the Treasury Board took upon itself, or received from Council, the authority to review a host of small administrative decisions. The installation of each new telephone in government offices and the purchase of each motor vehicle by government departments and, later, of punch card equipment, all had to have the approval of the board. The payment of damage claims, of allowances for various purposes, and of compensation for animals slaughtered because of disease, as well as a variety of other matters, had to come before it.[30]

It must be recognized that most of these administrative transactions, including those relating to personnel, did not take up much of the time of the ministers on the board at their meetings. They were included in large looseleaf books placed before the ministers but were usually designated as routine or were so described by the secretary of the Treasury Board. But any inquisitive minister could raise a question about them, which they sometimes did as a means of checking on the work of the secretary and staff. The secretary went over all these papers in advance, being advised orally by his staff as to which cases were routine, that is, conformed with regulations or standards already settled, and which merited consideration by ministers. The ministers also discussed cases that had been rejected by the board or its staff but that had to be reconsidered at the request of a minister not on the board, who occasionally attended the meeting. All this detail required a great deal of paperwork and indicated a failure by the board to spell out proper standards for administrative powers, which could have been delegated to departmental officials. There was, however, an unwillingness both to trust the judgment of departmental officials and to hold those officials properly accountable for their discretion on administrative matters.

Government contracts for construction, purchases, or services were normally considered by the Governor in Council rather than the board, probably because they were of wider interest to ministers, who were concerned with the inevitable issues of patronage and its relationship to tenders and the regional distribution of work. It was not until 1952, after the enactment of the Financial Administration Act, that the Governor in Council authorized the board to approve contracts without further sanction by Council.

One specialized and important statutory function of the Treasury Board was the examination and preliminary approval, on behalf of the Governor in Council, of proposals from the revenue departments for the remission of taxes, fees, and penalties under the sweeping powers given the government under section 33 of the Consolidated Revenue and Audit Act. These remissions provided the answer to many detailed problems of taxation which could not readily be spelled out in the taxing statutes, but which could be the subject of serious abuse if not carefully and consistently controlled.

It was under the stress imposed by the Depression of the 1930s that the Treasury Board became important. It did not streamline its operations or delegate authority, but in the later years of the decade it added good, young men to its staff. Consequently, when the even greater stress of World War II came, it was able to carry the load under Ronson's direction. In later years it developed along different lines under other leadership but remained an important and controversial central agency of government. In 1966 the Treasury Board, its chairman, secretary, and staff, were separated from the minister and Department of Finance. A new Cabinet portfolio of president of the Treasury Board was created, and the secretary had the status of a deputy minister in his own right.[31]

Chapter Nine

New Programs: Debt Adjustment and Housing

The widespread severe hardship caused by the Depression led the Dominion government to take on new responsibilities and to expand the scope of its involvement in the economy. One was the adjustment of outstanding farm debt that was beyond the ability of farmers to pay during the Depression. Canadian farmers were hit hard by the Depression; the severe decline in farm prices and incomes made the payment of debts a difficult and often impossible task.[1] Although this problem was most acute in western Canada, many farmers throughout the country found themselves in the same situation. In fact often they were afforded some relief because creditors decided that foreclosure would be pointless, given the market situation. Further alleviation was provided by provincial legislation aimed at preventing creditors from realizing on their security. The inability of farmers to meet debt payments persisted, however, and it became increasingly apparent that some means by which farmers could adjust their debts in accordance with their ability to pay was badly needed.

The Department of Finance was involved in dealing with this debt adjustment problem not only because of its general responsibilities for financial institutions, interest rates, and economic affairs, but also because it included the superintendent of bankruptcy, who administered the Bankruptcy Act. This old act did not permit creditors to put farmers into bankruptcy, and while farmers could choose bankruptcy if they wished, fees and legal expenses usually were so substantial that they were deterred from this route. Consequently, in hard times farmers normally sought some protection from their creditors by special provincial laws, since matters relating to debts, mortgages, and property fell within provincial jurisdiction.

The 1930s was not the first occasion when farmers experienced difficulties with debts.[2] During World War I, the inability of borrowers to make payments prompted provincial legislation providing a moratorium on debts. In Saskatchewan and Alberta, the two provinces most affected by fluctuating farm incomes, legislation was introduced in the 1920s to help farmers who were heavily in debt.

In the early 1930s more extensive legislation was enacted by provincial governments to meet the serious problems of the rapidly increasing number of farmers who could no longer meet debt payments. By 1931 the Saskatchewan government, for one, found that its arrangements for negotiated settlements were not adequate to handle what was becoming a widespread problem. In the next year the debt adjustment commissioner was authorized to issue certificates preventing creditors from taking any legal action without either his permission or that of a judge of the district court. In 1933 and 1934 the powers of the Debt Adjustment Board were significantly increased. In Alberta, an appointed director continued to negotiate debt adjustment settlement between debtors and creditors. A Board of Review, to which creditors could apply in lieu of a judge, was created in 1931. The government of Manitoba first appointed a director of debt settlement in 1930, under the provisions of an act designed specifically to aid heavily indebted farmers. In 1932 and 1933 Ontario, Quebec, British Columbia, and Nova Scotia enacted debt adjustment legislation, but it was of general application; farmers received the same treatment as any other debtor class. In New Brunswick and Prince Edward Island no special legislation was passed.

THE FARMERS' CREDITORS ARRANGEMENT ACT

By 1934 the farm debt problem had become so widespread and so devastating that the Bennett government introduced special legislation to help alleviate it. In doing so, provincial jurisdiction over property, mortgages, and debt had to be respected. Any Dominion legislation had to fall within the limited federal authority over bankruptcy, insolvency, and interest.

The first bill presented to Bennett for his consideration permitted only voluntary arrangements between the farmer and his creditors. Bennett wanted a more far-reaching measure and reportedly sent the bill back saying that he wanted legislation which would empower some authority to adjust both principal and interest to the productive value of the farm, an idea which apparently threw Deputy Minister of Finance Clark "into a panic."[3] The task of revising the bill fell to Clark and F. P. Varcoe, a senior counsel of the Department of Justice. It was apparently discussed with representatives of credit institutions, who finally pronounced it sound.[4] On June 4, 1934, Bennett introduced a resolution in the House of Commons which eventually led to the passage of the Farmers' Creditors Arrangement Act.

The aim of the bill was straightforward, as Bennett explained in the

House: "The object, of course, is to keep the farmer on the farm; if possible to keep him cultivating the land upon which he had lived."[5] The new legislation that would make this possible was essentially a bankruptcy measure, but of a special kind. The administrative costs of the actions were to be met from public funds, not by the farmer or his creditors. Special official receivers were to be appointed in the judicial centres of the farming communities. A farmer unable to meet his liabilities as they came due could submit a proposal for a composition, extension of time, or scheme of arrangement for his debts to an official receiver, who would then convene a meeting of the creditors and assist in arriving at an agreed adjustment or settlement. The agreement would be put into effect by the county or district court. If agreement could not be reached, the official receiver would report the case to a Board of Review. These boards, which were to be established in each province by the Governor in Council, would consist of a provincial judge with jurisdiction in bankruptcy, who would act as chief commissioner, and two other commissioners, one representing creditors and the other, debtors. If the board was unable to formulate a proposal acceptable to both the debtor and the creditors, it could then decide upon a settlement which would be enforced by the local court.

The bill included a separate, important section based on the Dominion government's jurisdiction over interest. It provided that whenever a rate of interest exceeding 7 percent was stipulated in a mortgage on farm real estate, the debtor could tender payment of the principal amount owing (although not yet due) plus the interest to the date of payment and three months' additional interest in lieu of notice. After this offer was made, no interest in excess of 5 percent could be charged or recovered.

To complement the measures in the Farmers' Creditors Arrangement Act, Bennett introduced amendments to the Farm Loan Act enabling the Farm Loan Board to make loans at lower rates available to credit-worthy debtors.[6] These new provisions proved of substantial help to farmers; it is noteworthy that the number and aggregate amount of mortgage loans made by the board increased nearly tenfold between 1933 and 1936.

Both the Farmers' Creditors Arrangement Act and the amendments to the Farm Loan Act passed through the House of Commons with little serious opposition. Bennett displayed great knowledge and skill in explaining this legislation.

Operation of the Act

The Department of Finance was given the responsibility of administering the new legislation, probably because it was also responsible for the Bankruptcy Act. Initially M. A. MacPherson, a well-known and experienced Saskatchewan lawyer and politician, came to Ottawa and assisted the department for eight months in implementing the legislation. He drafted the necessary rules and forms, and he found suitable persons to serve as the official receivers and members of the Boards of Review. He prepared a letter of instruction from the minister to the official receivers and a pamphlet for farmers, explaining the purpose of the act and the procedures for making use of it. MacPherson was primarily responsible for bringing the legislation into effect quickly: in the Prairie provinces on September 1, 1934, in Ontario and Quebec on October 1, and in the other provinces on November 1. The superintendent of bankruptcy was given the supervision of the official receivers in their role as trustees. Some time after MacPherson's important initiating role, H. F. Gordon became director of the work under the act. By April 1939 he had two senior clerks and a staff of eleven and was also administering the Municipal Assistance Act, which had been introduced in 1938.

The first report on operations under the act,[7] covering approximately an eighteen-month period ending March 31, 1936, stated that 19,091 farmers had submitted proposals to official receivers, 18,840 creditors' meetings had been held, and 11,011 proposals had been settled, of which 4,893 had been agreed settlements mediated by the official receivers and 6,118 had been determined by the Boards of Review. As well, 4,298 settlements had been worked out informally by the official receivers, and "many thousands" had simply been arranged between farmers and their creditors outside the act. An analysis of a large number of settlements showed that the total debt reduction averaged about 30 percent.

In subsequent years several important amendments were made to the act. In 1935 it was provided that, except with the agreement of the creditor, the act would not apply to debts incurred after May 1, 1935. To avoid a likely confrontation with the government of British Columbia over jurisdiction, an additional act was passed, which stated that, except for cases approved by the British Columbia Court or confirmed by the province's Board of Review before the passage of this new act, the Farmers' Creditors Arrangement Act would no longer be enforced in that province.[8] Three years later, important amendments to the arrangement act provided for the appointment of additional Boards of Review in any province with too much work for one board. A subsection stated that no further proceedings were to take place after June 30, 1937, in Manitoba and British Columbia, and in all other provinces, except Alberta and Saskatchewan, after December 31, 1938. This act remained in effect until 1943. It was then rescinded, as were its amendments and the act exempting its application in British Columbia, and a new Farmers' Creditors Arrangement Act was passed, which consolidated many of the provisions of the earlier legislation and included some additional amendments.[9]

THE HOUSING PROGRAM

In 1935 the Bennett government was persuaded by parliamentary pressure to establish a national housing program to alleviate the deplorable housing situation resulting from the Depression. The Department of Finance was the source for and locus of administration of this legislation.

Before the 1930s the Dominion government's involvement in housing was very restricted.[10] It was generally accepted that this matter was the responsibility of the provinces or municipalities or both. By 1914 rapid urban growth, inflated real estate values (partly as a result of speculation), a significant influx of poor immigrants, and, above all, bad planning combined to create a severe shortage of adequate housing, particularly for lower income groups. The Dominion government did not become involved in this problem until 1919, following publication of the report of the Royal Commission on Industrial Relations, which concluded that the housing shortage was a chief factor in encouraging social unrest in the country. Using its powers under the War Measures Act, the Dominion government authorized $25 million of loans to the provincial governments, which would allocate funds to their municipalities for the purpose of stimulating the construction industry. This program was of very limited success, particularly because it failed to provide housing for the lowest income groups, the sector most in need of assistance. Residential construction, however, increased significantly during the 1920s, though this was due not to government intervention but to a general improvement in the economy. In 1929, the peak year, 64,700 new housing units were completed.[11]

After 1929 the volume of residential construction activity declined to less than half that of the prosperous building period of the late 1920s. The problem of a growing shortage of adequate housing was further aggravated by the increasing unemployment resulting from the depressed economy. Professor A. E. Grauer of the Department of Social Science in the University of Toronto described the situation in his 1939 report:

> After 1930 the sharp break in construction, resulting from the recurrence of depression, meant an increasingly acute problem of housing accommodation. The depressed condition of business and the decline of salaries virtually stopped building of middle-class residences, while the fall in wages and the phenomenal increase in the number unemployed radically reduced the capacity of the lower income groups to pay rents. The effects were evident in a decreased number of available homes, the doubling-up of tenants in congested residential areas, and the deterioration of low rental houses through the inability of landlords to make necessary repairs.[12]

In several of the larger Canadian centres critical reports were prepared condemning the deplorable state of local housing conditions and calling for increased government assistance to right the situation. The subject was raised in Parliament early in the session of 1935 by T. L. Church, a Conservative member from Toronto, and both the Liberal and Conservative parties supported the demand for action. A special committee of the House of Commons was appointed to investigate the matter.

The Special Committee on Housing held eighteen meetings and listened to the testimony of twenty-three witnesses representing the Dominion government, municipalities, boards of trade, and other private and public organizations. Clark, the key official representing the Dominion government, had acquired much experience in the real estate field from his earlier employment with S. W. Straus and Co., an American firm specializing in the financing of urban building and development.[13] In his presentation before the committee, he stressed the need for action, not only to improve the housing situation itself, but also to relieve unemployment by stimulating the construction industry. He urged caution however in approaching the popular but complicated question of slum clearance. His elaborate suggestion for lending Dominion funds for construction purposes involved setting up a National Housing Board to encourage the creation of local housing corporations, which in turn would finance the construction of houses and apartments. A simpler method he also proposed included establishing a national insurance corporation to guarantee the last quarter of an 80 percent mortgage.[14]

On April 16, 1935, the Special Committee on Housing tabled its final report in Parliament. The report was somewhat confused, but it conclusively recommended Dominion government action in the housing field. "The community as a whole has some responsibility for the housing of its people," the report asserted, and a "national emergency" would soon develop if the number of houses available was not increased immediately.[15] Most important, the report stated that "unaided private enterprise" could not construct the number of houses required to meet the demand of lower income families.[16] Thus, the Dominion government was obliged to intervene. The report argued that a federally assisted housing program would have a "moral value" and a "cash value" for Canadians.[17] An increase in the number of rental homes for lower income families not only would alleviate the housing shortage but would create employment in the construction industry, thereby reducing the amount of money spent on unemployment relief. Better housing would reduce the incidence of disease and crime, which so frequently accompanied slum housing conditions, and, in so doing, would save taxpayers further money. The committee recommended the establishment of a national housing policy to be administered and controlled by a housing authority empowered to allocate funds authorized by Parliament for this work.

Clark gladly accepted the responsibility for preparing the policy, a responsibility he retained throughout the 1930s. As originator of the program, Clark was given the often difficult task of convincing representatives of Canada's leading lending institutions of the merits of his proposals. His success was partly due to the assistance of David Mansur,[18] a representative of the Sun Life Assurance Company, who supported Clark's innovations when most of the other lending institutions opposed them. When Clark's program was put into effect but before the Finance Department had an administrative system in place to handle it, Mansur assisted Clark by reviewing the loan applications in detail on an informal but effective basis. It is not surprising that Mansur became one of Clark's closest friends and one of his most ardent supporters.

Dominion Housing Act of 1935

Clark's housing program was first embodied in the Dominion Housing Act of 1935. It involved the appropriation by Parliament of $10 million for a loan fund to aid in the construction of houses. The minister of finance was authorized to enter into contracts with approved lending institutions by which they would make available a new type of mortgage loan for building homes. These loans would cover up to 80 percent of the cost of construction or the appraised value of the property, whichever was less. The Dominion Treasury would provide one-quarter of the amount to be loaned, while the company would put up the remaining three-quarters. Although no interest rate was specified in the act, the Dominion government hoped that with the cooperation of the lending institutions the rate on the total amount would not exceed 5 percent. This lower rate was made possible by the government charging only 3 percent on the amount it advanced (approximately the cost to the Treasury), while the companies asked for 5⅔ percent for their portion of the loan, a commercial rate adequate to cover borrowing and operating charges. The act stipulated that any losses would be borne on a defined sharing formula depending on the principal amount still outstanding.

There were several innovative features in the mortgage loans made under the new legislation. First, the terms of the loans were to be for ten years and could, by agreement, be renewed for another ten. This was an important change; until that time mortgages had usually been for only three or five years. Second, the principal was to be repaid by amortizing it over a twenty-year period in blended payments of interest and principal. The act stated that there were to be monthly payments of principal, interest, and taxes, which was a new feature in Canada, although it had already been introduced in the United States. Monthly payments, opposed by most of the lending institutions at the time Clark proposed this feature, became the standard mortgage practice of many of Canada's lending institutions.

An important aspect of Clark's housing plan was the attention given to the quality of construction. The minister of finance issued minimum standards of construction, which were to be observed and enforced by inspections by the lender during construction. More detailed memorandum specifications, including both minimum requirements and more desirable standards for all aspects of housing construction, were also made available. Two architectural competitions were held for house designs; one led to an illustrated booklet of plans and the second, to detailed working plans of the winning designs, which the government sold at a nominal price.

The Dominion Housing Act was a relatively simple act, but difficulties were encountered with its implementation. First, by the time the legislation was passed and the machinery put in place for administering the new mortgages, the normal building season for 1935 was almost over. As well, there were some major drawbacks to the act.[19] Several lending institutions refused to take part in the new mortgage scheme because the interest rate was limited to 5 percent. Other lending institutions claimed that they did not have the administrative system in place to handle mortgage applications outside major centres and, consequently, applications from small, remote communities were often neglected. Particularly in the western provinces the Dominion government had difficulty getting the cooperation of the lending institutions. From the borrower's point of view, many wishing to obtain a mortgage did not have the 20 percent of the capital required under the provisions of the act. It was this problem which led to the criticism that although the act encouraged the construction of houses, it did not encourage construction for lower income wage earners. The act was also criticized because the mortgages covered only new construction and not renovation work. But despite these shortcomings, the act did in fact promote housing construction and over five thousand units were built as a result. Defending the legislation in 1937, Clark wrote that it was "already making what is believed to be a significant contribution to the amelioration of the housing problem and it has many important possibilities still to be explored."[20]

Home Improvement Loans

On September 6, 1936, Prime Minister King announced that the government had accepted a recommendation of the National Employment Commission that a home improvement program be started to generate employment throughout the country and that legislation would soon be introduced to put this program into effect. Because of the public support for immediate re-employment measures and because the Canadian chartered banks agreed in September to cooperate fully with the Dominion government in carrying out its plans, the home improvement program went into effect in November. It was not until the 1937 session, however, with the passage of the Home Improvement Loans Guarantee Act, that the program was legally sanctioned and made retroactive.

This act answered one of the criticisms of the Dominion Housing Act in that it provided a government guarantee on loans to property owners who wished to repair or improve their homes. The Dominion guarantee was limited to 15 percent of the total amount of the loans made by any approved lending institution, and the statute stipulated an aggregrate limit of $7.5 million for the guarantee. Borrowers were allowed loans of up to $2,000 on single houses and larger amounts on multiple dwellings. A discount rate of 3¼ percent for a one-year loan repayable in equal monthly instalments was established, and appropriate rates were drawn up for loans of other durations. The maximum term of loans for single houses was three years and for multiple houses, five years. Although the Department of Finance was given the responsibility for administering the guarantees under the act, the National Employment Commission organized and promoted the program until 1938 when the Finance Department assumed control. The program proved popular with home owners; in 1937, its first full year of operation, over $12 million was loaned.[21] The act remained in effect until 1940 when the funds appropriated by Parliament for its operation were exhausted.

NATIONAL HOUSING ACT, 1938

The Dominion Housing Act was replaced in 1938 by a more comprehensive act, the National Housing Act, aimed primarily at providing housing for low income groups. The new act, designed to complement the home improvement program, was divided into three parts. Part 1 re-enacted most of the chief provisions of the 1935 act with certain amendments and additions made to solve some of the problems with the original legislation. The aggregate amount that could be advanced by the minister of finance for mortgages for construction was increased from $10 million to $20 million (less the amount already provided under the 1935 legislation). Loans covering up to 80 percent of the lending value of the house (that is, construction costs, including land, or the appraised value of the house, whichever was less) continued to be granted. So that those living beyond the normal administrative areas of the lending institutions might benefit from this act, the government paid twenty dollars a loan to cover the additional expenditures incurred by companies making loans in small communities.

Part 2 of the act provided for Dominion assistance of up to $30 million for the financing of housing to be leased to low income families at less than economic rates. The government offered loans for such construction to limited dividend housing corporations and to local authorities at low interest rates, 1⅓ and 2 percent respectively, if municipalities agreed to limit taxes on these properties to 1 percent during the terms of these loans. The limited dividend corporations were to put up a 20 percent equity on the cost of construction, and the Dominion government would cover the remaining 80 percent with a loan. For local authorities, the equity was 10 percent and the government share, 90 percent. A further incentive to construct low-cost housing was provided in part 3 of the National Housing Act, which authorized federal payment for three years of a certain portion of municipal taxes on houses built between June 1, 1938, and December 31, 1940, at a cost of not more than $4,000.

With the outbreak of World War II, the new features of the National Housing Act never really had a chance to be effectively implemented. But even though its practical application was limited, the act was of major importance in that it signified a frank admission on the part of the Dominion government that federal assistance was essential in the provision of adequate housing. During and after the war, the government would again take up the commitment it had made in the 1938 act by greatly expanding its housing program both in scale and in scope.

THE CENTRAL MORTGAGE BANK

In 1938, as the general economic recovery continued to be disappointing, mortgages on both farms and houses were still in a precarious state. The general weight of farm debt, including arrears of interest, remained severely high in relation to the income of the debtor and the value of the farm. In the towns and cities the mortgage debt of those owning houses was in a similar situation, although it was more dispersed and less visible. The lending institutions and other creditors with mortgages on such houses were also facing risks of default, as the Depression continued and the number of persons unemployed and on relief remained high.

In these circumstances, Clark concluded that the Dominion government should make a more comprehensive effort to secure the writing down of mortgage debts to a more reasonable amount in relation to the value of the farms and houses. Creditors could not be compelled to do so, as the Dominion lacked the constitutional powers. It would require a voluntary arrangement with the government sharing the costs of writing off the excess debt as an inducement to the creditors. Clark devised such a plan early in 1939 and received Finance Minister Dunning's support. Then, with some difficulty, Clark persuaded the governor and deputy governor of the Bank of Canada to support it by including a provision within his bill reconciling the new legislation with that of the provinces. In due course Dunning convinced Mackenzie King and his Cabinet to accept Clark's plan in principle.

Clark next took the matter up with the mortgage-lending institutions, the major creditors whose voluntary participation would have to be secured. Most institutions were clearly opposed to Clark's plan. In February 1939, on behalf of the Dominion Mortgage and Investment Association, D'Arcy Leonard submitted a plan for the adjustment and refinancing of farm mortgages which was much more favourable to the lending institutions and more expensive for the government.[22] In reply, Clark presented a devastating analysis and critique of this proposal to Dunning, and he proceeded with the preparation of the legislation as before.[23]

Despite the persistent opposition of most of the lending institutions, which in all likelihood were behind the opposition the bill eventually encountered in the Senate, the Central Mortgage Bank Bill was introduced in the House of Commons by Dunning on May 6, 1939. It called for the establishment of a Central Mortgage Bank owned and controlled entirely by the government. This bank was to be run by the Bank of Canada; the governor and deputy governor of the Bank of Canada were to serve in the same positions in the new bank and also on the board of directors, along with the deputy minister of finance and three outside directors. The Central Mortgage Bank would be authorized to issue Dominion-guaranteed debentures up to an amount of $200 million. Any lending institution could become a member company in the bank if it agreed to certain conditions: it had to adjust all its mortgages held on farms to a 5 percent basis, and all those on homes not on farms to a 5½ percent basis if the amount owing did not exceed $7,000 for a single unit or $12,000 for a double. In addition, all arrears of interest in excess of two years, and all amounts owing on the mortgage account in excess of 80 percent of the appraised fair value of the property mortgaged, were to be written off.

Membership in the Central Mortgage Bank would be purely voluntary, but an attractive inducement was offered to the creditor companies (mortgage, loan, trust, or life insurance companies incorporated by Canada or any province or licensed to do business in Canada) to make these adjustments to realistic 1939 valuations and interest rates. The bill authorized the government to share the cost of the write-offs by giving the creditor company twenty-year debentures at 3 percent, guaranteed by the government and equivalent in amount to one-half of the reduction in the mortgage account. In addition to this compensation, the Central Mortgage Bank was to provide its members with "permanent discounting facilities."[24] The bank would be empowered to buy bonds, debentures, or other forms of indebtedness of its member companies and to set the interest rate at which member companies could lend money for new mortgages to farmers or owners of homes not on farms. It was intended that the bank would purchase the debentures of its member companies at a rate which would guarantee them an operating margin of not less than 1½ percent or more than 2 percent.

The act attempted to deal with the problem of duplicate adjustments or insecurity of adjusted mortgages created by provincial debt adjustment legislation. A provision stipulated that member companies would not have to adjust mortgages in any province "where in the opinion of the Central Mortgage Bank debt adjustment or other legislation unduly impedes, restricts or penalizes the exercise of the right of action or proceeding for sale under foreclosure of a mortgage,"[25] unless the province passed further legislation removing such restrictions for mortgages adjusted under the act.

The Central Mortgage Bank Bill encountered little opposition in the House. But the bill was severely criticized in the Senate, particularly by Arthur Meighen, then leader of the Conservatives in the Senate, who argued that legislation of such far-reaching application should not be rushed through Parliament. In Meighen's opinion, the bill was a first step towards the Dominion government's assuming responsibility for all mortgage debts in Canada, which he felt certain would lead to the bankruptcy of the Dominion. Although Meighen grudgingly acknowledged the need for debt adjustment for farmers, he could not understand why the government felt compelled to provide it for home owners.[26] Dunning accepted a number of Meighen's proposed amendments but he would not accept others, particularly one which would have eliminated altogether the coverage on homes not on farms. In the end, after a very tense day, the Senate accepted the views of the House, which had been unanimous except for C. H. Cahan, and approved the bill, its last action before war began in September 1939.

In retrospect, the Central Mortgage Bank Act is a vivid illustration of Clark's abilities and the influence he had upon Finance Minister Dunning. It is evident from the files that the plan was largely the work of Clark, although in allocating credit for it he characteristically emphasized Dunning's knowledge and long experience in the field of farm mortgages. Clark's dogged persistence in the struggle to convince the representatives of the lending institutions of the merits of the legislation paid off; in the end, it was reported by one of the outside directors that "Mr. Leonard's people" had become fairly well reconciled with Clark's program.[27]

The act came into effect by proclamation on July 14, 1939. David Mansur came to the Bank of Canada to assist in organizing the Central Mortgage Bank and was subsequently appointed general superintendent. But because the international situation was rapidly deteriorating towards war, the attentions of Mansur, as well as of Graham Towers, Donald Gordon, and Clark, were diverted from the bank to preparations for the war. On September 18, shortly after Canada declared war, the board of directors of the bank decided unanimously that "the uncertainties which inevitably arise, at least in the early stages of war, were such that it would be impracticable for the Central Mortgage Bank to come into active operation on the basis set forth in the Act."[28] Towers so informed J. L. Ralston, the new minister of finance, and Ralston must have decided, probably with Cabinet approval, not to fix a date on which the bank could enter into agreements with lending companies to adjust mortgages. The Central Mortgage Bank Act became a dead letter.

The problem of creating and enacting a nationwide, broadly applicable plan for the adjustment of debts acceptable to both debtors and creditors remained unsettled. By the time the war was over, farm income had increased to several times that of the 1939 level, total wages and salaries had doubled, and the real burden of both farm debt and old mortgages on houses had greatly decreased. The Central Mortgage Bank Act was repealed in 1945 and no new debt adjustment legislation was introduced.

The actions of the government in debt adjustment and mortgage reform in the 1930s did establish precedents for federal action late in the war. The Industrial Development Bank was created in 1944 to provide financial resources for industrial enterprises, especially small businesses. The Central Mortgage and Housing Corporation, which started operations in 1946, was designed to improve the administration of the National Housing Act and to create discounting facilities for mortgage financing. In both cases, agencies were created which supplemented the existing lending facilities.

Chapter Ten

Dominion-Provincial Discussions and Disputes

Relations between the Dominion and provincial governments in the 1930s were of unprecedented importance and left a legacy of interdependence and contention that has continued to the present. During the decade these relations centred mainly on the problem of unemployment relief (including farm relief) and its financial implications. The controversy began with Prime Minister King's famous House of Commons speech of April 1930 in which he said, most imprudently, under fire from the Opposition, that he would not give "a five cent piece" to provincial Tory governments for "these alleged unemployment purposes."[1] At the end of the decade the financing of unemployment relief was the dominant factor which in 1940 led the Rowell-Sirois Royal Commission on Dominion-Provincial Relations to radically propose that the Dominion should have the sole right under the constitution to use income taxes and succession duties. But although relief obviously involved the most serious financial consequences, the Department of Finance played a surprisingly inconspicuous role in relief policy itself and discussions of it with the provinces.

The constitution, the BNA Act of 1867, did not explicitly allocate jurisdiction over relief for the poor, including the unemployed, except for its references to the provinces having jurisdiction over municipal institutions and charitable and eleemosynary institutions and matters of a merely local or private nature. In the nineteenth century, when Canada was predominantly rural, poverty could be regarded as a local problem, and aid to the poor as charity, whether administered privately or publicly through municipal institutions. When large-scale urban unemployment first emerged in 1920, it was regarded as essentially a temporary postwar phenomenon. It was serious, however, and the municipalities provided relief to many unemployed; the provincial governments assisted many municipalities that needed help, and the Dominion came to their aid as well, to the extent of nearly $1.9 million spread over three fiscal years.[2] The

Dominion's share was usually one-third but in some areas, one-half. Dominion assistance was provided because "the abnormal economic and industrial conditions now existing and arising in a measure out of the late war alone afford justification for action on the part of the federal authorities."[3]

ACTION ON RELIEF

With the onset of the Depression in 1929, unemployment and reduced incomes were imposed on a society that already included many who were poor and vulnerable and for whom there was little organized means of help. Most of the unemployed were having to get along as best they could.

The King government did nothing about the relief problem before it was voted out of office, except to regret the unaccustomed intemperance of the prime minister's April speech. Bennett, elected in July 1930, was committed to deal with unemployment: "The Conservative party is going to find work for all who are willing to work, or perish in the attempt."[4] A special session of Parliament was called not only to deal with relief, but also to institute an across-the-board tariff increase to create jobs. Bennett's Unemployment Relief Act provided $20 million for 25 percent grants towards municipal work projects and for one-third of the cost of direct relief paid by municipalities. The administration of the program was disorganized, however, and at the expiry of the act at the end of the fiscal year only $4 million had been disbursed by the Dominion.

In July 1931 the Unemployment and Farm Relief Act, 1931, was passed, but, as before, the primary responsibility for relief remained with the provinces and municipalities. The special problems of the transient unemployed and of the drought-stricken southern Prairies led, however, to special Dominion assistance. Transient single men, usually employed in seasonal industries, could rarely satisfy the residence requirements for municipal relief. The relief act provided financial assistance for provincial road-building programs designed to draw single men away from urban centres. Bennett also agreed to finance the burden of relief for drought-stricken Saskatchewan as neither the municipalities nor the province had the necessary resources. Aid in Saskatchewan was distributed through an independent Relief Commission established by that government.[5]

By September 1931 the number of unemployed single men was still growing and the four western provinces called on Ottawa to assume at least 75 percent of the cost of transient relief. The Dominion government agreed to pay half the cost of approved municipal relief projects and lend the western provincial governments what they needed to make up the difference.[6] Complaints of incompetent provincial administration and political patronage in the distribution of relief work and demands from the premiers for increased assistance from Ottawa led to tensions between the Dominion and the provinces. During the winter of 1931–32 only the Conservative governments in Ontario and Nova Scotia and United Farmers of Alberta government escaped major controversy with Ottawa over relief administration.[7]

In April 1932 the provincial premiers came to Ottawa to discuss relief: what methods should be employed in order that the greatest good could be accomplished with the least possible expenditure of money and casting the least possible burden upon the municipalities, the provinces, and the Dominion. At the meeting the premiers ratified a switch in policy from relief work to direct relief embodied in the Relief Act, 1932, which was given Royal Assent in May. The change to direct relief was an economy measure; public works required expenditures for materials, equipment, and administration. To avoid the return of the transient unemployed to the cities expecting direct relief, at the meeting, the provinces proposed setting up relief camps "where work could be done, where men would not be left idle, places where requirements of food and other necessities would be given, and some amount of cash subsistence advanced by the dominion and the provinces." At the end of the conference, however, the only solution to the problem of single men to emerge was a farm placement scheme, which did prove mildly successful.[8]

During 1932 the unemployment situation continued to worsen, and the numbers on direct relief increased rapidly from about 600,000 in May to 1.2 million in December. They now included many skilled workers and middle-class members of society who had exhausted their personal assets and credit. Moreover the lack of proper administration of relief and the widely differing standards were becoming evident and were seriously criticized. Some emphasized the inadequacy of what was provided, while many others argued that the administration was so poor that much was being wasted. Miss Charlotte Whitton, a leader of professional social workers, was hired by Bennett to investigate the situation. After a four-month tour of the West, she reported to Bennett that almost 40 percent of those receiving relief there did not really need it. While her proposal was for greater use of professional social workers in the administration of relief, the effect of her findings was to discredit the direct relief program as a whole and to lead to efforts by Bennett and his government to enforce economy upon the provinces and municipalities.[9]

Bennett called a formal Dominion-provincial conference for mid-January 1933 to discuss relief and related issues. Two weeks before it began, the four western provinces presented a united demand that Ottawa accept the cost of financing both the municipal and provincial shares of relief costs. Credit for further loans by the western provinces had been denied both by the banks and the Dominion finance minister, and without some source of funds, the provinces warned, they would have no alternative but to discontinue relief.[10] W. C. Clark, after only a few weeks in office as deputy minister of finance, admitted the seriousness of the provinces' financial crisis and recommended that they "commit themselves to some definite programme for putting their financial houses in order in the very near future."[11] In his view the provinces had to take the initiative in working out a cooperative scheme with the Canadian bond houses to carry out a program of long-term financing.

The conference convened on January 17, 1933, faced with a long agenda. A number of committees were struck, which reported back to the conference as a whole. Subjects discussed, in addition to relief, included the provision of a uniform company law, the relative legislative jurisdiction of the Dominion and the provinces over old age pensions and other social insurance, jurisdiction over insurance companies, more uniformity in statistical information, and the regulation of motor trucks and buses that competed with railway services. None of these topics was of primary interest to the Finance Department, but several later came up in Dominion-provincial meetings.

The most important issues were relief and its financing and unemployment insurance. The conference resolved that the federal government should continue to assist the provinces with matching grants covering one-third the cost of direct relief. Bennett would go no further. It was also decided that the Dominion should cooperate with any province that set up a commission to administer relief (as Saskatchewan had), and the provinces agreed that some should get better terms from the Dominion than others because of their greater needs. The conference also concluded that more municipal and public works should be undertaken instead of depending heavily on direct relief.[12]

At Bennett's insistence unemployment insurance had been put high on the agenda of the conference. In a speech to the House of Commons in April 1931, Bennett had promised a national system of unemployment insurance. Problems of jurisdiction, the lack of necessary information about the work force, as well as the magnitude of the problem of unemployment, had combined to retard the preparation of any legislation. Clark had strong views on the issue; as mentioned previously, he reportedly agreed to become deputy minister of finance only when he had found that the prime minister was prepared in principle to introduce unemployment insurance.[13]

In a memorandum prepared for Bennett before the 1933 conference, R. K. Finlayson, the prime minister's private secretary, who had consulted with O. D. Skelton of External Affairs, Clark, and R. H. Coats, the Dominion statistician, recommended that a royal commission be appointed to make a thorough statistical and actuarial survey before Ottawa made proposals to the provinces on unemployment insurance. He also suggested that any unemployment insurance scheme that was adopted "should aim to limit the State's financial responsibility to the task of administration; labour and industry sharing the responsibility for premium payments."[14]

In a letter written to Bennett as the conference was meeting, Clark advocated, as Finlayson had, the separation of unemployment insurance from relief: "If you segregate these cases of unemployment relief from the insurance scheme, you will make it much easier for your provinces to give you the new constitutional powers for which you are asking . . . they will, I think, be prepared to accept the major responsibility which they now have for unemployment relief."[15] Clark conceded, however, that unemployment insurance was not an immediate solution to the problems of unemployment relief. An insurance program could not be expected to do everything, especially in its early stages and in times of unprecedented depression.

The question of jurisdiction was not settled at the 1933 conference. Bennett asked the provinces to agree to transfer jurisdiction and contribute to an insurance scheme even though no plan had been prepared. Not surprisingly, the provinces refused.[16] A shrewd observer suggested that Bennett's proposal was made in the hope that the provinces would reject it, enabling him to drop it for a time without unpleasant political consequences.[17]

The conference had made no progress in solving the acute financial problems of the western provinces, which the Dominion had met as they arose by loans. It was unwilling, however, to recognize the provinces' situation as a continuing emergency beyond their control. In March 1933, the very bottom of the economic crisis in North America, Bennett wrote to the premiers of the western provinces, telling them that to obtain further aid from his government each province would have to agree to balance its budget or at least hold its deficit to no more than a million dollars.[18] Watson Sellar, comptroller of the Treasury, visited the western provincial governments in April to report to the Treasury Board on their financial prospects. Their budgets, he said, were "balanced on hope" and not much could be expected of their ability to make savings. He recommended against any direct Dominion control over their expenditure and could propose only that Ottawa keep up the maximum possible fiscal pressure.[19]

This fiscal pressure was applied and led to a crisis in Manitoba. In the end it was settled without default, and Manitoba got loans from Ottawa for relief and other purposes amounting to some $2.5 million during the 1933–34 fiscal year.[20] The other western provinces also received loans, as well as the Dominion share of relief expenditures.

In July 1933 the Dominion government signed agreements with the provinces that each would contribute one-third of the costs of direct relief, leaving the municipalities to meet the remaining third. The efforts of the

Bennett government to escape its share of the cost of relief did not succeed, despite its campaign of fiscal pressure on the western provinces. Severe drought in Saskatchewan added to the Dominion's burdens, as that province could not afford to finance the extra cost of farm relief. Nor did Clark succeed that year in forcing the governments of the western provinces to a commitment to put their finances in order.[21]

At the end of 1933, the worst year of the Depression, the premiers of the four western provinces called for another Dominion-provincial conference. By then they wanted to discuss a complete federal takeover of relief for homeless transients and a constitutional amendment to establish unemployment insurance.

The conference was held in January 1934. Again, unemployment relief was its primary concern. The minister of labour informed the premiers that the Dominion government had decided to cut off all federal contributions of a share of the cost of direct relief in the coming spring but a national program of public works would be implemented to take up some of the slack. Bennett exhorted the premiers to economize and finally he "launched into a diatribe against the provincial leaders for their extravagance and sloppiness."[22]

The worsening financial position of the provinces, particularly their increasing debt, was also discussed. Papers prepared for the Dominion delegation included analysis of provincial debts, a summary of the pros and cons of a possible debt conversion program, and descriptions of the Australian economic adjustment program and the Australian Loan Council. Bennett again urged "stern economies in Provincial expenditures to help maintain the financial integrity of the nation."[23] No consensus on this subject emerged. While the eastern provinces could face the prospect of having to finance their own deficits, the western provinces could not. They had to have loans from Ottawa, as well as grants for relief.

It was not until summer that the Bennett government introduced its change in sharing relief costs. In the meantime there was a long crisis with Premier Duff Pattullo of British Columbia over Ottawa's insistence that he reduce his prospective deficit in order to get federal loans for relief costs or debt obligations. Pattullo had been elected in November 1933 on a public spending policy to deal with unemployment and social assistance. Although determined to proceed with it, he could not borrow what he needed in the market. On the other hand, Bennett was not prepared to finance Pattullo's election program or to lend him money unless he reduced his deficit. Pattullo warned that if a federal loan was not received by the end of March, he would default on his April 2 interest payments. Bennett would not give in and Pattullo began arrangements for the default. The Bank of Commerce, the province's fiscal agent, was very worried about the dangers in this confrontation and offered to finance Pattullo's interest payments for some weeks while he worked out a solution with Bennett. The president of the bank added a warning to both parties of the serious dangers to the Canadian economy if defaults were allowed to occur.

The deadlock between Pattullo and Finance Minister Rhodes continued for several months; Rhodes granted two small credits to meet debt obligations in the meantime. Fortunately an improvement in the B.C. economy in 1934 and consequently in the provincial revenues brought down the prospective deficit to the level on which Rhodes had insisted. Pattullo had discovered his fiscal dependence on Ottawa, but Bennett and Rhodes had found that they had to recognize the real fiscal difficulties of the western provinces.[24] In that fiscal year, 1934–35, all four western provinces received loans under the relief acts.[25]

The change in the form of the federal contribution, from a share of the actual payments to a round-sum grant-in-aid for relief, was first scheduled for June 15, 1934, but then postponed until July 15 and later to August 15, on a reduced basis as a result of Cabinet pressure. At the end of July, at Bennett's request, the premiers converged on Ottawa. Bennett took the offensive. The sharing system would continue no longer, he said. Beginning August 15, each province would be given an unconditional grant to be used for relief under its own control. The amount would be determined by the Dominion government, taking into account both the need for relief in the province and the ability of its government and municipalities to meet the costs. After estimating relief costs for the rest of the year, each premier was interviewed by Bennett and told what he could have. In nearly all cases these amounts were less than what the provinces had been getting. Naturally the premiers were shocked and angry but Bennett would not delay. Over the next few months he was prepared to change some of the amounts set for particular provinces but not the nature of the payments or the general scale. The change in form and principle led to substantially different proportionate changes in what the provinces would receive from Ottawa. The total amount paid out per month by Ottawa declined.[26] However, it is noteworthy that for the fiscal year 1934–35 as a whole total Dominion expenditures on direct relief were substantially larger than those in previous years, and the system of grants-in-aid was continued by the Liberal government after it came into power in late 1935.

Again in 1934 Bennett decided to proceed with the preparation of an unemployment insurance bill and draft legislation was ready by the end of April. The plan was intended to be actuarially sound, although it was conceded that past predictions of unemployment rates had proved to be far from reliable. Coverage was not extended to the whole labour force; unskilled seasonal workers and professionals were excluded. A commission would administer the plan and would be supervised by an advisory committee acting as financial watchdog.

Because the problem of jurisdiction remained, in August 1934 the prime minister invited the premiers to a conference to discuss the possible reallocation of powers conferred by the BNA Act. Bennett asked the premiers under what terms they would be prepared to surrender their exclusive jurisdiction over unemployment and social insurance. The conference was indefinitely postponed, however, after none of the premiers expressed enthusiasm for the idea and several were lukewarm, if not hostile, a predictable reaction after the confrontations over relief financing earlier in the summer.[27]

The "New Deal"

In January 1935 Bennett surprised Canadians with a series of five radio broadcasts. Bennett sought to emerge as an ardent reformer. He described how bad things had been during the Depression, the measures that had been taken by the government, and the distinction he saw between recovery measures to increase employment and prices and reform measures to improve the capitalist system. Among the measures he proposed were unemployment insurance, a new contributory old age pension system, and health insurance. He would take action on the recommendations of the Price Spreads Commission upon submission of its report, if it made a good case. He also proposed to establish an Economic Council. In his final address he spoke about the difference between the laissez-faire Liberal party, and his own, which stood for the reform of capitalism.[28]

These flamboyant speeches were the object of much puzzlement and concern both in Ottawa and across the country. Were thcy a program for Parliament in its final year or a platform for an early election? The issue was quickly resolved. Parliament was opened soon after the addresses, and the Throne Speech, which exaggerated the degree of recovery achieved, stated that reform measures would be submitted to that session "as part of a comprehensive plan designed to remedy the social and economic injustices now prevailing."[29]

The speeches and the reform program were the products of collaboration between Bennett, R. K. Finlayson, and W. D. Herridge, Bennett's brother-in-law and the minister at the Canadian legation in Washington. Herridge had been impressed by the ideas prevalent in the Washington of Roosevelt and the American New Deal. The political appeal of the American program was underscored by the Democratic landslide in the congressional elections of November 1934.[30] Bennett's legislative program was also influenced by two decisions of the Judicial Committee of the Privy Council on appeal from the Supreme Court of Canada. In these two cases—one concerning jurisdiction over aeronautics and the other, over radio broadcasting—the Judicial Committee ruled in favour of the Dominion Parliament, mainly by reason of the general power granted Parliament under the peace, order, and good government clause of section 91 of the BNA Act. These rulings encouraged Bennett and other Canadian lawyers and politicians to believe that the Judicial Committee might well approve other legislation that was not clearly within the specified powers of Parliament or the provinces. Unemployment insurance might possibly be such a case.

Bennett's program of reform was of course influenced by political considerations as well as his own conversion. The emergence of the CCF, the rise of Social Credit in Alberta, and the provincial successes of the Liberals indicated growing political opposition. Bennett's break with the popular Conservative, H. H. Stevens, in 1934, as well as the upcoming election, prompted Bennett to take a bold initiative.[31]

In the 1935 parliamentary session Mackenzie King supported Bennett's reforms and restrained Liberal debate on them, while reserving judgment on their constitutionality. The Employment and Social Insurance Act was speedily passed in early March.[32] It established an unemployment insurance system and an Employment and Social Insurance Commission which had advisory and investigatory powers over national health insurance and payment of "assistance" to unemployed persons not qualified for insurance benefits. Other reform measures passed during the session included the Dominion Trade and Industry Commission Act intended to carry out many of the detailed recommendations of Stevens's Price Spreads Commission. Six conventions of the International Labour Organization were ratified to lay a legal basis for acts to establish minimum wages, a weekly day of rest, and an eight-hour working day.

After the election of October 14, 1935, however, King was back in office. One of the first actions of the new government was to refer Bennett's "New Deal" measures to the Supreme Court to ascertain whether they were ultra vires. The Supreme Court's decisions had to be appealed to the Judicial Committee of the Privy Council to get final rulings, which were handed down on January 28, 1937. As many had expected, the Judicial Committee struck down most of them as ultra vires, including the Employment and Social Insurance Act and the three labour acts intended to implement conventions of the International Labour Organization. The Dominion Trade and Industry Commission Act was also declared ultra vires because of its main provision, which authorized the Governor in Council to legitimize agreements regulating prices and production where wasteful or demoralizing competition exists. On the whole, there was little left of the reform legislation. The generally negative decisions of the Judicial Committee were an object of much criticism and expert argument. Even if the decisions had gone the other way, it would have done little to expedite recovery from the Depression, although unemployment insurance would have begun several years earlier than it did.

DOMINION-PROVINCIAL CONFERENCE, DECEMBER 1935

Immediately after his election victory and even before taking office, Mackenzie King invited the premiers to a conference, which after some delays eventually took place in December. The Dominion government and five provincial governments were new, having been formed since the 1934 conference. All were Liberal governments, except John Bracken's coalition in Manitoba and the inexperienced Social Credit government led by William Aberhart in Alberta. The change of government, however, did not imply a new approach to the problems of relief financing. King, like Bennett, wanted to keep federal expenditures to a minimum, and he had criticized Bennett's relief policy on the grounds that it allowed the provinces to waste vast sums of federal money. Bennett, it will be recalled, had repeatedly urged the provinces to reduce their expenditures on relief and even went so far as to suggest that four separate legislatures in the western provinces were unnecessary. When the Liberals formed the government, Dunning stated that one of his key tasks as finance minister was the "prevention of provincial raids upon the federal treasury."[33]

King's government had little time to prepare for this important conference. On a number of issues ministers professed their unpreparedness in order to defer committing the government, but they did their best to draw the provinces out. On other matters the government had prepared positions for which it sought approval or arrangements for further consideration. It distributed a draft agenda of seven questions in late November, which was accepted. The conference, beginning December 9, lasted a working week. It was comprehensive and harmonious. One successful result was the establishment of the Permanent Committee on Financial Questions, consisting of the provincial treasurers and Dominion minister of finance, which was to meet again in January before the opening of the provincial legislatures.

Some advance preparation in financial matters had been done. Finance Minister Dunning had been well briefed by Clark on the state of provincial finances, on the problem of assisting the western provinces in meeting their maturing bond issues, and on problems relating to the overlapping use of various tax fields by the Dominion and the provinces. He was given papers on the Australian Loan Council and a suggested loan council for Canada, prepared by Finance and the Bank of Canada, and on the duplication of taxation, written by Finance and National Revenue.[34] Because of his wide experience Dunning came into office again as minister of finance full of confidence in his ability to deal with Dominion-provincial relations. As deputy minister, Clark had been worrying about the financial position of the western provinces, which his department had been financing by extraordinary measures under Bennett's government, including advances made under the relief acts to assist these governments to meet debt maturities for which they did not have cash and could not borrow in the market. As early as January 1935 Clark had put on paper an idea he had already spoken of to Bennett or Rhodes: a proposal for the four western provinces to sell three- to five-year notes, guaranteed by the Dominion government, to fund over $100 million of floating debt to the Dominion and to their banks. This plan, Clark argued, would reduce the interest burden on the provinces and provide the Dominion with a large amount of cash. Clark believed this assistance would have to be accompanied by some degree of federal supervision of their finances while the guaranteed loans were outstanding.[35] Nothing came of this idea during Bennett's remaining months in office, but Clark was ready with a more extensive proposal if the new Liberal government wanted to have a new policy on financing the western provinces, which it did.

Meanwhile, a Social Credit government with very different and radical views about money and debts had been elected to office in Alberta by a landslide vote on August 22, 1935. Even before it took office, the holders of provincial savings certificates had cashed them or tried to do so, cleaning out all of the Alberta government's cash and bringing about default on the remaining certificates. When Aberhart took office, the cupboard was bare. He tried to get an immediate large loan from Bennett during the Dominion election campaign, but the prime minister felt the most it would be proper to do was to advance Alberta $2.25 million to cover its urgent requirements up to the date of the election. On December 5, immediately before the conference, E. C. Manning, acting premier, sent a letter to the principal bond dealers in Canada, explaining the desperate financial situation of the provincial government and people and asking the holders of Alberta securities to consider an arrangement that would bear less heavily on the province. The letter suggested, as an example for consideration, a perpetual security—a market bond with no maturity date—to cover half the debt of $160 million, with the remainder to be replaced by serial bonds, all to bear interest at a substantially reduced rate of 2¾ percent. This action, of course, destroyed what was left of the credit standing of the Alberta government and lent considerable urgency to the search for some solution to the debt problems of the western provinces generally.[36]

In a memorandum to Dunning written just before the December conference, Clark recommended the immediate establishment of a National Employment Commission to act primarily as an advisory and coordinating body. Since the problem of direct relief would continue until substantially all the employable unemployed could be absorbed into productive industry, Clark argued, a commission could in the meantime eliminate waste and make relief administration more just and efficient.[37] A National Employment Commission was not a new idea, however; it had been part of the Liberal party platform since 1933. One was proposed at this 1935 conference by Labour Minister Norman Rogers. The commission was intended to assist the provinces and municipalities in organizing a nationwide registration of all relief recipients, to establish standards and regulations which the provinces should meet to qualify for federal assistance, to supervise the distribution of Dominion grants, and to plan and coordinate a consistent program of public works and employment projects. The provincial premiers, anxious to receive the additional funding promised by the Dominion government, readily agreed to Rogers's proposal of the establishment of the federal commission. Monthly federal relief grants to the provinces were increased by 75 percent from December 1935 to March 1936, but in April 1936 King and Dunning, shocked at the size of the federal deficit, convinced the Cabinet to revert to earlier levels.

Finance was not directly involved in a general discussion at the conference on the procedure for amending the constitution, but it is worth noting that substantial progress was in fact made at a lengthy meeting of attorneys-general in February 1936. Agreement on an amending formula was fleshed out in detail by a subcommittee of specialists. The developed proposal was approved at a further meeting of attorneys-general on March 2, though in the absence of a New Brunswick representative. No further action was taken on this proposal. King probably sensed there was little chance of getting New Brunswick's approval, in view of Premier Dysart's attitude that the amending formula would allow the central and western provinces to operate in concert and impose changes against the will of the Maritime provinces. Perhaps King also thought it would be difficult to get formal approval from Quebec in the final months of the Taschereau government or from that likely to succeed it.[38]

The most urgent and important discussions at the subconference on financial questions were those on the financial position of the provinces and on a possible National Loan Council. Facts and figures showed the very serious situation of the Prairie provinces (although Cockcroft, treasurer of Alberta, said little at this stage), the difficult but improving situation of British Columbia, and the deficit position of even Ontario, Quebec, and the Maritimes. Dunning fairly quickly moved the discussion to the possible establishment of a National Loan Council through which provinces with serious financial difficulties would be able to refund their outstanding debt into provincial bonds guaranteed by the Dominion and therefore carrying reduced interest rates. The exposition made clear that this action would not require the prior assent of the holders of the provincial debt, although in general the proposal was that, because of the guarantee, the creditors would be offered securities of equivalent market value. The Dominion would expect the participating provinces to jointly indemnify it for half of any loss it might incur in implementing its guarantee, and participating provinces would be required to pledge the subsidies payable to them under the BNA Act by the Dominion as security against such loss. All future borrowing by participating provinces would be guaranteed by the Dominion but would be subject to the approval of the National Loan Council on which the Dominion would have half the voting power.

The proposal was put forward for discussion only. A minority of provinces wanted to participate, but all seemed prepared to have the BNA Act amended to authorize the Dominion guarantee and to permit the provinces to pledge their subsidies as security. There was criticism of the joint indemnification of the Dominion for its guarantees and a preference for loan council arrangements being confined to individual participating provinces. Several provinces felt that the plan involved an element of repudiation of debt and did not wish to participate. Others felt it would not do enough to meet their very serious budgetary situation. The subconference presented a watered-down and noncommittal public report to the conference.

During the final session of the conference, Premier Bracken made a strong speech on the need for action in which he included a moving statement of his province's efforts to meet its own situation:

> So far as we in Manitoba are concerned, we have imposed taxes to the limit, and beyond the limit, of the capacity of our people to pay. We have had an income tax for a considerable time, and on top of that we found it necessary to put a wage tax; and in addition to all that we have practised economy as far as we possibly can. We have cut expenditures to the bone. That is about all we can do, and in spite of that we have only managed to balance our budget apart from relief.
>
> What are the alternatives before us? Either we must get alternative sources of revenue, or someone must relieve us of the responsibility of some of these social services. Failing these two, we see nothing ahead of us but eventually some time in the future, default. We have headed that off for five years and we purpose heading it off until the end; and I am hopeful that as a result of this conference, we shall be able to meet our financial problem and at the same time maintain the credit of Manitoba without impairing the credit of Canada.[39]

National Employment Commission

In April 1936 the act authorizing the establishment of a National Employment Commission (NEC) was passed by Parliament. In the preamble to the act, it was charged with the responsibility to "find ways and means of providing remunerative employment, thus reducing the numbers at present on relief, and lessening the burden of taxation." This statement reflected King's expectation that the commission would dramatically reduce relief costs, leading the way to a balanced budget, by supervising the administration of relief and thereby eliminating "obvious abuses, rackets, overlapping and the like."[40] The commission, chaired by Arthur Purvis, a prominent and able industrialist, was granted the authority to control the disbursement of Dominion government expenditures on relief and to undertake the first nationwide registration and classification of all relief recipients.

While the commission conducted its study, the Dominion government continued to provide financial and material aid to the provinces for relief. Agreements were made for the construction of numerous public works projects, including the Trans-Canada and other provincial highways. In July 1936 the National Defence relief camps were closed, and many men from the camps were offered employment with the Canadian Pacific or Canadian National Railways. Special agreements were made between the Dominion government and the provinces (except Ontario and Nova Scotia) to place others from the camps on farms. The Dominion government also agreed to pay 50 percent of the costs of operating forestry and other works undertaken by the governments of British Columbia, Alberta, Manitoba, and New Brunswick for the specific purpose of employing single persons unsuitable for farm labour. In addition, special assistance was given to the governments of the Prairie provinces in 1936 and 1937 because of the acute drought.

By September 1936 the National Employment Commission had made a number of specific proposals but only one, the Home Improvement Plan, had been approved by year's end. In July 1937 the NEC published an interim report which included the results of its nationwide registration of relief recipients and made a series of recommendations designed to get people off the dole. Again, few of the recommendations were approved. The commission was proposing not only to continue spending money on relief, but also suggesting a significant extension of federal responsibilities. King, however, saw the key to recovery in the reduction of federal expenditure and responsibility and had expected the NEC to assist in saving money.[41]

The commission's final report was presented in January 1938, but before its completion King was informed of its major recommendation. Mary Sutherland, a member of the commission, forewarned King of the intention of most of the commissioners to recommend that the Dominion assume full responsibility for the provision of relief to all unemployed employable persons (besides unemployment insurance to which the government remained committed in principle; in November 1937 it had again proposed to the provinces a constitutional amendment giving Parliament exclusive jurisdiction over the subject). King was both alarmed and dismayed by the financial implications of the recommendation. He argued that it was beyond the terms of reference of the commission (which appears to have been the case) and that it showed the political naiveté and irresponsibility of the commissioners (which was not the case). King blamed Purvis, who he thought was too much of an insensitive businessman, and W. A. Mackintosh, another member of the commission, whom King dismissed by saying that he "may be a good professor [of] economics, but knows nothing about politics."[42]

The commission's views had apparently been discussed with Labour Minister Rogers, who defended them when King reported Sutherland's conversation in a meeting of the Cabinet. King's faith in his minister of labour was undoubtedly shaken. He insisted that Rogers see Purvis and get the commission to change its decision. Rogers resisted, although he did talk to Purvis. In due course Purvis and Mackintosh suggested some changes to their colleagues, which persuaded them to hold to their view against that of Sutherland, as expressed in her dissenting memorandum, which opposed Dominion responsibility for full financing or administration of relief for the employable unemployed.

In essence the majority report of the National Employment Commission stated that when the proposed change in the constitution led to the establishment of a nationally administered system of unemployment insurance and an employment service, it would require "a supplementary system of Unemployment Aid to meet those phases of unemployment need which experience abroad has shown cannot be covered by Unemployment Insurance."[43] The commission stated that such a supplementary system would be best administered by the Dominion. This further step would require the Rowell-Sirois Royal Commission on Dominion-Provincial Relations, which had been appointed August 1937, to determine the financial basis upon which such a system should be established, and, in light of all relevant considerations, the wisdom of further constitutional and financial changes. Sutherland alone dissented from these carefully worded conclusions, and her views were strongly commended by the prime minister to his colleagues.[44]

But King was not displeased with the final result of the commission's recommendations. Although the commissioners had refused to abandon their view of the desirability of Dominion government responsibility over the provision of relief, they had backed down in that they had admitted that because of the financial implications, the matter required further study by the Rowell-Sirois Commission. Thus, the determination of whether the relief system proposed by the National Employment Commission was financially feasible was shunted off to another royal commission. Unemployment insurance had the same fate. In June 1938 King announced that the promised legislation would have to wait until the Royal Commission on Dominion-Provincial Relations submitted its report, since not all the provinces had agreed to the necessary amendment.[45] That commission is discussed more fully in chapter 12.

Provincial Loans and Loan Councils

The Permanent Committee on Financial Questions, established by the 1935 conference, met on January 13 and 14, 1936. As a result of the debate on a National Loan Council in December 1935, Dunning decided to propose at this meeting only a separate loan council for each province that might wish to have the Dominion guarantee its bond issues, either to convert its debt generally or to meet maturities as they came due. However, he also proposed a National Finance Council, which would include the treasurers of all the provinces and the minister of finance and which would have advisory powers and coordinate financial and borrowing policies generally. Proposals on refunding, loan councils, and the terms and conditions on which the Dominion would be prepared to guarantee provincial borrowing provoked debate. Some provinces thought the conversion proposals smacked of debt repudiation. Most did not think they would need or wish to seek Dominion guarantees on the terms proposed. Some thought they might have no alternative, although refinancing would not solve their very serious budget problems. All were prepared to support the Dominion proposal to amend the BNA Act to authorize these guarantees and to clarify the disputed provincial taxing powers. A press release was issued on January 14 recording these proposals and the area of agreement, as well as the willingness of the Dominion in principle to collect provincial income taxes.[46]

Immediately after the meeting, the Dominion, acting on an agreement between Dunning and Alberta Treasurer Cockcroft, advanced that province $1,557,000 it required to meet a maturity of $2 million on January 15, 1936,[47] the same day the Dominion issued a large public loan in New York. Shortly after, British Columbia was advanced $4.3 million so that with its other available funds it could meet a maturity of $5 million on February 15.[48] These were the last advances made to provinces by the Dominion to enable them to meet maturities. Dunning had stated at the permanent committee that the government's policy was to discontinue this practice. The authority to make loans for this purpose had been provided by the broad powers in Bennett's relief acts to spend money for maintaining peace, order, and good government, and it was intended to let these powers expire at the end of March. Instead, an amendment to the BNA Act, approved in principle by the Committee on Financial Questions in January and in detail by the attorneys-general at a meeting in early March, would authorize the guarantee of provincial loans subject to specific approvals by a loan council for that province. The guarantee could also require the pledge of subsidies payable under the BNA Act to the province.

The implications of this change in policy led to a major confrontation with the government of Alberta. It had a debenture issue of $3.2 million maturing April 1, 1936, and had available only $550,000 to meet it, unless it received help from Ottawa. Alberta could not borrow in the market, given the statements by Manning and Aberhart on the province's ability to service its existing debt. On March 12 Alberta Treasurer Cockcroft wrote to Dunning, requesting a further advance of $2,650,000 on the same terms as had been agreed to in January. The letter reached Dunning just after newspapers reported that Premier Aberhart announced that his government would introduce legislation to reduce unilaterally the interest rates payable on the debt of the province, without reference to the proposed loan council arrangements. In light of this action, Dunning telegraphed Cockcroft that he could not justify the loan to Parliament and the country. Dunning also telegraphed Aberhart, proposing a meeting with the western premiers or treasurers to clarify the situation. Aberhart replied that he could not meet at this time but urged the Dominion to arrange the loan and to discuss the situation later. Dunning again rejected the request and tried to obtain agreement on a loan council. More exchanges of telegrams followed. Mackenzie King recorded in his diary that after a great deal of soul-searching the Cabinet decided to stand firm and allow Alberta to default if it would not accept the loan council plan.[49] However, Aberhart, who apparently disagreed with his provincial treasurer, felt it necessary to demonstrate his adherence to Social Credit views, which were inconsistent with the controls involved in a loan council arrangement.[50] As a result, Alberta failed to meet its April 1 obligations, the first default by a Canadian province on its debentures.

In late May the Alberta government decided to reduce unilaterally by executive order the interest on its debt (including that in default) to one-half the contractual rate (but not less than 2 percent). A bondholders' committee was formed and endeavoured to persuade Alberta that it could and should meet its contractual obligations. In fact it was not until 1945 that Alberta was persuaded to pay all that it had earlier refused to pay.

The government of Saskatchewan had a maturity of $3 million due on May 1, 1936, for which it did not have sufficient funds, nor could it borrow them in the market. By this time, however, the law did not permit the Dominion to lend to the provinces, except to meet its agreed share of relief expenditures. Because of its desperate position (which was to get worse before it improved), the Saskatchewan government was prepared to accept the loan council scheme, despite the uncertainties implied in it. Graham Towers, governor of the Bank of Canada, felt that a second provincial default so soon after that of Alberta might be a major threat to Canada's credit rating abroad, and he was prepared to have the Bank of Canada lend Saskatchewan the funds required to meet its maturity on the written undertaking that the bank would be repaid by a loan under the loan council scheme when it was enacted. King and Dunning agreed, no doubt with considerable relief.[51]

The resolution requesting the British Parliament to amend the BNA Act to authorize the Dominion to guarantee provincial loans on specified conditions and to extend and clarify provincial taxing powers was introduced in the House of Commons on May 14, 1936, and was passed the following day despite opposition by Bennett and his Conservatives. In the Senate, however, where there was a Conservative majority, there was much opposition to the provisions on provincial taxes. After a critical examination of the resolution in committee, the government moved amendments to the tax provisions, but despite these concessions the resolution was defeated. As it happened, Prime Minister King had come to regret the loan council scheme as a means of trying to control the provinces, even before it had passed in the House of Commons, and was "immensely relieved" when the Senate defeated the measure.[52] Thus the loan council proposals, as well as changes in provincial tax powers, came to an end.[53]

The minister and Department of Finance were now left without a policy or powers to assist or control the financial difficulties of the western provinces. Dunning tried to salvage what he could from the collective study of the preceding winter by the provincial and Dominion ministers. He asked the provincial treasurers to meet with him as a voluntary and advisory National Finance Committee. In a long letter of June 25, 1936, he outlined eight general subjects worthy of consideration, ranging from Dominion-provincial financial relations and a better tax system to improved accounting and statistical practices.[54] The provincial treasurers agreed and the meeting was held on December 9, 10, and 11.

At the Bank of Canada, however, Alex Skelton, the director of research, must have been relieved by the Senate action. On March 20, 1936, the bank had produced a lengthy paper on federal-provincial finances, almost certainly by Skelton, in which the proposal for provincial loan councils was severely, indeed, intemperately, criticized. He gave some support to purely temporary, emergency alternatives, such as the Dominion accepting more responsibility for financing relief and other social support measures. For the longer term, however, he suggested trying to make something effective out of the proposed advisory National Finance Council by equipping it with a very able and well-informed secretariat. If this were done well, "it should rapidly become the real National Finance Council."[55] The memorandum said that the Bank of Canada had a considerable interest in making the proposed national council effective. It is not clear how far Skelton's opinions were known to Clark and Dunning. It would be surprising if they did not learn of Skelton's National Finance Council proposal in June, if not before. At that time Clark did not have enough experts to run the department itself properly, much less accomplish what the bank memorandum had proposed.

This 1936 memorandum enables one to appreciate the willingness, indeed the desire, of the bank to undertake the tasks which it and its director of research later undertook. In the summer of 1936 the bank made a beginning on detailed research when it brought in A. E. (Dal) Grauer of the Department of Social Science, University of Toronto, and a friend of Skelton's at Oxford. He produced a long report on the distribution of taxing powers in Canada, much of it factual, although not technical. But it reached some very specific conclusions, which seem to have reflected Skelton's views as well as those of its author. The concluding section begins: "The centralization and reorganization of the income tax would be the single improvement calculated to increase revenues most and it would be a step entirely in accordance with the theory of taxation."[56] The best means of achieving this end, in Grauer's opinion, was for the provinces to yield exclusive use of the income tax to the Dominion in consideration for the Dominion relieving them of some responsibilities or handing over to them a portion of its income tax receipts. While Grauer admitted that his suggested reapportionment of the taxing power indicated a strong predilection towards a centralized state, he felt that any conclusion based on economic reasoning would show that bent. On grounds of equity, as well as economics, it was his view that the main direct taxes on income and wealth should be vested in the central government as a means of offsetting regional inequalities and meeting regional fiscal requirements.

Early Steps towards the Rowell-Sirois Commission

The Grauer study fell into receptive hands in the Bank of Canada and the Department of Finance. The discussion it precipitated appears, however, to have been concerned less with the wisdom of his suggestions and the possibility of getting the provinces to agree than it was with the means to be used to obtain the support of the Dominion government itself.

Skelton and Towers rather quickly concluded that the best way of securing major improvements in the division of responsibilities for expenditures and of revenue sources would be to set up a royal commission of inquiry. They had discussed this idea with Clark and Dunning before

Towers confirmed, in a letter to the finance minister on October 20, 1936, that he had decided that such a commission should be established and that if this were done, a policy of temporizing with the public debt situation of the western provinces could be justified. He favoured some form of special Dominion assistance such as Clark had suggested in their discussions. Towers enclosed with his letter a memorandum, "Notes on a Possible Commission of Enquiry," a revision of a draft by Skelton on October 14.[57] On November 25 Skelton produced a further memorandum entitled "The Case for a Royal Commission Inquiry on Provincial Finances."[58]

Dunning favoured the commission proposal and broached the subject to the prime minister as early as November 14.[59] Clark was undoubtedly in favour of the project himself and on December 7 prepared for Dunning a memorandum entitled "Royal Commission on the Economic Basis of Confederation."[60] Included were the broad terms of reference for such a commission, similar to those Skelton had proposed, and his interpretation of what these would imply for the task of the commission. He suggested Chief Justice Newton Rowell of Ontario as chairman, with two distinguished British experts as alternatives, and provided ten names of other possible members, including, for example, Professor L. F. Giblin, the renowned but eccentric Australian economist. He also emphasized the need for a very able secretariat and expert research staff. Though Clark set forth the advantages and disadvantages of such a course of action, his disadvantages were largely understated. Here and there throughout his report he used Skelton's arguments, sometimes verbatim, but there is no doubt of his own understanding of the issues and his commitment to the project. Dunning must have decided not to make any such proposal to the National Finance Committee when it met the next week, lest it be rejected; instead he left it to the provinces to raise the subject and encouraged the expression of views upon it. These tactics worked well.

NATIONAL FINANCE COMMITTEE MEETING, DECEMBER 1936

The meeting of the National Finance Committee on December 9, 10, and 11, 1936, must be counted as one of the most successful Dominion-provincial meetings of the decade.[61] Despite Dunning's statement that he was not authorized to enter into commitments, de facto decisions were reached on a number of important questions, some of them embodied in agreed resolutions. One of the first and most urgent was a unanimous request by the provincial governments that the government of Canada enact legislation to end the gold clause obligations, as discussed in chapter 8. Others included the reform of public accounts of the various governments to make them easier to compare, greater coordination in the timing of public bond issues, and a review by the Dominion of the administration of the Old Age Pensions Act and an extension of pensions to the blind at an earlier age than seventy years.

A lengthy discussion took place between the provincial representatives and the governor of the Bank of Canada on the operations and monetary policy of the bank and also possible arrangements by which the bank might provide continuing advice and assistance in marketing the securities of provincial governments, as it did for the Dominion. There were also detailed explanations of the financial position of the Dominion and provincial governments, and a wide variety of suggestions were made for special action by the Dominion.

On the major question of the appointment of a royal commission to inquire into the economic and financial basis of Confederation, Premier Bracken made a specific proposal for such action or, alternatively, for a commission to examine the situation in the four western provinces. Bracken's broader proposal was supported by Premiers W. J. Patterson of Saskatchewan and W. Aberhart of Alberta. There was some support from British Columbia, New Brunswick, and Prince Edward Island, provided the inquiry was broad enough. Nova Scotia did not object. The Ontario representative, a junior minister, had no instructions on the matter, and Quebec saw little need for any such commission. It was agreed that interested provinces should discuss the matter with the others. Dunning managed to prolong discussion on the proposal without committing the Dominion government. Towers made a brilliant intervention at a key stage to emphasize the need for developing a better knowledge and understanding of the Dominion-provincial fiscal problem. He pointed out that it was clear that if nothing were done, one must expect further provincial defaults, a very costly way of dealing with the difficult problem outlined by the provinces. In the end, there was no consensus for or against the inquiry proposal, but there had been enough debate to pave the way for the Dominion to act.

After the meeting, Dunning promptly turned to secure Cabinet's approval for the royal commission. Since the plight of the western provinces had been the object of recurrent consideration by Cabinet, Dunning was able immediately to bring the question before it. Backed by Towers and Clark, and with his own Saskatchewan experience, Dunning was a determined and persistent advocate of a broad inquiry on the economic basis of Confederation.

His first opportunity to present the idea to Cabinet came on December 15, 1936. The Cabinet, however, was not disposed to decide upon the idea, primarily because its members were unprepared to assess the consequences that might flow from the default of two provinces. Indeed, Mackenzie King and many of his colleagues were able to convince themselves that Canada's credit would be enhanced by the default of Manitoba and Saskatchewan,[62] their argument being that a federal refusal to bolster the flagging credit of such provinces would be viewed by the financial world as an exercise of sound fiscal judgment and courage in economizing.

Dunning, Towers, and Clark disagreed and felt further action had to be taken. On the following day, Towers called on the prime minister to advise strongly against the federal government allowing Manitoba and Saskatchewan to default and to urge upon him the appointment of a commission to inquire into the financial position of all provinces.[63] Towers suggested to King that while such a commission's report was being prepared, the government or the Bank of Canada should advance to Manitoba and Saskatchewan sufficient funds to meet their current liabilities. The impact of Towers's arguments and suggestions was not immediately apparent, but, at succeeding meetings of Cabinet, King's apprehension of default increased.

As 1937 began, King's diary reveals considerable division and indeed confusion in Cabinet. For instance, the entry for January 8 indicates that whereas ministers such as J. L. Ilsley, N. Rogers, J. C. Elliott, and A. Cardin were prepared to allow Manitoba and Saskatchewan to default, others such as Dunning, T. A. Crerar, E. Lapointe, C. D. Howe, and King himself had come to feel that the repercussions of such an occurrence were too risky. They now feared that defaults by Manitoba and Saskatchewan would all too likely cause mounting debt repudiations by municipalities, school districts, and private enterprises throughout western Canada and even elsewhere and that no government in Canada, even the federal government, would be spared from the ensuing national and international reactions. Furthermore, such fiscal repercussions would be most unfortunate in a year in which the federal government had to refinance the last $326 million of its World War I tax-free Victory Loan. Nevertheless, the Cabinet remained divided on the issue of the appointment of a royal commission. What the diary does reveal is that King had by then joined Dunning as a strong advocate of a commission although Lapointe, while agreeing provincial defaults had to be prevented, was still resolutely opposed.

Assistance to Manitoba and Saskatchewan

In face of the division and indecision within Cabinet, King ultimately felt obliged to come to a decision on its behalf. He advised Dunning to attempt to arrange with Manitoba and Saskatchewan the refinancing of their indebtedness at lower rates of interest. To facilitate such refinancing, the Dominion might, King instructed Dunning, undertake to guarantee the interest on the provincial bonds if the provinces assigned their BNA

Act subsidies and possibly some provincial revenues to the Dominion as security for that guarantee. Though this suggests King had forgotten the BNA Act fiasco of 1936, Dunning invited Premiers Bracken and Patterson to Ottawa to review their provincial finances. They met on January 18 and 19, 1937, with Dunning, Clark, and Towers.

Just what happened at this meeting is difficult to determine. It is known that Dunning, Towers, and Clark had been opposed to any unilateral reduction of interest rates on provincial securities. They felt that the temporary benefit accruing from the lowered rates would be more than offset by long-term distrust of provincial obligations that such a repudiation would generate in the foreign and domestic bond markets. Current circumstances were unlikely to have changed their opinion, for the Department of Finance had arranged to sell some $85 million of bonds in the New York market on January 21.[64] This issue would bring a large fiscal gain from the substitution of new federal bonds with taxable interest of 2¼ and 3 percent for maturing Victory Bonds that bore 5 percent nontaxable interest. Dunning and his advisers would not have been prepared to endanger that operation by allowing Manitoba and Saskatchewan to lower unilaterally the interest payable on their outstanding issues. Bracken sensed the Dominion's situation and, to his own surprise, found himself in a negotiating position of some strength, despite the fact that he had but recently emerged from a general election in a minority position and was obliged to depend on the newly elected Social Credit bloc for survival.[65] Bracken found that the suggestion Manitoba might be forced to follow Alberta's example and repudiate the interest on its outstanding obligations had a noticeable impact on the federal representatives. The upshot of the meeting was an understanding between the parties that if Manitoba (and Saskatchewan) refrained from defaulting on their indebtedness, the Dominion would appoint the proposed royal commission and, during the time the inquiry was being conducted, would provide the two provinces with funds to meet their obligations.

Dunning had difficulty in securing approval for this plan from King, mainly because of King's reluctance to override Lapointe's fear of setting up a royal commission to solve provincial problems. As a means of persuading Lapointe to change his mind and resolving ministerial differences, King conceived the idea of having the Bank of Canada report on the financial position of Manitoba and Saskatchewan and advise on steps to remedy it. The matter was in this undecided state when the meeting with Bracken and Patterson ended and Bracken had to return to Winnipeg. It appears that Dunning and Clark gave Bracken assurance that by the time his train reached Winnipeg, they would be able to advise him if the Bank of Canada was to proceed with the financial investigation.[66] They were under some pressure, for Bracken had said he would have to know before the first session of the Manitoba legislature, tentatively set for February 18, whether his government would be in a position to avoid a default.

While Dunning had approved King's proposal, Towers initially balked. The governor had already made King fully aware that the Bank of Canada favoured the appointment of a royal commission, but he was reluctant to have the bank employed as a mere device to serve a political purpose. The matter was not to rest there, however. Disturbed over this conversation with King, Towers consulted Clark and returned to inform King that he was now prepared to advise the bank to undertake the study King had suggested. Pleased at the outcome and with his strategy, King concluded in his diary that "the more I think of it, the more I believe the quicker the old situation is known and understood, the sooner we will be rid of it."[67]

Under the pressure of time, Towers, Skelton, and other bank personnel gathered in Winnipeg and immediately began to prepare the survey of the province's past and current financial state. The report was completed quickly and was sent to Bracken on February 11, 1937.[68] On the following day, Towers sent letters of conclusions to Bracken and Dunning. In each case he said, "We do not see any solution other than that which might be provided by a comprehensive enquiry into the financial powers and responsibilities of all our governing bodies, and we are therefore led to the unqualified recommendation that a Royal Commission should be appointed for this purpose." Towers added, "Pending the report of such a Commission, it would appear to us that in the case of the Province of Manitoba the Dominion Government, in view of all circumstances, would be justified in extending temporary financial aid." In the knowledge that his letter to Dunning would be seen by King and Lapointe, Towers thought fit to use the stance Bracken had employed at the January meeting: "I believe that Mr. Bracken feels that he must present a definite programme of some kind to his Legislature when it meets on February 18th, and that if a decision in regard to the appointment of a Royal Commission has not been reached by that time, he will probably announce his Government's intention of cutting interest rates. Once such a position is taken, it is difficult or impossible to retreat from it and this emphasizes the urgent necessity for a decision by the Dominion Government prior to the 18th instant."[69]

Given this report and recommendation, King acted with unusual dispatch. On February 16 the Cabinet decided, "inside of half an hour, that we would have a Royal Commission investigate financial relations of the Provinces and assist Manitoba and Saskatchewan pending report."[70] The prime minister announced the decision to the House of Commons that afternoon.[71] He implied that temporary grants would be provided, pending the report of the royal commission, and a recommedation would be made to the House when the Supplementary Estimates were brought down. R. B. Bennett immediately protested, as a citizen of Alberta, against this discrimination, charging that Dunning had led that province to default by refusing it money but was now providing Saskatchewan and Manitoba with assistance that would save them from having to follow the same course.

Even before Supplementary Estimates providing for temporary grants of $750,000 to Manitoba and $1.5 million for Saskatchewan were considered by the Commons on April 9, Alberta had requested the Bank of Canada to report on its financial position. Submitting its report on April 7, the bank stated that because Alberta had reduced its interest payments by $3.4 million, it was able to balance its budget with a scale of taxation no higher and a scale of expenditure no lower than that in Manitoba and Saskatchewan. The bank consequently saw no justification in Alberta's budget position for recommending temporary aid. Again, Bennett and others voiced charges of discrimination, which were vigorously denied by Dunning, though the grants to Manitoba and Saskatchewan were approved without a vote being forced. Surprisingly there was no explanation or discussion in the House of how the specific figures for the grants had been determined.

A few months later Saskatchewan, on top of all its previous difficulties, suffered the worst crop failure of its history. Two-thirds of its population were on relief, and total relief expenditures by all governments amounted to about double the total provincial and municipal revenues (excluding subsidies).[72] As a result, Parliament voted additional special subsidies of $2 million each year in the spring of 1938 and 1939. In the spring of 1939, there was some anxiety in Ottawa about the ability of Saskatchewan to refinance $3 million of debentures falling due May 1, 1939. Clark arranged a meeting for a number of the leading bankers with Dunning in April.[73] As reported in the Saskatchewan budget of February 1940, this 1939 refinancing was accomplished by the sale of a similar amount of debentures at 4 percent through a syndicate in Toronto. This 1939 issue was in turn refinanced, along with another in 1940 for a two-year term, which was sufficient to carry Saskatchewan through its critical period.

In retrospect, it is hard to judge whether Bennett's charge of discrimination against Alberta was justified. King and Dunning were probably too hasty in their change of policy in early 1936 about loans to the provinces to meet maturing obligations. They did maintain a readiness to lend for relief purposes, but Aberhart, wishing to show a balanced budget, had refused to borrow on this basis. Aberhart seemed determined to cut his interest costs even if he had to do it by unilateral default. The provinces had understandable reasons for refusing to commit themselves to a loan council plan before the BNA Act amendment was appproved by Parliament and before the necessary Dominion legislation and terms of agreement were provided. The Dominion government, and apparently the Department of Finance, had not thoroughly studied the problems to be faced in applying the loan council scheme, including those difficulties recognized in the Bank of Canada memorandum of March 20, 1936. Alberta was unlucky in the timing of its critical need for financing in March 1936 and the result certainly looked like discrimination. By April 1937 it was easier to distinguish the case of Alberta from the other two, as the Bank of Canada did, and it is noteworthy that in the end Bennett accepted Dunning's statement that there was no intention to discriminate. Bennett nevertheless insisted that both the government and the Bank of Canada had in fact done so in 1936.[74] He suggested that there should have been a conditional item in the Estimates to provide a grant to Alberta if it paid its interest in full and put itself in the same position as Manitoba and Saskatchewan had. Dunning, at the end of the debate in April 1937, indicated that if Alberta did pay its interest in full and at the end of the year needed the $600,000 the Bank of Canada estimated it probably would, he was quite sure no Dominion government could refuse to propose to the House, at the proper time, terms precisely the same in principle as those accorded to the other provinces in like circumstances.[75]

Alberta took no action that year, or soon after, to qualify for this equivalent treatment Dunning had proffered. But in 1945 the Alberta government of Premier E. C. Manning, urged on by Clark, reached agreement with its bondholders on a settlement of those bonds on which defaults had taken place. Under its terms bondholders were compensated for the portion of the contractual interest they had not received. When the province had implemented this settlement, J. L. Ilsley, then minister of finance, secured parliamentary approval to pay grants of $600,000 a year for 1937, 1938, 1939, and 1940, on the same basis as those received by Manitoba and Saskatchewan. In addition, Alberta received a large amount to cover the increased payments it could have claimed under the debt service option of the tax rental agreements had it been paying full interest on its bonds. By December 1945 Ilsley was able to report to Parliament about Alberta: "They have conducted extensive and successful refunding operations in the United States. Today their credit appears to be excellent, and personally, as Minister of Finance of Canada, I think it is a great thing that now, when people have bonds which are signed either by the Dominion government or by any of the provincial governments, they have every reason to believe that the interest will be paid in full and that the principal will be paid in full on maturity."[76]

Four decades later in this age of the Alberta Heritage Fund, and following upon the many years of widespread and continued prosperity in western

Canada and the elaborate structure of federal-provincial fiscal arrangements, it is hard to believe that for long periods in the thirties the western provinces were unable to borrow in the market and that the emergency actions of the middle and late 1930s were debated so vehemently in Cabinet and in Parliament. Even the majority of the Senate, which was supposed to have a special regard for regional interests, showed what can only be viewed in retrospect as an unfeeling disregard of provincial interests and responsibilities in the bitter debate of 1936 that killed the resolution to amend the BNA Act.

Chapter Eleven

The Emergence of Tax Collection Agreements

Tax collection agreements, now a commonplace feature of federal-provincial relations, were first reached in 1936. The concept owes its origin in federal circles, not to the Rowell-Sirois Commission, but to W. C. Clark. It was developed after Clark became deputy minister of finance in early November 1932 and after R. B. Bennett announced in the House of Commons on November 22, 1932, that a Dominion-provincial conference would be held in January 1933. At that time Bennett indicated that the conference agenda would include the intergovernmental division of the fields of taxation. Preoccupied with imperial trade matters and a December trip to the United Kingdom, Bennett failed to leave explicit instructions on the preparation of conference material, and Clark had to take the initiative. After consultation with Bennett's private secretary, Rod Finlayson, Clark had the topic entitled "Duplication of Dominion and Provincial Taxation: Remedies" placed on the conference agenda. He and Fraser Elliott, the commissioner of income tax, then prepared background papers for the prime minister.[1]

In these papers, both Clark and Elliott indicated their concern with the intergovernmental overlapping that had emerged and was likely to continue in the income tax field. Many Canadian taxpayers, both individuals and corporations, were subject to two and in some cases three income taxes: federal, provincial, and municipal. Clark suggested two possible remedies: a new allocation of tax fields between governments or the evolution of intergovernmental agreements for cooperative exploitation of the tax fields. While Clark preferred that the federal government assume sole occupancy of the income tax fields, as it would allow taxes to be used as a tool of social policy through redistribution of wealth, he recognized that the provinces also had fiscal needs. If fiscal necessity required that the provinces remain in the income tax fields, Clark at least wanted cooperative administrative arrangements. He thought such arrange-

TABLE 7
PROVINCIAL ENACTMENTS OF INCOME AND CORPORATE TAXES

	Personal Income Tax	Corporation Income Tax	Other Corporation Taxes
Prince Edward Island	1894	1920	1894
Nova Scotia	1961	1939	1912
New Brunswick	1961	1938	1892
Quebec	1940	1932	1882
Ontario	1936	1932	1899
Manitoba	1923	1930	1900
Saskatchewan	1932	1932	1907
Alberta	1932	1932	1907
British Columbia	1876	1901	1901

NOTE: In some cases the tax was applied to the year preceding the date of enactment and in other cases to the year following. In the five easternmost provinces, corporate income tax either was applied to those corporations not subject to a special corporation tax or was an alternative to that tax, with the higher prevailing.

ments might be pursued to the extent that the federal authority would determine the taxable income of individuals and corporations for both jurisdictions and further might collect the taxes imposed by both. Elliott essentially agreed. While he thought it might be desirable that the federal government assume exclusive jurisdiction over income taxes and succession duties and the provinces over sales taxes, Elliott did not believe that the provinces would be prepared to give up any of their existing revenue sources. In the circumstances, he thought the best that might be achieved would be administrative improvements. For the Dominion and those provinces wishing to impose an income tax, a common tax return might be devised, which individuals and corporations would file with the federal authorities.

While it is doubtful that Bennett circulated either paper to those attending the 1933 conference, their substance does appear to have been discussed by him at thc conference proper and by Clark at the conference Committee on Taxation. Bennett precipitated the discussion at the conference by inviting the provincial ministers to consider ways of reducing duplication, whether of taxes or of tax administration. The sparse records indicate that Bennett placed greater emphasis on the simplification and improvement of tax administration, while Clark stressed the reallocation of tax sources.[2]

The discussion began with the minister of finance of British Columbia, James W. Jones. He repeated past provincial assertions that the personal and corporation income tax fields were assigned exclusively to the provinces by the constitution, and he protested emphatically against the permanent nature of the "temporary" 1917 federal intrusion into the income tax field. On this subject, Jones could and did speak with authority, for British Columbia's entry into the personal and corporation income tax fields had long antedated that of the federal govenment and any of the other provinces, with the possible exception of Prince Edward Island in the case of personal income tax. Table 7 shows the year in which the first provincial (as distinct from municipal) personal income, corporation income, and other corporation taxes were enacted.

No doubt anticipating Bennett's opposition to Dominion withdrawal from income taxation, Jones concluded with the proposal that, pending the Dominion's withdrawal, every arrangement should be made to permit the fullest cooperation between Dominion and provincial taxing authorities. This suggestion received support from Saskatchewan and Alberta, which had the previous year enacted personal and corporation income taxes, and from Ontario, which had just brought in a corporation income tax. The premier of Ontario, George Henry, made what Clark recognized as a promising observation: Henry thought it would be healthier to have the personal income tax levied by one jurisdiction rather than by a series of municipalities, as was the case in his province.

Conference and Post-Conference Matters

On the conclusion of this discussion the conference referred the matter to a committee for further study. Clark chaired the Committee on Taxation and the provinces were represented primarily by their treasurers. The possibility of a more equitable allocation of tax sources and the question of administrative cooperation that would reduce both the tax burden and the cost of collection were examined. The committee adjourned with the conference, after having decided to correspond about data and suggestions for a later meeting.

The later meeting was never held, partly because of Clark's absence in London at the World Monetary and Economic Conference in July 1933 and partly because of his inability to secure data from the provinces.[3] While Clark later suggested that the committee might meet again at the January 1934 Dominion-provincial conference, it did not. That conference was too concerned with unemployment and agricultural relief to consider matters such as the reallocation of taxes or improvements in their collection. Further, the provincial political climate was becoming increasingly hostile. Conservative administrations had already been swept out in British Columbia and Nova Scotia; they were to be defeated in Ontario and Saskatchewan by mid-summer 1934 and in New Brunswick and Prince

Edward Island by mid-summer 1935. And the Social Credit party was, in September 1935, to end the long political dominion of the United Farmers of Alberta in that province.

The prevailing atmosphere of political hostility and public distress nullified the further effort Bennett made. In the late summer of 1934, he tried once again to raise the issue of tax jurisdiction when he proposed a conference to consider constitutional amendments.[4] Among the suggested changes were a more logical allocation of revenue sources and a transfer to the federal government of responsibility for such social policy matters as old age pensions, unemployment, and social insurance. As mentioned previously, the response of several provinces, however, was so hostile or indifferent that Bennett was obliged to postpone the conference indefinitely.[5]

The issue of tax reallocation and of improvements in tax collection did not die with the defeat of the Bennett government in 1935. The Depression had made it the object of ever-widening interest and concern. At its July 1933 Regina convention, for example, the CCF party endorsed a drastic extension of income, corporation, and inheritance taxes (steeply graduated according to ability to pay), and the institution of more efficient systems for their collection.[6] Mackenzie King moved rapidly on this front after his election victory by calling a Dominion-provincial conference, which took place in December.[7]

Preparations for Another Conference

By November 19, 1935, when federal officials assembled under the chairmanship of Labour Minister Norman Rogers to consider an agenda and the preparation of conference papers, many provinces had already suggested topics.[8] One was the distribution of the income tax fields. As a consequence the topic "Questions relating to the Financial Relations between the Dominion and Provinces, and to Taxation" was placed high on the conference agenda, and Clark and R.H. Coats, the Dominion statistician, were asked to prepare the necessary background and policy papers.

In retrospect, less effort appears to have been spent devising policy and preparing papers for the conference than planning and organizing it. Mackenzie King's consultative approach was emphasized and repeatedly contrasted with Bennett's brusque treatment of the provinces to the point that form seemed to become more important than content. The conference was broken down into six subconferences, including mining, the tourist trade, agriculture, unemployment relief, constitutional issues, and financial questions. Each had its topics for discussion, its allotted ministers, its advisers, and its secretaries. And save for the conference's opening morning and closing afternoon sessions, the federal and provincial delegations were destined to spend the five days of the conference in one or another of the subconferences.

Dominion-provincial financial relations were allotted to the subconference on financial questions, and four federal ministers were assigned: Dunning, who, as minister of finance, served as chairman; J. L. Ilsley, minister of national revenue; T. A. Crerar, minister of the interior and of immigration and colonization; and W. D. Euler, minister of trade and commerce. Clark, Elliott, and David Sim served as the subconference's advisers and Kenneth Eaton and George Lowe of the Department of Finance as its secretaries.

For the new federal ministry and the five new provincial ministries, the conference and its subconferences were designed to provide the novices not with remedies but rather with an education in the nature of the multiple afflictions besetting Canada's governments and people.

Clark appears to have devoted his main effort to verbally enlightening his minister and his minister's colleagues about the dire economic condition of the country. Few background papers seem to have been prepared. A paper on the duplication of income taxation and its possible remedy gives evidence that the discussions at the 1933 conference had had an impact on federal officials.[9] For after reaffirming the belief that income taxes were the soundest and most desirable form of taxation, the paper conceded that the personal income tax was too important a source of revenue for either the Dominion or the provinces to forgo. The paper suggested centralizing in one administrative staff the responsibility for determining for all governments the taxable income of each Canadian taxpayer and for collecting this tax for the Dominion and those provinces that wanted to impose it. In such circumstances the provinces might either enact their own tax schedules or express their taxes as a percentage of the federal tax. While the paper preferred the latter, the tax on tax approach, it conceded that the practical difficulty of synchronizing changes in federal and provincial rates might make it desirable to adopt the tax on taxable income approach.

The paper adopted a different position on the corporation income tax. Its authors felt that provincial rate rivalry and disagreement over allocating corporate incomes among provinces argued strongly against the use of this tax by the provinces; instead, the Dominion should try to get the provinces to relinquish their constitutional right to impose it. The Dominion could "buy out" the provinces by paying them either a specified percentage of the yield of the federal corporation income tax or a specified percentage of federally determined corporate taxable incomes. The yield of either method would be distributed among provinces on a formula related, not to corporate profits, but to population.

These suggestions were not picked up and presented to the provinces by Dunning or Ilsley, although they would be on another occasion. During the subconference discussions, however, the rising interest of the provinces in imposing personal income taxes and in having them collected by the federal authorities became apparent. Whereas at the 1933 conference Quebec had professed no interest in a personal income tax, its treasurer, R. F. Stockwell, now thought that all provinces would have to levy such a tax and that federal collection would make for equitable taxation. After reiterating his predecessor's claim that the income tax fields belonged to the provinces, the B.C. minister of finance, John Hart, went on to recommend that, in the interest of economy, efficiency, and simplicity of administration, one income tax should be collected on behalf of both federal and provincial governments. The premier and secretary-treasurer of Prince Edward Island, W. M. Lea, proposed that the federal government collect his province's income tax, and his counterpart in Saskatchewan, W. J. Patterson, wanted the federal government to levy, collect, and redistribute both personal and corporation income taxes for provinces.[10] The receptive disposition of the federal ministers was abruptly disturbed when Premier Mitchell Hepburn of Ontario inquired point-blank if the federal government would be prepared to collect a province's personal income tax if it should enact the necessary legislation. Taken aback, Dunning and Ilsley, in a flurry of apparently concurring remarks, allowed themselves to go no further than to say the suggestion was worthy of investigation.

The query, however, generated an ultimate response. After an interval of continued discussion had allowed whispered consultation between federal ministers and officials, Dunning made a suggestion: the subconference should establish a continuing committee to give further study to proposals such as that of Hepburn and to formulate recommendations for possible action. Premier Bracken of Manitoba proposed that the continuing committee consist of the ministers of finance and treasurers of the federal and provincial governments, and the subconference concurred. The continuing committee was immediately assigned the task of drafting the subconference's report to the conference and of determining the date and place of further meetings.

While the subconference reported that no agreement had been reached on transfer of tax sources, it did affirm that there had been general agreement that cooperative administrative arrangements should be worked out that would reduce both taxpayers' inconvenience and the costs of collection. The report concluded that the continuing committee should constitute a permanent committee to continue the discussion on tax matters with a view to recommending appropriate government action. The conference accepted the report and agreed that the permanent committee should meet again in Ottawa in January 1936 before the federal and provincial legislatures assembled for their winter sessions.[11]

In the month between the conclusion of the conference and the reconvening of the Permanent Committee on Financial Questions on January 13, 1936, Ontario continued to pursue Hepburn's query. Would the federal government be prepared to collect a provincial personal income tax on Ontario's behalf? This concept was developed and pursued so rapidly that it seems probable that Hepburn had been contemplating such an innovation before he posed the question to Dunning and Ilsley at the conference. For, only four days after the conference ended, Hepburn announced that his government intended to pre-empt the personal income tax field from the municipalities, to impose a provincial personal income tax equivalent to 50 percent of the federal tax with effect for the 1935 year, and to have the federal income tax administration collect it if satisfactory arrangements could be made.[12] To make such arrangements, Hepburn sent to Ottawa his controller of finance, Chester S. Walters, and the secretary of the Ontario Budget Committee, Harold J. Chater. Two days later, on December 20, 1935, the *Toronto Globe* reported that on his return Walters had gone directly to a Cabinet meeting. After that meeting it was announced that the Ontario legislature would be summoned into session January 21 to enact a provincial personal income tax. When the Permanent Committee on Financial Questions met on January 13, it was revealed that Walters and Fraser Elliott had met three days earlier to review a draft personal income tax bill prepared by Ontario and to consider draft federal-provincial income tax forms prepared by National Revenue.

FEDERAL OFFER: PERSONAL INCOME TAX

At the meeting of the Permanent Committee on Financial Questions, no other province showed an immediate interest in adopting similar measures. This may have been partly due to the manner in which the Ontario arrangements were presented. Dunning, who invited Elliott to open the discussion on the unified collection of income taxes, had no doubt anticipated that Elliott would give a favourable presentation of the arrangements. But surprisingly Elliott criticized them: they would require the enactment of a provincial personal income tax act and continuing future amendments to ensure that the legislation would parallel in form and content the federal act. Instead he advocated an approach in which the federal government would, on a province's request, place a surtax on the federal tax within the province and remit the amount collected. The Ontario approach, Elliott felt, would endanger the secrecy of income tax administration and would increase the chances of complications and litigation that would hamper and undermine efficient tax administration. Elliott's presentation provoked surprise and annoyance. Chester Walters complained that, at their meeting three days earlier, Elliott had never raised the question of whether it would be preferable for the Dominion to impose an additional tax on behalf of the province or to have the province impose the tax and the federal administration collect it. Dunning was no less annoyed and broke into Walters's protest to assert bluntly that he would tolerate no doubt that the tax would be Ontario's, and though the federal administration might collect it, the province would have to impose it.[13]

Clark was as surprised as Dunning. For in papers he had prepared for his minister, he had recommended that any tax the Dominion agreed to collect for a province should be imposed by the province.[14] Clark had seen two alternative approaches. He preferred that the provinces accept the federal act's definition of taxable income and schedule of exemptions and impose a provincial tax expressed as a percentage of the federal tax. Alternatively, the provinces could enact the federal definition of taxable income and exemptions schedule but enact their own provincial rate schedule. In each case, the principle would be maintained that the provinces imposed their income tax on a basis accepted by themselves and that the federal government merely acted as a collection agency. If Elliott had thought that the Finance Department supported a provincial tax that took the form of a federally imposed surtax, Dunning had quickly shown otherwise. The discussion concluded with Dunning tabling a federal press release. The release stated that the Dominion agreed that the federal tax machinery might be used to collect provincial income taxes if those taxes were levied under provincial statutes and if the terms of each statute were acceptable to the Dominion.

Ontario's Personal Income Tax

The day after the press release was issued, Harry C. Nixon, the acting premier of Ontario and its provincial secretary, released copies of the draft Ontario Income Tax Act to the press and to members of the Ontario legislature. An accompanying statement revealed that the provincial personal income tax would supersede the existing municipal personal income taxes, apply to the 1935 year, and be collected by the federal Department of National Revenue. The Ontario legislature met on February 11, 1936—after a three-week delay owing to the death of King George V—and the next day the Income Tax Act of Ontario was introduced and given first reading. After some protracted procedural wrangling from the Conservative opposition, the bill cleared the Assembly and received Royal Assent on May 2, 1936.[15] National Revenue, which had been standing by, at once billed Ontario residents for both their 1935 federal and provincial personal income taxes.

The federal-provincial legal niceties took more time to complete. In June, Parliament empowered the Cabinet to enter into an agreement not merely with Ontario but with any province to collect such income taxes as it imposed.[16] On July 2, 1936, Ilsley and Hepburn signed the Canada-Ontario agreement under which the minister of national revenue and the commissioner of income tax for Canada undertook to exercise, in the place and stead of the treasurer and controller of revenue of Ontario, all the power and duties conferred on them by the Income Tax Act of Ontario.[17]

The Ontario legislation was essentially a copy of the federal income tax legislation. Aside from imposing its tax only on the incomes of persons resident or carrying on a business in Ontario, that act accorded the same personal exemptions and dependants' deductions as did the federal legislation. It imposed a rate schedule equivalent to one-half of the federal schedule and, with two exceptions, the income subject to tax was the same as under the federal act. The exceptions were that interest income from federal World War I Victory bonds, which was tax exempt under federal law, was subject to provincial tax just as it had been under Ontario municipal income tax bylaws, and that the federal income tax was deductible from each Ontario taxpayer's income before that income was subject to the Ontario tax. Under the July agreement, Ontario was to pay 2 percent of the provincial tax collected to cover collection costs for 1936–37, subject to such subsequent adjustments as the two parties agreed to.[18]

Federal Occupancy: Corporation Income Tax Field

On the question of federal-provincial arrangements governing corporate income tax, the federal policy approach was quite different. When the topic was raised in the January 1936 meeting of the Permanent Committee on Financial Questions, Dunning did not risk inviting an official to present the federal position but opened the discussion himself. He stated bluntly that the existing taxation of corporations was most unsatisfactory. Provinces were levying taxes on corporate net profits as well as on bases such as paid-up capital, gross income, premium income, and track mileage, and the resulting complexity and duplication created an inconvenience and expense out of all proportion to the yield of the tax. To end the complexity and expense, Dunning said that the federal government, in exchange for the provinces' undertaking to abandon this field, would be prepared to allot them a portion of the federal income tax on corporations.[19] This proposition had first been presented to Dunning by his department officials before the 1935 conference and again by Clark before this meeting.[20]

Dunning had not expected that any concrete decisions would be made at that time, but he had hoped that the difficulties in the corporate tax field would be sufficiently appreciated that a uniform system under one authority would ultimately be put in place. He thought that, to be successful, a uniform tax required all provinces to enter the joint arrangement, and he did not conceal his belief that while such a tax would be more productive, its allocation among the provinces would make it less lucrative to the central provinces than their current corporate tax structure. While R. F. Stockwell, treasurer of Quebec, and A. L. Macdonald, premier of Nova Scotia, in particular voiced doubts that their provinces would be prepared to sacrifice their independent taxing authority, the provinces did agree to cooperate in providing data from which Dunning might refine the federal proposal. The permanent committee accepted Dunning's suggestion that Clark collect such data. Each provincial treasurer was to provide Clark with an outline of each corporation tax his province imposed, its yield over several years, and the cost of its collection. From this data, Clark was expected to determine the increase in the federal corporation income tax rate that would have to be imposed to produce the same revenues the provinces had been receiving from their own taxes.

NATIONAL FINANCE COMMITTEE

Some eleven months passed before the income tax endeavours set in motion by the permanent committee were again considered at the federal-provincial level. The occasion was the first and, as events proved, the only meeting of the National Finance Committee, which Dunning had planned as the successor of the permanent committee.[21]

Fraser Elliott and Chester Walters had been invited to describe their initial experiences with the federal collection of the Ontario personal income tax.[22] Elliott had also been asked to give his views on the extension of the collection arrangement to embrace provinces that had adopted payroll tax deductions or different personal and dependants' allowances from those of the federal act.

Walters's report was all that the federal ministers and administrators could have wished. He said that the collection of the Ontario income tax had been conducted in a faultless manner. He referred to, but did not highlight (as had the head of the Ontario delegation, Mines Minister Paul Leduc, the previous day) the adverse impact on provincial revenues caused by the method chosen for imposing the provincial tax, no doubt because it was a decision with which he had been closely associated. The shortcoming in the system was evident in the fact that a provincial tax schedule set at 50 percent of the federal schedule was producing but 30 percent of the federal revenue.[23] While the shortfall was partly due to the fact the federal tax returns included tax for prior years to which the Ontario tax did not apply, it was mainly due to the fact that the Ontario law allowed a taxpayer, in determining provincial taxable income, to deduct from federal taxable income his federal tax payable.

Where Walters's appraisal of the Ontario-Canada tax collection arrangements had been complimentary, Elliott's was fulsome.[24] He became so expansive that, contrary to the position he and his minister, Ilsley, had taken at the January meeting of the permanent committee, he assured the provinces that if they accepted the federal definition of income, it mattered not if they adopted different personal exemptions or rate schedules. He asserted that his staff could administer provincial income tax systems in which the employer deducted provincial tax from employee payrolls. With this statement he stored up trouble for the future, as Manitoba was contemplating entering a tax collection agreement. Manitoba Premier Bracken, Treasurer Stuart Garson, and Attorney-General W. J. Major subsequently repeatedly sought and were given assurances by Elliott that his staff were both able and prepared to collect provincial income taxes that involved tax deductions from payrolls, a feature such as Manitoba's tax on wages. On this point Elliott later had to renege.

FEDERAL CORPORATE TAX OFFER

When the National Finance Committee turned to corporate tax arrangements, Clark presented the results of the study undertaken by the Finance Department after consultation with the provinces.[25] He proposed that all provinces should enter a tax collection agreement, for a fixed term of years, under which the Dominion would impose and collect on their behalf a uniform tax on corporation profits and certain other specific, though not necessarily uniform, corporate taxes. The latter category might include a universal tax on the capital of all corporations and special taxes on certain classes of corporations such as banks, insurance companies, trust and loan companies. Clark felt that the Dominion should limit the corporate taxes it imposed on the provinces' behalf to those currently levied by all of them; they could continue to exploit those taxes which were not widely imposed, such as those on telephone, gas, and electricity companies. Clark also felt that the special corporate tax rates the Dominion imposed for the provinces need not be uniform. The Dominion could levy higher rates for those provinces, such as British Columbia, which might suffer a revenue decline with the uniform national corporation income tax rate.

Dunning and Clark insisted that the proposal had to receive universal provincial acceptance, and it quickly became apparent that this was unlikely to be realized. Maurice Duplessis, the recently elected premier of Quebec, made it clear that his province intended to continue to collect its own corporate taxes, and Chester Walters and John Hart doubted that Ontario or British Columbia would be prepared to vacate this tax field or abandon any of their special corporation taxes. Clark was disappointed, if not surprised. While he continued to encourage a federal collection system, he made little further effort to have the provinces standardize their corporation income taxes or their other corporation taxes. As directed by the National Finance Committee, he did ask in January 1937 each province to name a representative to a committee to consider the practicality of the proposal, but he took no steps to have the committee assemble when Mackenzie King announced the government's intention to appoint a royal commission to investigate the constitutional allocation of tax revenues and of governmental functions. Nor did he or Dunning take steps to reassemble the National Finance Committee. It was the provinces, rather than the federal authorities, that eventually initiated the steps which led to further federal collection of provincial income taxes.

MANITOBA TAX COLLECTION AGREEMENT

Despite Elliott's assurances at the National Finance Committee meeting that his organization was able and prepared to collect Manitoba's taxes, including its special 2 percent tax on wages and incomes, the collection arrangements took longer to implement and were less complete than Attorney-General Major had been led to expect. The arrangements, which did not become effective until January 1, 1938, applied to incomes earned in 1937 and included the collection of uncollected taxes, interest, and penalties of prior years. The delay in the effective date from that initially contemplated by Major was due to several factors. Before entering a tax collection agreement with Manitoba, the Department of National Revenue had thought it prudent that the province consolidate its income tax legislation, which had not been done since 1924. Because of the Bracken government's precarious majority, opposition members in the Manitoba legislature took advantage of the opportunity to make determined efforts to repeal the special 2 percent tax on wages, which, despite Fraser Elliott's assurances to the contrary, National Revenue showed a reluctance to collect.

The impasse was ultimately resolved. Manitoba consolidated its income tax legislation and National Revenue undertook to collect, along with the province's income taxes, that portion of the special 2 percent wages tax that applied to the incomes of the self-employed.[26] Manitoba employers were to continue to deduct the 2 percent tax from the wages and salaries of their employees and remit it directly to the province. Although there was a subsequent reduction of the wages tax to 1 percent, an increase in the graduated personal income tax, and an enactment of a graduated corporation income tax, Manitoba's income tax continued to be collected by the Department of National Revenue until 1942 when Manitoba, along with the other provinces, came under wartime tax rental arrangements.

Other Collection Agreements

The trend initiated by Ontario and Manitoba was to attract other provinces. In 1937 Prince Edward Island, with little prior consultation, decided to enter a tax collection agreement with the minister of national revenue, and in 1940 the new Liberal government of Quebec as well as the Yukon Territorial authorities followed suit.[27] Quebec and the Yukon, like Ontario, were entering the personal income tax field for the first time, while Prince Edward Island, like Manitoba, had been in the tax field for many years. Because Montreal and Quebec City had municipal income taxes, Quebec undertook to pre-empt the tax field for its sole occupancy, as Ontario had done in 1936 when it ended local income taxes in some two hundred municipalities.[28] As in Manitoba, National Revenue required Prince Edward Island to consolidate and revise existing income tax legislation before it would undertake collection, and, as a result, the arrangements there did not become effective until January 1, 1938. While the negotiation and administration of these agreements were primarily the work of Ilsley and Elliott in National Revenue, Clark had ensured that the Department of Finance remained associated with the arrangements. Each agreement provided that the remittance of the provincial taxes collected by National Revenue was to be under the jurisdiction of the deputy minister of finance.

The tax collection agreements with Quebec, the Yukon, and indeed all of the provinces did not last long. In 1941 provincial income tax legislation and tax collection agreements were rendered null and void when the federal government assumed sole occupancy of the income tax fields and replaced the existing tax collection agreements with negotiated tax rental agreements. A precedent had been set, however, and federal-provincial tax collection agreements were destined to re-emerge when the war and the postwar tax rental agreements came to an end.

Chapter Twelve

The Royal Commission on Dominion-Provincial Relations

The final episode in Dominion-provincial relations in the thirties was played out, not by governments, but by the Royal Commission on Dominion-Provincial Relations. The minister of finance, his department, and the Bank of Canada were instrumental in the creation of that commission, as described in chapter 10. In the early years of World War II, the department, a subsequent minister, and the prime minister were to agonize over what should be done about the commission's proposals. While the deputy minister of finance helped to steer the commissioners along what he considered the right lines as they planned their work, he chose not to submit a brief or present formal testimony to the commission.

Because Prime Minister King was preoccupied with other matters, there was a lag of six months between his announcement in February 1937 of the government's intention to set up a royal commission and the passage on August 14 of Order-in-Council P.C. 1908 appointing the commissioners and defining their terms of reference. In March and April, King was involved with Ontario and the United States over the St. Lawrence Seaway; in late April he attended the coronation of George VI and a meeting of Commonwealth prime ministers in London; then, with British encouragement, he went on to visit Germany and met briefly with Hitler. When he returned to Ottawa early in July, he was confronted with a serious crop failure in the Prairies and other problems. It was only then that he took the necessary decisions on the royal commission. In the meantime, however, Alex Skelton had somewhat impatiently had his Research Department at the Bank of Canada prepare detailed studies on the issues he believed the commission would have to consider.

The first two choices as commissioners, Newton Rowell,[1] chief justice of Ontario, and John Dafoe, the celebrated editor of the *Winnipeg Free Press*, came to Ottawa early in August 1937 to discuss the commission with the prime minister. During this visit, O. D. Skelton (the father of

Alex) had Rowell and Dafoe to dinner, along with W. C. Clark and Graham Towers of the Bank of Canada, to discuss the commission and its task; Alex Skelton was also there to meet the commissioners and to speak about the preparations he had put in hand.[2] The names of all the commissioners and their terms of reference were not announced until August 16 after the order-in-council appointing them was issued. In addition to Rowell, who was designated chairman, and Dafoe, the other three were Thibaudeau Rinfret, justice of the Supreme Court of Canada; R. A. Mackay, professor of government, Dalhousie University, Halifax; and H. F. Angus, professor of economics, University of British Columbia, Vancouver.[3] These five commissioners made up a strong, well-balanced team despite R. B. Bennett's criticism that they were "a pack of Grits."[4] Even the constantly critical *Canadian Forum* commented that it appeared King really intended that something be done about Dominion-provincial relations.[5] Two weeks after the commission's appointment, the government, on Clark's recommendation and with Rowell's approval, appointed Alex Skelton as secretary of the commission and director of research.

Under Rowell's leadership, the commission quickly got off to a good start. Rowell first called on all the provincial premiers, who at that early stage agreed to cooperate fully.[6] From late November 1937 until early May 1938, he presided over public hearings. In addition he guided the planning of a very extensive research program which had been drawn up by Alex Skelton and his assistant director of research, John Deutsch. This was the first royal commission in Canada to have a large research program. It involved many of the leading Canadian academics: twenty-seven persons were named in the commission's report as participants in research on economic matters and nine on constitutional and legal matters. Eighteen research papers were published, including the very valuable collection of public accounts prepared on a comparable basis for the Dominion and the nine provinces.

Early Activities

The commission held extensive formal hearings across Canada. Hundreds of witnesses appeared, although it did not accept individual witnesses unless they were invited or represented an organization. Many senior Dominion government officials gave evidence but, following what was to become the department's usual practice, no one appeared from the Department of Finance. Graham Towers, governor of the Bank of Canada appeared, gave a statement, and was questioned at some length.[7] The report acknowledges the assistance of many Ottawa officials in answering private inquiries, and in particular it mentions A. K. Eaton of Finance. His inclusion is understandable, for the field of taxation, his specialty, was one of the few areas not well represented in the long list of witnesses and in those doing research on the staff of the commission. In accordance with its terms of reference, the commission's report contained much argument on the various taxes, and it is unlikely that all this material came from Skelton or Deutsch, even with the help of the 1936 Grauer memorandum.[8] Although there is little of consequence in departmental records to indicate that Clark, Eaton, or other departmental officials submitted recommendations of substance to the commission, there is some suggestion that Eaton (and perhaps others) helped in summarizing and commenting upon briefs and some of the draft research reports that were submitted.

Unfortunately the commission soon suffered serious casualties. Rinfret, the Quebec representative, had to resign because of ill health only three months after his appointment and was replaced by Joseph Sirois, a leading notary and professor of constitutional and administrative law at Laval University. This was a serious loss, for Sirois lacked the legal and judicial experience and reputation of Rinfret. Much more damaging was the severe stroke suffered by Chief Justice Rowell early in May 1938, some nine months after he commenced work on the commission. In a telephone conversation in June, O. D. Skelton suggested to King that W. A. Mackintosh be added to the commission (the wording of King's diary is not clear, but the context indicates it was probably as a commissioner).[9] King objected, as he no doubt still associated Mackintosh with the recommendation of the National Employment Commission concerning federal relief to unemployed employables, which he had so disliked. He then made the shocking suggestion that in Rowell's absence O. D. Skelton and Clark be kept informed by Alex Skelton of what was going on so that the government might direct the commission when it was obviously wise to do so. In a memorandum to King in July, O. D. Skelton stated that Rowell was still unable to speak or write and "there seems practically no likelihood of his being able to take any part whatever in the organization and preparation of the Report of the Commission." He viewed it as a very serious situation because Rowell was the driving force of the commission. Dafoe had "knowledge and wisdom, breadth of view and power of exposition, but it may be doubted whether he has now the physical vigour necessary to pull the work of the Commission together and produce a report that will serve as the basis of all future discussions and revision of Dominion-Provincial relations. Each of the other members has a contribution to make, but none of them can fill the Chief Justice's role."[10]

These words were not to be taken lightly, particularly because they came from the prime minister's principal adviser whose son was the secretary of the commission. Although O. D. Skelton said it would be up to the government to decide whether to fill the gap, he implied that it should do so. As one possibility, he suggested Chief Justice Duff of the Supreme Court, who, he argued, had ability, prestige and "an increasingly national but objective point of view." As an alternative, Skelton also suggested R. B. Bennett (who had just stepped down as leader of the Opposition), saying: "I am aware of the widespread feeling, not confined to government circles, against his frequent partisan or personal bitterness, and also Mr. Dafoe's view. I think, however, he would rise to the occasion and be keen to do a crowning job for his country and for his own reputation before he retires completely to private life."[11] This last was too much for King. He noted, "Subject matter of memorandum discussed in Council. Thought inadvisable to appoint anyone. Last suggestion not approved. WLMK."[12]

Rowell's formal resignation as both chief justice of Ontario and chairman of the commission, was finally submitted on October 19, 1938. Over a month later it was accepted and Sirois was appointed chairman. No one replaced Rowell as the Ontario representative. Just how much influence Rowell had on the commission's report is difficult to determine. Some fifteen years later Angus wrote that the commission's opinion was unanimous, but he added, "Whether the Chairman would have concurred we do not know, for he had scrupulously discouraged any discussion of the evidence before the hearings were completed."[13]

Leadership

After Rowell had gone, the leadership of the commission was diffused for a time, and when Sirois was made chairman, he was not strong enough to provide effective guidance and control. In fact Alex Skelton was the key figure in both the research and the drafting of the report, though Angus and Mackay also worked on the draft. Skelton's work habits were irregular—prodigious at times and suspended at other times. Mackay's letters to his wife in October 1938 and Angus's memoirs both indicate recurrent friction with Skelton, despite their respect for his ability.[14] Angus and Mackay expected trouble in getting Sirois to accept the principles involved in the proposals they were being persuaded by Skelton to support, but in the end Sirois did not hold out or dissent.

It is very likely that Skelton really led the commission after Rowell collapsed. Skelton was a strong man, with strong opinions; he saw things as black or white with no shades of grey. He was intelligent, intuitive, and convivial to a fault. He was friendly but did not like compromisers. He was well informed, both from study and from his numerous contacts; he made up his mind quickly. He was a superb writer, as the report bears witness, for much of it must have been his own words.[15]

It was the research that Skelton organized and led, rather than the hearings, that formed the foundation for the commission's report. Although the exhibits and testimony are referred to frequently in the volume on recommendations, particularly those on jurisdiction and administration, as well as the claims and proposals advanced by provinces, the main fiscal analysis is derived from the research initiated by the commission. The main fiscal recommendations were based closely (in retrospect much too closely) on the Public Accounts for the fiscal years ending closest to December 1937, which are used in book 2 of the report to illustrate the effects of the proposals. They refer hardly at all to exhibits or testimony.

RECOMMENDATIONS

The main decisions of the commission, underlying the recommendations of the report, were reached before the outbreak of war, apparently by mid-1939. The report stated, "The Commission decided, after deliberation, to complete the Report exactly as it would have been completed had War not been declared."[16] This is understandable, and probably was the only practicable course, although it did have a considerable effect on the prospects for getting the report accepted. Writing in 1955, Commissioner Angus indicated something of the attitude of the commission in carrying out its terms of reference:

> The unanimous opinion [of the commission] as to the best way to effect certain purposes was in no sense a suggestion of the lines along which agreement could most readily be reached between the Government of Canada and the nine provincial governments; nor, strictly speaking, did our advice imply either approval or disapproval of the purposes designated in our instructions. But on both these points some common sense allowance must be made. We knew that our advice, if accepted, would be made the subject of negotiation and that it would be futile to advise anything utterly impracticable; and we did, as good Canadians, accept the purposes expressed in wide and flexible terms. None of us desired either complete legislative union, or separation of the provinces as independent states. Commissioners, like all counsellors, may be assailed by an insidious temptation to conserve a reputation for sagacity by avoiding recommendations likely to be unfavourably received or to prove politically impractical. It is not always easy to remember that even a government is entitled to frank advice, if it asks for it, and that the government is itself the best judge both of what it approves and of what is politically practicable.[17]

While there are many recommendations of the commission scattered through volume 2 of the report, the central fiscal recommendations, known as Plan 1, are of historical importance and are summarized here.

1. The Dominion government should assume full fiscal, administrative, and constitutional responsibility for providing aid for unemployed employable persons and their dependants. Unemployment insurance (to which the Liberal government was already committed in principle) should be implemented as the main means to achieve this aim. The government should also set up a national employment service as an essential element in carrying out this responsibility. Those unemployed employables who were not entitled to insurance benefits and could not get work should receive "unemployment aid." This recommendation was practically the same as that which had been recommended, conditionally, by the National Employment Commission and which had been referred to Rowell on the prime minister's instructions. The Plan would require constitutional amendments to implement it. It would also involve rather general associated responsibilities for the Dominion in maintaining, promoting, and stabilizing employment.[18]

2. The Dominion should assume the net debt service cost of the provinces as of a date to be specified. The gross debt would be taken over and replaced with Dominion obligations, preferably of identical terms and conditions. The Dominion would receive annually from each province a fixed sum equal to the interest (and presumably dividends and profits) received in a specified base year by the province on its investments. There were many detailed qualifications and terms related to this general recommendation, the most notable being that a part of the municipal debt of Quebec would also be assumed, as these municipalities carried out functions normally fulfilled by provincial authorities or agencies in other provinces. One of the main purposes of this debt takeover was to enable the fiscal needs of each province to be calculated on the basis of its future behaviour without any need to allow for the burden of past deadweight debts or "undue extravagance." After the adoption of this recommendation, future direct and guaranteed borrowing by the provincial governments and their agencies and municipalities would normally be permitted only "in lawful money of Canada."[19] Borrowing in foreign currencies would not be allowed unless special permission was granted by the Dominion on the advice of what the commission called a Finance Commission. And if the cost of servicing a loan was to be taken into account in calculating future fiscal grants, the loan would have to be approved before issue by the Finance Commission, which would determine the fiscal grants.

3. The Dominion should assume the obligation to pay national adjustment grants to provincial governments whose fiscal needs required them. These grants would be calculated (and were initially calculated by the commission itself) to be enough to permit the province, if it wished, and its municipalities,

to provide education and welfare services equivalent in quality, although not necessarily in cost, to the national average of such services, to make developmental expenditures at their provincial 1928–31 average level, and to balance its budget, if it wished, without having taxation (provincial and municipal) appreciably exceed the national average in relation to income (in the economic "national income" sense). The grants would never be reduced below their initial level but might be increased after a review every five years by the independent, advisory Finance Commission. Emergency grants to meet extraordinary conditions that were clearly temporary, such as crop conditions in Saskatchewan, would also be paid on the advice of the same commission. All existing subsidies whether payable under the BNA Act or Dominion legislation would be terminated, including even those paid to provinces not likely to qualify for national adjustment grants, such as Ontario and British Columbia.

4. Under the constitution the Dominion should be given the sole right to levy personal income taxes, corporation income taxes and other specific corporation taxes, and succession duties. The provinces and municipalities would then be excluded from these tax fields. The Dominion would, however, accept a moral obligation to respect their remaining revenue sources, which would include real property taxes, gasoline taxes, automobile licences, profits and taxes on liquor sales, and revenues from the public domain. The commission argued against the use of sales taxes by the provinces but implied the Dominion would use such a tax. The Dominion would also be obligated to rebate to the provinces 10 percent of all profits from mining, including petroleum development, and from smelting and refining of native provincial mineral products.

These four points, which were the essentials of Plan 1, were considered and debated at length by governments and a host of other people, experts, politicians, and laymen. It was a radical prescription, persuasively set forth against a background of history and analysis the like of which Canadians had never seen. The document as a whole was recognized even by its critics, such as the distinguished economist and historian Harold Innis, as one that "should be read by all students of government in Canada."[20]

But despite the fact that the report was and still is a widely read Canadian classic, very few of its recommendations were put into effect. Some of them were reflected in the *Proposals of the Government of Canada* to the 1945 Dominion-Provincial Conference on Reconstruction, but these too were not implemented. Although it did have an important but indirect effect in leading to tax rental agreements, the report and its proposals for national adjustment grants did not, however, have any significant influence on the introduction of equalization grants in 1957.[21]

The central proposals were never a negotiable package. Fundamentally they were not fair to the provinces, or at least to the stronger provinces, such as Ontario and British Columbia, whose support would have been essential for their adoption, since constitutional amendments would have been required.

Essentially they were non-negotiable because the whole approach from which they emerged, despite being rich in research, assiduous in analysis, and elegant in presentation, looked backward, not forward. There was no consideration of the effects of the proposed changes on provincial finances in times of prosperity. There was no analysis of the impact of inflation on the settlement proposed, although inflation was always associated with major wars and one had just begun. There was no appraisal of the political appeal which the progressive personal income tax and succession duties would have for provincial governments compared with the other taxes the commission so denigrated. As a bargain it was never a starter, particularly since the Dominion had decided to bring in unemployment insurance with or without it, which would greatly reduce the amount of relief payable by the provinces in future. Yet the transfer of relief was the main carrot offered the provinces in Plan 1.

The commission considered some alternatives to Plan 1 in chapter 6 of its recommendations on public finance. These alternatives took as their starting point the recommendation of the National Employment Commission that full responsibility for assistance to the employable unemployed should be transferred to the Dominion, in addition to unemployment insurance. This was the most obvious need that emerged from the experience of the 1930s. The commission concluded that the assumption of this responsibility alone would be impracticable for the Dominion government and inadequate as a comprehensive system compared with the favoured Plan 1. It considered some possible additions to that alternative Plan, such as the national adjustment grants, but without looking seriously for constructive answers to the problems raised. Rereading its recommendations and arguments leaves one with the feeling that the commission was so enamoured with the perfection and permanence of its Plan 1 that it was unwilling to give serious consideration to any less sweeping plan, even if it might be more acceptable to the provinces and involve fewer constitutional changes. Fortunately the pressures of war and then the political compromises of peacetime enabled the federal system to work out satisfactory solutions to these severe problems of provincial finance, without invoking constitutional restraints upon either the provinces' borrowing or their taxing powers.

Chapter Thirteen

Organization, Management, Recollections, and Reflections

When W.C. Clark took charge in November 1932, it does not appear that he had any plan for reorganizing or strengthening the Finance Department, apart from establishing a central bank to take over the monetary functions.[1] But he knew that the Canadian economy was in desperate straits, that more than monetary policy would be needed, and he expected to play a role in advising on policy and possibly in putting it into effect. His actions in organizing and staffing the department evolved from these beliefs, from the decisions of the government affecting the department, and from the problems he encountered as time went on. Clark's own view of the general role of the department was much the same as the one Courtney had expounded and applied as deputy minister in the 1880s: it should divest itself of operating responsibilities so it could be a "Department of Supervision" and concern itself with policy and the performance of others.[2] Clark had two opportunities, arising from the establishment of the Bank of Canada, to apply his view on a large scale, and a third minor one. A very large emergency administrative task was also thrust upon the department in 1934, and another was put into effect upon his advice to the government. Meanwhile, he engaged, for his own staff and that of the commissioner of tariffs, a few economists who with him formed the nucleus of a team to deal with policy problems, and he began to recruit regularly bright, young university graduates to be trained as competent officers.

Changes in Organization, 1933–1939

Among the changes in the organization of the Finance Department from 1933 until the outbreak of war in September 1939 were a few that did not affect the department directly but widened the responsibilities of the minister of finance. The appointment of the Tariff Board was such a change.

It had been authorized by 1931 legislation but was implemented only in February 1933 when the three members of the board were appointed. Because of its special role and powers the board was a court of record and not part of the Finance Department. The existence of the Tariff Board ultimately reduced the load on the commissioner of tariffs in the department, Hector McKinnon, though in the early years of its work he acted as its secretary and in other advisory capacities.

The second major change in the organization of the department during this period was that required to implement the Farmers' Creditors Arrangement Act, starting in July 1934. Hundreds of official receivers had to be appointed and it was also necessary to appoint a registrar for each Board of Review, as well as a judge, as chairman of the board, and two commissioners. M. A. MacPherson did a prodigious job in finding people within a few months to fill these positions,[3] no doubt assisted by unemployment, the political network, and the liberty of being released, by statute, from the formalities of the Civil Service Act. Members of the Boards of Review were paid fees for their services as were the official receivers, some apparently on a monthly or annual basis, and were not regarded as employees of the Department of Finance. Indeed many of the official receivers worked in other positions, as specifically permitted by the act. The department maintained a small staff in Ottawa to administer the act.

The beginning of a third small but significant change took place in 1934 with the appointment of A. K. Eaton as taxation investigator to work on tax measures in preparation for the budget. His arrival did not lead to any formal change in the rather loose organization of the department during the thirties, but the function expanded during the war and was reflected in the postwar organizational structure.

After the enactment of the Dominion Housing Act in 1935, a Housing Branch to administer it was set up in the Finance Department. The organization began slowly; in October 1935 only its director, Frank Nicholls, an architect, was appointed. An assistant architect was hired in mid-1936 and a young economist, Harvey Perry, was assigned to work with Nicholls. The branch grew rapidly in 1937 and 1938 and by 1939 it had a staff of forty-nine, a third of whom were architects.[4]

Administration of the Old Age Pension Act, which involved checking provincial regulations and practices, and auditing expenditures of which the Dominion was to pay 75 percent, was transferred from the Department of Labour to the Department of Finance in 1935. The Department of Labour had devoted little resources to it. In Finance it was placed under the supervision of J. Wilke MacFarlane, an experienced accountant, and by April 1939 his unit included twelve persons, chiefly clerks working under the supervision of two accountants.

Offsetting these additions were two major and one minor transfer of units out of the department. The first was caused by the establishment of the Bank of Canada, for it, like other central banks, was to issue currency notes, not the government. Consequently the Currency Branch, with 120 employees, was transferred to the bank on March 11, 1935, when it began operations. A small number of vault staff, which looked after security deposits, remained with the department. C. E. Campbell, who had been comptroller of currency, became the head of the Currency Division of the bank. The second move was delayed until the bank had large enough quarters to make it possible. On April 1, 1938, the department's Loans and Interest Branch became the bank's Public Debt Division, with M. G. Anderson still in charge.[5] The transfer of these functions was explicitly provided for in the Bank of Canada Act. As Clark had been the chief author of that act, these moves were in accordance with his wishes.

The third transfer, that of the superintendent of bankruptcy and his small staff to the Department of the Secretary of State, was done on January 25, 1939, by an order-in-council under the Public Service Rearrangement and Transfer of Duties Act. Since the secretary of state's department already administered the Companies Act, the Patent Act, the Copyright Act, and the Trade Mark Act, all varieties of commercial and corporate law, this move provided a more suitable departmental environment for the superintendent of bankruptcy than that at the Department of Finance. The transfer also had the advantage of relieving the minister and deputy minister of finance of unnecessary minor responsibilities.

THE ORGANIZATION IN 1939

The organization of the Finance Department in April 1939 is outlined in chart 2, which is based upon a more detailed chart of that date prepared by the Organization Branch of the Civil Service Commission.[6] It reflects the main changes just described. It also reflects the separation of certain staff functions, such as the central registry and the supplies office. The personnel office consisted of a mere records clerk at that time; W. C. Ronson, in his role as assistant deputy minister, in effect served as the main personnel officer, delegating to his senior clerks at the Treasury Board the explanation of the personnel regulations. The financial staff function, as it related to the department itself, was more dispersed and was largely concentrated on preparing the Estimates, which usually involved the deputy minister himself, assisted by the accountants and Bill Smellie, the clerk of Estimates for the Treasury Board.

In comparing chart 2 with chart 1 for November 1932, it will be noted that the largest increases in the department up to 1939 came from the addition of the Housing Branch and the growth in the staff of the Mint

CHART 2

DEPARTMENT OF FINANCE, APRIL 1939

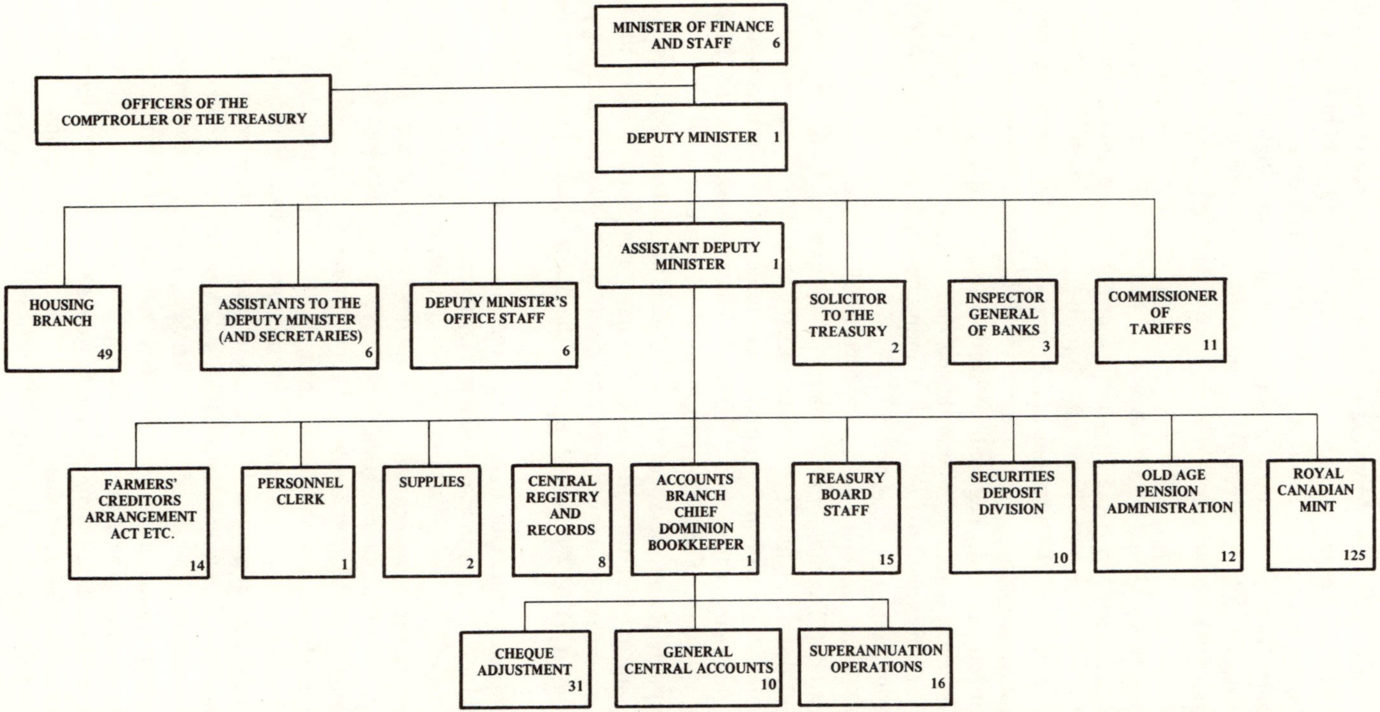

Drawn by R. B. Bryce from data in a detailed chart by the Organization Branch of the Civil Service Commission, plus auditor general's report for 1939–40.

Total number of persons: 330.

from 83 to 125. The Mint expanded partly because of the addition in 1936 of a gold refinery to serve the rapidly growing gold mining industry and partly because of the increased demand for coins. The staff of the Treasury Board doubled; it is noteworthy that half of the staff in 1939 were stenographers, needed to handle the very heavy task of typing accurately the hundreds of pages of cases placed before the ministers each week.

Between 1932 and 1939 the staff of the commissioner of tariffs also increased, from two to ten. The most important change was the appointment in 1936, by separate open civil service competitions, of two "tariff investigators," W. J. Callaghan and Arthur Annis, who had some experience or postgraduate education in the trade field. Annis worked with Hector McKinnon on trade negotiations during the late thirties, as mentioned in chapter 5, while Callaghan delved into the intricacies of the customs tariff and its relation to Canadian industries. Clerks and stenographers made up the rest of the increase.[7]

Two units declined in size between 1932 and 1939: the Cheque Adjustment Division, the dreariest of routine clerical work, and the administration of the Superannuation Act and related acts, routine work but some of it involving complicated statutes where mistakes were easily and often made. There is no evidence to indicate reasons for the reductions.

On the staff of the department in 1939 were a number of recently appointed, young clerks grade 4, besides the older experienced clerks who had advanced to this level. The new appointments were the result of a praiseworthy innovation by the Civil Service Commission, supported by Ronson. The 1934 annual report of the commission explains that policy:

> Reference was made in last year's report to a proposal to make some additions to staff in the middle or higher grades as is the case in the British Civil Service, and this proposal, with the conditions attendant upon it, has now been sanctioned by the Treasury Board. The Commission, therefore, proposes shortly to advertise open competitive examinations for a limited number of appointments as Clerk, Grade 4, requiring graduation from a university of recognized standing and much higher qualifications in general than are usually prescribed for a purely clerical position. It is true that many positions are now advertised requiring university graduation, and many new employees of a high order are imported into the Service. They are, however, usually in the professional and technical classes and have little connection with the administrative phase of the work. The present proposal is to make these administrative appointments to departments which have been gradually weakened through the loss of higher grade officials by death,

resignation or retirement and the lack of suitable employees to replace them.[8]

The first of these new graduates to enter the department was Harvey Perry—a very successful appointment indeed. He demonstrated outstanding ability during the war and for ten years after as Eaton's chief assistant on tax matters. He later became director of the Canadian Tax Foundation and one of Canada's best-known writers on taxation. Another half-dozen graduates in this category were appointed during the period up to 1940 and were moved about by Ronson to gain experience. He brought most of them into the Treasury Board staff as he needed them.[9]

Working Relationships

Something must be said about the relationships of the units in the Finance Department to the minister, deputy minister, and assistant deputy minister. The comptroller of the Treasury, Watson Sellar, reported directly to the minister when he had reason to do so, though this was not very often. Much more frequently he communicated with the Treasury Board, through Ronson as its de facto secretary, with whom he had close and friendly relations. His relations with Clark were cooler and generally at arm's length.

Chart 2 shows the commissioner of tariffs reporting to the deputy minister, rather than directly to the minister as he did before Clark's arrival. The commissioner took his instructions on administrative matters from the deputy minister and discussed questions on the preparation of the budget with the deputy minister, but he took his instructions directly from the minister or prime minister on trade negotiations. During the 1936 trade negotiations with the British, for example, McKinnon, usually with the other negotiators, generally met directly with the minister of finance, and, during the trilateral negotiations in Washington in 1938, with the Cabinet or even the prime minister alone.

Among the statutory duties and powers of the inspector general of banks was the requirement to inspect each bank at least once a year and report the results to the minister. He also probably informed the deputy minister about the reports. Although he was not responsible to the deputy minister to the extent that other officers in the department were, however, in the normal course of administration and of discussion of policies on the banks, and the revision of the Bank Act, the inspector general was responsible to the deputy minister as a matter of practice. It should be noted, parenthetically, that the salary of the inspector general—set at $15,000 a year when he was appointed in 1924, a salary substantially above those of deputy ministers at that time—was significantly higher than that of Clark as the deputy minister of finance in the thirties, though both his workload and general competence were lower than Clark's.

As illustrated in chart 2, a number of units reported directly to the deputy minister, Clark, rather than through the assistant deputy minister, Ronson. This arrangement differs from that in the chart prepared by the Civil Service Commission, which shows none reporting directly to Clark, except through Ronson, and a few, including the Farmers' Creditors Arrangement Act, reporting directly to the minister. Chart 2 takes into account the author's personal knowledge both of individuals and of their interrelationships at the time. The Housing Branch, for example, was Clark's own creation and he took some direct interest in its activities and relations with the financial institutions; he dealt directly with Nicholls.[10] The same was true in regard to the commissioner of tariffs and the solicitor to the Treasury. It was necessarily the case with the group described on the chart as assistants to the deputy minister, who had no chief other than Clark himself.

It will be noted in chart 2 that most units of the department, including the Mint, are shown as reporting to the assistant deputy minister. Since Ronson spent most of his time on Treasury Board matters, it is doubtful that he gave much time or attention to supervising the administration of these units. They probably came to him on personnel matters and for money. He ran his own staff and the department on an austere standard, which was what ministers desired him to do in the public service generally as the de facto secretary of the Treasury Board. His successor in that role in 1947 felt that more efficiency and effectiveness could be obtained by some changes that were not so conspicuously austere.

Assistants to the Deputy Minister

The group labelled assistants to the deputy minister in chart 2 includes a number of individuals whom Clark had selected to assist him directly in dealing with economic subjects and policy formulation. Clark's first known effort to secure an assistant of this kind was unsuccessful. He was impressed with the performance of Louis Rasminsky at the World Monetary and Economic Conference in the summer of 1933. Rasminsky, a young Canadian economist, was a member of the economic section of the League of Nations Secretariat. In November 1933 Clark wrote offering him a position in the department, one that O. D. Skelton described as "a minor post." Rasminsky declined. In December 1939 at a conference in Philadelphia Clark approached him again and persuaded him to visit Ottawa. This time he accepted a position in the Bank of Canada on April 1, 1940, to work for the Foreign Exchange Control Board.[11]

The first major appointment of an assistant to Clark came as a result of luck. Kenneth Eaton, a Nova Scotian, had served in World War I and then earned a B.A. at Acadia University, a B.Sc. in economics at London, and a Ph.D. at Harvard. In late 1933 he applied in one of the regular competitions for External Affairs officers. He qualified and, by reason of his war service preference, headed the list. It was found that he had specialized in taxation at Harvard. O. D. Skelton called his case to Clark's attention. The Civil Service Commission approved his appointment to Finance, first in a vacant clerical position in January 1934, and, some months later, in a new position with the provocative title of "taxation investigator." Eaton quickly got to work on tax policy and tax legislation, a field in which Clark had had relatively little experience and expertise. Harvey Perry moved into the group to work with Eaton and learn the subject. On occasion, however, Clark would call directly on Perry to undertake a particular project.

Another member of this group was George Lowe, who had been an accounting assistant in the department before Clark arrived. Clark was impressed with his versatility and ability to get things done; he used Lowe as an administrative assistant and a troubleshooter on nonpolicy problems, and had him appointed a head clerk. Lowe was able to expedite administrative matters, which he did well enough to mask real deficiencies in the management of the department. He had neither the authority nor the inclination to plan or organize the department.

The solicitor to the Treasury was not strictly in this new group, as he occupied a special office that had been established many years before. When David Johnson succeeded R. B. Viets as solicitor, both his legal and general abilities enabled him to hold his own in the policy discussions that took place in Clark's office.

Personal Recollections

I was the last man appointed before World War II to the group I have described as assistants to the deputy minister, but I was not part of any planned organization. In the spring of 1937 I came to Ottawa from Harvard to ask Clark for a job. He suggested I join the staff of the recently announced Royal Commission on Dominion-Provincial Relations, but I wanted a continuing job in the Finance Department. He asked me then to send him a number of things I had written. I heard nothing from Clark until six or eight weeks later when he telephoned me a few hours after I had accepted an offer from the Sun Life Assurance Company in Montreal. Although he offered to call the president of Sun Life to obtain my release, I told him I wanted to fulfil my commitment. About ten months later he invited me to see him and offered me a job on a level with Eaton's if I would go through a formal selection process. I had to write a difficult examination paper on Canadian monetary questions, which Clark himself had set, and was interviewed by a civil service board that included Clark, the governor of the Bank of Canada, the superintendent of insurance, and the commissioner of customs. After passing this senior scrutiny, I left Sun Life and arrived in the department on the weekend of the Munich crisis, October 1, 1938. My first task that Saturday morning was to go to the External Affairs library to study war risk insurance for ships, as Canada faced a potential tie-up if the crisis continued.

I found the department in 1938 a congenial and often exciting place to work. Eaton, Johnson, Perry, Lowe, and I all reported directly to Clark and could be, and often were, summoned at any time by an old-fashioned buzzer. We were expected to be versatile, to be capable of studying emerging problems, and to provide background papers and even advice. We had no junior assistants or library in the department, but we had a very stimulating boss. He never held regular staff meetings, and there was no indoctrination. In my own case, he gave me a number of quite interesting projects during the eleven months before the war, some in connection with the April 1939 budget, some on other legislation, on international matters, and on the domestic economy. There was also drudgery. Clark thought that all the letters to the minister and the department should be answered. It fell to my lot to prepare answers to scores of letters from monetary "cranks," some of which contained intricate monetary heresies and a variety of "social credit" plans, which required an understanding of economics to deal seriously with them. I found it tedious; these cranks were flattered by a response and wanted to continue the correspondence, but until the war intervened, Clark insisted on studied answers and continued correspondence.

Despite the obvious and ominous signs of approaching war, we were devoting most of our efforts to domestic issues of the day and were under no pressure to develop contingency plans for war. In this respect Finance was no different from the other departments. I was not aware of the plan being formulated at the Bank of Canada for foreign exchange control. Eaton and Johnson were doing some work, but not much, on problems of defence procurement and the need to avoid excessive profits on munitions contracts. This activity ended in futility. But Eaton and I, in that last prewar summer, were able to find an afternoon each week to play golf and to take vacations before late August brought the crisis to a head and plunged us into frenzied activity.

From what I have said, it is clear that most of the department in 1939 was still engaged in routine tasks, but three groups were working on policy issues. One was the group around Clark himself that I have described. The second involved Hector McKinnon and his two or three senior assistants.

The third included the new, young graduates, classed and paid as senior clerks, in the Treasury Board staff under Ronson, notably E. B. Armstrong, who was soon dealing with defence expenditures, and C. J. Mackenzie, who was working on government personnel measures.

It is evident in retrospect that, with the exception of the Housing Branch, Clark did little that was systematic and sustained to organize and staff the department. He was almost always preoccupied with policy problems and innovation. In this area he was very good and worked himself frequently to exhaustion, which was relieved to some degree by conversations with visitors from the business or academic world. But he did not organize to spare himself or find anyone in whom he had confidence to organize and manage the department for him. It is only fair to recall that Clark was frequently in pain with a bad back during those years. He smoked cigarettes endlessly and gulped down aspirin during the day. His work was his release from pain and perhaps, too, from anxiety over the dangers of a war that we could do nothing to prevent.

When his innovations required an institution to be set up, Clark could and would put his mind to it, as he did slowly with the Housing Branch and, of course, pre-eminently, with the Bank of Canada. In 1939 he was working, as noted, on establishing the Central Mortgage Bank, but he tied its administration to the Bank of Canada, not to his department. After the war started, he took a new interest in organizing the government as a whole for war, usually by setting up new agencies, staffed largely from outside the public service, but he devoted little attention to organizing the department itself for war. When the crises came, however, time after time he somehow managed to meet them by superhuman efforts on his own part and by bringing in a few men he knew to be able and trustworthy, such as Bill Mackintosh, Walter Gordon, and Mitchell Sharp.

Two tributes to Clark's prewar abilities and achievements remain in my memory. One is the fact that his portrait hangs in a place of honour among those of past governors in the boardroom of the Bank of Canada, mute but eloquent testimony to the respect he was accorded as the prime mover in the creation of the bank. The second is a story to be found in an excellent but unpublished book on R. B. Bennett written by his private secretary, Rod Finlayson.[12] It recounts how Charles Dunning, who had been out of Ottawa during the Bennett regime, was surprised to find this "academic" as his deputy when he again became minister of finance. He expressed some concern to Mackenzie King. Then, in the words of Finlayson:

> "Foxy Old Grampy" King telephoned R. B. and the conversation as related to me by the latter ran:
>
> "Bennett, there's a man in the Finance Department called Clarke

[*sic*]. What do you think of him?" "He's a good man," Bennett replied, "and the bankers hate him."

That set Clarke [*sic*] over all others and from then on King's door was open to him.

THE DEPARTMENT'S PERFORMANCE IN RETROSPECT

In 1867 the department got off to a good start under the strong, initial leadership of John Langton and Sir John Rose. The division of financial roles and responsibilities under the BNA Act was brought successfully into effect, though the final settlement of past accounts was long drawn out. The department's formal responsibilities were defined, but so broadly that they were of little guidance. In these early years the department was essentially an accounting and bookkeeping organization. It carried out ministers' decisions and the deputy minister audited the accounts of his own and other departments. These accounting functions seem to have been efficiently performed. Borrowing was mainly done in London through fiscal agents, who followed the instructions of a sophisticated minister. The personal relations in these formative years between Langton and Rose and other ministers on the Treasury Board were close, and as a result Langton, a man of wide-ranging interests and strong opinions, probably advised them informally on a number of subjects. When circumstances required it, the department was expanded under his management to carry out the supervision of insurance companies.

One of the most significant actions, for the long term, taken by Rose and Langton was their decision that no one on the staff of the department in the late 1860s showed sufficient ability to succeed Langton as deputy minister; they, therefore, brought in J. M. Courtney and trained him for this role. Courtney must be judged a success, though he was prudent and pragmatic rather than innovative or doctrinaire in dealing with policy problems. His qualities were appropriate to the Canada of the late nineteenth century. His main deficiency appears to have been in not seeking adequately to create an effective and systematic role for the department in the determination of the Estimates, along the lines practised by the British Treasury. He had the foresight to bring in well-educated, young men and train them for future advancement. He recognized that salaries in the public service were falling behind those in the prosperous private sector in the 1890s and after the turn of the century and, as chairman of a royal commission, recommended that public service salaries, particularly for senior officials, be made more competitive. But this proposal came too late to enable Finance Minister Fielding to find an experienced financial man outside government circles to succeed Courtney. Instead T. C. Boville, one of the well-educated young men trained within the department did so, but fortunately he had the assistance of an articulate and experienced lawyer from outside government, H. T. Ross, who filled the new role of full-time assistant deputy minister.

In Canada's fifteen prosperous years of dynamic growth and development before 1913, there was an excess of government encouragement and financing of railway building. A strong finance minister and department should have held it in check, so that the very costly settlements that led to the CNR in 1923 could have been avoided and the dreadful deficits of the Depression years would have been much less. But it would be quite unrealistic to blame Boville and Ross, or even Fielding himself, for these errors of overoptimism at the beginning of what Prime Minister Laurier had termed "Canada's century."

When war came in 1914, the department was not asked for advice on general policies, particularly monetary policy, which was important during the war. It had no monetary experts, though Ross was learning by experience. Inflationary financial policies were knowingly followed by Finance Minister White but under some restraint, which he exercised by moral suasion on the banks. The department could not have done this even if it wished to. It did manage to work out and administer the first corporate and personal income taxes under the surprisingly good leadership of its new adviser on tariffs. It succeeded, by enormous efforts and overtime work, to handle the huge Victory Loans issued in the newly discovered Canadian bond market. While therefore the department played no significant role in determining wartime economic policy, it met effectively the problems in carrying out what was decided by ministers, bankers, and other outside advisers.

Preparations for selecting a successor to Boville, who retired in 1920, were not as carefully made as the earlier changes. Ross's decision to leave the department in 1917 prevented him being the obvious choice, and J. C. Saunders was then moved into a position where he would have seniority. By 1920, however, the need for a deputy minister with an understanding of monetary affairs and banking, as well as other economic matters, must surely have been obvious, but Saunders was appointed and his deficiencies and those of his department soon appeared. By 1924 the acting minister was having to defend Saunders in Parliament against criticism of his abilities. In chapter 2 a number of examples of the department's weakness or mistakes have been given, but the comfortable fiscal situation of the government, the general prosperity of Canada, and its good reputation in the financial markets of New York meant that these deficiencies did not do much harm. Mackenzie King himself was strongly in favour of orthodox finance, and the government's only bout of extravagance was the CNR program of 1929, which became part of the Depression problem. By the beginning of 1930, however, Saunders was dying and the assistant deputy minister was in a penitentiary. It was quite evident that a new deputy minister would have to be found who had a good understanding of monetary and other economic problems.

Watson Sellar really ran the department from 1930 to 1932, apart from tariff questions, which Hector McKinnon handled. Sellar met the domestic monetary and borrowing problems successfully with the help of B. J. Roberts and others but was out of his depth on the foreign exchange difficulties that arose when Britain went off gold. The department and the government had no policy except to let the Canadian dollar float. Sellar and Ronson carried out Bennett's expenditure policies at the Treasury Board and through the offices of the comptroller of the Treasury when they were established. No one in the department questioned the economic wisdom (let alone the social justice) of the severe austerity in expenditure that Bennett and Rhodes enforced or the imposition of increased taxes to cover as much as possible of the unavoidable expenditures.

Clark made some difference in monetary policy almost from the time of his arrival. He nudged interest rates down in 1933 and influenced their decline in the next several years by increasing bank reserves. He promoted the decision to establish the Bank of Canada and was the main draftsman of the bill to create it. He was active in designing the measures to alleviate the burden of farm debt and promote a new financing program for housing. He began the serious study of tax policy and particular measures intended to encourage private investment. But he remained a hard-liner on fiscal policy up to the crisis in 1938 arising from the report of the National Employment Commission. He also maintained a hard line on the need for utmost economy on the part of the provincial governments, in relief and other expenditures, but he did accept the necessity of saving them from default, until Aberhart deliberately brought that on Alberta.

Clark's views on fiscal policy changed in 1938 when most of the Cabinet, led by Norman Rogers, his Queen's colleague, rebelled at the continued austerity in the face of the persuasive counterarguments of Arthur Purvis and W A. Mackintosh in their National Employment Commission report, which had been based, but not overtly, on Keynes's *General Theory*. Dunning had been worsted in the argument, but he was won over to Keynesian views within less than twelve months. His April 1939 budget must have been one of the first clearly Keynesian budgets in any country. It was too late to be put to the test, however, since World War II broke out in September. By the late 1930s the budget and the policy measures in it were the main concern of the deputy minister and others in the department, including Eaton, Perry, Johnson and, in 1939, myself, as well as senior officers from the Department of National Revenue.

THE PERFORMANCE OF THE DEPARTMENT DURING THE WAR

It was during World War II that Clark and his loosely organized department won their spurs. He had just enough versatile officers to meet the immediate problems that arose. Some of them moved quickly to positions with wartime economic agencies, for example, Hector McKinnon to the Wartime Prices and Trade Board. Most remained in the department doing whatever was most urgent. Clark himself served as a member of a number of boards, notably the Foreign Exchange Control Board organized by the Bank of Canada with Graham Towers at its head. Clark's own organization was the Economic Advisory Committee, established by order-in-council, of which he was chairman and which included about a dozen of the most important economic officials as members. In the early years of the war it dealt with a wide variety of issues referred to it by the Cabinet or occasionally by particular ministers. Clark brought his old friend and colleague W. A. Mackintosh (Bill), one of Canada's very best and least dogmatic economists, to be his senior special assistant. Walter Gordon came in to the department for about a year to work on a variety of special projects, and Mitchell Sharp in 1942 mainly to specialize in grain and other agricultural and food problems but also to deal with other matters when needed. Later other, younger economists were hired to help in the postwar planning.

During the war, the upper ranks of the department were mainly concerned with policy matters. Other departments or agencies carried on the operations: tax collection by the Department of National Revenue and borrowing by the National War Finance Committee. Officers at Finance maintained informal contacts and arrangements with officials in other departments and agencies, as well as through established boards or committees, and some met regularly with ministers in Cabinet committees. Relations with the British Treasury were very close and active, from the beginning of the war to the end, for the department was involved in financing Britain on a large scale, an operation that required attention to innumerable details. Clark's own relations with the U.S. secretary of the Treasury were also very close and important from 1940 to 1944.

The department's performance during the war years will be dealt with in future publications. The important point to recognize here is that Canada's economic policies and performance during the war were very good. The country managed to sustain war production at a very high level and the export of food and essential arms and materials to Britain at the level required. Tax levels were very high, but were accepted. Borrowing programs were successful. Price controls were more effective than those of Britain and the United States. Rationing was fair and, with one exception, worked well. To keep an effective ceiling on retail prices, effective wage controls had to be maintained. While defending controls for the many low wage categories, the need for family allowances was recognized. It was a radical social program for that time, but the man who really sold it in the key Cabinet meeting was none other than W. C. Clark, the deputy minister of finance. It was in his department that the detailed plan for the program was drafted.

In the postwar period Canada enjoyed twenty years of prosperity with only minor spells of modest unemployment. Suffice it to say that the experience of W. C. Clark, Hector McKinnon, Ken Eaton, Harvey Perry, and others in the loosely organized Finance Department during the difficult 1930s created a versatile policy-forming group with a strong esprit de corps. During the war this seasoned group expanded and took a leading part in the much larger Ottawa organization. When the war was over, the department had enough experienced officers, or could find them among those with whom it had worked, to organize and staff the kind of department that was needed to serve Canada well during an exciting period of economic and social development and international leadership.

Appendix

MINISTERS OF FINANCE

Alexander Tilloch Galt	July 1, 1867–November 7, 1867
John Rose	November 18, 1867–September 30, 1869
Sir Francis Hincks	October 9, 1869–February 21, 1873
Sir Samuel Leonard Tilley	February 22, 1873–November 5, 1873
	October 17, 1878–November 10, 1885
Richard J. Cartwright	November 7, 1873–October 8, 1878
Archibald W. McLelan	December 10, 1885–January 26, 1887
Sir Charles Tupper	January 27, 1887–May 22, 1888
George E. Foster	May 29, 1888–July 8, 1896
William S. Fielding	July 20, 1896–October 6, 1911
	December 29, 1921–September 4, 1925
Sir Thomas White	October 10, 1911–August 1, 1919
Sir Henry Drayton	August 2, 1919–December 29, 1921
	June 29, 1926–July 12, 1926
James A. Robb	September 5, 1925–June 28, 1926
	September 25, 1926–November 11, 1929
Richard B. Bennett	July 13, 1926–September 25, 1926
	August 7, 1930–February 2, 1932
Charles A. Dunning	November 26, 1929–August 7, 1930
	October 23, 1935–September 5, 1939
Edgar N. Rhodes	February 3, 1932–October 23, 1935
James Layton Ralston	September 6, 1939–July 4, 1940
James Lorimer Ilsley	July 8, 1940–December 9, 1946
Douglas C. Abbott	December 10, 1946–June 30, 1954
Walter Harris	July 1, 1954–June 21, 1957
Donald M. Fleming	June 21, 1957–August 8, 1962
George C. Nowlan	August 9, 1962–April 22, 1963
Walter L. Gordon	April 22, 1963–November 10, 1965
Mitchell W. Sharp	November 11, 1965–April 20, 1968
Edgar J. Benson	April 20, 1968–January 27, 1972

John N. Turner	January 28, 1972–September 9, 1975
Donald S. Macdonald	September 26, 1975–September 15, 1977
Jean Chrétien	September 16, 1977–June 3, 1979
John C. Crosbie	June 4, 1979–March 2, 1980
Allan MacEachen	March 3, 1980–September 10, 1982
Marc Lalonde	September 10, 1982–September 17, 1984
Michael H. Wilson	September 17, 1984–

Deputy Ministers of Finance

John Langton	May 12, 1870–July 31, 1878
John Mortimer Courtney	August 1, 1878–November 1, 1906
Thomas C. Boville	November 1, 1906–March 31, 1920
John C. Saunders	April 1, 1920–April 4, 1930
William Clifford Clark	October 24, 1932–December 27, 1952
Kenneth W. Taylor	January 1, 1953–June 30, 1963
Robert B. Bryce	July 1, 1963–March 31, 1970
Sol Simon Reisman	April 1, 1970–March 31, 1975
Thomas K. Shoyama	April 1, 1975–January 31, 1979
William C. Hood	February 1, 1979–September 1, 1979
Grant L. Reuber	September 15, 1979–March 25, 1980
Ian A. Stewart	March 25, 1980–October 31, 1982
Marshall A. Cohen	November 1, 1982–August 31, 1985
Stanley Hartt	September 1, 1985–

Notes

Abbreviations

BCA	Bank of Canada Archives
Bennett Papers	Papers of R. B. Bennett on microfilm, PAC, MG26 K
CJEPS	*Canadian Journal of Economics and Political Science*
DFR	Department of Finance Records in PAC, RG19
DPCR	Dominion-Provincial Conference Records in PAC, RG47
HC	House of Commons
King's diary	Diary of W. L. Mackenzie King, PAC, MG26 J13
King Papers	Correspondence of King, PAC, MG26 J3
	Memoranda and notes of King, PAC, MG26 J4
PAC	Public Archives of Canada
PANS	Public Archives of Nova Scotia
PAO	Public Archives of Ontario

Notes to Chapter One

1. Canada, *Public Accounts*, 1868, p. 54.

2. For a summary biography, see *Macmillan Dictionary of Canadian Biography*, 4th ed. (London and Toronto, 1978), p. 286. The most detailed and important account is *The Life and Times of Sir Alexander Tilloch Galt* by O. D. Skelton, first published in 1920 by Oxford University Press, but later edited and republished in the Carleton Library series (Toronto: McClelland and Stewart, 1966). A more recent work is *The Galts: A Canadian Odyssey*, by H. B. Timothy (Toronto: McClelland and Stewart, 1984).

3. Skelton gave a detailed account of this incident on pp. 200–207 of the Carleton Library edition of his biography of Galt noted above.

4. It is surprising to find that Macdonald revealed to the House of Commons on November 18 that he had first asked W. P. Howland, the minister of inland revenue, to take the Finance portfolio after Galt's resignation, but Howland had been unwilling to accept the heavy responsibility. HC *Debates*, November 18, 1867, p. 90.

5. D. M. L. Farr, "Sir John Rose," *Dictionary of Canadian Biography* 11 (Toronto: University of Toronto Press, 1982): 767.

6. It is possible that Tilley was asked to introduce the tariff measures because Rose had expressed strongly protectionist views as a private member of the Provincial Assembly in 1866. This was noted by Mr. Holton in the House at the time Macdonald announced the appointment of Rose. Tilley was from New Brunswick.

7. On Langton as auditor, much has been written. Note H. R. Balls, "John Langton and the Canadian Audit Office," *Canadian Historical Review* 21 (1940): 150; also numerous references by J. E. Hodgetts in *Pioneer Public Service: An Administrative History of the United Canadas, 1841–1867* (Toronto: University of Toronto Press, 1955), and by Norman Ward in *The Public Purse: A Study in Canadian Democracy* (Toronto: University of Toronto Press, 1962).

8. Evidence of Langton's wide-ranging intelligence and many of his ideas can be found in his correspondence, mainly with his brother William, a leading Manchester banker, which has been published as *Early Days in Upper Canada: Letters of John Langton*, ed. W. A. Langton (Toronto: Macmillan, 1929). Unpublished material can be found in the Langton Collections at the Public Archives of Ontario and the University of Toronto Archives.

9. *Statutes of Canada*, 1869, chap. 4.

10. *Statutes of Canada*, 1870, chap. 7.

11. Hodgetts, *Pioneer Public Service*, p. 278 n9; Order-in-Council P.C. 3, 1867.

12. HC *Debates*, May 4, 1869, p. 169.

13. Preface by Courtney to *Reminiscences* by Sir Richard Cartwright (Toronto: William Briggs, 1912).

14. University of Toronto Archives, Langton Papers, B65-0014/004(11), letter of John Langton, December 1, 1867.

15. This correspondence was published in Sessional Paper no. 46 in vol. 5 of the *Sessional Papers* for the second session of the first Parliament (1869).

16. Merrill Denison, *Canada's First Bank* (Toronto: McClelland and Stewart, 1967) 2: 157.

17. See R. M. Breckenridge, *The History of Banking in Canada*, National Monetary Commission (Washington: Government Printing Office, 1910) reproduced in E. P. Neufeld, *Money and Banking in Canada*, Carleton Library, no. 17 (Toronto: McClelland and Stewart, 1964).

18. Donald Creighton, *John A. Macdonald*, vol. 2, *The Old Chieftain* (Toronto: Macmillan, 1955), pp. 37–38. See also W. G. Ormsby, "Sir Francis Hincks," *Dictionary of Canadian Biography* 11: 406–16. Hincks was born in Ireland in 1807 and immigrated to York, Upper Canada, in 1832. He became manager of a small bank and later founded a newspaper. In 1841 he was elected to the Legislative Assembly of the United Canadas and in 1842–43 was appointed receiver general. In 1848 he was made inspector general, equivalent to minister of finance in the Baldwin-LaFontaine government. In 1851 he became prime minister in the Hincks-Morin government, which was obliged to resign in 1854.

19. PAC, Records of Royal Commission on Public Service, 1911, RG33-83, vol. 18, "Report on Superannuation," printed, signed by John Langton, chairman, and dated December 4, 1869. The report was written forty-one years before the

royal commission was set up but was found in the files of that commission.

20. In 1888 Courtney wrote a memo explaining the workings of the Superannuation Act, which had been amended the year before, as it affected the Finance Department. He justified the plan as a means of removing the inefficient and allowing the appointment and promotion "of younger men who are au courant with current affairs." See DFR, vol. 3042, file 3320, "Memo respecting Superannuation," May 3, 1888.

21. See "Finance Department," in DFR, vol. 2670, file "History of the Department."

22. DFR, vol. 3042, file 3312, "Memorandum respecting the Finance Department," by J. M. Courtney, June 7, 1888, p. 10, and *Civil Service List of Canada* (Ottawa, 1887), p. 30.

23. "Report of the Royal Commission on Life Insurance," *Sessional Papers*, 1907, no. 123a. On pp. 192-95 of this report section 11 describes the powers and duties of the Insurance Branch of the department. On the whole it reports favourably on the work of the branch, although in its detailed investigation this commission found many improprieties and irregularities in the business of the companies, only some of which had been found by the branch. In general the commission recommended that the branch be permitted to grow and that the law be amended to allow the minister to impose graduated penalties upon companies which were in no danger of insolvency but which were breaking detailed provisions of the law, in particular, for example, investment transactions.

24. *Statutes of Canada*, 1878, chap. 7. For its similiarity to the British act, see Herbert Balls, "John Langton and the Canadian Audit Office," p. 175.

25. Sections 19-22, 30, 34, and 35, as well as more general sections of "An Act to Provide for the Better Auditing of the Public Accounts," *Statutes*, 1878, chap. 7.

26. Ward, *The Public Purse*, p. 71. For an illustration of the tension between Courtney and McDougall, see DFR, vol. 3160, file 10320, "Memo re Finance Department," February 1899.

27. From the auditor general's report for 1878-79.

28. Samuel Leonard Tilley was born in 1818 in Gagetown, New Brunswick, and educated at the grammar school there. He went into business in St. John at the age of twenty. In 1850 he became a member of New Brunswick Legislative Assembly and was returned twice thereafter, becoming leader of the government between 1861 and 1865. He attended the 1864 conferences on Confederation. His government was defeated on the Confederation issue in 1865 but was returned to power in 1866. After Confederation he became minister of customs in the Dominion government in 1867 and minister of finance from February 1873 until the resignation of the Macdonald government in November 1873. He was lieutenant governor of New Brunswick from that time until the election of 1878, in which he was again elected. *Macmillan Dictionary of Canadian Biography*, 4th ed.

29. For the arguments in the debate, see J. Harvey Perry, *Taxes, Tariffs and Subsidies: A History of Canadian Fiscal Development* (Toronto: University of Toronto Press, 1955), vol. 1, chap. 4 generally and in particular p. 65 where Perry quotes Cartwright for the Liberals and Tupper for the Conservatives in the budget debate of 1878. See also T. G. Marquis, *Sir Leonard Tilley* (Toronto: Ryerson, 1930), p. 23.

30. Tilley, HC *Debates*, March 14, 1879, pp. 411-12, and PAO, Sir Alexander Campbell Papers, Tilley to Campbell, September 14, 1889.

31. W. A. Mackintosh, *The Economic Background of Dominion Provincial Relations*, Carleton Library Edition (Toronto: McClelland and Stewart, 1964), pp. 30-31.

32. PAC, Tilley Papers, MG27 I D15, vol. 20, Young to Tilley, November 1, 1878. See also J. J. B. Forster, "Tariffs and Politics: The Genesis of the National Policy, 1861-1879" (Ph. D. diss., University of Toronto, 1981), pp. 466-67.

33. Creighton, *John A. Macdonald* 2: 259.

34. See the concluding paragraphs of his reports transmitting the Public Accounts to the minister of finance, printed in the *Public Accounts* from 1879-80 to 1890. Apparently his remarks applied to the department excluding the Insurance Branch, of which part of the costs were paid by the insurance companies in accordance with the statutes.

35. George Foster, later Sir George, was born in 1847 in New Brunswick. He was educated at the University of New Brunswick and taught classics there for some years before being elected to Parliament as a Conservative in 1882. He remained minister of finance until 1896. Between 1911 and 1921 he was minister of trade and commerce in the Borden and Meighen governments.

36. DFR, vol. 3042, file 3312, "Memorandum respecting the Finance Department and Matters Connected Therewith," June 7, 1888. In the memorandum, Courtney makes several comments hinting at his dissatisfaction with the previous minister of finance, Sir Charles Tupper. In October 1886 Courtney had written Sir Richard Cartwright of the election rumours in Ottawa and stated that he was "much and selfishly interested." If Tupper became the next minister of finance as Courtney expected, it would mean the end of Courtney's connection with the Finance Department. Courtney must have changed his mind, as Tupper was the minister for over a year before the appointment of Foster in May 1888. PAO, Cartwright Papers, J. M. Courtney to R. J. Cartwright, October 23, 1886.

37. Courtney's readiness on this subject may have been prompted by a handwritten letter dated February 2, 1888, which he received from the prime minister. The prime minister noted the continuing failures of banks in Canada and asked Courtney for suggestions for dealing with the banking system either by way of legislation or by way of administration to establish a better state of things. DFR, vol. 3042, files 3287, 3312. In his memo to the new minister, Courtney said, "Mention has been made of a sub-committee of the Banking and Commerce Committee to enquire into this subject but I confess that I rather dread a sub-committee of Parliament. I would much rather have a committee of business men if a committee is necessary."

38. In another memorandum, eleven years later, Courtney was able to report some progress. The volume of work of the department had increased significantly and yet efficiency had improved. Accounts previously in arrears were now regularly adjusted and, despite the expansion of its responsibilities, the staff had been reduced, and Finance was the only department to have shown a stationary or reduced expenditure since 1878. Courtney, proudly if parsimoniously explained the means of achieving his success: "These results have been arrived at by improved organization and modern methods. Useless and unnecessary work has been

abolished . . . the power of promotion has been sparingly and judiciously employed." DFR, vol. 3160, file 10320, "Memo re Finance Department," February 1899.

39. "Report of the Royal Commission on the Civil Service," *Sessional Papers*, 1908, no. 299. Its recommendations are succinctly given on pp. 44-46.

40. Sir George Murray, "Report on the Organization of the Public Service of Canada," *Sessional Papers*, 1912, no. 57a.

41. PAC, Boville Papers, MG30 E415, "Autobiographical Account of T. C. Boville." Boville wrote this informal memoir for his niece sometime in the 1930s. He had a high opinion of Fielding: "Of all the ministers of Finance for whom I worked Mr. Fielding was the King."

42. *Statutes of Canada*, 1910, chap. 32.

43. See DFR, vol. 3353, file 17554-17565.

44. The Canadian Bankers' Association had been organized informally in 1890 after the revision of the Bank Act that year. It was formally established as a public corporation by statute in 1900, with various defined objectives and powers, including the operation of clearinghouses for cheques. Through this association, the banks sought to coordinate their views and actions, especially on legislative matters and relations with the government.

45. Robert W. Breadner was born in Lower Canada in 1865. After attending high school, he entered the Post Office in 1884. He transferred to the Customs Department in 1892 and advanced rapidly to chief clerk, then to Dominion appraiser, and to inspector of customs in 1906. In 1908 he left the department to become manager of the Tariff Department of the Canadian Manufacturers' Association. He re-entered the civil service four years later, again as Dominion customs appraiser and a member of the Board of Customs, a type of appeal body for customs transactions. He became commissioner of taxation in 1916. Watson Sellar, who knew him well, wrote in a memoir of Breadner and the Income Tax Division: "It was headed by a lonely man who worked nightly in an office where every chair was constantly piled high with files. Mr. Breadner did not know how to delegate and he was prone to depend on his prodigious memory . . . inside the Government, there was some concern over the possibility that major controversies were being arbitrarily compromised with less regard to the law than the likelihood of collection." PAC, Watson Sellar Papers, MG31, E5, vol. 4, Memoir, p. 66. After a Customs scandal in 1926, he was appointed commissioner of customs in 1927. In 1934 he returned briefly to the Finance Department in an advisory role. He was the subject of a considerable discussion, on balance friendly and favourable, in the House of Commons on February 20, 1934, pp. 762-68.

46. This is estimated on the basis of the auditor general's report for 1918-19 and probably allows too little for temporary clerical assistance. The same report shows thirty-one local and regional offices with over two hundred employees in all.

47. See PAC, Sir Thomas White Papers, MG27II D18, vol. 7. In 1923 an investigation of the organization and methods of the income tax administration was made by George Edwards, a leading chartered accountant, who reported favourably on them. In 1924 the administration of the income tax was transferred from Finance to the Department of Customs and Excise. As early as 1918 White had thought that the administration of the income tax and the profits tax should

be moved outside the department. See the White Papers, vol. 7, file 24, memorandum from White to Breadner, and DFR, vol. 4363, file "Departmental Organization," Report by George Edwards, July 4, 1923.

48. Most of these measures were passed by order-in-council in the tense atmosphere immediately preceding the declaration of war. The prime minister and the minister of finance met with the leading Canadian bankers on Monday August 3, 1914, and the new orders, approved by Cabinet that evening, were in effect Tuesday morning. Assistant Deputy Minister Ross was summoned back to Ottawa from his holidays in Cape Breton after war was declared to assist in the drafting of the legislation that authorized these emergency measures retroactively. See Sir Thomas White, *The Story of Canada's War Finance* (Montreal: Canadian Bank of Commerce, 1921), pp. 5–10, and DFR, Letterbook 2895, p. 521.

49. The files reveal that in March 1917 White received word that the British Treasury was dissatisfied with the time being taken in Ottawa to deal with some of this gold. He reacted immediately by instructing the Canadian high commissioner to inform the Treasury that if the British did not appreciate the service they had been receiving freely from his staff in Ottawa, they should make immediate arrangements to have their gold sent directly to New York for safekeeping. This elicited an immediate soothing response from the chancellor of the Exchequer that no criticism or dissatisfaction at all had been intended and that his advisers felt this laborious work had been carried out with an expedition which reflected the greatest credit on all concerned. See PAC, Robert Borden Papers, MG26 H, vol. 10, file OC71, White to Perley, March 22, 1917, and Dominion's Office to White, March 27, 1917.

50. PAC, Borden Papers, vol. 10, file OC71, Ross to Borden, November 16, 1916.

51. This information is taken from the chart of organization of the Department of Finance as of July 1918 prepared for the Organization Branch of the Civil Service Commission by Arthur Young and Co. It is found in PAC, Records of the Public Service Commission, RG32C1, vol. 1021.

Notes to Chapter Two

1. For unemployed wage earners, see Dominion Bureau of Statistics, *Canada Year Book, 1922–23* (Ottawa: 1924), p. 732. For net domestic income, see M. C. Urquhart and K. A. H. Buckley, *Historical Statistics of Canada* (Toronto: Macmillan, 1965), series E130.

2. Fielding, HC *Debates*, May 11, 1923, p. 2650.

3. W. A. Mackintosh, *The Economic Background of Dominion Provincial Relations*, Carleton Library Edition (Toronto: McClelland and Stewart, 1964), p. 73.

4. See Michael Bliss, "The Evolution of Industrial Policies on Canada: A Historical Survey," Discussion Paper no. 218, Economic Council of Canada, 1982.

5. The Progressives were first elected to the House of Commons in 1921. It was a western movement rooted in agrarian discontent and distrust of big business and the traditional parties. After the 1925 election the Progressives held the balance of power, along with Labour and Independent members, and King was forced to woo them in order to remain in power.

6. H. Blair Neatby, *William Lyon Mackenzie King*, vol. 2, *The Lonely Heights, 1924-1932* (Toronto: University of Toronto Press, 1963), p. 125.

7. James A. Robb (1859-1929) was minister of finance in 1925 and again in 1926-29. He was born and educated in Huntingdon, Quebec, and became a prosperous flour miller. From 1908 to his death in November 1929, he represented Huntingdon and Chateauguay-Huntingdon in the House of Commons as a Liberal. He was minister of trade and commerce in the first Mackenzie King government, and occasionally acting minister of finance. Early in 1928 Mackenzie King confided in his diary that he thought Robb relied completely on his departmental officials and did not know the significance, let alone the details, of what he was proposing (see Neatby, *William Lyon Mackenzie King* 2: 246). This is the first evidence of prime ministerial concern of too great an influence of the Department of Finance and appropriately it was focused on tariff measures.

8. These trade agreements included a major treaty with France, which set a pattern for treaties with a dozen other European countries.

9. Neatby, *William Lyon Mackenzie King* 2: 124.

10. PAC, Advisory Board on Tariff and Taxation, 1926-30, RG36-11, vol. 56, file 0-10-5 and 0-10-6. In vol. 57, file 0-10-23, there is a memorandum of March 6, 1929, giving much of the history of the board and its activities.

11. This refers to the chart of organization of the Department of Finance as of July 1918 prepared for the Organization Branch of the Civil Service Commission by Arthur Young and Co. It is found in PAC, Records of the Public Service Commission, RG32C1, vol. 1021.

12. HC *Journals*, 1923, Appendix 5, pp. 751-72.

13. DFR, vol. 318, file 101-60-104, "Memorandum re Theft of Coupons in Connection with Loans Issued in New York," June 16, 1925 (unsigned carbon copy).

14. Queen's University Archives, C. A. Dunning Papers, box 38, folder 319, "Special Investigation into Defalcations and Irregularities in the Department of Finance," Report by Walter Duncan, Special Investigating Officer, Ottawa, 1929-30. The report is dated March 3, 1930, and addressed to the Hon. Charles A. Dunning, minister of finance.

15. DFR, vol. 4363, printed Report by the Board of Audit, December 16, 1927. Chairman Gordon W. Scott, members L. E. Potvin and E. J. Howson.

16. The evidence and exhibits submitted by Duncan to Dunning were not found in the Dunning Papers in the Queen's Archives. Their whereabouts seem to be unknown and possibly they were destroyed because they were so bulky and of such limited interest after the trial and report.

17. See Derek Chisholm, "Canadian Monetary Policy, 1914-1934: The Enduring Glitter of the Gold Standard" (Ph.D. diss., Cambridge University, 1979), pp. 99-103.

18. Ibid., p. 144.

19. Chisholm in his thesis (based on Canadian Bankers' Association files) describes the legislation as originally drafted by Sir Thomas White for the association. It would have made the trustees of the Central Gold Reserves the agent of the minister in making advances to banks under the act (see ibid., pp. 148-49). If so, the bankers overreached their influence and did not succeed. Chisholm reports (p. 149) that Viets proposed to Fielding the three-year limitation

on the suspension of the redemption of Dominion notes in gold. For this he cites a memorandum of April 28, 1923, in DFR, vol. 261, file 101-53-6. Viets's proposal was apparently based on a reasonable inference from U.K. Treasury suggestions, in connection with the settlement of its war debts to Canada, that the U.K. would have returned to the gold standard by 1926.

20. HC *Debates*, 1923, vol. 5, pp. 4405–9.

21. HC, Standing Committee on Banking and Commerce, *1924 Minutes of Evidence*, testimony of Saunders, p. 366.

22. Ibid., pp. 343–83.

23. DFR, vol. 825, file 725, memorandum to Robb, May 21, 1926.

24. HC, Standing Committee on Banking and Commerce, *1928 Minutes of Evidence*, testimony of Hyndman, p. 54.

25. Chisholm, "Canadian Monetary Policy," p. 199.

26. Ibid., p. 202.

27. W. C. Good was born in 1876, graduated with a B.A. from the University of Toronto in 1900, and became a farmer. He was vice-president of the Farmers' Publishing Company and a member of the United Farmers of Ontario party. He was elected to Parliament as a Progressive in the general election of December 1921. He spoke frequently in Parliament on economic issues.

28. Good, HC *Debates*, June 11, 1925, p. 4145.

29. Robb, HC *Debates*, July 1, 1924, p. 3900. Watson Sellar commented in a memoir that Saunders "made no pretence of understanding politicians, so was scared of them." PAC, Watson Sellar Papers, MG31, E5, vol. 4, Memoir, p. 47.

Notes to Chapter Three

1. Much of this description of pre-Depression conditions was drawn from C. P. Kindleberger, *The World in Depression, 1929–39* (London: Allen Lane, 1973). See also K. Galbraith, *The Great Crash* (Boston: Houghton Mifflin, 1954), and Brookings Institution, *The Recovery Problem in the United States* (Washington: Brookings Institution, 1936).

2. Galbraith, *The Great Crash*, pp. 179–91, and Kindleberger, *The World in Depression*, p. 117.

3. League of Nations, *Monthly Bulletin of Statistics*, August 1936, p. 347, as quoted in Brookings Institution, *The Recovery Problem in the United States*, p. 550.

4. Ibid., pp. 654–55.

5. Kindleberger, *The World in Depression*, p. 117.

6. League of Nations, *World Production and Prices, 1935–6*, pp. 17–18, as quoted in Brookings Institution, *The Recovery Problem in the United States*, p. 548.

7. Ibid., p. 549.

8. Ibid., p. 652–53. Data in the Brookings study were from monthly issues of U.S. Bureau of Labor Statistics, *Wholesale Prices*.

9. The level of export prices in relation to that of import prices is known as the terms of trade. Changes in the terms of trade can be estimated by dividing the price index of exports by that of imports. Table 2 does this in column 9, which is the figure of column 7 divided by that of column 8. Since the price of exports declined from 1929 to 1930 much more than the price of imports,

Canada's terms of trade declined from 184 to 100. The decline continued down to 90.8 in 1932, owing mainly to the greater fall in food and raw material prices than in manufactured goods prices. Canada's terms of trade gradually recovered until 1937 when they experienced a sharp rise, after which they declined substantially for the next two years. Speaking broadly, Canada's terms of trade after 1945 were more favourable than they had been during the Depression and indeed better than they had been in the late twenties.

10. League of Nations, *World Production and Prices, 1935-6*, pp. 17-18, as quoted in Brookings Institution, *The Recovery Problem in the United States*, p. 549.

11. Ibid., pp. 562-63.

12. In writing this section I have relied substantially on Kindleberger, *The World in Depression*, and the Brookings Institution, *The Recovery Problem in the United States*. Milton Friedman and Anna J. Schwartz, *A Monetary History of the United States, 1867-1960* (Princeton: Princeton University Press, 1963), has been useful for monetary conditions in the United States, and Peter Temin, *Did Monetary Forces Cause the Great Depression?* (New York: Norton, 1976), for the Depression in the United States generally. I have, however, basically relied on my own Keynesian analysis of the Depression in United States and elsewhere, which I carried out as a graduate student at Cambridge and later at Harvard from 1932 to 1937.

13. U.S. Bureau of the Census, Historical Statistics of the United States, *Colonial Times to 1970 Bicentennial Edition*, part 2 (Washington, D.C., 1975), series F52, p. 229.

14. Ibid., series E40 and E42 (1926 = 100), p. 200.

15. Ibid., series D86, p. 125.

16. The description of the downturn in the Canadian economy was drawn mainly from A. E. Safarian, *The Canadian Economy in the Great Depression*, Carleton Library Edition (Toronto: McClelland and Stewart, 1970). See also E. Marcus, *Canada and the International Business Cycle, 1927-39* (New York: Bookman Associates, 1954).

17. E. Forsey, "The Pulp and Paper Industry," *CJEPS* 1 (August 1935): 504. See also Safarian, *The Canadian Economy in the Great Depression*.

18. An account of the Canadian wheat situation can be found in C. F. Wilson, *A Century of Canadian Grain: Government Policy to 1951* (Saskatoon: Wheat Producer Prairie Books, 1978). See also G. E. Britnell, *The Wheat Economy* (Toronto: University of Toronto Press, 1939).

19. In cases where statistics given in the text are not included in the tables, the sources of these statistics are cited in notes.

20. M. C. Urquhart and K. A. H. Buckley, *Historical Statistics of Canada* (Toronto: Macmillan, 1965), series C47-55, "The labour force and its main components," p. 61. See also p. 56 for a description of the sources for this series.

21. Urquhart and Buckley, *Historical Statistics of Canada*, series F91-103, "Canadian balance of international payments, all countries and by major areas, capital accounts, 1927-37," p. 164.

22. Ibid., series H113-136, "Chartered bank assets, 1923-33," p. 236.

23. Ibid., series H1-10, "Currency and chartered bank deposits, 1913-60," p. 230.

24. S. E. Nixon, "The Course of Interest Rates, 1929-1937," *CJEPS* 3, no. 3 (August 1937): 421-34.

25. Wilson's *A Century of Canadian Grain* was particularly helpful in writing this section.

26. Safarian, *The Canadian Economy in the Great Depression*, table 40, "Selected statistics on Canadian wheat, crop years 1926-7 to 1937-8," compiled from data in Dominion Bureau of Statistics, *Handbook of Agricultural Statistics*, pts. 1 and 2.

27. Wilson, *A Century of Canadian Grain*, p. 305.

28. Britnell, *The Wheat Economy*, pp. 48-68.

29. Royal Commission on Dominion-Provincial Relations, *Report*, book 1, *Canada, 1867-1939* (Ottawa, 1940), p. 169.

30. *Canada Year Book, 1931* (Ottawa, 1931), p. 227.

31. The following sources were helpful in writing about relief in the 1930s: A. E. Grauer, *Public Assistance and Social Insurance: A Study Prepared for the Royal Commission on Dominion-Provincial Relations* (Ottawa, 1939), appendix 6; Michiel Horn, *The Dirty Thirties: Canadians in the Great Depression* (Toronto: Copp Clark, 1972); L. C. Marsh, *Health and Unemployment* (Toronto: McGill University, 1938); idem, *Canadians In and Out of Work* (Toronto: Oxford University Press, 1940); L. Richter, ed., *Canada's Unemployment Problem* (Toronto: Macmillan, 1939); James Struthers, *No Fault of Their Own: Employment and the Canadian Welfare State, 1914-1941* (Toronto: University of Toronto Press, 1983); National Employment Commission, *Final Report* (Ottawa, 1938); annual report of the Dominion director of unemployment relief, 1931-32; annual reports of the Dominion commissioner of unemployment relief from 1933 to 1941.

32. Urquhart and Buckley, *Historical Statistics of Canada*, series C47-55, "The labour force and its main components," p. 61. See also Department of Labour, *Report of Dominion Commissioner of Unemployment Relief, 1941* (Ottawa: 1941), appendix D.

33. A detailed description of the beginning of the recovery of the Canadian economy can be found in Safarian, *The Canadian Economy in the Great Depression*, the source from which much of this account is drawn. See p. 188 for excess capacity in general, pp. 202-4 for newsprint, pp. 208-10 for electric power, pp. 212-13 for railways, and p. 214 for automobile construction.

34. I would include the following as strong ministers in King's government of 1935. The veteran Thomas Crerar from Winnipeg, former leader of the Progressive party in the West, became minister of mines and resources. Charles Dunning, premier of Saskatchewan from 1922 to 1926, minister of railways and canals in King's government from 1926 to 1929, and minister of finance from 1929 to 1930, was appointed minister of finance. James Gardiner, premier of Saskatchewan in 1926-29 and again in 1934-35, became minister of agriculture, a post he held for over twenty-one years. Ernest Lapointe, King's Quebec lieutenant, who had served in all King's Cabinets since 1921, and again became minister of justice, an office he had held off and on from 1924 to 1930. C. D. Howe, American-born engineer, professor at Dalhousie, practising engineering in Port Arthur, Ontario, first elected to the House of Commons in October 1935, was appointed minister of railways and canals and minister of marine. Norman Rogers, lawyer and academic, professor of political science at Queen's University from

1929 to 1935, and secretary to Prime Minister King from 1927 to 1929, became minister of labour (and King's "white haired boy"). James Lorimer Ilsley of Kentville and Halifax, N. S., lawyer, first elected to Parliament in 1926, re-elected in 1930 and 1935, was appointed minister of national revenue: he was frequently acting minister of finance during Dunning's illness or absence and became minister of finance in July 1940.

35. Dunning, HC *Debates*, May 1, 1936, p. 2362.

36. Ibid., p. 2384.

37. The physical change in inventories in 1933 was a decline of 91 and in 1937 an increase of 57, accounting for most of the difference. The residual errors of estimate were about the same in the two years.

38. For a comparison of the Canadian and American recessions of 1937-38 and a discussion of the extent of recovery in Canada, see Safarian, *The Canadian Economy in the Depression*, pp. 220-31.

39. Urquhart and Buckley, *Historical Statistics of Canada*, series Q289, "Physical output of selected manufactured commodities, 1917-1959," p. 484.

40. *Statutes of Canada*, "The National Employment Commission Act, 1936," chap. 7. The National Employment Commission consisted of Arthur Purvis (chairman), Tom Moore (vice-chairman), W. A. Mackintosh, Alfred Marois, A. N. McLean, Mary Sutherland, and E. J. Young.

41. Wheat prices quoted are for No. 1 Northern at Port Arthur.

42. Owing to Dunning's illness, Ilsley had to represent Finance in the critical scrutiny of this Prairie legislation. It was one of my assignments to assist him in doing so, despite my ignorance of the subject, and this was my first experience with the man who was an outstanding minister of finance during most of the World War II period.

43. When expressed in constant (1949) prices, the GNE for 1939 was higher than that of 1929. This increase, however, is more than accounted for by the remarkable fact that wheat stocks on farms and in commercial channels declined in 1929 but increased greatly in 1939. When these grain inventory changes are disregarded, the constant price GNE in 1939 was 3½ percent less than that of 1929.

44. Urquhart and Buckley, *Historical Statistics of Canada*, series C47-55, "The labour force and its main components," p. 61.

45. Ibid., series Q1-11 "General statistics for all manufacturing industries, selected years, 1870-1910 and 1917-59," p. 463.

46. For the number of employees in 1939, see ibid., series N82-88, "Principal statistics of the Canadian metallic industries, 1923-60," p. 425.

47. For the United States, see Kindleberger, *The World in Depression*, pp. 274-76.

48. Safarian, *The Canadian Economy in the Great Depression*, p. 238 n6.

49. C. P. Stacey, *Arms, Men and Governments: The War Policies of Canada, 1939-45* (Ottawa: Department of National Defence, 1970), pp. 100-107.

50. Marcus, *Canada and the International Business Cycle*, p. 156.

51. Department of Trade and Commerce, *Private and Public Investment in Canada, 1926-51* (Ottawa, 1951), pp. 31-33.

Notes to Chapter Four

1. Born in Huntingdon, Quebec, in 1894, Robert Watson Sellar was educated at Huntingdon Academy and the Wetmore Law School in Regina. He served as an apprentice printer with his father's newspaper, *Huntingdon Gleaner*, before attending law school in Regina in 1914. Sellar served overseas from 1916 to 1919. From 1924 to 1929, he worked as secretary to J. A. Robb, after which, in 1930, he was appointed assistant deputy minister of finance. Two years later he became comptroller of the Treasury, and in 1940 he was appointed auditor general of Canada, a position he occupied until reaching the mandatory retirement age of sixty-five in August 1959. Soon after, he wrote an interesting memoir recounting his observations of Ottawa in the 1920s. PAC, Watson Sellar Papers, MG31, E5, vol. 4, Memoir.

2. Queen's University Archives, C. A. Dunning Papers, box 8, folder 72, Dunning to W. M. Martin, March 6, 1930.

3. Further references to King's diary will be cited in the notes only when the date of the passage is not given in the text.

4. In his diary on April 30, 1930, King wrote that it was on this day that the Cabinet was informed of the removal of the duty on tea, the last item of the budget made known to the Cabinet.

5. King's diary, February 14, 1930. King's decision to call an election as soon as possible was based partly on the advice of Mrs. Bleaney, his fortune-teller.

6. The "Tariff Board" of which King wrote in his diary was the Advisory Board on Tariff and Taxation.

7. This action by King was particularly ironic because J. H. Thomas, some years later, was found to have leaked British budget secrets and lost both his position and reputation. See A. J. P. Taylor, *English History, 1914-45* (Oxford: Clarendon Press, 1965), p. 359.

8. There is no information on the preparation of the tax measures for the 1930 budget in either the PAC or the Dunning Papers. A detailed account of these measures, however, can be found in HC *Debates*, May 1, 1930.

9. See, for example, DFR, vol. 3527, "Cooperative Associations and Income Tax," by R. B. Viets, January 19, 1930.

10. King's diary, May 1, 1930.

11. Ibid.

12. Interviews with Arthur Annis, October 1979, and with David Sim, May 16, 1979.

13. O. J. McDiarmid, *Commercial Policy in the Canadian Economy* (Cambridge, Mass.: Harvard University Press, 1946), p. 275, and Bennett, HC *Debates*, September 16, 1930, p. 239.

14. Bennett, HC *Debates*, September 16, 1930, p. 238.

15. Ibid., pp. 245-52.

16. R. D. MacLean, "An Examination of the Role of the Comptroller of the Treasury," *Canadian Public Administration* 7 (March 1964): 1-133, and H. R. Balls, "The Development of Government Expenditure Control: The Issue and Audit Phases," *CJEPS* 10 (November 1944): 465-75.

17. PANS, E. N. Rhodes Papers, file 2D02, pp. 54745–863, memorandum from Sellar to Rhodes, November 14, 1931.

18. The defalcations noted in chap. 2 were relatively small in amount and were due to mistakes in operating the system, not to inherent defects in the system itself.

19. Bennett Papers, M1013, pp. 196161–68, memorandum for Bennett on government accounting, December 15, 1930.

20. The committee felt that an order-in-council under the Public Service Rearrangement and Transfer of Duties Act could have corrected the weaknesses in the system.

21. Bennett, HC *Debates*, June 23, 1931, p. 2937.

22. MacLean, "An Examination of the Role of the Comptroller of the Treasury," p. 55.

23. Bennett, HC *Debates*, June 23, 1931, p. 2939.

24. MacLean, "An Examination of the Role of the Comptroller of the Treasury."

25. W. L. White and J. C. Strick, "The Evolution of the Treasury Board's Role in Government," *Policy, Politics and the Treasury Board in Canadian Government* (Don Mills: Science Research Associates [Canada], 1970), pp. 20–31.

26. MacLean, "An Examination of the Role of the Comptroller of the Treasury," p. 26; White and Strick, *Policy, Politics and the Treasury Board*, p. 21; and Sir George Murray, "Report on the Public Services of Canada," *Sessional Papers*, 1912, no. 57a.

27. White and Strick, *Policy, Politics and the Treasury Board*, p. 24. A Cabinet secretariat was established during World War II.

28. J. E. Hodgetts, William McCloskey, Reginald Whitaker, and V. Seymour Wilson, *The Biography of an Institution: The Civil Service Commission of Canada, 1908–1967* (Montreal: McGill-Queen's University Press and the Institute of Public Administration of Canada, 1972), p. 139.

29. W. L. White, "The Treasury Board in Canada" (Ph.D. diss., University of Michigan, 1965), p. 80.

30. Ibid., p. 111.

31. HC *Debates*, February 5, 1932, p. 2.

32. Bennett, ibid., February 8, 1932, p. 59.

33. There is an unsigned memorandum on this subject, dated October 1, 1931, in the Rhodes Papers, which was almost certainly written by Ronson (file S06, p. 51332). It is probable, given the similarity and the timing, that the idea came from the British National Economy Act of 1931, which was introduced by the new National government early in September in order to balance the budget. This futile last-minute action in Britain was part of its effort to remain on the gold standard but was finally passed after Britain had been forced off gold. The act required a 10 percent reduction in the salary of all those paid by the state, from Cabinet ministers to those on unemployment relief. For a description of this act, see Taylor, *English History*, pp. 287ff.

34. Bennett, HC *Debates*, February 26, 1932, p. 561.

35. Rhodes, HC *Debates*, April 6, 1932, p. 1766.

36. Order-in-Council P.C. 44/1367, June 14, 1932.

37. C. J. Mackenzie, "The Treasury Board," speech delivered to the Junior

Administrative Officers' course, Civil Service Commission, December 7, 1947, mimeograph, p. 10, Department of Finance Library.

38. Hodgetts et al., *The Biography of an Institution*, p. 150.

39. Royal Commission on Administrative Classifications in the Public Service, *Proceedings* (Ottawa, 1946), pp. 59-60.

40. H. Blair Neatby, *William Lyon Mackenzie King*, vol. 2, *The Lonely Heights, 1924-1932* (Toronto: University of Toronto Press, 1963), p. 321. O. Mary Hill, *Canada's Salesman to the World: The Department of Trade and Commerce, 1892-1939* (Montreal: McGill-Queen's University Press and the Institute of Public Administration, 1977), p. 518. *Canadian Annual Review of Public Affairs, 1930-31* (Toronto: Canadian Review Co., 1931), pp. 307-9.

41. Neatby, *William Lyon Mackenzie King* 2: 353.

42. Ian Drummond, *Imperial Economic Policy, 1917-39: Studies in Expansion and Protection* (Toronto: University of Toronto Press, 1974), p. 461 n7.

43. H. H. Stevens, HC *Debates*, February 25, 1932, p. 514.

44. Bennett Papers, M998, p. 105794.

45. Ibid., p. 105875.

46. PAC, External Affairs Records, RG25, vol. 770, Clark to Skelton, June 2, 1932.

47. These documents, which were prepared for the use of the Canadian delegation at the conference and circulated to the other visiting delegations, can be found in DFR, vol. 4666. Within this box, the bound volumes 6 and 7 contain the papers on monetary issues.

48. The committee of which Stevens was chairman did not mention silver in its report to the conference, nor did Bennett in his speech to the committee (as reported in Ollivier's edition of the proceedings of the conference). The committee was concerned with broader and more urgent issues of monetary policy and the low levels of prices generally. Action was taken on silver by the World Monetary and Economic Conference in London in 1933, which is described in chap. 7, "Monetary Measures and the Bank of Canada."

49. Imperial Economic Conference, 1932, *Report* (Ottawa, 1936), p. 143.

50. W. A. Mackintosh, "William Clifford Clark: A Personal Memoir," *Queen's Quarterly* 60 (Spring 1953): 1-16, and R. B. Bryce, "William Clifford Clark: Notes and Memoranda," *CJEPS* 19 (August 1953): 413-23.

51. Clark's main teaching interests at Queen's were money and banking and international trade. He occasionally contributed articles to the *Journal of the Canadian Bankers' Association*, including one in 1919 entitled "The International Exchange Situation," and one in 1921, "Business Cycles and the Depression of 1920-21." Later in the 1920s *The Straus Investors Magazine* published some of his articles, and in 1931 "Flight from the Gold Standard" appeared in *Queen's Quarterly*. Unfortunately there appears to be no comprehensive list of his publications in the Public Archives or elsewhere.

52. Clark wrote an article on this subject, "The Grain Elevator in the Canadian West," *Queen's Quarterly* (July-September 1916). It may be noted that Clark and his two successors, K. W. Taylor and R. B. Bryce, did postgraduate work in economics but never completed their dissertations. Despite this, Clark was normally addressed as "Dr. Clark" in Ottawa, presumably after he was given an honorary degree by Queen's University in 1935.

53. Interviews with D. C. Abbott, former minister of finance, in 1982, and with George Watts of the Bank of Canada on what he had learned from Graham Towers.

54. PAC, Finlayson Papers, MG30 E143, R. Finlayson, draft memoirs, "Life with R. B.: That Man Bennett," p. 144.

55. *Statutes of Canada*, 1931, "An Act respecting the Establishment of the Royal Canadian Mint," chap. 48.

56. In Montreal the functions of the office of Assistant Receiver General were carried out, under contract, by the Montreal City and District Savings Bank.

57. Bennett John Roberts was born in Newfoundland but received his education at the University of Toronto. He entered the public service as private secretary to Finance Minister Sir Thomas White in 1917. After White left politics, Roberts remained with the department, becoming secretary in 1922, comptroller in 1929, and was assistant deputy minister in 1935-36. He was appointed to several boards and commissions including the Canadian Farm Loan Board. In 1940 he became the financial adviser to the British Commonwealth Air Training Plan. In later years he was chairman of the National Harbours Board (1955-58) and president of the St. Lawrence Seaway Authority (1958-60).

Notes to Chapter Five

1. Bennett, HC *Debates*, June 1, 1931, p. 2172.

2. Ibid., p. 2173.

3. Ian Drummond, *Imperial Economic Policy, 1917-39: Studies in Expansion and Protection* (Toronto: University of Toronto Press, 1974), p. 464.

4. The Canadian Manufacturers' Association was founded in 1871. In its early years it was, according to S. D. Clark in an article in *CJEPS* 4 (1938): 505ff., frankly a political pressure group representing only a small sector of the Canadian economy. As the manufacturing industries grew, the association came to provide information and advice to its members as well as to promote their interests. It was incorporated by a private act of Parliament in 1902. The association later acquired and developed expert full-time staff to deal with tariffs, taxation, transportation, insurance, industrial relations, and matters affecting its members and manufacturers generally, including exporters. It has issued many publications, including its monthly magazine *Industrial Canada*.

5. O. Mary Hill, *Canada's Salesman to the World: The Department of Trade and Commerce, 1892-1939* (Montreal: McGill-Queen's University Press and the Institute of Public Administration of Canada, 1977), pp. 521-22, and Drummond, *Imperial Economic Policy*, pp. 192-94.

6. Drummond, *Imperial Economic Policy*, p. 192.

7. Hill, *Canada's Salesman to the World*, pp. 520-21.

8. Bennett Papers, M1176, p. 122760, Bennett to R. W. Breadner, April 12, 1932.

9. Hill, *Canada's Salesman to the World*, p. 523.

10. Ibid., A. J. McPhail quoted on p. 518.

11. Ibid., p. 528. Original quotation taken from E. Watkins, *R. B. Bennett* (Toronto: Kingswood House, 1963).

12. Drummond, *Imperial Economic Policy*, p. 232.

13. Legislation had been passed in 1931 by the Parliament of Canada to establish

such an independent quasi-judicial board but it had not been implemented before the conference.

14. It is difficult to piece together a coherent account of the complex and confused negotiations between Bennett and the British representatives on the specific tariff concessions made by Canada in the agreement. Many details have been assembled by Drummond in his book *Imperial Economic Policy*, which he has woven into a connected account using British sources. This study, however, is much clearer on what Canada was seeking from the United Kingdom and on Bennett's willingness to accept the principle of "domestic competition" than it is on the immediate concessions in the tariff. Much less evidence can be found from the Canadian side, and it is difficult to fit it into the time frame that emerges from the British sources. Two Canadian sources are based on firsthand accounts: Hill's *Canada's Salesman to the World*, and Finlayson's as yet unpublished study, "Life with R. B.: That Man Bennett" (PAC, Finlayson Papers, MG30 E143), apparently written in the mid-sixties. Both agree that Bennett was getting advice before and during the early weeks of the conference predominantly from protectionist sources within and outside the government, notably from Ryckman, the minister of national revenue, and his outspoken deputy, Breadner, and also privately from Herridge, Finlayson, and Leopold Amery, a former secretary for Dominion affairs, who came over on his own initiative to promote agreement. At some unspecified point, Bennett turned away from Ryckman and Breadner and sought advice on the negotiations from McKinnon, who by this time he recognized as both expert and objective. Hill, who interviewed McKinnon and L. D. Wilgress (Trade and Commerce), states that N. A. Robertson (External Affairs) and Wilgress were asked by Bennett to be associated with McKinnon in preparing a list of concessions the British would accept. I find this wholly credible, given the sources of her information and the subsequent activities of these three men.

15. Drummond, *Imperial Economic Policy*, appendix 2, pp. 296-99.

16. Ibid., pp. 239–42.

17. O. J. McDiarmid, *Commercial Policy in the Canadian Economy* (Cambridge, Mass.: Harvard University Press, 1946), p. 284.

18. Article 22 of the Anglo-Canadian agreement, as quoted in Drummond, *Imperial Economic Policy*, p. 473 n162.

19. Phyllis Turner came from a miner's family in Rossland, B.C. After studying economics and political science at the University of British Columbia in the 1920s, she won a fellowship for postgraduate work at Bryn Mawr College in the United States and one to the London School of Economics. In England she married and had two children. Widowed in 1931, she returned to Canada and was appointed to the staff of the Tariff Board in 1934, to become its chief economist in 1937. During the war, she was administrator of oils and fats under the Wartime Prices and Trade Board. In 1945 she married Frank M. Ross of Vancouver. She served on the Board of Governors and Senate of the University of British Columbia and from 1961 to 1966 she was chancellor of that university. Her son, John Turner, became minister of finance in January 1972 and, briefly, prime minister in 1984.

20. Hill, *Canada's Salesman to the World*, p. 541.

21. PAC, Finlayson Papers, "Life with R. B.: That Man Bennett," pp. 165–66.

22. Joint statement by Roosevelt and Bennett, April 29, 1933, as quoted by Herridge in a communication addressed to C. Hull, secretary of state of the United

States, November 14, 1934, *Documents on Canadian External Relations, 1931-35*, vol. 5 (Ottawa: External Affairs, 1973), p. 177.

23. Bennett, HC *Debates*, February 19, 1934, p. 742.

24. Herridge to Hull, November 14, 1934, *Documents on Canadian External Relations, 1931-35* 5: 176-83.

25. Ibid., p. 183.

26. Hull to Herridge, December 27, 1934, ibid., p. 1984.

27. L. D. Wilgress, *Canada's Approach to Trade Negotiations* (Montreal: Private Planning Association, 1963), p. 10.

28. Ibid.

29. Communication with Arthur Annis, January 1980. For the substance of the dispute, see Hill, *Canada's Salesman to the World*, pp. 555-56.

30. Drummond, *Imperial Economic Policy*, p. 413.

31. King's diary, April 19, 1936.

32. Ibid.

33. Wilgress, as quoted in Hill, *Canada's Salesman to the World*, p. 548.

34. The problems and discussions on British imports of farm products, especially cattle and beef, from Canada are well set forth in Drummond, *Imperial Economic Policy*, pp. 380-85.

35. Skelton, under secretary of state for external affairs, to H. Marler, Canadian minister in the United States, February 18, 1937, *Documents on Canadian External Relations, 1935-39*, vol. 6 (Ottawa: External Affairs, 1972), p. 580.

36. Wilgress, *Memoirs* (Toronto: Ryerson, 1967), p. 108.

37. Ibid. p. 109.

38. Interview with Annis, October 1979.

39. Wilgress, *Canada's Approach to Trade Negotiations*, p. 12.

40. Ibid., p. 13.

41. McKinnon was probably referring to the Dunning budget of 1936, which was described earlier in this chapter.

42. It is only fair to note that this same kind of reform had started in a cruder way in 1926 with the Advisory Board on Tariff and Taxation.

Notes to Chapter Six

1. Mr. Ross Tolmie told me this in discussion of source material.

2. For further information on the tax measures of the budgets, see J. Harvey Perry, *Taxes, Tariffs and Subsidies: A History of Canadian Fiscal Development*, vol. 2 (Toronto: University of Toronto Press, 1955), appendices.

3. Bennett, HC *Debates*, July 16, 1931, p. 3857. At this time financial conditions in Europe were deteriorating rapidly towards the situation which forced Britain off the gold standard in September.

4. Ibid., June 1, 1931, p. 2174.

5. Although undoubtedly an expert on income tax and an effective tax administrator, it seems evident that Walters did not serve Bennett well as adviser in regard to tax policy in the 1931 budget. It may be noted that Walters resigned as commissioner about a year later, for reasons which do not appear on the record, and was appionted to an obscure position in the Department of National Revenue

for the balance of the fiscal year. Auditor general, *Report*, 1932–33, vol. 2, p. R24. Years later, when the context made it relevant, Clark instructed me to have as little to do with Walters as possible.

6. HC *Debates*, July 16, 1931, p. 3855.

7. Ibid., February 8, 1932, p. 59.

8. Ibid., June 1, 1931, p. 2171.

9. See also chap. 4, "Bennett and the Department's Interregnum," for an account of Rhodes's proposed reductions in controllable expenditures in the budget speech of April 6, 1932. A biographical sketch of Rhodes is provided in chap. 4.

10. Rhodes, HC *Debates*, April 6, 1932, p. 1768.

11. Ibid., p. 1766.

12. Ibid., March 21, 1933, p. 3218. The action taken in regard to the deficit of the CNR in 1931 and 1932 was in accord with the principle laid down in the Canadian National-Canadian Pacific Act (chap. 33 of the *Statutes of Canada*, 1932–33, section 12) which required that income deficits of the CNR in future should not be funded but met from appropriations by Parliament. This legislation was passed to implement the recommendations of the Royal Commission on Railways and Transportation appointed in November 1931. Reporting in September 1932, the commission recommended that the general direction of the CNR be vested in three trustees and that the CNR and CPR cooperate in joint measures to economize on expenses.

13. PANS, Rhodes Papers, Minister's Office file no. 2E02, files on Estimates, 1933–34, from Ronson to Rhodes, June 10, 1933.

14. Rhodes, HC *Debates*, March 22, 1935, p. 1977.

15. Rhodes Papers, file 2T02.

16. A. Kenneth Eaton was the first senior officer to be brought into the Department of Finance by Clark, who had quickly recognized the need for an economist with special knowledge of taxation, which he himself lacked.

17. Rhodes, HC *Debates*, March 22, 1935, p. 1961.

18. Ibid., p. 1977. The alert reader will note the discrepancy in the figure given for the budget deficit in the text and that given in table 6. The text gives the deficit as stated in the budget speech given before the end of the fiscal year, while table 6 gives the figure reported in the final accounts for 1934–35.

19. Dunning, HC *Debates*, May 1, 1936, p. 2383.

20. Ibid., p. 2384.

21. For a biographical sketch of Crerar, see chap. 3, n34, of this study.

22. The technical effects upon mining operations of this exemption were open to serious criticism. After a prolonged public debate with the industry, this exemption was ended in the tax reform of 1971, a move proposed by the Carter Royal Commission on Taxation, which I strongly supported as deputy minister of finance. My criticism of this exemption was partly based on earlier conversations with my father, a leading figure in the mining industry for many years, who privately believed that this was a poor form of tax incentive for mining ventures.

23. See HC *Debates*, February 15, 1937, p. 876, for introduction of the amendment, and February 19, 1937, p. 1073, for the defeat of the amendment.

24. King's diary, December 18, 1936.

25. H. Blair Neatby, *William Lyon Mackenzie King*, vol. 3, *The Prism of Unity,*

1932-1939 (Toronto: University of Toronto Press, 1976), pp. 180–83. James Eayrs, *In Defence of Canada*, vol. 2, *Appeasement and Disarmament* (Toronto: University of Toronto Press, 1965), pp. 134–45.

26. Dunning, HC *Debates*, February 25, 1937, p. 1238.

27. Ibid.

28. Neatby, *William Lyon Mackenzie King* 3: 250-51.

29. DFR, vol. 3677, file 101-54.

30. Ibid., p. 3.

31. For more on the National Employment Commission, see chap. 3, "The Economic Course and Impact of the Depression," and chap. 10, "Dominion-Provincial Discussions and Disputes," of this study.

32. H. Aitken et al., *The American Economic Impact on Canada* (Durham: Duke University Press, 1959), pp. 53–54.

33. National Employment Commission, *Final Report* (Ottawa, 1938), p. 34.

34. Economists may be interested in Mackintosh's comments in his 1959 article, "Recent American Influence in Canada," in Aitken et al., *The American Economic Impact on Canada*, pp. 51–68, in which he discusses criticisms of this part of the commission's report.

35. The Department of Finance Records do not contain any papers which reveal that the department was advising Dunning to take this position.

36. King's diary, April 1, 1938.

37. Ibid.

38. Ibid., May 2, 1938.

39. Ibid., May 5, 1938.

40. Ibid., May 6, 1938.

41. Ibid., May 9, 1938.

42. Ibid., May 16, 1938.

43. Ibid., May 20, 1938.

44. Ross Tolmie, who was a solicitor in the income tax administration at the time, says this exemption from the gift tax of an amount equal to one-half of the donor's income less his income tax paid was made in response to a proposal by Bennett. Bennett was known to be a very generous man who made numerous gifts.

45. King's diary, June 15, 1938.

46. Ibid., June 16, 1938.

47. Dunning, HC *Debates*, June 16, 1938, p. 3924.

48. King's diary, June 16, 1938.

49. Dunning, HC *Debates*, April 25, 1939, p. 3149. For the substance of the 1938 wheat policy, see chap. 3 of this study.

50. Dunning, HC *Debates*, April 25, 1939, p. 3446.

51. After the war had begun, this device was eliminated.

52. Dunning, HC *Debates*, April 17, 1939, p. 2840.

Notes to Chapter Seven

1. Bennett Papers, M1045, pp. 203373ff., memorandum from Sellar to Bennett on senior personnel of the Department of Finance, January 1932.

2. PANS, Rhodes Papers, file D02 Department of Finance, memorandum from Sellar to Rhodes, December 10, 1931.

3. These figures have been taken from F. A. Knox, *Dominion Monetary Policy, 1929-34: A Study Prepared for the Royal Commission on Dominion-Provincial Relations* (Ottawa, 1939), and do not agree in detail with the later estimates in M. C. Urquhart and K. A. H. Buckley, *Historical Statistics of Canada* (Toronto: Macmillan, 1965). In particular the later figures show a larger net monetary gold inflow. The main result, however, is consistent in the two sources.

4. It may be recalled that the Finance Act had been introduced as a war measure in 1914 and made permanent in 1923; it permitted a bank needing more cash reserves to borrow Dominion notes from the Finance Department against approved collateral.

5. Derek Chisholm, "Canadian Monetary Policy, 1914-1934: The Enduring Glitter of the Gold Standard" (Ph.D. diss., Cambridge University, 1979), p. 214. Initial source: president's letter to the minister, February 8, 1930, Canadian Bankers' Association Archives (Toronto), file "Summer Meeting 1930."

6. DFR, vol. 105, file 101-7, memorandum by Sellar, February 25, 1930.

7. Chisholm, "Canadian Monetary Policy," pp. 220-21. Initial source: Henry Ross, "The Finance Act," June 7, 1930, Canadian Bankers' Association Archives.

8. DFR, vol. 105, file 101-7, memorandum from Sellar to Bennett, September 5, 1930.

9. Chisholm, "Canadian Monetary Policy," p. 223. Initial source: DFR, vol. 1681, Dominion of Canada Ledger, 1908-37, p. 502.

10. DFR, vol. 105, file 101-7, memorandum by Sellar, May 4, 1931.

11. C. P. Kindleberger, *The World in Depression, 1929-39* (London: Allen Lane, 1973), p. 163.

12. *Canadian Annual Review of Public Affairs, 1932* (Toronto, 1933), p. 431.

13. Bennett Papers, M1044, p. 202200.

14. Ibid., memorandum, undated and unsigned but almost certainly by Sellar, pp. 202184-90.

15. Born in New Brunswick in 1887, S. Randolph Noble entered the Royal Bank in 1903. In 1917 he became general inspector of foreign branches, and from 1922 to 1944 was assistant general manager. Noble was appointed sugar administrator to the Wartime Prices Board in 1939. From 1942 to 1944 he served as vice-president of the Commodity Prices Stabilization Corporation Ltd. He then became general manager of the Industrial Development Bank, a position he held until 1954. Despite a lack of university education, Noble was one of the bankers who understood international markets best and was one of those responsible for making the Royal Bank the most liberal of the Canadian banks in monetary policy and reform.

16. Bennett Papers, M1044, p. 202177, "Notes on the Present Financial Situation," by S. R. Noble, September 26, 1931.

17. Ibid., pp. 202184-90, memorandum, almost certainly by Sellar.

18. Ibid., pp. 202295-300, memorandum, presumably by Skelton.

19. Ibid., M1014, p. 196652.

20. Ibid., M1044, pp. 196732-48, memorandum on Canadian currency policy, by T. E. Gregory, October 10, 1931.

21. *Canadian Annual Review, 1932*, p. 432.

22. Ibid.

23. Bennett Papers, M1015, p. 197095, memorandum from Sellar to Meir, March 18, 1932.

24. Ibid., M1015.

25. Ibid. p. 112596ff., "A Suggestion as to Canada's Immediate Problem," by Clark, n.d.

26. G. S. Watts wrote a series of articles in the *Bank of Canada Review* about central banking in Canada: "The Origins and Background of Central Banking in Canada" (May 1972), pp. 15-27; "The Legislative Birth of the Bank of Canada" (August 1972), pp. 13-26; "The First Phase of the Bank of Canada's Operations: 1935-9" (November 1972), pp. 7-21; "The Bank of Canada during the War Years" (April 1973), pp. 3-17; "The Bank during the Period of Postwar Adjustment" (November 1973), pp. 3-25; "The Bank of Canada from 1948 to 1952: The Pivotal Years" (November 1974), pp. 3-17; "The Bank of Canada in 1953 and 1954: A Further Stage in the Evolution of Central Banking in Canada" (January 1976), pp. 3-14.

27. DFR, vol. 592, file 155-30, vol. 2, memorandum by Sellar, May 30, 1932.

28. Chisholm, "Canadian Monetary Policy," p. 256.

29. Bennett, HC *Debates*, November 8, 1932, p. 927.

30. S. E. Nixon, "The Course of Interest Rates, 1929-1937," *CJEPS* 3, no. 3 (1937): 421.

31. Ibid.

32. Rhodes, HC *Debates*, April 18, 1934, p. 2271.

33. Kindleberger, *The World in Depression*, chap. 9, "The World Economic Conference," pp. 199-231.

34. *Documents on Canadian External Relations, 1931-35*, vol. 5 (Ottawa: External Affairs, 1973), joint statement by Bennett and Roosevelt for the press, April 29, 1933, p. 252.

35. Monetary and Economic Conference, "Agreements regarding Silver" (Ottawa, 1934), p. 3.

36. Bennett Papers, M962, pp. 62566-62647.

37. Royal Commission on Banking and Currency, *Proceedings*, vol. 1 (Ottawa, 1933), p. 2.

38. Ibid., confidential, private sitting, p. 109.

39. Bennett Papers, M1400, pp. 436794-801. For mention of Bennett's personal payment for the broadcast, see L. Grayson, "The Formation of the Bank of Canada, 1913-38" (Ph.D. diss., University of Toronto, 1974), p. 216.

40. *Statutes of Canada*, 1934, "An Act to Incorporate the Bank of Canada," 24-25 George V, chap. 43, sections 9 and 10.

41. Royal Commission on Banking and Currency, *Report* (Ottawa, 1933), paragraph 206.

42. *Statutes of Canada*, 1934, "An Act to Incorporate the Bank of Canada," 24-25 George V, chap. 43. For a draft copy of the bill, see Bennett Papers, M1314, p. 388434.

43. H. Blair Neatby, *William Lyon Mackenzie King*, vol. 3, *The Prism of Unity 1932-1939* (Toronto: University of Toronto Press, 1976), pp. 54-55.

44. HC, Committee on Banking and Commerce, *Minutes of Evidence*, June 5, 1934, pp. 954ff.

45. King, HC *Debates*, June 21, 1934, p. 4195.

46. Bennett Papers, M963, pp. 63895-98, "Memorandum *re* Mr. King's Remarks regarding Possible Conflict between Government and Bank of Canada," by Clark.

47. Bennett, HC *Debates*, June 22, 1934, p. 4223.

48. Ibid., p. 4225.

49. Osborne's comment was recorded in an article by Grant Dexter in the *Winnipeg Free Press*, August 7, 1957, entitled "Where Control Lies."

50. Ibid.

51. BCA, SP/G: T-5, G. F. Towers, speech before the Montreal Junior Board of Trade, March 14, 1938, pp. 3-4.

52. HC, Banking and Commerce Committee, *Proceedings* (Ottawa, 1954), testimony of Towers, p. 714.

53. Ilsley, HC *Debates*, June 13, 1941, pp. 3936-37.

54. *Statutes of Canada*, 1966-67, "An Act to Amend the Bank of Canada Act," chap. 88, section 6.

55. Raminsky, "Statement by the Governor of the Bank of Canada issued August 1, 1961," reprinted in Bank of Canada, *Evidence of the Governor before the Royal Commission on Banking and Finance* (Ottawa, May 1964), p. 131.

56. Bennett, HC *Debates*, June 14, 1934, p. 4087.

57. Ibid., p. 4086.

58. Ibid., p. 4105.

59. Grayson, "The Formation of the Bank of Canada," p. 284.

60. R. S. Sayers, *The Bank of England, 1891-1944*, vol. 2 (Cambridge: Cambridge University Press, 1976), p. 515.

61. In late 1938 I was appointed financial investigator in the department, which involved some duties regarding monetary questions. It fell to my lot to prepare letters for Clark or the minister on monetary questions, including many answers to letters from monetary cranks of which Canada had quite a number in those days. I also assisted Clark with answers to parliamentary questions on monetary as well as other economic subjects and assembled statistical information for him. I had little official business to take up with the Bank of Canada before the war began in 1939, but I made many informal contacts with members of its Research Department.

Notes to Chapter Eight

1. Debt management is the main theme of Sir Thomas White, *The Story of Canada's War Finance* (Montreal: Canadian Bank of Commerce, 1921).

2. This decline in total debt and funded debt outstanding took place even though the net debt in the early 1920s increased because of a substantial decline in the "active" assets (mainly loans to railways) deducted in reaching the total.

3. Sterling and U.S. dollar obligations were valued at par of exchange, i.e., the pound at \$4.86 (Canadian) and the U.S. dollar at \$1.00 (Canadian). Holdings in sinking funds of about \$54.5 million held against sterling debts and \$1.7 million held against Canadian dollar debts have been deducted.

4. Royal Commission on Dominion-Provincial Relations, *Report*, book 1 *Canada, 1867-1939* (Ottawa, 1940), p. 154. (The differences in tense of the verbs are in the original.)

5. Public Resolution no. 10, 73rd Congress, June 5, 1933.

6. This legislation declared that it was contrary to public policy to enter into such contracts and that they would be prohibited in future, although Bennett, the leader of the Opposition, criticized this prohibition as an unnecessary restriction on the freedom of Canadians to make contracts, notwithstanding the precedent of the American legislation of 1933. HC *Debates*, April 8, 1937, pp. 2754-58.

7. The minister of finance initially set the amount of the issue at $156 million, but he increased the amount in response to the public demand before the closing date. Rhodes, HC *Debates*, April 6, 1932, p. 1757.

8. DFR, vol. 594, file 155-33-15L.

9. Ibid., Clark to Pope, August 11, 1933.

10. A truly arcane constitutional point arose in connection with this August 1933 issue. In the London market, it was a material advantage for an issue of "stock" to be eligible for investment by trustees. This was made possible for issues by dominion governments which conformed with the Colonial Stock Act of 1900. To ensure that no subsequent dominion legislation would conflict with the terms of this old act, the obsolescent power of disallowance by the imperial government was relied on. After passage of the Statute of Westminster in 1931, disallowance might not have been possible had it not been agreed at a 1929 imperial conference that the U.K. government would continue to have the power to disallow dominion legislation that conflicted with the Colonial Stock Act, notwithstanding the Statute of Westminster. An old order-in-council of the government of Canada (P.C. 740, March 22, 1900) consenting to disallowance in such circumstances was allowed to remain in effect after 1931, and, as a result, the 1933 registered stock was an eligible investment for trustees in Britain. DFR, vol. 594, file 155-33-15L.

11. DFR, vol. 598, file 155-52.

12. Rhodes, HC *Debates*, April 18, 1934, p. 2288.

13. General information about bond issues is normally given in the budget speech for the following year and more details are available in the *Public Accounts* for the fiscal year in which the issue was made.

14. The department's files contain some letters and memoranda from Towers and Henderson to Clark, and some memoranda from Clark to the minister, but very little information about the oral discussions. Clark did put one memo on file in 1938 about a decision on the pricing of a government-guaranteed CNR issue, indicating that he thought it could be sold at 97¼, while Henderson thought the price should be only 97 in view of the experience with some CNR issues in the market. Clark wrote that he decided he should accept the advice of Henderson, who was speaking on behalf of the Bank of Canada, on a matter so closely touching market judgment.

15. DFR, vol. 3978, file F-1-6, memorandum by Henderson, August 27, 1936.

16. Dunning, HC *Debates*, April 25, 1939, p. 3147.

17. The amount of guaranteed railway securities outstanding and held by the public at March 31, 1930, was approximately $806 million. The amount of other

guaranteed securities held by the public was about \$31 million of which \$9.4 million was for the CN (West Indies) Steamships Ltd. and \$18.5 was for the Harbour Commissioners of Montreal.

18. Royal Commission to Inquire into Railways and Transportation in Canada, *Report* (Ottawa: King's Printer, 1932). Note chap. 5, pp. 62–67, on conclusions and proposals. The report recommended many things not noted in the text of this book, only indirectly relevant to the Department of Finance.

19. See C. D. Howe, HC *Debates*, January 29, 1937, p. 398.

20. Standing Committee on Railways and Shipping, *Proceedings*, no. 3, March 2, 1937, p. 72. Clark had another highly technical role in this complex situation as one of five official trustees constituting the CNR Securities Trust. They held, on behalf of the minister of finance, the original securities which were being removed from the books of the CNR. These securities had been issued by the railway companies taken over by the CNR or the government. The purpose of this Securities Trust was to retain for the government its priorities as a creditor of the original companies vis-à-vis other possible claimants.

21. DFR, vol. 3978, file F-1-6, memorandum by Clark, February 7, 1936.

22. Written comment by E. B. Armstrong, 1981.

23. Both the Salaries Deduction Act and the sweeping staff control regulations had been introduced before Clark arrived. I think he would have favoured the former, but I am inclined to doubt whether he would have approved of the very arbitrary staff control measures.

24. The friction between the Civil Service Commission and the Treasury Board during this period is described in chap. 7 of the excellent history of the commission by J. E. Hodgetts, William McCloskey, Reginald Whitaker, and V. Seymour Wilson, *The Biography of an Institution: The Civil Service Commission of Canada, 1908–1967* (Montreal: McGill-Queen's University Press and the Institute of Public Administration of Canada, 1972). See p. 148 for Ronson's views on the transfer of the Organization Branch.

25. Royal Commission on Administrative Classifications in the Public Service, *Proceedings*, vol. 1 (Ottawa, 1946), pp. 48–91.

26. The attendance of ministers at the Treasury Board is recorded in the minutes sent to the Privy Council Office for incorporation with other recommendations from the Council itself for the approval of the governor general. They show that Finance Minister Rhodes was absent from five of twenty-six meetings in 1934. In 1936 Finance Minister Dunning was absent from two of thirty-nine meetings.

27. There are relatively few Minutes of the Treasury Board itself in its records for this period. Most of what it produced went to the Privy Council from which it emerged as orders-in-council approved by the governor general.

28. Royal Commission on Administrative Classifications in the Public Service, *Proceedings* 1: 48–91.

29. For example, on November 5, 1935 the salary of W. J. Bennett, private secretary of C. D. Howe, was approved.

30. One of the Treasury Board's responsibilities is of special interest in this historical context. On June 2, 1936, the Treasury Board issued a Minute dealing with the destruction of public records, a perennial problem, as office space was short and very limited facilities for dead storage existed. The board required that

documents of genuine historical value be retained indefinitely. The Dominion archivist was to be notified on the intention to destroy documents and could object to the destruction of particular papers or files. If the department responsible disagreed with the archivist, the dispute would be referred back to the board. As I recall, the board normally sided with the archivist. Later an interdepartmental committee on public records was established with a process to ensure systematic review and preservation.

31. *Statutes of Canada*, 1966, 14-15 Elizabeth II, chap. 25.

Notes to Chapter Nine

1. For a discussion of the problems facing the Canadian farmer, see chap. 3, "The Economic Course and Impact of the Depression." Table 4 on the fall in farm prices and incomes can also be found in chap. 3.

2. A detailed description of debt adjustment legislation is provided in W. T. Easterbrook, *Farm Credit in Canada* (Toronto: University of Toronto Press, 1938).

3. PAC, Finlayson Papers, MG30 E143, R. Finlayson, "Life with R. B.: That Man Bennett," p. 239.

4. Bennett, HC *Debates*, June 4, 1934, p. 3638.

5. Ibid., p. 3639.

6. The Canadian Farm Loan Act, passed in 1927, had created the Farm Loan Board for the provision of mortgage credit to farmers. The board commenced operations in the summer of 1929 but was subsequently criticized for being overly cautious. Loans were limited under the statute to amounts that in the opinion of the board the borrower could repay. With the decline in farm prices, the market and appraisal values of the land and the farmers' prospective profits were reduced, thus decreasing the borrowing capacity of the farmer. The 1934 amendments empowered the board to take additional security, to make time extensions, or to make other arrangements deemed necessary to help capable farmers make ends meet.

7. *Sessional Papers*, vol. 334, May 4, 1936, no. 208 (not printed).

8. *Statutes of Canada*, 1935, 25-26 George V, chap. 61.

9. Although the 1943 Farmers' Creditors Arrangement Act has been amended from time to time, it is still on the statute books today, including the section permitting the advance repayment of mortgages with interest rates of over 7 percent. However, the administration of the act was transferred to the Department of Justice in July 1954 and later to the Department of Consumer and Corporate Affairs.

10. A good summary of the Dominion government's involvement in housing policy can be found in A. E. Grauer, *Housing: A Study Prepared for the Royal Commission on Dominion-Provincial Relations* (Ottawa, 1939). See also O. J. Firestone, *Residential Real Estate in Canada* (Toronto: University of Toronto Press, 1951).

11. Firestone, *Residential Real Estate in Canada*, table entitled "Dwellings completed, with and without public assistance, Canada 1921-49," p. 125.

12. Grauer, *Housing*, p. 39.

13. While employed with S. W. Straus and Co., Clark and J. L. Kingston, an architect colleague, wrote a short yet fascinating book entitled *The Skyscraper:*

A Study in the Economic Height of Modern Office Buildings (New York and Cleveland: American Institute of Steel Construction, 1930).

14. HC, Special Committee on Housing, *Minutes of Proceedings and Evidence*, April 4, 1935.

15. Idem, *Report to the House*, April 16, 1935, pp. 6, 20.

16. Ibid., p. 20.

17. Ibid., p. 21.

18. David Mansur later became general superintendent of the Central Mortgage Bank and, after World War II, the very influential president of the Central Mortgage and Housing Corporation. Much of the information in this paragraph was provided by Mansur.

19. For a number of letters written by Clark in 1936 on some of the problems with the Dominion Housing Act, see DFR, vol. 3979, file H-1-3.

20. Grauer, *Housing*, p. 42. Original source: *Social Welfare* (June–September 1937): 36–37.

21. DFR, vol. 3979, file H-1-10, p. 47, "Summary of Dominion Government's Housing Program."

22. DFR, vol. 3975, file C-5-1-1, proposal by D'Arcy Leonard, February 25, 1939.

23. Ibid., Clark's response to Leonard's proposal, n.d.

24. Dunning, HC *Debates*, May 6, 1939, p. 3667.

25. *Statutes of Canada*, 1939, 3 George VI, chap. 40.

26. A. Meighen, Senate *Debates*, June 3, 1939, pp. 578–79.

27. DFR, vol. 3975, file C-5-1-1, F. W. Wegenost to P. A. Chester, September 8, 1939.

28. Ibid., Towers to Ralston, September 21, 1939.

Notes to Chapter Ten

1. King, HC *Debates*, April 3, 1930, p. 1228.

2. See sections relating to the Department of Labour in the auditor general's reports for 1920–21, 1921–22, and 1922–23.

3. P.C. 191, January 25, 1922.

4. James Struthers, *No Fault of Their Own: Unemployment and the Canadian Welfare State, 1914–1941* (Toronto: University of Toronto Press, 1983), p. 46.

5. H. Blair Neatby, "The Saskatchewan Relief Commission," *Saskatchewan History* 3 (Spring 1950): 41–53.

6. Struthers, *No Fault of Their Own*, pp. 54–57.

7. Ibid., p. 58.

8. W. A. Gordon, HC *Debates*, April 28, 1932, p. 2452. Under the farm placement program the Dominion government paid five dollars a month to each single man placed on a farm in the four western provinces for the winter months and paid half the stipend allowed to the farmer for room and board. Eventually 10,456 men found work during the life of the 1932 act. See Struthers, *No Fault of Their Own*, pp. 67–68.

9. Struthers, *No Fault of Their Own*, pp. 74–79.

10. Bennett Papers, M1448, pp. 487585–87, E. A. Macpherson, provincial

treasurer, Manitoba, to R. B. Bennett, January 7, 1933.

11. Ibid., pp. 487589-90, W. C. Clark to R. K. Finlayson, January 7, 1933.

12. See DFR, vol. 2672, file "Dominion-Provincial Conference 1933."

13. Bennett's speech was in response to a resolution introduced by a Labour MP, Abraham Heaps, proposing the immediate establishment of unemployment and health insurance. In his speech, Bennett described the need for time to make the necessary agreements with the provinces as well as gather information but he did promise an insurance scheme at "the earliest possible moment" HC *Debates*, April 29, 1931, pp. 1095-104. For Clark's views, see chap. 4, n53.

14. Bennett Papers, M1459, pp. 504027-40, R. K. Finlayson to R. B. Bennett (n.d., circa December 1932). R. H. Coats, Canada's first Dominion statistician, has been described as "one of the few intellectuals and genuinely able men in the public service of the 1920s." Coats had come to Ottawa in 1902 as associate editor of the *Labour Gazette* and subsequently became the Department of Labour's chief statistical officer. He was appointed Dominion statistician in 1915 and under his direction the collection of statistics became centralized in one government agency. See O. Mary Hill, *Canada's Salesman to the World: The Department of Trade and Commerce, 1892-1939* (Montreal: McGill-Queen's University Press and the Institute of Public Administration of Canada, 1977), and J. L. Granatstein, *A Man of Influence: Norman A. Robertson and Canadian Statecraft* (Ottawa: Deneau Publishers, 1981).

15. Bennett Papers, M1459, pp. 501802-3, W. C. Clark to R. B. Bennett, January 18, 1933.

16. See Struthers, *No Fault of Their Own*, pp. 90-91. It is interesting to note that the assumption, at least by the provinces, that all constitutional changes would require provincial approval dates from the 1930s. The 1931 conference, which discussed the Statute of Westminster, was significant, as the federal government admitted the need for consultation with the provinces about any amendments to the constitution. See Christopher Armstrong, *The Politics of Federalism: Ontario's Relations with the Federal Government* (Toronto: University of Toronto Press, 1981), pp. 140-48.

17. Grant Dexter in the *Winnipeg Free Press*, as quoted in Struthers, *No Fault of Their Own*, p. 91.

18. Ibid. The letter is to be found in the Bennett Papers, M1282, pp. 351089-91, Bennett to J. T. M. Anderson, March 9, 1933.

19. Struthers, *No Fault of Their Own*, p. 93.

20. Rhodes, HC *Debates*, April 18, 1934, p. 2279.

21. Bennett Papers, M1448, pp. 487589-90, W. C. Clark to R. K. Finlayson, January 7, 1933.

22. Armstrong, *The Politics of Federalism*, p. 152.

23. National Library of Canada, microfiche M52, no. 24, Documents of the Dominion Provincial Conference on Relief, 1934.

24. The account of the confrontation with Pattullo is based upon Struthers, *No Fault of Their Own*, pp. 111-14.

25. Rhodes, HC *Debates*, March 22, 1935, p. 1973.

26. This account of the change in the form of relief is based primarily on the discussion in Armstrong, *The Politics of Federalism*, pp. 153-55, supplemented

by detail from Struthers, *No Fault of Their Own*, pp. 115-18.

27. *Canadian Annual Review of Public Affairs* (Toronto, 1935), p. 36.

28. R.B. Bennett, *The Premier Speaks to the People* (Ottawa: Dominion Conservative headquarters, 1935). See also Bennett Papers, microfilm M1401, pp. 437366ff.

29. HC *Debates*, Speech from the Throne, January 17, 1935, p. 3.

30. Donald Forster and Colin Read, "The Politics of Opportunism: The New Deal Broadcasts," *Canadian Historical Review* 60, no. 3 (September 1979): 324-26.

31. H.H. Stevens, Bennett's volatile minister of trade and commerce, headed an investigation of price spreads in 1934, emerging as the champion of the "little guy." Bennett and Stevens disagreed and Stevens quit the Conservative party, eventually forming his own Reconstruction party. In the election of 1935, Stevens was elected as its only representative.

32. HC *Debates*, March 12, 1935, pp. 1638-39. See also Forster and Read, "The Politics of Opportunism," and H. Blair Neatby, *William Lyon Mackenzie King*, vol. 3, *The Prism of Unity 1932-1939* (Toronto: University of Toronto Press, 1976).

33. See Struthers, *No Fault of Their Own*, pp. 139-41.

34. DPCR, vol. 62, file C-1-5-1, memorandum by Clark on Australian Loan Council and paper entitled "Duplication of Taxation in Canada: Extent, Objections and Possible Lines of Solution."

35. DFR, vol. 3986, file Pl-10-1, memorandum from Clark to R.K. Finlayson, January 3, 1935.

36. DFR, vol. 731, file 205-2, Report of Alberta Bondholders Committee by Courtland Elliott and J. W. Walker, July 17, 1936, appendix A.

37. DPCR, vol. 62, "Miscellaneous—General" file, Clark to Dunning, December 5, 1935.

38. See Armstrong, *Politics of Federalism*, pp. 205-6.

39. DPCR, vol. 60, Dominion-Provincial Conference, 1935, *Record of Proceedings* closing session.

40. *Statutes of Canada*, "The National Employment Commission Act, 1936," chap. 7 and HC *Debates*, April 3, 1936, p. 1787.

41. National Employment Commission, *Final Report* (Ottawa: 1938), appendix A, and Struthers, *No Fault of Their Own*, pp. 153-72.

42. King's diary, December 21, 1937.

43. National Employment Commission, *Final Report*, p. 28.

44. King's view of the National Employment Commission recommendations was in opposition to those of both O. D. Skelton and Clark who, like Mackintosh and Rogers, were from Queen's. On January 25, 1938, King wrote in his diary: "These men, all of whom are Queen's University, Department of Economics, have come together, and have been working jointly to seek to bring about a change in constitutional relations which will lead to a centralization of powers and away from the present order of things."

45. In August 1940 the Unemployment Insurance Act was passed even though the outbreak of war and the defeat of Quebec Premier Duplessis had changed the circumstances. The recommendations of the Rowell-Sirois report of May 1940 were not related to the decision to proceed with the legislation. See Struthers, *No Fault of Their Own*, pp. 187-204.

46. DPCR, vol. 73, file C-1-5-2-1.

47. *Canadian Annual Review, 1935-36* (Toronto, 1939), p. 338.

48. Budget speech, Legislative Assembly of British Columbia, November 6, 1936.

49. Neatby, *William Lyon Mackenzie King* 3: 160. Original source: King's diary, March 25, 28, and 30, 1936.

50. J.R. Mallory, *Social Credit and the Federal Power in Canada* (Toronto: University of Toronto Press, 1954), p. 133.

51. Neatby, *William Lyon Mackenzie King* 3:160 Original source: King's diary, April 25, 1936.

52. Neatby, *William Lyon Mackenzie King* 3: 160. Original source: King's diary, May 14 and 15, 1936.

53. In December 1936 Dunning stated before the National Finance Committee that representatives of four provinces had informed him that they were not prepared to support the loan council scheme without the taxation changes and, consequently, the Dominion government decided that the opposition to the proposal was too great to proceed. DPCR, vol. 73, file C-1-5-2-2, Proceedings of the National Finance Committee, December 10, 1936.

54. DFR, vol. 3985, file P1-1-2.

55. BCA, John Deutsch Collection, JD6, file "Provincial Finance," "Federal-Provincial Finance," p. 11.

56. BCA, file 2B-170, "The Distribution of Taxing Powers in Canada," by Grauer, August 30, 1936, p. 45.

57. BCA, file 2B-400, "Provincial Debt Conversion and National Finances and Terms of Reference for a Royal Commission on Provincial Finances," by Skelton, October 14, 1936.

58. Ibid., "The Case for a Royal Commission Inquiry on Provincial Finances," by Skelton, November 25, 1936.

59. King's diary, November 16, 1936.

60. DFR, vol. 22, file 101-85-15, "Royal Commission on the Economic Basis of Confederation," by Clark.

61. See DPCR, vol. 73, for the proceedings of the National Finance Committee, December 9-11, 1936.

62. King's diary, December 15, 1936.

63. Ibid., December 16, 1936.

64. See chap. 8, "Expanding Traditional Activities."

65. The party standings following the 1936 general election were as follows: Liberal-Progressives, 23; Conservatives, 16; CCF, 6; Social Credit, 5; and others, 4.

66. DFR, vol. 670, file 201-1-31-46, memorandum from Clark to Dunning, January 20, 1937.

67. King's diary, January 21, 1937.

68. BCA, LB 11.2.37-312, Towers to Bracken, February 11, 1937 (and enclosure).

69. BCA, LB 12.2.37-351, Towers to Bracken, February 12, 1937, and ibid., DPR/LB-1-20, Towers to Dunning, February 12, 1937.

70. King's diary, February 16, 1937.

71. King, HC *Debates*, February 16, 1937, pp. 921-22.

72. Royal Commission on Dominion-Provincial Relations, *Report*, book 1

Canada, 1867–1939 (Ottawa, 1940), p. 237.

73. DFR, vol. 3986, file P1-10-1.

74. Bennett, HC *Debates*, April 10, 1937, pp. 2938–40.

75. Dunning, ibid., p. 2945.

76. Ilsley, ibid., December 3, 1945, p. 2862.

Notes to Chapter Eleven

1. DFR, vol. 107, file 135-0-167, unsigned memorandum from Finlayson to Bennett, n.d., "Duplication of Dominion and Provincial Taxation," and Department of Finance Library, "Dominion-Provincial Conference 1933, Memoranda regarding Questions on the Agenda" (Ottawa, 1933), "Taxation Problems," by deputy minister of finance.

2. For the conference minutes and the report of the Committee on Taxation, see DFR, vol. 2672, Dominion-Provincial Conference of 1933, afternoon session, January 18, 1933.

3. DPCR, vol. 67, file C-1-4, Clark to Bennett, January 16, 1934.

4. Bennett Papers, M1184, pp. 121805–6, Bennett to Taschereau, August 31, 1934.

5. Ibid., press release, November 5, 1934, p. 121924.

6. W. D. Young, *The Anatomy of a Party: The National CCF, 1932–61* (Toronto: University of Toronto Press, 1969), appendix A, "The Regina Manifesto."

7. King Papers, J1, vol. 210, King to Pattullo, October 16, 1935; DPCR, vol. 59, secretary of state to provincial premiers, November 7 and 12, 1935.

8. See DPCR, vol. 59, for minutes of the organization meeting for the Dominion-provincial conference of 1935 and for provincial premiers' replies to the secretary of state's invitation of November 7. John Erskine Read, legal adviser to External Affairs, was secretary to the conference.

9. DPCR, vol. 62, file C-1-5-1, Dominion-Provincial Conference of 1935.

10. DPCR, vol. 65, Minutes of the Sub-Conference on Financial Questions, December 11 and 12, 1935; DFR, vol. 107, file 135-0-167, British Columbia, Minister of Finance, 1935 Brief on Taxation.

11. DPCR, vol. 65, Minutes of the Continuing Committee, December 13, 1935. The report of the sub-conference can be found in *Dominion-Provincial Conference 1935: Record of Proceedings*, December 9–13, 1935 (Ottawa, 1936), appendix A2.

12. *Globe*, December 18, 1935.

13. DPCR, vol. 73, file C-1-5-2-1, Proceedings of the Permanent Committee on Financial Questions, January 13, 1936, pp. D1-F5.

14. DPCR, vol. 62, file C-1-5-2-1, "Duplication of Taxation in Canada," and vol. 73, file C-1-5-2-1, "Suggestions regarding Clarification of and Broadening the Base of Provincial Taxation."

15. *Statutes of Ontario*, 1936, chap. 1.

16. *Statutes of Canada*, 1936, chap. 38; section 17, added section 76A to the Income War Tax Act which empowered the Governor in Council to enter into an agreement with any province for Canada to collect the province's income tax(es).

17. PAC, Records of the Privy Council Office, RG2, ser. 1, vol. 1987, Ontario-Canada Tax Collection Agreement, July 2, 1936. National Revenue did not secure

passage of the order-in-council approving the signed agreement until May 1937 (see P.C. 1081, May 14, 1937). As the federal legislative authorization was not to be secured until after the federal collection of the Ontario tax began, Ilsley took advantage of the passage of National Revenue's 1936-37 Estimates through the Committee of Supply to inform the Commons of the nature of Ontario's legislation and arrangements with Ottawa. HC *Debates*, March 19, 1936, pp. 1278-81.

18. DFR, vol. 739, file 220-4, memorandum by Purkiss to Clark, November 4, 1937. The 2 percent administration fee was subsequently adjusted by letter: $100,000 was paid for the 1936-37 fiscal year, $60,000 for the 1937-38 fiscal year, and $80,000 for each subsequent fiscal year.

19. DPCR, vol. 73, file C-1-5-2-1, Proceedings of the Permanent Committee on Financial Questions, January 14, 1936, p. J-6.

20. Ibid., Clark to Dunning January 12, 1936, enclosing "Suggestions regarding Clarification of and Broadening the Base of Provincial Taxation."

21. The differences in personnel and subject matter were so minimal that the *Hansard* reporters who recorded its first day's discussions (December 5, 1936) continued to dub them "Proceedings of the Permanent Committee on Financial Questions."

22. DPCR, vol. 73, file C-1-5-2-2, Clark to Elliott, November 1, 1936, and Clark to Walters, November 16, 1936.

23. Ibid., Proceedings of the National Finance Committee, December 11, 1936, pp. A1ff., and December 10, 1936, p. R5-S1. The deduction of the graduated federal income tax and, where applicable, the graduated federal tax on investment income and the federal 5 percent surtax removed an appreciable portion of each taxpayer's income from taxation by the province and dropped many taxpayers into a lower tax bracket.

24. Ibid., December 11, 1936, pp. B2ff.

25, Ibid., pp. G5ff.

26. *Statutes of Manitoba*, 1937, chap. 43, and 1937-38, chap. 39. For the Manitoba-Canada tax collection agreement, December 21, 1937, see P.C. 75, January 12, 1938. As a matter of interest, throughout the period of federal administration the exemptions and deductions under Manitoba's personal income tax and under its wages tax differed.

27. The authorizing legislation was *Statutes of Prince Edward Island*, 1937, chap. 18, and 1938, chap. 10; *Statutes of Quebec*, 1940, chap. 16; and *Ordinances of the Yukon Territories*, 1940, chap. 7. The dates the tax collection agreements were signed and their authorizing federal orders-in-council secured were Canada-Prince Edward Island, March 8, 1938, P.C. 1097, dated May 16, 1938; Canada-Quebec, August 31, 1940, P.C. 151/6613, dated November 18, 1940; and Canada-Yukon, June 15, 1940, P.C. 86/6885, dated November 26, 1940.

28. Quebec statute, 1935, chap. 112, imposed a municipal tax on the income of individuals resident or doing business in Montreal and the municipalities of the Montreal Metropolitan Commission with effect for the 1934 year. Quebec statute, 1939, chap. 102, imposed a similar tax on Quebec City residents with effect for the 1939 year. In Ontario personal incomes assessable under the Assessment Act had been taxed by some two hundred municipalities ranging in

size from the city of Toronto to Blenheim Township. See Ontario Assessment Act, *Revised Statutes of Ontario*, 1927, chap. 238, and Ontario, *Public Accounts*, 1937, for a listing of municipalities that had a municipal income tax.

Notes to Chapter Twelve

1. Rowell had been a member of the Ontario legislature and leader of the provincial Liberal party until 1917, when he joined the Union government in Ottawa as president of the Privy Council. On the formation of the Meighen government in 1920, he ceased to be a minister and on the dissolution of Parliament he returned to Toronto to the practice of law. There he remained until his appointment as chief justice of Ontario in 1936.

2. David W. Fransen, "Unscrewing the Unscrutable: The Rowell-Sirois Commission, the Ottawa Bureaucracy and Public Finance Reform, 1935-1941" (Ph.D. diss., University of Toronto, 1984), pp. 87-89.

3. Ibid., pp. 74-80, recount the steps leading to the decision to have five commissioners rather than three, and also the decisions to select Mackay and Angus. See pp. 89-90 regarding the announcement.

4. King Papers, vol. 206, file F1978, Briefing notes on the Royal Commission on Dominion-Provincial Relations.

5. Ibid.

6. Royal Commission on Dominion-Provincial Relations, *Report*, book 1, *Canada, 1867-1939* (Ottawa, 1940), p. 15. Later the Alberta and Quebec governments declined to participate in the hearings. Ibid., p. 16.

7. Fransen, "Unscrewing the Unscrutable," pp. 268-73.

8. BCA, file 2B-170, "The Distribution of Taxing Powers in Canada," by A. E. Grauer, August 30, 1936. This memorandum is described in chap. 10, "Dominion-Provincial Discussions and Disputes." It should also be noted that W. H. Wynne, formerly engaged by the Citizens Research Institute, did a special inquiry into taxation, apparently for that institute. He is mentioned among those who participated in research in economic matters. *Report*, book 1, p. 14.

9. King's diary, June 2, 1938.

10. King Papers, vol. 160, file F1446, memorandum from Skelton to King, July 16, 1938.

11. Ibid. R. B. Bennett for chairman had been suggested to King in March by George McCullagh, editor of the *Globe and Mail*, and also in April by George Perley and Sir Edward Beattie, as indicated in King's diary, but King had turned the suggestion aside. See Frasen "Unscrewing the Unscrutable," pp. 65-66.

12. Ibid., attached memorandum by King, July 19, 1938.

13. H. F. Angus, "An Echo of the Past: The Rowell-Sirois Commission," *Canadian Tax Journal* 5 (1953): 439.

14. Fransen, "Unscrewing the Unscrutable," pp. 288-93.

15. Professor J. A. Corry was probably one chief author of book 1. See *My Life and Work* by J. A. Corry (Kingston: Queen's University, 1981), pp. 104-7. Skelton seems clearly to have been the chief author of section B, "Public Finance," in book 2. Alex Skelton was a colourful and influential person but no one has written much about him. It is said that when he was finished at Oxford he had

the choice of two jobs—one teaching economics in Saskatoon, which he took, and the other to be yachting correspondent in the Mediterranean for *The Times*. It is a tragedy that he died a relatively young man in Nigeria as a member of a British royal commission in July 1950.

16. Royal Commission on Dominion-Provincial Relations, *Report*, book 2, *Recommendations*, p. 275. The report is not dated. It was published in May 1940.

17. Angus, "An Echo of the Past," pp. 439-40.

18. In estimating the cost saving to the provincial governments of this proposal the commission included the provincial and municipal shares of relief to employables and their dependants. The commission also included that cost of relief works regardless of whether the provinces and municipalities charged them to capital or to ordinary expenses.

19. Royal Commission on Dominion-Provincial Relations, *Report*, book 2, p. 83.

20. H. A. Innis, "Notes and Memoranda: The Rowell-Sirois Report," *CJEPS* 6 (November 1940): 571.

21. The reader is entitled to some explanation of this point. Equalization grants were introduced after it was decided in 1956 to separate the subsidy or fiscal need element of the tax rental agreements from the estimated yield of the taxes rented. It was Prime Minister St. Laurent's own decision, reached after lengthy discussions with Finance, and it reflected his view that the inclusion of such a subsidy in the tax rental agreements was seriously unfair to Quebec, which objected in principle to entering into such an agreement. I was the secretary to the Cabinet at the time and very much involved in the discussions on the subject.

Notes to Chapter Thirteen

1. For Clark's views on a central bank, see the discussion in chap. 7.

2. DPR, vol. 3042, file 3312, "Memorandum respecting the Finance Department," by J. M. Courtney, June 7, 1888. This memo was discussed in chap. 1.

3. M. A. MacPherson was described in chap. 9.

4. The auditor general's report for 1939-40 shows that employees in the Housing Branch were paid not only from an appropriation for the branch but also out of unappropriated funds under the authority of the National Housing Act. It is difficult to reconcile the numbers of employees given in this report with that in earlier reports; it seems to imply a rapid growth in 1938-39, financed by funds outside the regular appropriations voted for the branch.

5. See George S. Watts, "The Legislative Birth of the Bank of Canada," *Bank of Canada Review* (August 1972): 24.

6. The detailed Civil Service Commission organization chart is to be found in PAC, Records of the Public Service Commission, RG32, vol. 773. Several rearrangements of details have been made in drawing up chart 2, as noted in the text.

7. One of the stenographers was Anne MacRitchie, who became my secretary during the war and for eight years after it. Her competence and accuracy undoubtedly increased my efficiency during that important period.

8. Civil Service Commission, *Twenty-Sixth Annual Report—1934* (Ottawa, 1935), pp. 10-11.

9. See chap. 8. On the general policy, see Ronson's testimony to the Royal Commission on Administrative Classifications in the Public Service, *Proceedings*, vol. 1, (Ottawa, 1946), pp. 82–89.

10. I have been informed by D. B. Mansur, whose close relation with Clark and with the housing acts has been explained in chap. 9, that Clark showed little interest in the day-to-day work of the Housing Branch once he had it operating, and that one of the reasons for setting up the Central Mortgage and Housing Corporation in 1945 was to relieve the Department of Finance of this operating responsibility.

11. J.L. Granatstein, "The Road to Bretton Woods: International Monetary Policy and the Public Servant," *Journal of Canadian Studies* 16, nos. 3 and 4 (Fall–Winter 1981): 176 and n10.

12. PAC, Finlayson Papers, MG30 E143, R. Finlayson, draft memoirs, "Life with R. B.: That Man Bennett," p. 113.

Index